ROLOFF BENY · MICHEL TREMBLA[Y] · [FAR]LEY MOWAT

W. O. MITCHELL · JACK BATTEN ·

ROGER LEMELIN · DUDLEY WITNEY

STEPHEN LEACOCK · DAVID BEZMOZGIS

CONRAD BLACK · MORDECAI RICHLER

RUDY WIEBE · ROBERTSON DAVIES · E. J. PRATT

GABRIELLE ROY · CHARLES TEMPLETON

IRVING LAYTON · A. J. M. SMITH · RICHARD GWYN

MALCOLM LOWRY · PETER C. NEWMAN

GERALDINE SHERMAN · JOHN MACFARLANE

BRIAN MOORE · JUNE CALLWOOD · ADELE WISEMAN

CHARLES TAYLOR · ALICE MUNRO · YANN MARTEL

MARGARET ATWOOD · CAROL SHIELDS

MORLEY CALLAGHAN · SCOTT SYMONS

LUCY MAUD MONTGOMERY · DAVE GODFREY

HAROLD TOWN · DIONNE BRAND

AL PURDY · WOLE SOYINKA · CAMILLA GIBB

PETER WORTHINGTON · MARIA CAMPBELL

IN OTHER WORDS

How I Fell in Love with Canada

One Book at a Time

ANNA PORTER

Phyllis Bruce Editions

Simon & Schuster Canada

New York   London   Toronto   Sydney   New Delhi

SIMON &
SCHUSTER
CANADA

Simon & Schuster Canada
A Division of Simon & Schuster, Inc.
166 King Street East, Suite 300
Toronto, Ontario M5A 1J3

This Simon & Schuster Canada edition September 2018

SIMON & SCHUSTER CANADA and colophon are trademarks of Simon & Schuster, Inc.

For information about special discounts for bulk purchases, please contact Simon & Schuster Special Sales at 1-800-268-3216 or CustomerService@simonandschuster.ca.

Interior design by Carly Loman

Manufactured in the United States of America

10 9 8 7 6 5 4 3 2 1

Library and Archives Canada Cataloguing in Publication

Porter, Anna, author
In other words: how I fell in love with Canada one book at a time / Anna Porter.
Issued in print and electronic formats.
ISBN 978-1-4767-9513-3 (hardcover).—ISBN 978-1-4767-9515-7 (ebook)
1. Porter, Anna. 2. Authors, Canadian (English)—20th century—Biography. 3. Publishers and publishing—Canada—Biography. 4. Autobiographies. I. Title.
PS8581.O7553Z46 2018 C813'.54 C2018-901000-2
C2018-901001-0 ISBN 978-1-4767-9513-3

ISBN 978-1-4767-9513-3
ISBN 978-1-4767-9515-7 (ebook)

Permissions and credits appear on page 459.

For the two Jacks—McClelland and Rabinovitch

When home is not where you are born, nothing is predetermined.

MASHA GESSEN

CONTENTS

PART ONE
Becoming Canadian

A Soft Landing	3
Welcome to CanLit	17
The Rosedale Radical	25
The Unfortunate Incident of Ted's Name	31
Assembling a Book on the Linoleum Floor	35
All Those Glorious Manuscripts	41
Roblin Lake and After	49
The Happy Hungry Man	57
The Amazing Ms. Atwood	61
The Master Storyteller	69
Tough Times	75
Finding Home	81
The Very Young Matt	87
National Dreaming, or The Berton Extravaganza	91
How Pierre Berton Is Responsible for My Marriage	99
1972, a Year to Remember	105
For the Love of Words	111
Meetings with the Messiah	115
A Land of Poets	121
Peter's Establishment	125
A Northern Nation	133
The Best and the Brightest	137
The Disinherited	141
The Greatest Gift	145
Escaping the City	153
That Great, Always Recognizable Voice	159
Marian's Way	165

A Whole Lot Larger than Life   169

The Establishment Man   175

The Uneasy Balancing Act   179

Intermission   185

Talking about Feminism   191

Rebel Daughter   197

In Search of My Father   203

PART TWO

No Rose Garden

Looking for a New Gig   209

Sealing   217

The Challenge of Being Julian   223

Sylvia's Magic   227

Trying to Heal the World with Graeme and John and Monte   231

The First Lady   235

Michael's World   239

Finding the Key   243

Farewell to the Seventies   251

Taking a Leap in the Dark   257

Inviting the World to Love Canada   265

Dudley and Malak   269

Our Spanking New Premises   273

1984   279

Journalists and Politicians   283

Looking for Trouble   287

I've Always Told Stories   291

My Candidate   293

The Right Honourable Jean   297

The End of an Era   303

Saying Goodbye to Margaret   309

Imagining Canadian Literature   313

The Doubleday Gamble   317
From *Mortal Sins* to *The Bookfair Murders*   325
Five Years of Struggle to Come to Terms with an Illusion   329
Saving the World, One Book at a Time   333
Growing Pains   341
New Challenges   347
Basil Johnston's Ojibway Heritage   353
The Canadian Way of Death and of Living   357
The Witness   359
"Money-Grubbing Has Become Respectable"   363
The Last Decade of the Last Century   369
Farley: The Next Chapter   373
The Last Berton Party   377
The Incomparable Dalton Camp   381

PART THREE
Passages

Memory, Secrets, and Magic   389
Key Porter's Twentieth Birthday   393
The End of M&S   397
Welcome to the Twenty-first Century   401
Endings   407
From Publisher to Writer   409
Europe's Ghosts   413
Keep the Promise   419
A Footnote to Canadian Publishing History   421
The Inimitable Jack Rabinovitch   423
For the Love of Books   429

Acknowledgements   433
Index   435
Permissions and Credits   459

PART ONE

Becoming Canadian

A Soft Landing

Y FIRST GLIMPSE of Canada was the highway from the airport to Toronto, early-winter grey, barren, treeless, with squat industrial buildings. It was gloomy even for an outsider with no plans to stay. The turbaned driver tried jolly small talk about his busier friends in Montreal and, when he heard where I'd come from, sang a bit of "England Swings (Like a Pendulum Do)." Unlike the suspicious customs woman, he made no comments about the battered blue suitcase with no handle that contained all my worldly possessions. He deposited it in front of a gold-braided doorman outside the Royal York Hotel and accepted a meagre tip in shillings. I had nothing left for the doorman but he liked my outfit so much he didn't care. Nor did the next chap in a less fancy uniform who hefted the suitcase onto his shoulder with one hand. He had come from Munich, via Zurich and London. Like me, he wasn't sure where he would go next.

I had arrived after Expo madness, after Canada's Centennial celebrations, just before the end of the sixties. I came from swinging London: Beatlemania, Bee Gees, Wimpy bars, Mick Jagger, Keith Richards, Trafalgar Square happenings, hippies and free love, weed parties, "mod" counterculture, and late nights on the King's Road.

I wore my white vinyl knee-high boots, a mauve minidress, a short bunny-fur coat, ironed-straight long blond hair—all perfectly acceptable in London—and I thought I looked professional enough to rate being hired by the Canadian branch plant of the American publisher Collier Macmillan as a copy editor. I had worked for their London office as a college sales rep for a couple of years, travelling all over the UK and Northern Europe—none of which qualified me for copy-editing. Still, my erstwhile boss, the indomitable Fred Kobrak* at Collier Macmillan International's UK office, figured if I could pass for a college rep in Scandinavia, I could pass as a copy editor in Canada. He advised me to look earnest, not one of my obvious attributes, and try to fit in. If it didn't work out, he said, he would arrange for an interview at the New York office, and if that too failed, I could go back to Scandinavia and sell more copies of Samuelson's *Economics*.

Prior to Collier Macmillan I had put in a few months pretending to proofread at Cassell's on Red Lion Square, while they pretended to pay me. I suspect the reason I had taken the proofreading job was that Cassell's published Robert Graves, whose poetry and fiction had served me well during sleepless nights. Needless to say, he did not frequent the proofreading department, though I did see him once in the lift (elevator). He was tall, wore a rumpled raincoat under a rumpled face framed by wispy white hair, and like everyone else, was staring into elevator space. I was so excited I could barely mutter that I had been a fan for many years. He looked at me briefly and said, "Really?" Just one word from the great literary giant and a missed opportunity for this memoir.

My New Zealand passport listed my name as Anna Szigethy and place of birth as Hungary, where my family had lived for several hundred years, though some of our homes had found themselves in other countries after the First World War. The 1920 Treaty of Trianon had distributed more than half the country among its neighbours, leaving many former Hungarians feeling like emigrants or exiles. Though there were plenty of other

---

* After he retired as president of Collier Macmillan International, Fred went on to work for the Frankfurt Book Fair. At last count, he had attended fifty-six Frankfurt Book Fairs, consecutively.

traumas to talk about when I was a child, the tragedy of Trianon—a mere sideshow to the Versailles Treaty that ended the war—was still mentioned in tones of heavy mourning. It had been Hungary's punishment for having allied itself with the Kaiser's Germany.

As most of the beneficiaries of Hungary's Trianon losses (Yugoslavia, Czechoslovakia, and so on) became our fellow Socialist Republics after the Second World War, my grandfather Vili was careful not to mention the unfairness of the treaty unless we were outside our apartment. Inside, as he never tired of warning me, "the walls have ears." He explained that in the late 1930s, our country had gone somewhat crazy and joined Nazi Germany in yet another world war. That's why we were invaded in 1945 by the Soviets, who then stayed.

In keeping with our conquered state, Hungarian schools taught Russian from about grade one on, and children were ill advised to skip those classes, particularly those youngsters with politically suspect backgrounds, such as mine. Soviet-trained Communists, who were in charge after 1946, were bent on reversing the old social order and kept a wary eye on everyone who had owned anything in prior years. Vili had been a magazine and book publisher and had dabbled in liberal politics. My missing father had owned some sort of factory (I still have no idea what). He had been scooped up in 1945 by a gang of Soviet soldiers with orders to fill quotas for Hungarians to work in Siberia. We rarely talked about him.

Vili was my childhood hero. He was a tireless and inventive storyteller, an amateur magician, a former champion sprinter, a wrestler, and one of the best sword duelers in Hungary. He was so strong, he could lift two of his daughters at once, holding only one leg of each chair they were seated on. He had no trouble winning every race he ever invented for me, though he gave me ample handicaps.

Vili taught me to listen to stories, to love hearing them and, later, reading them.*

---

* My book *The Storyteller: Memory, Secrets, Magic and Lies* is about Vili and his profound influence on my life.

Stories became my passion. I had started to read soon after I started to walk. Fantastic folktales about witches and dragons (my grandfather had insisted that there was a particularly fiery dragon still living in Transylvania, where our family came from); wily Turks and heroic Hungarians; then books by Karl May, Zsigmond Móricz, Vörösmarty, Arany, Jules Verne, Flaubert, Balzac, Molnár (I was particularly fond of *The Boys of Paul Street*), Stendahl (after defeating an army of janissaries, I planned to become a musketeer); and, from the top shelves of my mother's library, Maupassant. In time, my Russian and English, German and French education would add to the growing lists of books I loved.

AFTER SOME YEARS as a slave labourer in the Soviet Gulag, my father was sent home. My memory of his return is a bit hazy but I do recall that he ruined my Christmas by interrupting what promised to be a lighthearted occasion. A complete stranger, he was shabbily dressed; he stank of stale tobacco and horse manure. He had yellow teeth and broken knuckles. I was surprised during the night to find a revolver under his pillow. He did not seem happy to see me.

I was relieved when he left a couple of days later. I was discouraged from talking about him even to my friends. Not only had he been in the Gulag, he would now manage to cross the border illegally into Austria. My mother, Puci, and I (I was only about five, too young to make my own decisions) attempted to join him, but we were caught, interrogated, and jailed in Szombathely. That was the first time I was arrested.* I was there for only a few weeks but they kept my mother for eight months. Trying to leave a Communist paradise was punishable by jail.

Since we had failed to follow him, my father sent divorce papers and vanished from our lives. My mother tended to forgive him—he was so much older than she was, he had suffered in the slave labour camp, he could never hope to come home, and so forth. I had no interest, then, in seeing him again.

---

* The second time was in late 1956 when we spent two nights in jail.

With such a suspect family history it was obvious that I had to shine in Russian classes in Hungary. My family wanted me to be seen as a perfect example of Communist youth, white shirt, blue kerchief, and all. Sometimes I could even carry the flag with the hammer and sickle. I was honoured to be hanging giant banners of comrades Stalin, Lenin, and Rákosi, our very own Communist leader. None of them was pretty, but Rákosi with his bald, sloping, neckless head and forced smile outdid the other two.

In spite of all our efforts to conform, the state caught up with Vili in 1954, tried him on trumped-up charges, and condemned him to eighteen months of hard labour. Though he and my grandmother were allowed to leave the country a few months after his release, I had become seriously discouraged about our future in Hungary. In 1956 when the anti-Soviet demonstrations began, I spent a lot of time in the streets with protesters. At first the crowds were jubilant, but then the shooting began. I was at Kossuth Square when the secret police shot into the crowd, and I saw one of my friends die. I saw Soviet tanks roll over people. In a doorway where I had hidden, a Russian soldier held my hand as he died.

When our tiny flat took a direct hit, my mother* decided it was time to leave. This time we crossed the border on foot to Austria successfully. New Zealand eventually accepted us as refugees, as we were sponsored by my mother's oldest sister, Sari, who had also sponsored my grandparents. It was her brilliant idea that shortly after our arrival I should be incarcerated in a Catholic boarding school, where I would quickly learn English. She was right about the English, but I also learned that the Communists weren't all wrong about religion. Vili answered my sad letters from school and sent me a few stories about very brave Hungarians who endured hardship in battle and were rewarded by kings. But there were no kings in New Zealand.

---

* My mother, though she had married again after my father left, didn't have any more children because of the political turmoil. Her second husband was a Communist engineer who arranged Vili's release.

I decided it would have been far easier to be a freedom fighter than a refugee.

MY MOTHER SOON married a Dutch New Zealander, many years her senior, with three children of his own and no interest in more. Alfons was a handsome, charming, opinionated, argumentative presence. He had spent the war years as a Japanese prisoner and never recovered from the experience. Nor had his children. Later, after overcoming our mutual suspicions, his daughter Ines and I became friends and still are. She was vivacious, funny, warm, and adventurous, though she too had spent her early childhood hungry and afraid. She and her two brothers had been with their mother in a Japanese prisoner of war camp in Java. She remembered scrounging for scraps of food in the garbage behind the guards' quarters. They tolerated her because she was so tiny.

After surviving the Sacred Heart Convent School in Wanganui, New Zealand, I started university, supporting myself with a range of jobs. I took English literature from an indulgent professor at Canterbury University in Christchurch. He had been impressed with my morning job cleaning toilets at Princess Margaret Hospital and my afternoon job modelling clothes for department stores. I wasn't particularly good at either job (my only experience of being fired was when the New Zealand Wool Board ended my modelling stint because of late-night carousing with a bunch of former '56 Revolutionary Hungarian poets in my Wool Board–courtesy hotel room), but the jobs fed me while I struggled through Old English with Beowulf and Sir Gawain; discovered I could understand Chaucer and Shakespeare; and enjoyed Coleridge, Shelley, and other assorted Romantics, Austen, Thackeray, James, T. S. Eliot, Woolf, and Joyce. The truth is I loved them all. I took a few French and German courses because they were easy and, less enthusiastically, I took Russian as my minor because, unlike others in the class, I already had a good working knowledge of the language. At the end of my second year, I got a job stacking books in the large Whitcombe and Tombs warehouse and was promoted to also entering the retail price, giving change to customers, and wrapping.

Thinking back on my early New Zealand days now, I realize that the people I had most wanted to be with were all members of the large Ward clan. There were six blondish, fair-skinned siblings and a very motherly mother who worked two jobs to support them all. I used to spend hours drinking tea, eating biscuits, and talking with her when she returned from her night job. My best friends were Mary and Dunstan, but I loved the feeling of blending in to a large, functioning family.

It was Mary Ward who had found me the cleaning job on the mental ward of the Princess Margaret Hospital. She had an "in" because she also worked there while going to university. Her brother Dunstan introduced me to the works of e. e. cummings, Robert Graves, and Alice Munro. Dunstan lives in Paris now, teaching English literature, writing poetry and books about the work of Robert Graves—the man I met once in an elevator.

After graduation, Ines and I set out from New Zealand together to see if we could make it in London, which is where young Aussies and Kiwis went almost as a rite of passage to adulthood. My jobs at Cassell's and at Collier Macmillan were stopgap measures, not career moves. As Ines remembered, the only reason we worked was so that we could eat, drink warm beer, and make friends.

I had now arrived in Canada with a New Zealand passport, a British work permit, and an American publisher's guarantee of work in either Toronto or New York. I was full of the bravado that young people felt at the end of the sixties when the world seemed to offer us so many options.

AFTER A SLEEPLESS night surrounded by florid wallpaper and dim lights, I set out at seven a.m. to explore the area around the Royal York. The young trees along Front Street looked as forlorn as I felt with the sharp wind blowing about my legs, scrunched newspapers flying along the pavement, a few half-frozen birds hunched over the bare branches. There was a small triangular park near the hotel. A man in an army greatcoat spread out on one of its benches, humming to himself, offered to share his sandwich. "You're gonna be mighty cold in that wee dress, young lady," he said, and invited me to share his coat. He sounded Irish but told me he was from Newfoundland and trying to hustle up enough money to go home again.

Some years and many park changes later, he was still in Berczy Park—I have no idea why the city keeps remaking it—and still collecting bus fare for his return home. I had none to offer the first time we met but I used to give him money later. By then we had both stopped pretending it was for bus fare.

In no small part thanks to Fred Kobrak's influence, Collier Macmillan decided to hire me despite my lack of experience. My beautifully printed degrees were not much help with adapting American children's textbooks for use in Canadian classrooms, but they did need someone to do the job and, I assume, they figured I could learn. Sadly, my Russian was as useless as my knowledge of the Romantics.

I hadn't the slightest idea what Canadian usage was, though replacing "as American as apple pie" with "as Canadian as maple syrup" was not very challenging. Such minor changes to an American reading series, I was told, would allow Collier Macmillan to submit the books for approval to departments of education in various provinces. If the selection committees liked the prototype, an "adoption" would follow. Adoptions meant that schools in an entire province would be obliged to buy the books, making the company a ton of money and providing bonuses all around.

As an assistant to the assistant editor I didn't rate an interview with Vern, who ran the Canadian operation, but he did meet me on my way to the washroom one day and nodded acknowledgement that I had been successfully transferred. By then I had acquired sheets and pillowcases from a co-worker (Morty Mint, who years later would run Penguin Books Canada) and a small room in an apartment-to-share on Broadway Avenue across from North Toronto Collegiate, a high school celebrated for its vigorous sports and music programs. Even with my window closed, I rarely missed an evening practice.

The assistant editor was a transplanted Englishman called Peter. The "editor" was somewhere in New York: he had no interest in supervising our work in Canada. Peter found the whole notion of adding a *u* to *or* words such as *harbor*, changing *sidewalk* to *pavement*, eliminating all signs of *gotten*, and demanding changes in drawings of policemen and mailmen (different uniforms) utterly amusing. He encouraged me to insert the occasional *shall* just for the hell of it, though he was sure some "committee" would object on the grounds that certain words had fallen out of usage here. Peter had never met a member of any "committee" but thought of them as groups of exceedingly pretentious retired schoolteachers with British aspirations.

Wide-shouldered, pot-bellied, pink-cheeked, he was glad to be rid of the "old country" and its fusty ways. But he still had a lingering fondness for pubs with warmish beer and pianos they let him play. He was quite a virtuoso, singing along to tunes he remembered from his youth. He knew fine versions of "We'll Meet Again" and "The White Cliffs of Dover" and played a toe-tapping, irresistibly tinkly "Greensleeves." Late afternoons he would announce that we needed to do urgent research, so we went on pub crawls that included the Jolly Miller, the Black Bull, and sometimes the Brunswick House. Peter's idea of a great pub was one teeming with people, bad bar food of the Scotch egg variety, and a piano. I knew all the words to "Farewell to Nova Scotia" long before I had any idea where Nova Scotia was.

Strangely, I had a formal letter of introduction to a Canadian journalist from a British character actor who had distinguished himself playing a Dalek in *Doctor Who*.[*] My actor friend, ironically, was a very tall, hefty guy with sandy hair and a mellifluous voice. He was optimistic that a part more interesting than a Dalek was bound to come along soon.

The Canadian journalist, David, another English expat, was a slim, cheerful man with sandy hair that curled above his ears, a narrow face that creased all the way up when he smiled, and opinions on everything, including parking tickets, public transportation, and the quality of food in the eatery he had chosen. He talked of the current political fiasco—as he saw it—of Pierre Elliott Trudeau's over-the-top popularity, his suspi-

---

[*] Daleks were the ubiquitous squat robots with mechanized voices proliferating in *Doctor Who* episodes.

ciously easy wit in two languages, his swift turns of phrase, his appeal to the ladies, and the certainty of his becoming Canada's next prime minister.

As minister of justice in Lester Pearson's Liberal government, Trudeau had introduced a bill in Parliament that decriminalized homosexuality. The papers, David said, had been full of Trudeau's casual but clever statement that "there is no place for the state in the bedrooms of the nation." I started to read the local newspapers and listen to CBC radio.

Trudeau's reception at public appearances was somewhat like that of the Beatles: adulation, some screaming and shouting, a few tears, all of this met by his self-deprecating smile that succeeded in making his opponents seem fuddy-duddy. He would run for the leadership of the Liberal Party in April 1968 and win easily. A large number of us gathered in David's living room to watch the Liberal Party Convention. The others were all journalists, some with spouses, who knew everyone vying for the top political job in the country. Needless to say, I knew none of the candidates, but it was easy to see that Trudeau was the star. He was charmingly superior in interviews, physically attractive, and a verbal gymnast.

He became the most dashing, least long-winded, most talked-about prime minister not only in Canada but in the world. When I travelled back to New Zealand, everyone wanted to talk about his many lady friends, his famous shrugs, his talk of "the just society," his Marshall McLuhan quotes, the rose in his lapel, his sandals, his self-possession, his "cool" demeanour. Even cynical David found "Trudeaumania" enjoyable, and he thought that Trudeau was the man to put an end to Quebec separatism. He was, after all, a fellow Quebecer; he knew all there was to know about the province. He understood it instinctively.

It was David who first explained to me how different Quebec felt from the rest of Canada, but it took much longer for me to understand the ideas driving Quebec's desire to be a country, or the notion of two nations in one. The country where I was born has one language—Hungarian. New Zealanders have only one country; and while the South Island may bitch about the North, they both bitch in unison about Australia with a combination of superiority and envy not unlike, as I learned, how English Canadians feel about Americans.

The 1970 October Crisis—the kidnapping of British Trade Commissioner James Cross and Deputy Premier Pierre Laporte by the FLQ and the murder of Laporte—would harden relations for years.

SOMETIME DURING MY first several months of Canadianizing American textbooks, I decided to look for another job. I am not sure where I learned about an opening for a researcher at the Canadian Broadcasting Corporation, but I suspect it may have been David who first mentioned it. Since I had no experience in television or research, my application must have been a work of art, because they offered me an interview.

I was interviewed by Moses Znaimer, a young man about my age, with longish dark, curly hair; soft brown eyes; and a fleeting, somewhat lopsided smile. He spoke so quietly you had to lean in to hear him. Thin, with stylish clothes, he was so laid-back that at one point I wondered whether he had stopped the interview and was thinking about something much more interesting. He seemed to have a short attention span; later he told me he had a low boredom threshold. As I went on about my education, I was sure I was losing him. He mentioned that he too spoke five languages, but unlike me, I assume he did so without resorting to a dictionary. One of them, luckily, was Russian. He had been born to Eastern European Jewish parents in Tajikistan; like me, he had been a refugee. Having come to Canada via Shanghai without much luggage, he had worked as a stevedore before getting a gig with the CBC.*

He was working at that time for a show called *Take 30*, which I had not yet seen, but I swore it would become my constant study from that day on, if only he considered me suitable for a job.

He said that he was thinking about what television could and should

---

* Moses also had many degrees, including an MA from Harvard.

be. He wanted a different way to use the new technology, one that would attract rather than repel viewers. He thought that most TV on offer in Canada was dull and that the CBC was particularly moribund.

We had tea in a Japanese tea place on Queen Street West where the waitress made a great fuss over tea pouring and even more fuss over Moses. It seemed like an odd ending to an interview, but I thought it best not to comment on it. After the tea, Moses drove me home in his Jaguar.

He said he'd let me know about the job.

I didn't hear from Moses until much later. By then, I had resigned from Collier Macmillan; been to Mexico with my roommate, Lou; flown to Lima to visit an old boyfriend from London who had taken over managing his father's liquor import business; gone up to Cuzco and Machu Picchu; contracted typhus; and flown home to Christchurch, New Zealand, to recover. Moses's telegram to Christchurch suggested that there might be a job for me, but I was too ill to come back for another interview.

We stayed sporadically in touch after he left the CBC, while he was making plans for his new television channel.*

Launched in 1972, Citytv soon became the most innovative, most talked about, most imitated kind of television in the country. Moses went on to launch MuchMusic, CityPulse24, Bravo!, FashionTelevision, and Musique-Plus. Then he took over VisionTV, CARP, and *Zoomer* magazine and eventually incorporated ZoomerMedia. As his early media ventures had been aimed at boomers in their youth, the new venture aims at the same people, now older. Moses calls them "Zoomers" (Boomers with Zip). *Marketing* magazine named him one of the Top 10 Canadian Media Moguls of the Past 100 Years. His website features a tuxedoed Moses and, my favourite, a barefoot Moses with closed eyes and ponytail, meditating.

He never mentioned a job to me again and I had become so enmeshed in publishing that, except for a passing thought in 1978, I didn't ask. But

---

* Moses worked for a while for Ben Webster, an imaginative entrepreneur who believed in animal communication, holistic medicine, and the spirit world. Ben became a friend of mine and a millionaire.

I sometimes wondered how life would have played out had I worked at Citytv. How long would it have taken before I stopped acting as if I had an abiding interest in television and applied again for work in publishing?

Some years after our first lunch, my journalist friend David invested a bit of his hard-earned dosh in a new board game invented by a couple of his equally impecunious fellow journalists. It was called Trivial Pursuit and it has a brilliant history of its own.

Welcome to CanLit

I AM NOT entirely sure why I didn't love New Zealand. Though it was suspicious of outsiders, it had been kind enough to take me in when I was a refugee in 1957; it taught me English; it provided me with an education; it provided a very credible third husband for my mother, who had been without one for a few years. It had given a home to my beloved grandfather, though he believed he was only in exile, ready to return to Hungary as soon as the Soviets left. It had offered me two lifelong friends and taught me how to cook lamb; to serve oysters, crayfish, and beer; to do the haka; to appreciate rugby and the All Blacks, who were the best in the world. Its generosity extended to a free university education and a chance to be co-editor of *Canta*, the Canterbury University student newspaper. Despite all that, I had found the country insular, static, and lacking in curiosity. I couldn't wait to leave the first time and now, again, I was eager to get back to Canada.

My roommate, Lou, had suspected I would be back and kept my bedroom and Morty Mint's sheets and pillows more or less unoccupied on Broadway Avenue.

While job-hunting, I heard about an opening at McClelland & Stewart from a senior guy at an educational publishing house who had interviewed me and thought I was singularly unqualified for educational publishing.

Jack's publishing house, he told me, was much more likely to hire some-one with my enthusiasm and lack of appropriate experience. Besides, it was an exciting place to be. The 1967 Centennial, he said, had produced a whole new wave of Canadian nationalism and a slew of Canadian books. Jack McClelland was at the centre of all that activity. As it happened, he explained, Canadians were even starting to like their own literature.

To make sure I got a foot in the door, he called Frank Newfeld,* M&S's vice president and art director, and assured him I would be worth an in-terview. Frank (thick black hair with bits of white, trimmed moustache, a military gait, very serious face) had an office at the far end of the low-slung, tin-roofed, warehouse-style building in an industrial hinterland of East Toronto where I would spend the next ten years of my life. I suspect Frank, in turn, recommended me to Jack McClelland because I spoke passable German, some French, reasonable Russian, and had an unpronounceable Hungarian name (Szigethy, my father's only legacy). Frank mentioned that he was from Czechoslovakia. After the Second World War he had served in the Israeli army, was wounded in action in 1949, and eventually ended up in Canada. He looked like a man with a sense of fashion, with his well-cut vest, flared jacket.

Jack interviewed me in the dining room of the Westbury Hotel on Yonge Street, his usual lunchtime hangout in the sixties and early seventies. He had a corner table that, I discovered, was reserved for him whether he was there or not. It was a dark room with hovering waiters, white tablecloths, flowers in slender vases centred on each table—the perfect setting for a Second World War hero on his second martini and an ambitious refugee with a desperate need for a job.

He was tall and broad-shouldered with longish, floppy blond-white hair, blond eyebrows, light-blue eyes, and freckles; even his hands were freckled. He had a tanned face with white laugh lines, a rumpled grey suit, white shirt, blue tie, and great manners that spoke of English family tradi-

---

* Frank won more than 170 international awards during his long career. His fascinat-ing memoir, *Drawing on Type*, was published by Porcupine's Quill in 2009.

tions. He stood when I came to the table. There were four cigarette butts in the ashtray already and he was lighting a new cigarette. There was a pile of paper in front of him, several hundred typed pages that he had been reading before I arrived.

"Quite an outfit," he said, appraising my London garb. "What will you have to drink?"

I said I'd have what he was having, which seemed to be the perfect answer, except that I had not known he was drinking a martini, not something I was used to at the time, though only a few months later, I could take two without losing consciousness. In London and Christchurch, I used to drink beer. It was cheaper. In Budapest I was too young to be drinking anything alcoholic.

Once I recovered from my martini-induced coughing fit, I started into a long, eloquent, and largely fictitious list of all that I had accomplished in my previous jobs.

"What have you been reading?" he asked after I had finished talking. I drank more of my martini and waxed eloquent about the merits of Russian and British classics, while Jack ordered food.

I told him I had just read a book by Alice Munro and another by Margaret Laurence. I had also read a Mowat but didn't realize he was Canadian.

Jack was charming and polite, though keen on the liberal use of four-letter words, a hangover, he explained, from his years in the navy. This explanation was followed by his observation "I can't imagine why the fuck Frank recommended you for this job."

"I guess he thought I would be really good at it. I already know a great deal about production . . ." I warbled on, singing my own praises, inflating my few years on the fringes of book publishing. I even included stacking books at Whitcombe and Tombs in Christchurch, my short stint inscribing Dewey Decimal designations on the spines of books at the Royal Geographic Society library in Wellington (I had escaped to Wellington when my mother married Alfons), stacking more books in the Canterbury University Bookstore. Naturally, I inflated my Collier Macmillan stint. The waiters hovered and Jack appeared to listen, head to one side, blond eyebrows knitted—a look he had perfected for long, one-sided conversations.

Later he told me he had been delighted with my résumé. I had listed years of employment with a variety of firms, where I might, indeed, have worked, but not for long and not as an editor. He thought that inventiveness was what he needed, with M&S's finances sinking and no new money on the horizon. Besides, publishing was a young person's game. Creativity, he said, declines as you age and you are no longer capable of new ideas.

Jack had also started young, in 1946, after captaining a motor torpedo boat that harassed German U-boats in the North Atlantic. His father owned M&S then, a firm mainly in the business of distributing American books in Canada, though it did publish a few authors such as Lucy Maud Montgomery. Jack had a dream of publishing great Canadian writers. It was a huge risk, but he was young. Such risks, as he never tired of telling me, are for the young.

After lunch he decided to inspect sailboats in Toronto Harbour and invited me to come along. He spent a good ten minutes examining a single-masted wooden yawl, gleaming white in the sunshine, its long prow bobbing gracefully in the water. He talked a bit about line and thrust or some such. At the time I thought Jack knew something about sailboats. It was not until a few months later that Farley Mowat disabused me of that notion.

I am not sure what all he said but I remember he was excited about that season's authors, and about Canada in general. The second martini had claimed most of my ability to speak.

He hired me after closely examining the second boat we had come to and deciding not to buy it. I didn't care that he hadn't mentioned exactly what the job was. I was ready to start any time. It seemed to me that being paid for reading was going to be an amazing gift from the gods.

The one condition of my showing up for work a week later was that I had to read all the books in M&S's New Canadian Library. Jack thought my knowledge of Canada was deplorably minuscule and he was sure that the best way to learn about the country was reading Canadian writers. Of all his achievements, Jack said, he was proudest of the New Canadian Library. He had begun it in 1954 with the appointment of Malcolm Ross, a professor at Dalhousie University, as general editor. Ross had been Jack's professor at a University of Toronto summer course.

Starting a series of paperback reprints of Canadian fiction was taking a leap into the dark, Jack explained. The initial public response had been cool. In the first year fewer than three hundred copies of each book were sold. But by the mid-sixties, with a new awareness of being Canadian and a new generation filled with self-confidence, the books had begun to sell.

I started with Gabrielle Roy, because Jack had said she was the most brilliant novelist, as well as the most beautiful woman in Canada, perhaps the world. He said he had been in love with her since the first time she looked into his eyes in Saint Boniface, Manitoba. "She was small, dainty, beautifully groomed, extremely bright and perceptive," he said. Her first novel, *The Tin Flute—Bonheur d'Occasion* in the original French—had been awarded both the Governor General's Award and the Prix Femina in France. It had sold about 700,000 copies in the United States alone, in large part owing to its wise selection by the Literary Guild book club.

I went on to Frederick Philip Grove (not one of his favourites and I could see why), Morley Callaghan, Thomas Haliburton, Sinclair Ross, Charles G. D. Roberts, Stephen Leacock, Ralph Connor, Mazo de la Roche (didn't do much for me), Ernest Buckler (loved him), A. M. Klein, and Mordecai Richler's *Cocksure* (funny, sardonic, takes a whack at swinging London), which was not in the New Canadian Library but Jack thought it would be a relief from Grove. I read about thirty books and enjoyed myself. I had never considered reading to be a chore.

A week later I arrived for work at 25 Hollinger Road, a grim stretch of warehouses in a quasi-industrial part of the city east of the Don Valley. Marge Hodgeman, Jack's long-time secretary, walked me to a small office with a desk and a window overlooking the parking lot, and mentioned that this was where Jack had placed me. It was just outside the editorial compound, where there were no windows and only plywood partitions defining each person's area. You could hear every cough and sniffle, throw paper darts over the partitions, share bits of manuscript, left-over sandwiches. There was the steady drone of manual typewriters. Editor Charis Wahl, who started her M&S stint in 1975, dubbed it the "Franz Kafka Memorial Suite."

The first person to emerge from the compound to greet me was Pamela

Fry. Speaking with the remnants of an English accent, she told me that she herself had written a couple of British-style mysteries. She had short dark-red hair and wore long, loose dresses and shawls. Her specialty was fiction, but she also worked on children's books. She was the oldest among the editorial staff, most of whom were my age or younger. A few years after she left, she was replaced by Lily Poritz Miller, small, feisty, opinionated, and usually right. Unlike Pamela, whose general approach to Jack was to humour him, Lily engaged him in written debates, some of which she even won. She worked with some of our most interesting and most challenging authors—Leonard Cohen, Sylvia Fraser, Michael Ondaatje, Alistair MacLeod, to mention a few. In 1975–76 she edited Alistair's *The Lost Salt Gift of Blood* and, ten years later, his *As Birds Bring Forth the Sun.*

Peter Smith, thin, serious, bespectacled, was the senior non-fiction editor.* Sam Totten, who had the office next to mine, was the formidable head of education, a balding older man who wore tailored suits and spoke with great deliberation about "juveniles" and ministries of education. When I hired Linda McKnight as "education editor" I had to seek Sam's approval. Linda managed to impress him with her very precise diction and her ability to listen without interrupting. She would rise through the ranks to director of publishing and president. She was the best and brightest at a time when we were all at our best and brightest.

Once, while looking for a pencil sharpener in Sam's desk, I discovered a well-thumbed copy of William S. Burroughs's *Naked Lunch*, a book then still considered scandalous, though no longer banned. After that, I was no longer terrified of him.

It took me a while to figure out what everybody did and how they all felt about my sudden appearance. One person I know was pleased was the overworked reader of "the slush pile," manuscripts that arrived unbidden at the rate of about eight or nine per day. It was a job held by a long succession of people, most of whom couldn't take it for longer than a year. Philip

---

* Peter ended up working for the National Gallery and the federal government after leaving M&S. Many M&S graduates went on to prestigious jobs in the arts.

Marchand, who had the job at the time, was sure that no matter what other duties I had, I would share his reading burden. Clearly, he needed help. Phil went on to be the book columnist at the *Toronto Star*.

Frank Newfeld's art department was at the end of the long corridor leading to the warehouse. It was Frank who came up with the title of "production editor" for me. He had a fierce temper, unlike Jack, whose usual mode of expressing displeasure was sarcasm. I didn't know that most of the walls in the building were plywood until Frank put his fist through a wall of my office in the middle of an argument about a book cover he had designed. Frank felt compelled to show me how strongly he felt about the original design. That may have been the first inkling I had that an art director was a powerful figure at a publishing house. As time went on, I learned that Frank was the king of book designers and that he picked his fights carefully and usually won.

Bob Wilkie, a distinguished Scot with a pleasant burr who ran marathons, was production manager. He was a bit surprised by my appointment as production editor but, unlike Frank, he was easygoing and didn't mind. A few weeks later, perhaps inadvertently while dictating a letter to someone he wanted to fob off on another person, Jack made me "managing editor."

Scott McIntyre was head of advertising, promotion, and publicity. A cheerful guy with light brown locks and a ready smile, he had been at M&S for a couple of years already and seemed very much part of the high-voltage excitement of the place. Scott left midway through 1969 to join Jimmy Douglas's firm selling our books in the West, but our paths would intertwine for years.

The Rosedale Radical

ONE OF MY first jobs at M&S was printing multiple copies of Scott Symons's *Civic Square*, a manuscript typed on the wax paper of a Gestetner duplicating machine. It's hard to explain how the damned thing worked: there were inked rollers that sometimes relieved themselves of superfluous ink, making the paper copies messy and virtually unreadable, so that each sheet had to be inspected and replaced if necessary. My hands and arms all the way to the elbows were covered in ink. Scott Symons was there for part of the arduous process but kept himself away from the infernal Gestetner.

He was about my height with muscular shoulders and arms, a tanned face with intense brown eyes that he would focus, squinting to make sure I knew he was serious—very serious, even when he appeared to be kidding about some parts of his personal story. He talked about growing up in a big house in Rosedale, a Red Tory, grandson of Perkins Bull, a famous bulwark, he said, of Toronto society; as expected of him, he had married into the upper class. His wedding, he told me, had been a disaster. Since then, I have heard various versions of the event, but irrespective of who made the nastiest speech and who shouted "Shame, shame!" it was Scott who was at the centre of this story, a rebel among the respectable, loathsome Protestant gentry of his day. By the time of *Civic Square*, he had left his wife and son to begin his journey of self-discovery.

While he talked incessantly and with great passion about his life, we made three hundred sets of the 848-page beast, then stacked each one into a blue Birks-style box. (Birks was a very chic, expensive downtown Toronto jewellery store.) Scott personalized the top sheet of each set of pages with a red felt-tipped pen, drawing stylized testicles, penises, flowers, decorative curlicues, and signing his name. We then closed the boxes and wrapped a Birks-style white ribbon around each one. *Civic Square* was heavy-handedly anti-Toronto-establishment, so the packaging served to attract attention to the story inside. Scott was planning to deposit one of the blue boxes in an offering plate at St. James Cathedral, his father's church.

Originally, Scott told me, the book was to be called *The Smugly Fucklings* but Jack had objected, as he objected to the overall length and repetitions in the manuscript, though he decided to publish it anyway. John Robert Colombo,* an experienced freelance editor Jack often entrusted with difficult manuscripts, had done his best with *Civic Square*, but it was never going to become a big seller.

Jack, Scott assured me, admired his flourishes of inimitable prose, his clear-eyed view of the milieu he had been born into, and his absolutely honest rejection of it. Scott loved Jack's courage in publishing his first novel, *Place d'Armes*, in 1967, and now *Civic Square*. *Place d'Armes* had been a call to arms, he told me, a statement of such brilliance that Canada's bloodless establishment quavered in its pristine sheets. While Jack was not the only person who recognized Scott's brilliance, he was in a position to publish and promote what Scott wanted to say about Canadian society's stultifying, emasculating ways.

Since we had to spend many hours with the Gestetner and the boxes, I came to know Scott reasonably well. Trinity College School in Port Hope, he assured me, had failed to break his spirit, though it had broken his body. Scott had been a brilliant gymnast: gymnastics suited his solitary ways, he said. He had practiced every day to keep his muscles tuned. One day he

---

* John had been one of M&S's best book doctors before he became famous for his books of quotations. Now his website lists more than two hundred books.

flew off the high bar, fell, and broke his back. That was not the only reason he had hated Trinity. Despite its appreciation of his intellectual abilities, despite the scholarships and suggestions he should go to Cambridge, he saw it as a hidebound place where future elite leaders learned their limp ways. At the University of Toronto he became a stellar member of the Zeta Psi fraternity—the erudite, wild boys—who thought they had a chance to discomfort the comfortable.

Scott went on to study at the Sorbonne, was appointed a curator at the Royal Ontario Museum, and enjoyed occasional bouts as a journalist. His first love, he told me, had not even been his wife (I never understood why he had married) but a fellow male student with whom he had stopped short of enjoying sex. He was still too much infected by "the disease of society's mores."

His best friend (not a lover) since early school days was Charles Taylor, a brilliant journalist who would later manage the considerable estate, including thoroughbred racehorses left by his father, E. P. Taylor.* Charles's 1982 book *Radical Tories: The Conservative Tradition in Canada* would look back at the ideas of Scott and other Red Tories, including philosopher George Grant and poet Al Purdy. Charles's definition of a Red Tory: "a conservative with a conscience."

Charles saw *Civic Square* as a kind of testament: Scott's break with conventional society and a rejection of all its comforts and traditions. Charles admired his courage.

When I met him, Charles had already published a book about China, based on his experiences as *The Globe and Mail*'s man in Beijing. We became friends over my trying and failing to persuade him to write another, about thoroughbred racing. As far as I could tell, horses and horse breeding were the only things Charles liked about his father's activities. He looked splendid in his formal Kentucky Derby garb. His Windfields Farm had been the birthplace of Northern Dancer, one of the most famous thoroughbreds in racing history.

---

* E. P. Taylor, the former brewery king, had become one of the richest men in Canada and, later, in the Bahamas.

Scott absconded with a seventeen-year-old boy to Mexico, where he was chased by *federales* determined to return young John to his distinguished family in Montreal. John's parents had charged Scott with inducing a minor into immoral acts.

After they returned from Mexico, Scott and his lover used to visit our apartment in the late evening, when he was sure no one had followed them. They made quite the pair: John, with long legs and red hair, sleek as a young colt; Scott in his trademark soiled black sweatshirt and his large silver medallion on a silver chain. Scott would be whispering stories about narrow escapes from the *federales*, his attempts to keep writing in impossible circumstances, assuring me that he was still—as far as Canadian society was concerned—"a very dangerous man," a revolutionary who could change the world. He fulminated about the "death-dealing puritanism that lies at the base of the Canadian identity."

I tried to like *Civic Square* because I liked Scott, but I found it wearying, shrill in tone, and, as Jack had told Scott, unrelentingly repetitious. Given that the late sixties were still anxious about sex, that there were banned books and homosexual behaviour was just being decriminalized, Scott was brave to have written his books, and Jack was brave to have published them. But I didn't think they were good books. Still don't. Yet, looking back, I admire Scott's courage to challenge society, and his belief that words can be dangerous: that's why tyrants are always eager to imprison or kill writers who confront them with words.

I WOULD WORK with Scott again in 1971. This time, it was a huge book called *Heritage: A Romantic Look at Early Canadian Furniture.* He knew his subject well and loved each piece he described. His only problem was that he couldn't bring himself to sit and type, so we developed a working pattern where Scott marched about my small office glaring at the parking lot, talking, and I typed. Then I edited what he had said and read it to him. I remember Scott pacing, smoking his pipe, dribbling ash down his black sweatshirt, standing still for a moment, starting again, never missing the continuity of his words, though he did stop now and then to tell me about his love for "the boy" and how he had been liberated at last from the stultifying social strictures of this country, a country he had loved enough to try to change.

In the finished book each chunk of copy, except for the introduction, is accompanied by one of John de Visser's stunning photographs.* Despite the strange way we produced it, I think *Heritage* is Scott's best writing.

We stayed in touch while he was in BC with his lover, doing odd jobs for a living. When they broke up, he came to Toronto again, looking sad and dishevelled but determined to continue with "his mission." Though he was openly and proudly homosexual, he insisted he was not "gay." He was seeking a "new kind of man," sentient, not effeminate, a male ideal that he thought might exist in other countries.

He chose Morocco.

His last book, *Helmet of Flesh* (1989), a novel set in Morocco, was neither scandalous nor a critical success, and no amount of editorial attention could save it from its author's overwrought prose.

---

* John de Visser's photographs are some of Canada's defining images. I had a chance to work with him on a number of books, including *Winter* with Morley Callaghan and *Canada: A Celebration.*

The Unfortunate Incident of Ted's Name

A FEW WEEKS after I was hired at M&S, I discovered how to spell Ted Allan's name. Unfortunately it was too late. We had been preparing a revised edition of *The Scalpel, the Sword*, the biography of iconic doctor Norman Bethune, by Ted Allan and Sydney Gordon. It had been an arduous task, as Ted and his co-author no longer spoke to each other and both wrote longish, abusive letters complaining about each other's lack of professionalism. Several times the project dropped off the schedule and was revived only after Jack's mollifying talks with both authors. Sydney lived in East Berlin at the time and Ted lived in London. Both had been die-hard Communists. Sydney was still a true believer,* but Ted had wobbled after Soviet troops attacked Hungary in 1956.

I had okayed for press the redesigned (several times, because the authors couldn't agree) cover of the book. It was not until Ted Allan received his author copies and yelled on the phone at me that I discovered the mis-

---

* Andreas Schroeder wrote in *Founding the Writers' Union of Canada* that Gordon came to Canada every year for the AGM to take notes and, presumably, report back to the Stasi. He stopped coming in 1976 after a union motion condemning the Soviets for persecuting writers.

take. His name was misspelled. The books had rolled off the press with "Ted Allen" on the cover.

Ted was a celebrated playwright, novelist, and short story writer (he had been published in *The New Yorker*), a Communist-Republican journalist and volunteer in the Spanish Civil War. He'd been on the Hollywood blacklist during the 1950s McCarthy era and was a close friend of Jack's close friends Mordecai and Florence Richler. One of Mordecai's early novels, *A Choice of Enemies*, draws on the people both he and Ted had known in London's world of expat Canadians eking out a living. Ted had been the most successful of them all.

Ted had every reason to assume that editors and designers at M&S would be familiar with his name, especially as this was a revised edition of an already successful book (I confess I had not previously heard of the famous doctor). Bethune had also been a Communist and a surgeon who, like Ted, had volunteered to help the Republican side during the Spanish Civil War. He operated close to the front, perfecting a method of blood transfusions for the critically injured. It was the same method he used later in China, operating on Mao's soldiers in 1938 and in 1939 during the Sino-Japanese War.

Ted was apoplectic. He demanded to talk to Jack.

Jack ordered me into his office while the two of them talked on the phone. As was his habit, Jack leaned as far back in his chair as the back wall would allow, his feet planted on his desk, his shirtsleeves rolled up, his top button undone, tie askew, a full ashtray close to the hand holding a cigarette. The office was clouded in blue smoke.

After patiently listening to Ted for what seemed to me at least twenty minutes, Jack inhaled deeply and said, "Ted, I have just shipped twenty thousand copies of your book and I can tell you we are not about to reprint because of one small mistake. Perhaps you could change your name."

Then he laughed. Ted, a future winner of the Stephen Leacock Memorial Medal for Humour, did not laugh. He kept talking and shouting so loudly that I could hear him where I sat meekly near the door.

Jack listened. Then, astonishingly, he said, "Picky, picky, picky, Ted," and hung up.

Later, when I saw the Academy Award–winning film *Lies My Father Told Me*, I understood Ted better. It's a warm, delightfully quirky heartbreaker of a story based on Ted's long-ago childhood in Montreal. Ted wrote the original script, and he even played a bit part as Mr. Baumgarten, one of the old Jewish characters. I felt a connection: both our grandfathers had been storytellers.

I spent hours with Ted to see if he could turn the film's story into a novel, but he was too busy on scripts—he was working on four or five at the time—so the novelization was ultimately written by his son, Norman. You can read the whole novel on Norman Allan's website. There you can also find Ted's delightful children's book about a squirrel-mouse who is a retired acrobat, *Willie the Squowse.*

YEARS LATER TED used to visit me at Key Porter Books, the company I would co-found. He complained about the 1990 Bethune film based on his book and screenplay, about Donald Sutherland's ego, and about the damage done by the Cultural Revolution in China. He had found Mao's wife, the actress Jiang Qing, terrifying when she was in power and pathetic afterwards. He liked to talk about the difficult story of his life.* He had been shocked by Nikita Khrushchev's so-called secret speech at the Twentieth Congress of the Communist Party in 1956, the speech that revealed some of Stalin's purges, the murders of fellow Communists he no longer trusted. Ted still felt terrible guilt about testifying against a comrade at his trial by fellow Communists in Spain in the 1930s. He had sworn false testimony in the belief that his words would help heal a rift in the Party.

---

* Ted's story in *This Time a Better Earth* is worth a serious read. It describes his difficult childhood, and his guilt about having taken his beloved sister to an asylum for the insane. It evokes a time of heroes who fought for a cause they believed was right and worth dying for. Not enough has been written about the Mackenzie-Papineau Battalion of Canadian volunteers in the International Brigades that fought against Franco in the Spanish Civil War.

My own feelings about Stalin and Khrushchev (and Lenin and Marx and even Engels) had been consistent since I'd first heard their names as a child in Hungary. My mandatory lessons about the birth of Communism, about the Great Leader, Stalin, and the shiny-headed Mátyás Rákosi failed to improve my first impressions. Vili and his friends joked about them all, but only where they were sure no informer would overhear them. I suspect Ted liked to tell me about his own Communist sympathies because he felt he needed to explain himself to someone who had witnessed the 1956 Hungarian Revolution.

Assembling a Book on the Linoleum Floor

MANAGING EDITOR WAS only the first of my five or so titular promotions. I was executive editor for a few months, then editorial director, then editor-in-chief, with vice president added for extra spice. Each time, I think Jack figured a new title meant he didn't have to give me a raise. He was right. Those days at M&S were so jam-packed with new faces and manuscripts that I barely had time to think about money. Jack, on the other hand, thought about it most of the time. The firm was running out of cash, he said, and what was left wouldn't be wasted on staff stipends. If anyone felt it was not enough, he or she could leave. He considered it a privilege to be at M&S with the country's best authors. And it was, indeed, a privilege.

With two notable exceptions, Jack was unable to fire anyone. The closest he came was clipping printed advertisements for suitable jobs and placing them on the desks of those he wanted to be rid of. One notable exception involved one of our many vice presidents, who told Jack he had to make a choice between himself and me. I stayed. The second firing would rock the entire company, but more about that later.

Periodically Jack would complain about the general incompetence of people who worked for him, as when he announced to a roomful of booksellers at the company's annual big fall list launch party at the Royal York Hotel that he was, sadly, "surrounded by idiots." We, his senior staff, duti-

fully arrayed behind him on stage, took it reasonably well, though someone had to restrain Peter Taylor, our director of marketing, from grabbing
the mic and making a few observations of his own.

Peter was irrepressibly witty, always full of ideas for how to sell books,
never lost for words, friendly to newcomers like me. He was thin, wiry,
and almost completely bald. His novel *Watcha Gonna Do Boy . . . Watcha
Gonna Be?* was published by M&S before he came on board. We became
friends as soon as we met.[*]

The building itself, at 25 Hollinger Road, was cruel and unusual pun-
ishment for even the most dedicated employees. Brick with a tin roof, it
was perishingly cold in the winter and nightmarishly hot in the summer.
Some days in mid-winter the snow-removal crews would leave out most of
East York or decide not to de-ice the roads off Eglinton Avenue, east of the
Don Valley Parkway, so that even showing up for work was an act of courage in face of civic indifference. Midsummer, the place turned into a sauna.
Jack would sometimes be shirtless, as would a few male staff; the women
wore as little as possible and hovered over fans. The floors were covered in
linoleum that sweated as we did.

IN THE EARLY summer of 1969, in preparation for the publication of Harold Town's *Drawings*, after an excruciatingly sweaty debate in the boardroom, I laid out the sticky, curling, damp photostats of Harold's drawings
along the continuous corridor. The line started before reception, went past
Jack's office, turned the corner, carried on past Sam Totten's office and
the editorial bunker, all the way to the door of the art department. Since I
spent most of the day on my knees, arranging drawings, I was glad that I
had given up my London miniskirt and worn long cotton pants—rather
than my new quite fashionable, beige imitation-leather pants—that didn't
ride down when I was bent over.

---

[*] Years later, Key Porter published his still very funny *Bald Is Beautiful*. (With so
many balding boomers, surely it's time for a new edition.)

Frank Newfeld had already planned the design of the book; Robert Ful-ford, art critic and columnist for the *Toronto Star* and recently appointed editor of *Saturday Night* magazine, was writing the text.

It's hard to overstate Harold Town's fame at the end of the 1960s. In 1968 alone he had had eight one-man shows and been part of many others featuring the work of his generation's best-known artists, Painters Eleven. He had represented Canada at the Venice Biennale; he was profiled every-where, revered, collected, and discussed; he won international awards; he reviewed other people's work, appeared on talk shows, debated, fought, argued, and lambasted those who dared to criticize or contradict him.

He was not only one of the country's most celebrated artists but also a man given to great flights of belligerent verbal abuse with a full lexicon of sexual and scatological references, including some I had not heard even in the company of American servicemen stationed in the United Kingdom. My London boyfriend had been a captain in the US Air Force, a veterinar-ian in civil life, and delightful company. Some of his less gentle-hearted friends, however, did manage streams of interesting invective.

Harold's drawings were even more eclectic than his language. He had experimented with a variety of styles and media: heavy blacks, light pencil sketches, pastels, gouache, charcoal, brush, ink, in a wide range of colours and surfaces. He did soft portraits, such as one of Allen Ginsberg, figures in motion, dancers, and the surreal Enigmas—grotesque figures with tem-ples for heads and objects sticking out of their asses—Picasso-style nudes, horses, ancient warriors, queens, and some pure whimsy, such as "Michel-angelo Composing a Sonnet by Candlelight."

He was a lanky, broad-shouldered man, pale, with soft mousy-brown hair and grey sideburns that ran down the sides of his face all the way to his chin. He had an intense, fixed look with a pair of long lines between his eyebrows that made him seem angry even when he was not. That day, he wore white pants and some sort of pleated twill jacket in defiance of the heat.

Jack had warned me about Harold's insatiable ego, his inability to com-promise, and the likelihood that we would be sorting through pictures for the rest of the day, the night, and maybe the week. Harold considered each drawing to be of such superior quality that leaving out even one was an insult to his genius.

While Bob Fulford admired Town's prodigious talent, he did not think that everything he had ever produced was a work of unparalleled brilliance. One of his ways of dealing with Harold's flights of verbal fancy was to listen, chew on his pipe, nod sagely, and postpone the decision until it had become obvious, even to Harold, that the book could not accommodate all his drawings.

Bob's experience as editor of the venerable magazine *Saturday Night* must have taught him a great deal of patience. The eighty-two-year-old magazine was an institution but, according to Jack, in a very precarious financial state. One wrong move and this could be its last year. In a strange way, Jack both delighted in and sympathized with *Saturday Night*'s plight, as M&S was in a similarly precarious situation.

Balding, with black-framed glasses that had a habit of slipping down his nose while he was in contemplation, Bob also had a smiling, thoughtful, and cheerful attitude to the whole improbable day. Frank had, surprisingly, held his temper in check for the better part of an hour, then left. Harold and Bob appeared not to notice the heat or the dampness. Each was determined to wrestle the other into submission—Harold to include more than the designated number of works, Bob to urge discernment.

My job was to get down on the floor and move the sheets of sticky paper in and out of order, or just onto a pile of what Harold bitterly called "rejects."

Harold didn't directly address me while I was squatting or kneeling, but he did have a few choice words he urged me to pass on to my boss when the "son of a bitch" dared show his face again. Jack had mentioned that he loved Harold but did not much like him. He was tired of the tirades and of picking up the tab every time they went out for drinks. He thought Harold was depressingly cheap when it came to paying his own way.

Jack was also critical both of the fact that Harold had a "lady" in addition to his wife and annoyed that Harold often reneged on paying her for her research work. I met Iris Nowell, Harold's lady, one evening when the four of us had dinner in a restaurant on King Street. Harold harangued

Jack for his lack of attention to the quality of paper in *Drawings* and the amount of promotion he felt entitled to and didn't get. For some mysterious reason, then, Harold sang "Bye, Bye Miss American Pie," with its anti-Vietnam overtones and unforgettable image of "the day the music died."

Iris was blond, with soft grey eyes, quiet, smart, and very attentive to Harold. When she expressed an opinion about something, he berated her:* I think the subject was dogs or cats. Harold hated all pets but especially dogs and cats. He wanted Iris to write a book about the dangers they posed to humans. He talked about movies he hated, about Toronto landmarks slated for destruction by bureaucrats who knew the value of nothing, about critics—particularly art critic Clement Greenberg, who had promoted the work of Jack Bush, a Canadian artist whom Harold despised—and about a proposed book on his own famous Christmas trees. They were miracles of lights and construction displaying hundreds of fabulous old things he had collected over the years. Even after a tree toppled under the weight of its decorations, the surviving objects remained treasures in Harold's studio.

But back to the linoleum floor. Bob Fulford, who must have appreciated my efficiency in placing damp paper in straight lines and my dumbfounded diplomacy about the final choices in *Drawings*, invited me to lunch a few weeks later. He was then, and is now, the most interesting and erudite conversationalist, one of the most quoted people in the country. He discussed art, museums, Jane Jacobs's ideas for cities, Expo 67 and why it was such an important event, the Canadian Broadcasting Corporation and what it should be broadcasting, movies, and filmmakers. Unlike some of the writers I met later in Toronto, Bob was an anti-Communist, and we found we shared a suspicion of the Soviet Union verging, at least on my part, on vehement dislike.

To my great relief, we did not talk about Harold's drawings.

Bob had been writing a movie column for some years as Marshall Delaney. I tried to persuade him to write a book about films and filmmakers

---

* Iris Nowell has written several books, including *Hot Breakfast for Sparrows: My Life with Harold Town* and *Harold Town*.

for M&S. Though I failed to convince him, eventually he did publish his *Marshall Delaney at the Movies*, but not with us.

DRAWINGS WAS PUBLISHED in time for Christmas, 1969. It was a handsome book but suffered a little from "show-through": some of the strong blacks were showing through the paper under the finer drawings on the reverse side of the page. Harold was, predictably, unhappy. Jack, in a mischievous moment, assured him that the choice of paper would have been a part of my job. Harold raged and shouted and refused to speak to me for a while. Perhaps because of my childhood, I am not comfortable around violence, whether physical or verbal, and Harold, as I said, was very good at invective.

I knew I had been forgiven when he set me up for a date with his close friend Sig Vaile. Siggy was quiet, restrained, and charming. He told lovely stories about his growing up in Ontario along with a few amusing Harold tales, but we were, clearly, not destined for each other. We belonged to different worlds, though we managed to have a couple of very pleasant dinners at rather swish restaurants. At the time, I was still somewhat involved with a young Jewish lawyer named Harvey, whose parents actively disliked gentiles, particularly Hungarians.

Harold was disappointed but not discouraged. He assumed that my relationships were of a temporary nature and that eventually I'd be looking for someone he would find acceptable.

All Those Glorious Manuscripts

W E USED TO get an average of fifty manuscripts a week, more in early January when would-be authors delivered on their own New Year's resolutions. Of that lot, few made it to a second reading, and maybe one was eventually published. Reading them was disheartening but Jack felt it was perfect for editors-in-training. I can't remember all our slush-pile readers, but I know Philip Marchand was succeeded by a coterie of equally talented young people: David Berry, who remembers that every inch of the floor-to-ceiling shelves was filled with manuscripts, most of them barely readable; Patrick Crean (later at Somerville House, Key Porter, Thomas Allen, HarperCollins); Greg Gatenby (founder of the International Festival of Authors); and Wailan Low, who married poet Earle Birney, went on to study law, and became a judge.

Everyone was encouraged to take home manuscripts from the slush pile, in case we missed an important new voice we should be publishing. One of Jack's many stories of missed opportunities was Sheila Burnford's *The Incredible Journey.* The way he used to tell the story, he had read the manuscript and thought who in hell would believe such an incredible tale. Three spoiled pets traversing the wilderness in search of their home. Five million copies and a movie later . . .

My own best slush-pile find was Dennis T. Patrick Sears's *The Lark in the Clear Air*; he was an original voice and a formidable new talent. Not a young writer, he had already lived a couple of hard-working lives, and his next book, *Aunty High Over the Barley Mow* (1977), was his last. The multi-talented Jennifer Glossop (she could edit fiction, non-fiction, illustrated books, and children's stories) finished editing Dennis's second manuscript after he died. Jennifer was one of my first hires. Without dwelling on the irony, she mentioned years later that she had started at M&S on April Fool's Day, 1970.

Every evening I took home a couple of huge white canvas bags full of manuscripts and read till the early hours. Some we had already decided to publish; others had been recommended for a second read. It was the beginning of a habit that lasted for my entire life in the book business.

That's where I read Rudy Wiebe's huge manuscript of *Big Bear* in one night. I had planned to stop for a couple of hours' sleep, but couldn't put the damned thing down. It was riveting then and is still riveting now, though other books have been written about the great Cree chief and his defiance of white authority. Charis Wahl was appointed Wiebe's editor, but the copy editing was farmed out to a meticulous freelancer. I had the unenviable task of presenting the author with the marked-up manuscript in Calgary. Rudy thanked me, then went to his room, and returned a few hours later with all the pencil marks rubbed out. Charis, who had disagreed with the copy editor's work, was pleased, and *Big Bear* was published with Rudy's long sentences intact.

I read Gabrielle Roy's slender *Windflower* under the dim lights of our Broadway Avenue balcony. It was almost word-perfect. I read Margaret Laurence's *The Olden Days Coat* and her short-story collection *A Bird in the House*, Brian Moore's *The Revolution Script* and *Catholics*, Eric Arthur's text for *The Barn: A Vanishing Landmark of North America*, and hundreds, no, thousands of other manuscripts during those years.

Everyone at M&S seemed to be imbued with a sense of mission, as if part of a magnificent experiment, with Jack as the exalted master magician, and the rest of us inspired apprentices. The experiment was publishing Canadian authors: novelists, poets, academics, children's writers, historians, anthropologists, journalists, and politicians.* We published anthologies, essay collections, reprints in the New Canadian Library, art and photography books, memoirs. Despite the financial problems, we continued to publish more than a hundred books a year, and we were wildly optimistic about the fate of every one of them.

During the summer, the warehouse, which occupied most of the building, was slightly cooler than the rest of the building because it had a lot of large fans: we were anxious to preserve the books. They were the only things of real value in the building, Jack used to say. The books, unlike the rest of us, were insured.

Our editorial meetings were endurance tests. They took place in the brown-walled corner boardroom of the building, where it was almost impossible to open any windows. The marketing staff brought notepaper and the editors filed in and talked about what they were editing; they tried to get sales projections from the marketing people, who were, at best, defensive. They didn't want to commit themselves to predictions. Peter Taylor was usually quite direct and merciless in assessing a book's sales potential. Paul Dutton, M&S jacket and advertising copywriter (and, with bpNichol, Steve McCaffrey, and Rafael Barreto-Rivera, one of the sound poetry group The Four Horsemen), often attended because he had to come up with copy.†

---

* I spent a day in a car with former cabinet minister Judy LaMarsh in 1969. We had just published her book, *Memoirs of a Bird in a Gilded Cage*, and we were travelling to dozens of interviews. By coincidence, I did the same job for her in 1979 during my last weeks at M&S and her last weeks of life. She died in December that year. The first trip she had talked about how much she loathed Pierre Trudeau, the second about not wasting even an hour of whatever time we had. Changing the world was not a quick task and women had a long way to go.

† More central to his career, Paul was a poet. Their early performance pieces were always well attended. The group stopped performing after bp died, but Paul went on to perform alone and with other groups in various countries. When I last talked with him, he was on his way to the Lvov music and poetry festival.

When Jack was there, the whole room focused on what Jack said and very few of us argued with him. One time when he was lauding the virtues of a long piece of what he considered "commercial fiction" and I suggested it was crap, he left, sweeping his papers off the table. He didn't come back that day but he insisted we publish the "crap."*

Each editor was expected to work on at least twenty manuscripts a year and supply each book-to-be with heartfelt recommendations for the sales department. Both Jack and Peter had a tendency to slip into grief over a lackluster list or too-low-key presentations. They wanted displays of passion and commitment.

On the brown boardroom's wall, someone had written: "It is the duty of all good M&S employees to devise the most expeditious way to cross the river from one bank to the other. However, when you are up to your ass in alligators, it is hard to recall that your original objective had been to drain the swamp."

IN 1969 JACK asked me to work with Peter Mellen, a very young professor of fine arts at the University of Toronto, who was planning a big book on the Group of Seven. They were Canada's iconic landscape painters, the first to portray Canada as it really is—a rugged Northern country. Their artistic ambition had been to produce something "strong and vital, and big,"† like the land itself. It would be hard to imagine a more appropriate education in what was quintessentially Canadian than this project. The art of the Group of Seven was very different from European paintings I had seen in galleries in London and Paris: more dramatic, wilder, less restrained even than the work of the Impressionists. In my earliest experience, Hungarian art had been mostly storytelling, detailed, and representational, portraying scenes from Hungarian history.

---

* I won't mention the author's name. No point in hurting her feelings, nor in being sued for libel.

† From the "manifesto" of the Canadian Art Club.

The Group of Seven was designed by Frank Newfeld with the young David Shaw, who would succeed him as M&S's art director.

My copy of the book has a finely penned note of thanks from Peter for my "help and patience" and A. Y. Jackson's shaky signature. It was appended when Jack and I drove to Kleinburg to meet with Robert and Signe McMichael of the McMichael Canadian Art Collection. A. Y., one of the founding Group of Seven artists, was in residence at the time. Polite but preoccupied, he was at work on a large painting near the open door of one of the rooms of the building.

My FIRST M&S sales conference was also an education in Canadian geography. The reps came from every region of the country, and our editors knew how to make sure that each one of them took away something from the conference that would spur their sales efforts on behalf of individual authors. I remember Jim Douglas (later co-founder of Douglas & McIntyre) scribbling notes and Allan MacDougall (later of Raincoast, the Canadian publisher of the Harry Potter books) throwing paper airplanes at Scott McIntyre, and Keith Andrews (from Montreal) with his handlebar moustache, who wore his bowler hat for the entire day. It was well known that no bookseller, department store, or chain store book buyer could give a rep more than two minutes to present a book, so key words, regional angles, comparisons to known bestsellers were vital. The editors, of course, took at least ten minutes to present each title to the general irritation of the salespeople. Delighting in my discovery of the Seven plus Tom Thomson, I took even longer to talk about *The Group of Seven.*

Most reps dozed part of the day, but not our Alberta rep, Ruth Fraser. She had been an editor herself and had presented her books to other reps, so she understood how difficult it was for someone close to a book to sum it up in only two minutes. She had spent years working with Maria Campbell editing *Halfbreed,* Maria's revelatory memoir of sexual abuse and poverty, followed by alcoholism, drugs, and prostitution. Ahead of its time, the book drew attention to the racism, brutalization, and oppression of Métis women in Canada and led the way to changes both in government policies and in Métis self-perception.

Since its first publication in 1973, *Halfbreed* has become a classic, taught in schools and debated among scholars, though as I read about the thousands of Indigenous women who have been murdered or disappeared during the past forty years and counting, it seems not to have made enough of a difference.

Ruth Fraser had been a student of W. O. Mitchell,* a multi-talented spinner of tales in many forms. She was a "facilitator" at W. O.'s weird but very enjoyable writers' workshops at the Banff Centre. It was Ruth's idea to invite me as a young publishing professional to read and comment on the bits and pieces emerging from the workshops.

The writers were all young and enthusiastic. They found W. O.'s approach, which he called "freefall" and others called "Mitchell's messy method," somehow liberating. It certainly eliminated performance anxiety and writer's block. Students were told to start typing or writing whatever came to their minds and eventually a story would emerge. Words would float out of their subconscious, and often those words would be the right ones to express what they were reaching for. To test the theories on young would-be writers, he had them read what they had written to other, equally inexperienced and uncritical students. Then he added a few "professionals" to the mix. That was my own baffling role, but I loved it—not so much because of the experience of hearing and reading those young writers, but because of the mountains.

The first time I saw the Rockies, I was thunderstruck. On the way to Banff, I had to ask Ruth to stop the car and let me out to look at them. I was spellbound and I have never tired of the sight. Hungary's mountains, the Carpathians, have lodged mostly in Romania since the end of the First World War, so I didn't have a chance to see them till many years later when my daughter Julia and I went in search of our ancestors. New Zealand's

---

* W. O.'s work has stood the test of time. Readers wanting to know why could start with *Who Has Seen the Wind* and, if they love the book, go on to read the others.

Mount Cook is a long way from Christchurch, Wanganui, and Wellington, where I spent my teen years. Okay, so Mount Cook is impressive, but not as massive, wild, breathtaking as the Rockies. Once I'd been there, I pined every year for another chance to go to Banff.

Fortunately for me, Ruth and I remained friends and she managed to invite me several times to the workshops—usually when my friend and novelist Sylvia Fraser was also there as a professional writer.

Roblin Lake and After

I N HIS INTRODUCTION to the aforementioned *Drawings*, Bob Fulford had written that Harold Town was "a heroic figure attracted to heroic figures." Other than wearing a heavy twill jacket during the summer, though, I found his heroism difficult to discern. At book launch parties, he stood apart. He hated to be touched and frequently threatened anyone who, in some conversational gambit, laid a hand on his arm or shoulder, with immediate destruction. He would mention or demonstrate his judo moves. Fortunately I never observed whether he had really learned judo. The closest I came to witnessing a punch-out was when Harold told photographer Roloff Beny that he would kill him if Beny touched his jacket again.

Once he threatened to hang young Doug Fetherling over the railing of the apartment I shared with Lou. I am not sure what annoyed him so much about Doug,* who did not reciprocate the animosity. Perhaps it was that Doug was a scruffy-looking American draft dodger with a stammer who didn't always have a room of his own. He had been sleeping on our

---

* Later he changed his name to George.

couch while he looked for a flat to rent.* A poet, a critic, a journalist, Doug eventually wrote more than forty books as a general observer of our times and his own life.

One memorable evening in 1970, Jack drove Harold and me to Prince Edward County for a friendly meeting with Al Purdy. We arrived at Purdy's A-frame house on Roblin Lake near Ameliasburgh in the late afternoon. Al offered us some sweet wine he said he had brewed himself; his wife, Eurithe, set out crackers. There was talk of a collaboration between Harold and Al.

Jack proposed a collection of poems—one poem by each of Canada's best poets, chosen by Al and accompanied by Harold's portraits. Both Jack and Al smoked steadily. They talked a bit about the most successful example of such a cooperation between artist and poet, Irving Layton's best-selling *Love Where the Nights Are Long*, love poems selected by Irving with drawings by Harold.

Al wondered whether Harold would illustrate Purdy's forthcoming book, *Love in a Burning Building*, but Jack didn't think Purdy's poetry was romantic enough. "Too hard-boiled," he said. Besides, Harold did not view himself as an illustrator.

The new collection, as Jack imagined, would feature only the most "significant" (Jack's word) Canadian poets, including Earle Birney, Leonard Cohen, Irving Layton, Raymond Souster, E. J. Pratt, maybe Milton Acorn, and John Newlove, but the choice was to be Al's. Jack claimed he had no opinion on who should be in, but Harold, of course, did have a lot of opinions. I thought it was best for me not to have an opinion either, though I did love some of the poetry they discussed. I was awed by Al and wary of Harold.

Discussions about the choice of poets and poems started politely

---

* Though I used to see Doug/George at a variety of book-related events, we tended to stand awkwardly next to each other rather than talk. I don't think it was his stammer or that he would leave long silences between sentences, but it took until 2003 for us to have a good conversation.

enough in the living room, then moved outside, to a somewhat marshy outcrop by Roblin Lake, where Harold held forth on the quality of the poets and Purdy's "unaccountable" (according to Harold) insistence on including himself in the galaxy of the best. Harold wore a large dark cape and marched about, emphasizing his points by an ever-escalating range of vitriol.

Al, no blushing violet, and taller and wider than Town, rose to the occasion and demonstrated to Harold that he could match him both verbally and physically, if that was called for. Jack, drinking the vodka he had brought, mostly stayed out of the fray.

I have no idea why Harold had chosen that moment to tell a long, rambling story about a bunch of skiers or snowmobilers he had terrorized with a long whip. It was too dark to see Al's face, except for the part lit up by his burning cigarette, but his stiff shoulders said appalled or outraged. His big hands were scrunching the papers he had brought out earlier.

For me, the night ended at dawn. Both combatants were still on the field when Eurithe ushered me up to a bunk on the second floor of the A-frame. I have no recollection of how or at what time we made it back to Toronto, what with Jack still drunk and Harold still talking and waving his arms to show his rage at Al's presumption. I must have driven the car.

Surprisingly, the project limped along for a while, with Harold drawing several of the selected poets. It came to an end only when Jack proposed a royalty split of seventy-five per cent to Harold and twenty-five to Al. Jack explained that Harold would not be able to sell the portraits—I have kept the drawing of a lovely brown and white Earle Birney—and Purdy was not writing new poetry for this volume.

Purdy insisted on fifty-fifty. After all, he was the country's most celebrated poet; he had been publishing poetry since 1944; he was the winner of the Governor General's Award (for *The Cariboo Horses*) and, like Harold, he was a sought-after prose writer for magazines and newspapers. His chief reason, though, for persisting in a demand for equal royalties was that he had come to loathe Harold.

One memorable occasion when the two men almost met again was in my Broadway Avenue living room. Purdy and I were working our way through the proofs of *Love in a Burning Building* when Jack and Harold arrived. While they knocked on the door, Al dashed to my bedroom and hid in the clothes closet until they left.

In the end, Jack ponied up a token one thousand dollars for Purdy not to go away mad and they never mentioned the damned thing again. Or at least not until Purdy slyly told his short version in the Preface to *Love in a Burning Building* and a more elaborate version in *Reaching for the Beaufort Sea.*

To my untrained eye, Al Purdy was the kind of heroic poet I had grown up admiring. He too was in love with his country. He talked about his poetry mapping the country, starting from the specific, the particular, expecting it would reach the broad, the general, as it always did. He was quintessentially Canadian. In one of his letters he says Canadians have been disguised as other people for a hundred years, and suddenly we are beginning to realize such disguises are useless. His poems celebrate Canada's landscape, its place names, and the Canadian way of speaking.

He wrote about the country in a way no one had written about it before. In a letter to Dennis Lee, he said he had "opened up the country thru poetry." Just read his poem "Say the Names."

    —say the names say the names
    and listen to yourself
    an echo in the mountains
    Tulameen Tulameen
    say them like your soul
    was listening and overhearing
    and you dreamed you dreamed
    you were a river
    and you were a river
    Tulameen Tulameen . . .

It is difficult to describe to anyone who was not fortunate enough to have heard and seen him read how Al Purdy read his poems. A big, shaggy man with uncombed hair, big shoulders, white sleeves rolled up, beefy hands, a booming voice, glasses slipped down low on his nose, he did not declaim as so many poets do but talked to you, as if he had just met you and decided to tell you what he had been thinking about. He looked as if he had just wandered onto the stage accidentally and would be so much more comfortable somewhere else, perhaps leaning on a bar instead of a lectern.

Al's family had moved to an old rundown house in Trenton, Ontario, after his father died. Al was about three years old, but he remembered the sagging floors, the wooden barn that filled the backyard, farm wagons clopping by on their way to the market, the black Trent River, the Crimean War cannon on a hill, and most of all his whisky-drinking, tobacco-chewing hellraiser of a grandfather, who was then about the size and shape Al grew into much later. He wrote about "Old Rid" in *Morning and It's Summer*, the slim book he sent me in 1983, with a whimsical dedication: "For Anna—16 years after hiding in her clothes closet."*

He was a natural storyteller. He talked about working at a range of menial jobs; he had been all over the country, at first as a kid riding the rails, seeking work during the Depression. He drank with novelist Malcolm Lowry in BC, made friends with Earle Birney ("genial and expansive"), met Irving Layton ("the Montreal magnet") in Montreal. He and George Bowering became friends. He wrote about the Arctic for Peter Newman's *Maclean's*; to make ends meet, he also wrote for *Weekend* magazine and *The Canadian*. (Sadly, both are long gone.) He travelled to Cuba with an assortment of other lefties, including Pierre Trudeau.

Known as a brawler, he commemorated some of his more interesting fights in poems. My favourite is "At the Quinte Hotel":

---

* He got the date wrong, but it was a lovely gift.

I am drinking
I am drinking beer with yellow flowers
In underground sunlight
And you can see I am a sensitive man
And I notice that the bartender is a sensitive man too . . .

But in many ways, his self-representation as a tough working man is misleading. He was a voracious reader and dedicated book collector. He had signed first editions of most of his contemporaries. He read Persian, Greek, and Gothic history as well as anthropology. He read Rilke, D. H. Lawrence, Creeley, Williams, Hardy, Pound, Pratt, Auden, Eliot, Thomas, Yeats (he loathed Whitman), Yevgeny Yevtushenko, and many more. He would have been pleased with my later publishing of Yevtushenko's autobiographical novel *Don't Die before You're Dead.*

He used to invite young writers to the A-frame on the shore of Roblin Lake, where he plied them with food, American beer, wild grape wine, and opportunities to share their poetry. Next to the A-frame, but not too close, he built a one-room study, a separate building where he could write.

During the late eighties Al spent a year at the University of Toronto. He thought it was ironic that a person with such little education should be invited to a university to talk with students about poetry. Far from the simple man of the soil, the image he cultivated in public, he discussed literature with any graduate without fear of being less than what he was.

The wonderful documentary *Al Purdy Was Here* opened at the Toronto International Film Festival in 2015. It is a celebration of Al's life, his poetry, and the A-frame he built with an assist from Milton Acorn—another fine poet, though I could never look at him the same way after he had vomited

---

* The Russian poet drew a huge crowd in Hamilton for the Key Porter book launch in 1995, with elderly women throwing flowers at his feet as he performed in both Russian and English. Like a rock star, he launched himself into the seats and lay, prostrate, on adoring ladies' laps.

on my shoes the day he received his Governor General's Award for Poetry at the Governor General's official residence in Ottawa.

I have a cherished memory of Al from the late seventies. We were walking along Yorkville, where we found a patio table at a restaurant and ordered beer. Al stretched out his long legs, lit a cigar, and started to talk about where he had just been and where he was going. He may not have been conscious of attracting a crowd, but since this was Yorkville trying to preserve its hippie reputation, some people slowed down and listened to Al talking poetry. Most of them were in their twenties. They didn't know the poems but they clapped every time Al took a long breath. One of the poems he recited that day was "The Country North of Belleville," his voice rising and raging:

> This is the country of our defeat
> and yet . . .

It was the poem Dennis Lee read at the Al Purdy Tribute at the October 1997 International Festival of Authors.

The Happy Hungry Man

I N HUNGARY, POETS were revered. Children learned to recite poems even before they learned to read, there are streets named after poets and life-size statues of poets all over the country. Most of my beloved poets were unabashedly nationalistic. I had grown up with poetry, admittedly the kind of nineteenth-century Hungarian poetry that scans in iambic pentameters and renders Hungarians tearful with patriotism or nostalgia. I had loved János Arany, Sándor Petőfi, Mihály Vörösmarty, and Endre Ady. I used to know every word in Vörösmarty's verse play, *Csongor és Tünde*. So many years later, I can still recite a few lines.

My grandfather used to take me to the Gerbeaud coffee house on the square named for Vörösmarty and I would spend hours walking around his massive statue with stone versions of some of his characters. The statue of Sándor Petőfi, hero of the 1848 uprising against the Hapsburgs, is not far from Vörösmarty's. A romantic figure, young, always in love, he died fighting for the country's independence from the Hapsburg Empire. My chief ambition before the 1956 Revolution was to be a poet.

I gave up that dream together with my first language in 1957 when I landed in New Zealand but I had not given up my love of poetry.

* * *

GEORGE JONAS WAS the first Hungarian '56er I met in Canada. It was at a party to celebrate his birthday. He wore dark glasses, though it was dark enough in the apartment where the party was held, a leather jacket, and leather pants with, incongruously, a collared shirt and tie. He was about six foot two, with a fringe (really), brown hair, high cheekbones, and a cigarette holder. He smoked constantly, lighting one cigarette after another. He had a soft voice and a relaxed Hungarian accent. He was working at the CBC then, producing radio and TV dramas and documentaries. Since 1962 he had written, produced, and directed about a hundred dramas. He would add a hundred more before he left the CBC.

More important in my estimation of George, he was a poet. His first poetry collection, *The Absolute Smile*, had been published by the new House of Anansi in 1967. His second, *The Happy Hungry Man*, was published in 1970. Margaret Atwood was his editor but, as she recalled, he didn't need much editing. These few lines were my favourite:

The happy hungry man believes in food
The happy homeless man believes in a home
The happy unloved man believes in love
I wouldn't mind believing in something myself.

George and I became friends by increments. We would meet for lunch and talk about music, fascism, Hungarian humourists, old films, George Orwell, poetry, Canadian law, motorcycles, the joys of flying, and politics. We had both survived a revolution and both of us were enamoured with Canada, but he thought my views of the world were, at best, naive, at worst, dangerous. He feared that I had retained too much socialism. I thought he was too far to the mordant right and lacking in sympathy for the poor.

But we always agreed on poetry. We would recite long Petőfi poems— ones with a bit of humour—and Heine, Rilke, sometimes even Pushkin. As for his own poems, I love "Memories":

The Room has four walls, the room is empty,
And there is nothing left in the room.

Around the room the house is dying
The way worlds die.
I lived here, I am told. I don't remember.

What I remember is nothing to speak of:
A summer perhaps, and a flow of streams.
Now I am tired. Elephants
Sit on my dreams.

One of George's best-loved poets, George Faludy, had also landed here after '56. He had been the most famous poet of the 1950s in Hungary. His translation of the little-known fifteenth-century French vagabond poet François Villon made him into a celebrity. Faludy had served hard time in both Nazi and Communist prisons*: George called him "an equal opportunities resister." A small man with wildly unruly grey hair, Faludy was a frequent visitor to George's midtown apartment. When he met my mother, who could still recite his Villon poems by heart, he was impeccably polite and even flirtatious, though he was travelling with his gay lover at the time.

George Jonas introduced me to the work of Sándor Márai and Stephen Vizinczey, both of whom I still read today. Vizinczey had emigrated to Canada when George did, but unlike George, he had found Canada stifling. His first novel, *In Praise of Older Women*, was self-published. Vizinczey used to personally cart copies to bookstores, where they were snapped up by eager book buyers. Though Márai died in penury in the United States, his novel *Embers* became an international bestseller twelve years after his death.

Both George and I kept Márai's diary next to our beds for late-night reading. I also keep T. S. Eliot there, the collected W. H. Auden, and now, the George Jonas *Selected Poems*. Poetry sustains me.

---

* I used to send copies of Faludy's autobiography, *My Happy Days in Hell*, to various publishers in the UK and United States, in hopes of seeing it back in print. I am delighted to find it now, available online from Amazon.

The Amazing Ms. Atwood

I FIRST MET Margaret Atwood in 1969. I didn't know then that she was a genius. I did know that she had written some remarkable poetry and that *The Circle Game* had won a Governor General's Award. We were meeting because somewhere in the mad labyrinth that was McClelland & Stewart the manuscript of her first novel had been lost.

There are various versions of the lost *Edible Woman* story. Jack favoured the one that started with his sending Margaret an obsequious letter asking whether she would consider submitting to M&S a novel she had mentioned in a recent newspaper interview. She replied that she had submitted it to M&S some two years earlier. He then discovered that the manuscript had been in a drawer of his desk all along. In another version she had received an offer of publication from M&S and agreed to the terms. There ensued two years of silence. It was not until she demanded the return of the manuscript that it was found.

Jack tried to placate her with a nice letter but, since I was the managing editor, it was my job to smooth things over with the understandably grumpy Ms. Atwood. It was a helluva way to start a relationship that has lasted through forty-eight years and the publication of (so far) twenty novels and collections of short stories and essays, thirteen volumes of poetry, seven children's books, and two graphic novels.

When she arrived, Margaret was accompanied by Pamela Fry. Pamela was Margaret's first editor at M&S (followed by Jennifer Glossop and, then, for many years, Ellen Seligman).

I had read *The Edible Woman* the night before and was still pondering the fate of its heroine, now divested of her male companions and determined not to be absorbed into their lives. I loved its humour, its utterly disrespectful treatment of sex ("'How was it for you?' he asked casually, his mouth against my shoulder. He always asked me this. 'Marvellous,' I murmured; why couldn't he tell? One of these days I should say 'Rotten' . . ."), and the final scene when Marion makes a cake in the shape of a woman and presents it to Peter. "'You've been trying to assimilate me. I've made you a substitute, something you'll like much better. This is what you wanted all along, isn't it? I'll get you a fork. . . .'"

I loved her sharp wit, her devastating observations of modern (then, and still valid now) life, and her unsentimental perceptions of men and women. I expected her to seem tough and world-weary. Instead, she seemed gentle, small, with long, curly dark-brown hair, white creamy skin, intense blue eyes, and a frequent smile. There is a moody, soft Charlie Pachter portrait of Margaret that captures both her toughness and her fragility.*

Charlie is, I think, Margaret's oldest friend. They had first met when they were both counsellors at a kids' summer camp. They still make each other laugh. I too find it impossible not to laugh at Charlie's utterly silly jokes. He told me that he has a jokes cache that allows him to find one for every occasion.

Margaret was almost as interested in finding out about me as I was in finding out more about her. We discovered that we shared a past as ineffectual waitresses. She had worked as a cashier and waitress in a coffee shop on Avenue Road. I had worked in a coffee shop operated, briefly, by my aunt Leah in Hastings, New Zealand. Leah, who had somehow managed to get married seven times, was one of my mother's two older sisters. She

---

* Charles (Charlie) Pachter is one of Canada's most famous artists.

had an espresso machine (rented) and was very good at making European-style coffee, but it was her looks that attracted most of the customers.

Margaret's father had been a forest entomologist who, for obvious reasons, did most of his research in forests. She had spent much of her childhood in the wilderness, didn't attend a full year of school until grade eight, and knew more about worms, snakes, tent caterpillars, and wood-boring beetles than everyone else. One of the characters in her novel *Cat's Eye*, first published in 1988, is a forest entomologist but he is not, as Margaret told me, based on her father.

Margaret had studied at the University of Toronto in a class taught by one of the world's great intellectuals, Northrop Frye, and she went to graduate school at Harvard. I studied at Canterbury University in Christchurch, on the South Island of New Zealand, where I could have become a hiker but didn't. I am not much of a wilderness person. Unlike Margaret, I can't even paddle a canoe. Other than a love of stories and the words that tell them, we didn't have much in common.

But Pamela had told me that Margaret could read palms, and a few days later in a coffee shop in Yorkville she offered to read mine. It was not a particularly comforting experience because she said "hmmm" a lot, from which I assumed she had noted I would have a short life but refrained from telling me.

Her tarot reading was more of a success. She was spot-on about some of my checkered past and convinced me that the Hanged Man card was not as dreadful as it seemed. Instead it suggested that I should break free of old patterns of behaviour, habits that restrained my development. Having just broken free of the UK and arrived in Canada, I was not at all sure I could follow the card's lead again, but it gave me something to think about.

Even as *The Edible Woman* was making its way through our production processes, Margaret was already working on *The Journals of Susanna Moodie*, a poetry collection first published in 1970 (not by M&S, sadly). I remember telling Margaret that there was a reason why my people didn't become settlers.

When *The Edible Woman* was published, M&S sent Margaret on the usual book tour, complete with television, radio, and print interviews. Her first book signing at a Hudson's Bay Company department store (yes, the Bay used to sell books) took place in the men's socks and underwear department. A few years later there were long lines of fans waiting for signed copies at the book department and in bookstores all across Canada.

I remember going to Montreal to meet with Quebec publishers and explaining to them in my enthusiastic but heavily accented French (I am told I have a pronounced Hungarian accent in French) why Margaret Atwood was one of the most important writers in the world. By 1975 Grasset in Paris had already published her and people lined up for copies of her books in French.

The New York Times characterized the novel as "feminist black humor," an invented category that made it easier for the reviewer. *The Edible Woman*, like much of Atwood's work, does not fit into any narrow category. She has broad emotional range and presents, often quite casually, arresting images that stick in one's mind. A poem called "You Fit into Me" has these lines:

You fit into me
like a hook into an eye
a fish hook
an open eye

After all these years, I still cannot get that image out of my mind. For a completely different mood, just read the "Owl and Pussycat, Some Years Later," her poem maybe for Charlie Pachter and herself (some others thought it was for them), growing older but still singing, whether anyone listens or not.

In seemingly fast succession, we published *Surfacing, Lady Oracle, Life Before Man, Bodily Harm, The Handmaid's Tale,* and *Cat's Eye*; Atwood had become a household name, the one writer most Canadians could name. Margaret has won the most Canadian and international prizes, including (seriously) the Swedish prize for humour.

In the beginning she used to send me her manuscripts to read. Now she no longer does, but I am one of the first thousand or so readers of every new book and I sporadically follow her on Twitter.

ELLEN SELIGMAN WOULD eventually become Margaret's Canadian editor. Ellen had come to Canada from New York, following a romantic dream. I remember her arrival at the M&S office for the first time in 1976. She sat in the narrow hallway of what we jocularly called "Reception." Tall, willowy, with thick dark hair and big eyes, she had an uncertain smile. She claimed that when I first saw her, I asked, "What the fuck are you doing here?" I don't remember that, but it's not impossible. After eight years, I had acquired much of Jack's vocabulary. I needed it to get through even the average days, and 1976 was hardly average. We had a huge list and were in the middle of production of *Between Friends: Entre Amis*, co-published with the National Film Board's Still Photography Division to honour the American Revolution's Bicentennial and the two hundredth anniversary of the American Declaration of Independence. The empress of the Still Division, the most powerful woman for Canadian photographers, was Lorraine Monk. A fascinating mix of extreme vulnerability and steely determination, she prided herself on setting the highest possible standards and was untroubled by the costs that often accompanied those standards.*

I hired Ellen an hour after she answered my question. Margaret says Ellen was meticulous, kind, and funny. "I always feel I'd hit the target when I made Ellen laugh," she said.

FROM THE FIRST time I saw them together, Margaret and Graeme Gibson seemed the ideal couple, talking to each other quietly, sharing observations, laughing at the same stories. My early memory of Graeme is at a House of Anansi party attended by the young editors and writers. Many of them worked there, editing and commenting on one another's work,

---

* Lorraine's expectations often created havoc at M&S.

sometimes slept there, certainly wrote there, and often fell in love there, as Margaret and Graeme had done.

Shirley Gibson, then still nominally married to Graeme, was also at the party. She had been one of the House of Anansi's early supporters, a revered editor, and active both in the literary and theatre worlds. She had been the first woman member of the Bookmen's Lunch Club (it has since been renamed the Bookpersons' Lunch Club), founded by Jack in 1962, a group where bookish people could talk about books. Bob Fulford, who was one of the original members, still joins us once a month.

Very tall, blue-eyed, with an easy charm and confidence, Graeme wore an elegant cape-style overcoat and corduroy trousers. He was intensely serious, with a wide-open laugh all the more cheering because it was infrequent. He was suspicious of me because I worked for M&S and Jack had mishandled his novel *Five Legs*.

Next to him, Margaret seemed small and deceptively fragile. Some journalists have described her as "elfin," an odd word for a woman with such a substantial presence. Graeme seemed protective of her. Though they sometimes escaped to their house on Pelee Island, I think their only long quiet time was the year they spent in an Alliston farmhouse, with neighbouring cows and a resident ghost.

An extraordinary aspect of Margaret's life is her formidable energy. In addition to the novels, her poetry, the operas, the television series, the Writers' Union, the book reviews, the public readings, the lectures, the speeches on topics that she considers vital, her Arctic journeys, the international promotional tours to please her publishers (my publisher friends in Germany, Australia, and Norway have been thrilled with her support), PEN, her investments in inventions (for example, LongPen) and enthusiasms (she had 1.26 million Twitter followers when I last checked), the Massey Lectures, and the movies and television series based on her books, she is an active environmentalist and travels widely to see birds. She managed to turn her tour for her novel *The Year of the Flood* into a series of staged summer camp–style public readings with performers—actors, singers, musicians—and dedicated the funds raised to the protection of bird habitats. Ron Mann made a forty-five-minute documentary, *In the Wake of the*

Flood, about the experience. Oh yes, and in 2016 she published two books: *Hagseed*, a remarkable novel of revenge and enchantments, and the first of her, so far, two graphic novels (with Johnnie Christmas and Tamra Bonvillain), *Angel Catbird.* Her 1996 novel *Alias Grace* was made into a six-part miniseries on CBC/Netflix.

Her dystopian novel *The Handmaid's Tale* was in its fifty-second printing in 2016. I assume it has now passed its eightieth printing, what with the Hulu television series, the awe-inspiring reviews, the magnificent photo of Margaret in *The New Yorker*, and even the habitual carping of the Canadian press. It was number one on Amazon twenty years after it was first published, when Amazon was still just a name for a fierce woman warrior. Yet throughout all this activity she has retained her sense of humour and her old friendships.

Recently I was rereading one of Margaret's essays, "True North," and I was caught by these sentences: "One way of looking at a landscape is to consider the typical ways of dying in it. Given the worst, what's the worst it can do?" Like much of her writing, this seems on the surface simple, light-hearted, almost mocking, but it isn't. It is quintessentially Atwood: ironic, while diving into the abyss.

I think of these lines and her list of the many nasty ways you can die every time I go north and walk away from our cottage. Death by blackfly. Death by starvation, by animal, forest fire, thunderstorm, freezing, drowning . . . "Every culture has its exemplary dead people." Ours seem to have been killed by landscape.

She is as confident speaking from a podium as she is paddling a canoe, and I know because I have seen her speak to spellbound audiences. I can even attest to the fact that she is an accomplished pastry chef. I think she, herself, could easily have made that woman-shaped cake in the last chapter of *The Edible Woman.*

The Master Storyteller

THE ONE FARLEY Mowat book I had read before I came to Canada was *Never Cry Wolf*. I had read it in New Zealand, where there were no wolves—a pity, since I was seized with the desire to save them, though I am pretty sure they would have made short work of New Zealand's iconic bird, the small, brown, flightless kiwi, whose last descendants were still lurking in the undergrowth on the South Island.

Farley was Jack McClelland's closest friend. They had both served in the Second World War. Jack had first crewed on a minesweeper, patrolling Nova Scotia, then commanded a Royal Canadian Navy motor torpedo boat. He was commended in dispatches and demobbed as a lieutenant. Farley had served in the Hasty Pees, a.k.a. Hastings and Prince Edward Regiment, battling its way up through Sicily, then the rest of Italy, through rivers of blood. He lost most of his friends and found himself "staring down a vertiginous tunnel where all was dark and bloody and the great wind of ultimate desolation howled and hungered." Those words are from the final pages of *And No Birds Sang*, his extraordinary memoir about coming of age in a world gone mad.

Devastated by man's ability to wreak mindless havoc, he tried to balance the horror by writing about Mutt, who would become the hero of *The Dog Who Wouldn't Be*, for a while my children's favourite book.

His travels to the Canadian North after the war had not improved his impressions of humanity. He wrote about the fate of the endangered people of the Arctic and the equally endangered wolves and, later, the whales and other animals that had once roamed our oceans and our land.

Jack used to tell the story of how Farley had first appeared in his office, a small, red-haired, wild man who wanted, more than anything, to be a writer. He thought words had the power to change the world. I believe that is what he was trying to do with *People of the Deer*, the book that opened the debate about the fate of the peoples in the so-called "barren lands," which had never been barren and where greed, incompetence, and injustice passed for government policies.

I FIRST MET Farley in 1969. It was summer and he was marching down that long, hot, gloomy corridor on Hollinger Road, waving and helloing at everyone. He walked with such aplomb that he seemed taller and heavier than his 180 or so pounds. He had greyish red hair over most of his face, uncombed bits on top. He was loud and cheerful. When he reached Jack's outer office, he hugged and kissed the somewhat flustered Marge, who guarded the entrance, then barged past her, yelling and swearing at "the old bastard" and inquiring "how the fuck" he was. Jack, as always, sat leaning back in his chair, his feet on his desk, a cigarette in one hand, the Dictaphone in the other.

He greeted Farley with a broad grin but didn't change position.

The Boat Who Wouldn't Float had just been published. It was the hilarious tale of Jack, Farley, and Farley's soon-to-be wife, Claire, trying to navigate a recalcitrant, leaking tub called *The Happy Adventure* around Newfoundland.

Jack had not been pleased with his own portrayal in the book—he thought it detracted from his reputation as a seaman—and Peter Davison, Farley's American editor, had not been pleased with the title. "A boat is a that, not a who," he had said in one of his more forceful notes to me. Peter was a gentle soul, a very fine editor, a respected poet, essayist, lecturer, and poetry editor of the *Atlantic Monthly*. Despite his objections, the title remained.

August 11, 1969

Dear Peter:

Well, what do you know—the title is back again to THE BOAT WHO WOULDN'T FLOAT . . . This is apparently what Jack and Farley came up with during their weekend together.

Yours,
Anna Szigethy

I had so far kept my last name, my father's only gift. People trying to contact me via the M&S switchboard had the unenviable task of trying to pronounce it, while the receptionist, used to the confusing sound of *s* and *z* and that baffling *thy*, would wait and enjoy their suffering. Farley would ask for "Anna Spaghetti," Al Purdy said "Szszsz, what the hell." Peter Newman, who was born Czech, rather enjoyed his perfect pronunciation of my name, as did Frank Newfeld (it's pronounced Sigetti). But they were the only two.

Boat won the Stephen Leacock Memorial Medal for Humour in 1970. It's impossible to read it, even today, without laughing out loud and without seeing those determined, larger-than-life characters as they wrestle with the obstinate little schooner.

MY FIRST BATTLE with Farley was over his manuscript of *Sibir: My Discovery of Siberia*, about his travels in the USSR during the coldest months of the Cold War. He loved the Russians, their energy, their welcoming vodkas, their poets, and their vociferous enjoyment of his books. He was thrilled that most of his books had been published in Russian. He said he had been bent on using up all his Russian royalties for food and drink while he was there. But they had obstructed his plans at every turn, insisting on offering him free food and booze in outsized portions, hosting him at banquets and applauding him at every opportunity.

I am not sure whether this story is true, but one of his hosts had told him that *Never Cry Wolf*, translated into Russian as *Wolves, Please Don't Cry*, had been so influential that the Russian people demanded an immediate end to the slaughter of wolves. Canadian wolves had not been so lucky.

Farley was as much in love with Russians as I was not. I had seen Soviet soldiers mow down civilians in Budapest with machine guns and flatten them with tanks in 1956. It had not been a pretty sight. Farley still thought of them as Second World War allies. Given our very different points of view and my desire to make changes in his manuscript, it is a miracle that we didn't come to blows. We fought and argued all afternoon, mostly in the Mowats' garden, then stumbled into the sunroom, where Claire had prepared some food we both ignored and some wine we both drank.

I drove home from Port Hope late, after we had settled into an exhausted peace and Farley had shown me his extensive collections of books and photos. During the ensuing years, we became cautious friends. Cautious in the sense that Farley didn't entirely trust anyone in business, not even the business of books.

I travelled west with him and Claire on a couple of his more arduous book promotion tours, planned with him and artist David Blackwood, for their book *Wake of the Great Sealers*, a eulogy for the Newfoundland fishermen who had once harvested cod and seals before they became scarce. I still have a couple of David's eloquent etchings on the second floor of our house. The three of us celebrated the unintended publicity stunt when the United States banned Farley from travelling there (he hadn't wanted to go anyway). After the birth of my own company, Key Porter Books, in the 1980s, I ended up being his publisher.

Farley's books have sold more than 50 million copies worldwide in umpteen languages and editions, yet he remained quintessentially Canadian: extremely serious about preserving life on the planet, serious about his art, but also funny about the silliness of everyday things other people value: money, cars, big houses, elegant clothes.

At first Farley, who was naturally shy, had been very uncomfortable with Jack's forced author performances, the publicity tours that demanded a writer should be centre stage, an entertainer ready with the quick quip, always up for whatever the occasion demanded. Farley compensated for his shyness with exaggerated bonhomie, too much rum, and legendary exhibitionism. A while ago in Montreal, a woman of about eighty told me how Farley once crawled down her dinner table (it was a benefit for the Writers' Trust) and buried his face in the cake. He was, of course, wearing his traditional kilt with no underpants.*

---

* Some years later, my daughter Catherine was enchanted when Farley asked her to dance at novelist John Irving's son's wedding. Farley was a lively dancer and he looked splendid in his kilt.

Tough Times

ONE PARTICULARLY DARK moment in 1970, three years after I joined M&S, while pondering what more he might have done to save the company, Jack suggested we try setting fire to the warehouse. Books, being dry, would burn easily and the company could collect insurance. We published, as he was fond of saying, authors, not books, and we could reprint what we needed.

Fortunately, the books were too damp and, after a few desultory attempts, we gave up and repaired to one of the bars at the Inn on the Park Hotel for refreshments. Back then, the Inn was something of a novelty, all steel and glass, in the industrial desert of Leslie and Eglinton.

I knew, of course, that M&S was painfully short of cash, but I did not realize how close we had come to bankruptcy until Jack announced to the press in 1971 that M&S would have to be sold to an American buyer. No Canadian buyers, he said, had offered to come to the table. You'd have to be living in some distant land not to be aware of Jack's brand of Canadian nationalism, so the news hit hard. Knowing Jack's flair for publicity, I thought that his announcement was merely a ploy to attract potential investors, and to light a fire under the recently formed Royal Commission on Book Publishing. It would certainly be more effective than the warehouse fire he had planned.

The Ontario government set up the commission in 1970, in response to the acquisition of the venerable United Church–owned publisher Ryerson Press by US-owned McGraw-Hill. As it happened, two future M&S authors—lawyer Lieutenant General Richard Rohmer, retired, and Conservative journalist Dalton Camp—were members of the commission. The third member was Marsh Jeanneret, director of the University of Toronto Press. All three could be counted on to be sympathetic to our woes.

Publishers, both large and small, presented position papers to the commission's public hearings. Both Jack McClelland and my future business partner, magazine publisher Michael de Pencier, submitted briefs urging the government to make room for Canadian books and magazines on convenience store and other newsstands.

The Royal Commission's Interim Report found that book publishing deserved government support because of its unique role in Canadians' understanding of who we were as a people. The report stated the fundamental lesson of Canadian publishing economics I had already learned: because book publishing is a capital-intensive industry, Canadian publishing companies are at a double disadvantage. Not only do they quickly reach the point where their total capital is tied up in author advances and inventories, often with relatively slow turnover prospects, but as a consequence, new opportunities go to the Canadian branches of foreign publishing firms, which have access to capital from their foreign owners.

As for M&S, they said it was "a national asset worthy of all reasonable public encouragement and support."

The government gave the company $961,000 as an immediate interest-free loan. All it demanded in return was that Jack should install on his board two directors of their choosing. It was fascinating to watch them fall under Jack's spell, as our various chief financial officers did, soon after entering 25 Hollinger. Larry Ritchie, for example, arrived in pinstripes, white button-down shirt, short power-cut hair. Within three months he wore chinos, white shoes, open-necked shirts, and had his hair permed. He installed huge potted plants in his office that tended to obscure the view of his desk and the fact that, in addition to looking at financial information, he had taken to doodling.

The loan didn't solve the financial problems, it just postponed them. It was a temporary fix. Jack needed more money to operate. The annual injection of cash delivered by bestsellers such as a Pierre Berton book or a Peter Newman book or a new Farley Mowat was no longer enough.

Various forms of assistance to Canadian publishing firms followed the Royal Commission. There were "operating subsidies," loan guarantees, both provincial and federal grant programs, export subsidies, travel grants, and flotillas of studies, but none of them eliminated the sense that we were always teetering on the brink of financial disaster. To quote Dickens, we were living in "the best of times" and "the worst of times." There had never before been such a plethora of excellent Canadian writing available, never had so many Canadian writers appeared on television and radio, been celebrated internationally, or won major awards, and yet the money kept running out (or into the stacks of books in the warehouse). Jack was forever looking for long-term solutions that could include the sale of the firm he had inherited from his father and made over into a national institution.

Indirectly, the commission was responsible for the creation of the Writers' Union of Canada when it decreed that writers could not appear before it. Margaret Laurence was the union's guiding spirit; Graeme Gibson supplied the reasons and the drive. "Back then, we didn't know one another," Graeme recalled. "We had no idea what our rights were. There were no agents . . ." Eighty writers attended the first meeting in June 1973. Margaret Laurence, who used to refer to writers as "the tribe," agreed to act as interim chair. Alma Lee was the first executive director. She would go on to found the Vancouver International Writers' Festival.

In 1970 there were still three substantial bookstore chains—Classic, W. H. Smith, and Coles—and many independent bookstores across Canada. However, despite Jack's formidable talents for promotion and the flourishing of young independent presses, Canadian books that were not on bestseller lists were still difficult to find on front-of-store shelves fully occupied by American and British books, and on tables laden instead by discounted imports. I went to several meetings with Classic Book Shops' owner Louis Melzack, trying to convince him that Canadian books needed more breathing space. Always polite and amiable, Mr. Melzack (I never called him Louis) explained that his stores would sell the books his customers would wish to purchase. I made the same argument to W. H. Smith in London, owner of Smith's, with the same results, though they did give me a very nice set of Smith's engraved glasses I have kept. Jack himself made the pitch to the irascible Jack Cole. Jack Cole and his brother Carl had opened their first store in Toronto in 1940; they had added a number of Coles outlets, and they published the ubiquitous Coles Notes that helped thousands of students across the country to graduate.

Jack believed that we could increase our profits by selling more of our books to other countries. We had a duty to attend international book fairs, to showcase our best writers, to try to persuade publishers to translate and publish Canadians. Since I could speak German, Russian, and French, I went to the annual Frankfurt Book Fairs where publishers hawked their authors and made or tried to make deals in the aisles, in their booths, and at late-night parties. In the seventies, when literary agents were scarce, we were promoting Canadian fiction and the few non-fiction books that were not about Canada. Pierre Berton, though he came a couple of times to Frankfurt, was not able to persuade publishers in other countries that they should at least consider his books.

We were a great deal more successful with illustrated books, George Swinton's *Eskimo Sculpture* and Fred Bruemmer's *Seasons of the Eskimo* and *Encounters with Arctic Animals*, for example. The fact that Fred was originally a Baltic German and that George Swinton was originally Austrian and that both of them spoke German fluently helped with German publishers. We even sold UK distribution rights to the wonderfully eccentric Christopher Hurst, whose main interest was not the Inuit but birds. The lesson I learned from selling Fred's and, later, Roloff Beny's books was that there was an international market for stunning photography books, as long as you were able to offer them at reasonable prices. Canada, it seemed, produced both great photographers and extraordinary fiction.

Jack hated Germany. He suspected that everyone his own age or older had been in the SS or in one of the U-boats his motor torpedo boat had tried to sink. Though he worked hard to meet people and they were, generally, interested in meeting him, he remained uncomfortable. William Collins* (Jack called him Billy) came marching down the isle between the booths, demanding to know where Jack McClelland was. And there was Jack in long conversations with Andre Deutsch about literary publishing in the UK and how much bigger the UK market was than Canada's. Andre was Philip Roth's, John Updike's, and Wole Soyinka's publisher. He thought Jack would have been very wealthy indeed had he decided to be a British publisher instead of a Canadian one. By strange coincidence, Andre had known my grandfather Vili in Budapest and thought well of him for trying to do his best in 1944 when it was dangerous to do anything to help Jews.

Jack sent me to New York several times during my first couple of years, always with a bag full of manuscripts and book descriptions. It was never easy to get in to see American editors, but once they got used to the idea that there were Canadian writers worth reading, I started making friends at Doubleday, St. Martin's, Avon, Random House, and among art book publishers such as the New York Graphic Society and Abrams, who thought it was rather quaint to be offered a book on barns.

The Barn was how I first met photographer and artist Dudley Witney. He co-ventured *The Barn* with architect Eric Arthur. I was in Eric's son's office the day Dudley first showed his slides and drawings and talked about the concept for a book that celebrated "vanishing landmarks of North America," the words that would become the subtitle of *The Barn*. He argued that barns were the most authentic pieces of vernacular architecture in North America.

Eric, a New Zealander, had come to Canada in his twenties and, much as I did many years later, fell in love with the place. The author of *Toronto, No Mean City*, he was an avid conservationist who had warned that many of our heritage buildings would disappear unless we cared about them and their (and our own) history.

---

* Then head of William Collins and Sons. Now the firm has been absorbed into HarperCollins.

Dudley and I became friends almost immediately—a friendship that has lasted a lifetime. Tall, thin, gangly, bespectacled, he is capable of folding himself into the smallest spaces. He can sleep almost anywhere, a useful ability when driving around the countryside with no motels he could afford. An Englishman from Oxfordshire, smitten with the Canadian outdoors, he is a keen observer of objects—both natural and man-made—a collector of people and impressions. He is a romantic with unbending determination. I understood his quirky English sense of humour and his deceptively straight-faced asides, and I loved his moody photographs. He was a strange mixture of nineteenth-century British philosopher John Stuart Mill and poet Percy Bysshe Shelley. Mill was intensely rational, Shelley the polar opposite: an idealist, a Romantic with a great love of beauty. Dudley was pleased with that description.

Several US publishers made remarks about manure and whether we would have brown covers, but we did, in the end, get an offer for a significant number of books.* Dudley and I celebrated with champagne as the first books rolled off the press.

---

* *The Barn* has been reprinted several times, both in hardcover and in paperback, and you can still pick up copies of the original edition, though the price can be steep.

Finding Home

I was beginning to realize I would be staying in Canada. It was an extraordinary time for the country and I was in the best place to enjoy it. Pierre Berton, who was named "Man of the Century" by the Canadian Authors Association, opined: "The country was in love with itself." Most days I listened to CBC radio and loved its broad coast-to-coast reach and unusual perspectives, its quaint musical interludes, its varied hosts, the dramas, the plethora of voices, its repeated time zones, even that half-hour difference with Newfoundland.

And in those shabby offices on Hollinger Road I was falling in love with Canadian writers. During my first years there, I met Margaret Atwood, Margaret Laurence, Earle Birney, Michael Ondaatje, Farley Mowat, Leonard Cohen, Marian Engel, Peter C. Newman, Austin Clarke, Mordecai Richler, Al Purdy, Irving Layton, Max Braithwaite, Sylvia Fraser, James Houston, Sinclair Ross, Marie-Claire Blais, Audrey Thomas, Rudy Wiebe, Charles Templeton, Pierre Berton, and Richard Gwyn. (We published Gwyn's *Smallwood: The Unlikely Revolutionary*, about the man who brought Newfoundland into Canada, and later *The Northern Magus*, still a great book on the most intriguing prime minister we have ever had.) Many others came down the damp corridors with manuscripts and galley proofs or just waited in the grim reception area for one of the editors or Jack or me to take them to the nearby Holiday Inn to talk. Of course we missed a few: Anne Hébert, though I pursued her relentlessly in Montreal and begged Sheila Fischman* to introduce us; Roch Carrier, also translated by Sheila; Robertson Davies; W. O. Mitchell; and Alice Munro, whom I importuned in vain at various bookish events. One of my stupid mistakes was not offering to publish Clark Blaise because, I said, "We do not publish short stories," though, in truth, I could have added "by little-known writers." *A North American Education* would haunt me for many years, and I often apologized to Clark when I met him.

Jack's mantra about publishing authors, not books, meant that M&S authors were to be treated like royalty, that the staff was told daily that we were replaceable, the writers were not. That real talent had to be nurtured. That Canada, after decades of neglecting its best and brightest, was now ready to honour them. There was, now, a direct relationship between literature and citizenship.

As I travelled the length of the country in the seventies, from Newfoundland to British Columbia, I began to understand how the people I met fitted into their landscapes. It was not difficult to see similarities between artistic visions of the land in paintings as disparate as those of Christopher Pratt and Tony Onley, or A. Y. Jackson and Alex Colville. And I could see how different writers—from Gabrielle Roy to Ethel Wilson, Margaret Atwood to Anne Hébert—grappled with the vastness of Canada and their own sense of belonging.

I was still baffled by Quebec separatists. Though I had heard the resentment of the *maudit Anglais*, listened to how Quebecers felt diminished by English Canadians, I did not think they would be happier as masters in their own house (*maîtres chez nous*). I used to spend a lot of time in Montreal meeting with publishers, editors, and writers, listening to their stories and observations. I read Pierre Vallières's *Nègres blancs d'Amérique* (published in

---

* Sheila Fischman is the best and most prolific translator in Canada and, I suspect, the world. She translated more than two hundred books and won every literary translation prize in the country.

translation by M&S) and listened to him give an impassioned talk at a Salon du Livre de Montréal, but still failed to see that Quebec would be happier on its own. I spent a day wandering about downtown Montreal with novelist and political activist Hubert Aquin, a grieving separatist, but it still made little sense to me. I went to hear firebrand separatist leader Pierre Bourgault at the Montreal International Book Fair. He was a strange all-white presence, but brilliant and passionate and, though he failed to convince me, I did get Jack's agreement to M&S's publishing one of his more incendiary books. We were also translating and publishing Marie-Claire Blais, Roger Lemelin, Fernand Ouellet, Antonine Maillet, and Jacques Godbout.

My own, admittedly brief, experience didn't divide Canada into two separate domains. The *deux nations* seemed more like family members debating, disagreeing, squabbling over rights and mutual respect, rather than borders. Canada is such a vast open country that there should be room for everyone's opinions without having to create new barriers. After my life within a system of absolute repression, Canada seemed to me to be governed for the people. Elections were free and unencumbered by reprisals. Writers were free to express their views.

Jack had added a patina of glamour to publishing. His exhausting championing of authors had moved their books from the back sections of "Canadiana" to the front sections with the bestsellers. He inspired new, young, upstart publishers. It was a time when you could dream up new publishing houses like the House of Anansi, Coach House, Oberon, Talonbooks, New Press (one of Dave Godfrey's babies,* co-founded with writers Jim Bacque and Roy MacSkimming), Hurtig Publishers, and ECW.† Their idea was to publish stories and poems, often experimental, by young Canadian writers. It was a time of optimism, a confidence that writers in Canada were finally valued, that Canadian literature was not periph-

---

* Godfrey had also co-founded Anansi and, later, Press Porcépic.

† Started by Jack David in 1974 as *Essays on Canadian Writing*. Jack didn't think Can-Lit had enough critical writing at the time. Robert Lecker came on board a year later. ECW published its first book in 1979.

eral but central to the nation. Jim Lorimer and two friends established James, Lewis & Samuel in 1971, a company with an edgy left-wing political agenda. Kirk Howard was so inspired by one of Jack McClelland's speeches about the need for Canadian economic and cultural independence that he set up Dundurn Press.

In 1970 Jack helped form the Committee for an Independent Canada with businessman and politician Walter Gordon, writer/journalist Peter C. Newman, and economics professor Abe Rotstein. The purpose of the committee was to focus public and, ultimately, government attention on the increasing foreign influence over the Canadian economy, our corporations, and our resources. Canada, they believed, was in danger of losing its independence to the United States. Jack was co-chairman with Claude Ryan, a prominent French Canadian journalist and politician. They were joined by Alberta bookseller and publisher Mel Hurtig and lawyer Eddie Goodman. Within a few months, the committee had accumulated 170,000 signatures on a petition for the government to limit foreign investment in Canada.

Jack was always quick to point out that he didn't want to put restrictions on foreign-authored books coming into the country. To the contrary, he said, we should encourage the reading of all great writers of whatever stripe. Yet, I thought, all you had to do was to browse the shelves of any bookstore in the country to see that we were flooded with foreign product. Canada needed to retain control of its own economy, and to level the playing field.

The Independent Publishers Association—distinguishing itself from the Canadian Book Publishers Council, most of whose members were branches of American firms—was formed in 1971. Five years later, it changed its name to the Association of Canadian Publishers. Strangely, Jack decided that M&S would not join. His explanation to me was somewhat petulant. He saw the newcomers as undisciplined, immature, and overly radical. He believed he could achieve more for M&S (and by implication for Canadian writers) than they could.

Canadian academics were beginning to demand that jobs at universities be filled, primarily, by Canadians to increase "Canadian content" in courses. New Press had published Robin Matthews and James Steele's controversial *The Struggle for Canadian Universities* in 1969, igniting the debate. Part of the authors' argument was that as long as most senior academic positions in Canada were occupied by Americans, it would remain difficult for graduate students to study their own country's history, society, and literature.

I hired Jim Marsh, ex of Collier Macmillan, to expand our Carleton Library series—one of Jack's projects intended to bolster Canadian studies at universities. Jim left in 1980 to become editor of the *Canadian Encyclopedia* at Hurtig.

WHEN JACK, EDDIE Goodman, Mel Hurtig, Walter Gordon, and executive director Flora MacDonald were invited to meet with Prime Minister Trudeau, Jack was hopeful that there would be a policy change. Trudeau listened, agreed with much of what he heard, and promised urgent action.

But not much happened.

It was difficult to push the government on these issues, when its focus remained on employment and on Quebec. Only a few of the committee's recommendations were taken into account when the Liberals created the Foreign Investment Review Agency in 1973 and the Canadian Development Agency.

Now, some forty-five years later, even these efforts to support Canadian companies would be impossible. Our governments are eager for new investment, whatever the source, and our cultural sectors are advised to seek digital salvation. Yet, even with the current porous state of Canadian nationalism, and the striving of economic elites for further integration with our more enterprising southern neighbour, some of the old myths and visions survive. And they help define who we are. Though this sometimes entails smugly comparing ourselves to the United States, it also entails seeing ourselves in the context of the land we inhabit.

Years ago, Graeme Gibson first recommended that I read George Grant's much debated *Lament for a Nation* (published by M&S in 1965) to gain a broader understanding of Canada. The danger that our country would be lost, that we would be swallowed up by the American "pursuit of material well-being" to the exclusion of all other values, seemed very real then, as it still does now. But Grant's notion that the Church would provide leadership for our society seemed baseless even then. I didn't think Canada needed that kind of leadership. And his assertion that our cultural institutions were not powerful enough to resist the draw of the United States has proven to be wrong.

In his review of *Lament for a Nation*, Mordecai Richler stated flatly that Canada's "independence from the United States was always illusory."

I believed then, as I still do, that Mordecai was wrong.

Though the kind of country Grant thought we should be is, indeed, a lost cause, I believe that the questions he asked about our identity are worth asking every few years, certainly with every new generation.

The Very Young Matt

M ATT COHEN ARRIVED with a letter of introduction from one of M&S's star authors, Peter C. Newman. Newman's massive page-turners—*Renegade in Power: The Diefenbaker Years* weighs in at 540 pages, and *Distemper of Our Times*, about the Lester Pearson years, is 660 pages—had topped bestseller lists. Each sold more than 100,000 copies, unprecedented numbers for Canadian contemporary political history. The letter said that Matt Cohen should be read "very carefully at McClelland & Stewart." Matt had already published a novel called *Korsoniloff* and a collection of short stories Peter couldn't name. *Johnny Crackle Sings* landed on my desk with an accompanying note from Jack telling me he had never heard of Matt Cohen and hadn't read the manuscript, but since it came from Peter . . .

I took it home that evening. It was mercifully slim, not quite two hundred pages, the story of a rock-and-roll singer, Johnny Crackle, and not at all the sort of thing I imagined Peter Newman enjoying. I, on the other hand, liked it a lot. The writing was fresh, funny; the story almost hung together; and I liked the author's ironic, distanced voice. I was even prepared to go along with his technique of telling the tale in snatches, though at that time, I preferred more traditional storytelling.

I wrote to Matt Cohen, suggesting a meeting.

My first sighting of him was in the doorway of my office. He was leaning against the door frame, his hands in his pockets, his dark hair a jumble of curls, thick black-rimmed glasses obscuring his eyes, an uncertain grin on his thin face. He was asking, haltingly, whether he was in the right place. He had difficulty telling me what place he had been seeking because he couldn't pronounce my name. He got hung up on the *sz* at the beginning. He didn't seem comforted when I told him he was correct.

He proceeded into my office, his hands still in his pockets, and perched uncomfortably on the narrow fake-leather chair across from my desk. He wore frayed, faded denim. The rest of him was as thin as his face. He seemed coiled, ready to flee at any moment.

He told me later that he simply had no idea what to say.

After his struggle with my name, his first word was "Well?"

When I told him I liked most of the novel but thought it would be easier for the reader if he could make a few changes, he just stared at me. When I told him we would like to publish it, he continued to stare.

"Publish it?" he asked at last, his voice rising. "You said you would publish it?" He was stunned. He didn't ask when or how; in fact, he looked as if the only question on his mind was why.

It wasn't until Matt had left that I recognized the smell he had brought into my office: fresh cow manure. It was not a smell you'd expect in a warehouse building east of Leaside, surrounded by concrete and roadworks. Matt was living on a farm near Kingston, Ontario, some two hours' drive from Toronto, but I didn't know that then. I thought he might be the kind of guy who trailed cow manure wherever he went. I also discovered later that he had quite forgotten the letter from Newman and couldn't believe his good luck in being invited to meet someone at McClelland & Stewart.

He lent me his only copy of *Korsoniloff*. It had been published by the House of Anansi, a publisher Jack often referred to as "alternative," though he didn't elaborate how or why he thought so. That assessment was not entirely wrong.

When Matt was not on the farm, he lived at Rochdale, a kind of student commune attached to the University of Toronto. One of Anansi's two founders, Dennis Lee, already legendary for his editorial skills, had also lived there for a while, as had some of the young writers whose work

Anansi published. Matt talked enthusiastically about Rochdale's residents, their sense of community, their aspirations, and their conviction that a revolution was in the works. I thought the sorts of revolutions I had known had no place here but we didn't talk about my Hungarian childhood then, as we didn't talk about Matt's childhood.

Matt was not given to easy confidences, but he loved to discuss ideas. He was, then, still much in thrall to George Grant.

I found *Korsoniloff* almost incomprehensible. Luckily Matt didn't ask me about it for some time. When he finally did, we were sitting in one of the bars at the Inn on the Park. Matt loved the red and maroon plush furniture, the heavy drapes, the thick brown patterned carpets, and the dim lights. He said it reminded him of some Western saloon that was trying to seem refined. There should be spittoons by the tables, he said.

When Matt finally asked what I thought about *Korsoniloff*, he didn't wait for my answer. "You hated it, right?"

"Well, I didn't exactly hate—"

"Right. You hated it." He was staring down at the table, his thin-fingered hands resting on either side of the ashtray full of my cigarettes. He didn't look up.

He was working with someone at Anansi on a collection of stories called *Columbus and the Fat Lady* that I liked a whole lot more, but we didn't publish short stories unless they were by a very famous author we had already published.

Johnny Crackle Sings was decently reviewed but hardly a success, yet Matt had already started to think about his next novel. We were to be friends for almost thirty years.

National Dreaming, or The Berton Extravaganza

THE MOST VIGOROUSLY promoted author of the late sixties and the seventies was Pierre Berton—Pooh Bear, as some of us called him behind his back. *The Comfortable Pew* was the first Berton book I read. Published in 1965 to howls of outrage from the religiously inclined, it had sold about 300,000 copies. I had not been religiously inclined since the year and a half I had spent as a charity-case boarder at the Sacred Heart Convent School in Wanganui. The standard uniform of pleated black skirt, black stockings, tie, and Panama hat inspired a rebellious spirit even in the otherwise placid New Zealand girls, let alone in someone like me, who was already rebellious. I had found the nuns sanctimonious and ignorant in about equal measure. They had stultifying attitudes toward women and work, and they taught creationism at a time when most people had at least heard of Darwin. In Hungary, where my general education began, there was, of course, no mention of the Bible when studying the beginning of time, but there were other nasty problems associated with living in a Communist dictatorship.

The Smug Minority was published the year before I arrived at M&S. It attacked the business elite for perpetuating out-of-date myths about women (place in the kitchen), work (its sanctity), poverty (it's your own fault if you are poor), etc. Canada, Berton argued, had been held back by

"selfish, narrow, short-sighted men unable to grasp the vision of the future, imprisoned by a bookkeeping attitude to life, creeping silently and
blindly along at the tag end of the parade of progress."

It had sold more than 100,000 copies.

Pierre was the ultimate nationalist, a man for his time, for the decade
when Canadians became more confident than ever before (or since). I
loved his defence of the RCMP: "To the Mounted Police, liberty was secondary to order; the pursuit of happiness was not as vital as the pursuit
of peace and security. . . . In my country the Mountie image is sacrosanct."
He accused the Americans—Hollywood—of inventing a Mountie closer
to their own beloved myth, a man who is stern, uncompromising, and always gets his man. Unlike American gunslingers, Canadian lawmen rarely
reached for their guns. After all, it's hard to reach for your gun while wearing two sets of mittens and a heavy parka.

WHEN I DISCOVERED that Berton's next highly anticipated manuscript was
about the Canadian Pacific Railway, I assumed it would be long, boring,
and corporate. It arrived on Christmas Eve 1969. I read it over Christmas
and wrote Janet Craig, Berton's own editor, that it was brilliant, riveting,
vivid, and on such an unlikely subject that I hadn't expected I would be
captivated by it. *The National Dream: The Great Railway, 1871–1881*, of
course, is not about the railway as much as it is about what it meant for
Canadians to have a line connecting the country from east to west, a line
that kept the expansionist Americans at bay.

The most obvious secret of Berton's success is his style. He is a storytelling phenomenon. *The National Dream* is full of memorable characters, the
men who dreamt that such a grand undertaking was possible, and the men
whose talents and foibles are laid bare in the telling of their stories. Open
the book and you will want to read on: "It is New Year's Day, 1871, the year
in which Canada will become a transcontinental nation, and in most of
British North America it is bitterly cold. In Ottawa, where it is 18 below,
the snow, gritty as sand, squeaks eerily beneath the felted feet of morning
church-goers." Or his description of Sir Charles Tupper, "a master of the

bludgeon," the "robust Nova Scotia doctor with the hard, unblinking eyes and the creased, pugnacious face." No one had ever written Canadian history like this. It was not until I read Basil Johnston about a decade later that I wondered why Indigenous people were missing from Pierre's grand narratives, as they were missing from most histories of that time.

I first met Pierre in his small office at the Royal York Hotel. He was a striking figure, six foot four, with white hair, bald patch covered by a careful comb-over, white mutton chop sideburns, usually a paisley silk bow tie, blue eyes, somewhat bronzed face (he wore makeup for television), and a bemused look that suggested he was interested in but unconvinced by whatever you said. He launched straight into a story about a BC cleric who had become a cult figure, and another about a hooker in the Klondike who became a millionaire. He was awkwardly flirtatious, though he also talked about his large family, and his wife, Janet, who was, he said, his best proofreader.

At some point he started to talk about his family's planned travel down the Yukon River following his father's route in 1898 to Dawson. The trip didn't happen till later but, through the haze of the railway books, he was already thinking about it.[*] He always had several books percolating in his mind and kept his researchers hard at work collecting original material for future books.

I think Pierre had been favourably disposed to me because one of his best friends had been a Hungarian: George Feyer, a cartoonist and artist with an irrepressible sense of humour who had accompanied Pierre on a trip to Hungary. He had liked being with Feyer, so he had liked Budapest. Elsa Franklin, Berton's manager, television producer, close friend, chief promoter, and business partner, hadn't been on that trip and had no illusions about Hungarians.

The first time we met, she barely glanced at me, then handed Jack a manuscript and told him, "Tell your girl to take this and make a copy." I

---

[*] *Drifting Home*, published in 1973, is still my favourite of Berton's sixty or so books. It's the most personal, the most affectionate toward his family, and the least concerned about presenting wild men with wild dreams—other than, perhaps, his own.

had just been introduced as editorial director, but as far as Elsa was concerned, I was just an office girl.

All of Berton's manuscripts were delivered on time, perfectly copied, with footnotes, bibliographies, acknowledgements in place, and usually accompanied by the redoubtable Elsa, whom the *Star* described as "a sexy, busty, green-eyed doll." But she was nobody's doll around M&S.

She had operated a small chain of bookstores in Vancouver and was confident she knew how to promote writers. Although she had had no television experience, she became the producer of *The Pierre Berton Show* and was now the force behind the hour-long interview series that had become a fixture on Canadian TV screens. It had been running since 1962 and displayed no sense of exhaustion. Pierre's interview style was an easy combination: he challenged, probed, argued, expressed his own views, but always allowed his guests to express theirs. One still-fascinating example of a Berton interview: Bruce Lee in 1971. I would like to have watched live Mickey Spillane, David Niven, and Yousuf Karsh as well. It's a pity that those archives are not accessible today.

Berton was also a member of the *Front Page Challenge* panel—one of the longest-running television shows in North America. Guests included such luminaries as Malcolm X, Errol Flynn, and Indira Gandhi.

In 1969 it was impossible to walk or drive around Toronto without bumping into Pierre's face. He was on streetcar ads, placards, billboards, and on top of his newspaper column five times a week. While pursuing his TV career, public speaking gigs, daily columns, and tireless publicity tours, he managed to write a book a year. (M&S's shaky finances—his sales accounted for about 20 per cent of the company's income— depended on his annual miracles.) He wrote them all with prodigious speed. Jack once called him "a writing factory."

Many of our authors felt that Berton's influence had become too great and that Elsa's persistent demands on his behalf exacerbated his tendencies to require royal treatment. Even Charles Templeton, Berton's friend and co-debater on the CFRB radio show they jointly hosted, was concerned that Elsa might alienate potential allies, although in fact Pierre's career did not seem to suffer.

Despite all the attention paid to his and Elsa's every request, Berton complained ceaselessly in long angry letters to Jack, who was afraid that Berton could easily find another publisher. It was his fear of Berton's wrath that led Jack to fire Catherine Wilson, our much-loved head of publicity. Elsa Franklin had accused her of botching Elsa's preparations for a Berton launch party by scheduling for the same evening a launch for poet John Newlove's impressive but very bleak poetry collection *Lies*.* As everyone at M&S realized, Catherine would not have been aware of Elsa's plans, but Jack told me he had no option but to comply with the pressure to let Catherine go. I think Peter Taylor never forgave Jack for instructing him to deliver the bad news to Catherine.

After that debacle, Farley Mowat threatened to sever his ties with Jack and he ended whatever friendship he had enjoyed with Pierre and Elsa. Frankly, I didn't think there was much of a friendship between them in the first place. They were rivals for the top of the bestseller lists and rivals also for attention at McClelland & Stewart.

The Bertons' summer lawn parties at their Kleinburg home were a veritable smorgasbord of Canada's who's who. Invitees included the McClellands and the Bodsworths;† political journalist Allan Fothering-ham, sportswriter Trent (Bill) Frayne,‡ and June Callwood;§ radio producer Geraldine Sherman and Bob Fulford; the Haileys;¶ Fred Davis;**

---

* *Lies* won the Governor General's Award for Poetry.

† Fred Bodsworth's most famous book is *Last of the Curlews*—one of the most moving nature books I have ever read. He could imitate fifty or more birdsongs and could spot a silent bird even in thick foliage.

‡ His friends were encouraged to call him Bill and he was, I think, the best Canadian sportswriter of the last century.

§ June called Bill "Dreamy."

¶ Arthur Hailey, the author of blockbusters such as *Hotel* and *Airport*, had been a good friend of Pierre's since his days as a lowly journalist in Canada.

** *Front Page Challenge* ringmaster.

Betty Kennedy;* writer Sylvia Fraser; CBC's Knowlton Nash and Lorraine Thomson; sometimes Harold Town and Murray and Barbara Frum; always Charles Templeton, Elsa Franklin, and others in the Berton-Franklin firmament.

As for any personal relationship between Elsa and Pierre, though speculations abounded, I never saw them as much as embrace. What I did know was that whenever Elsa called late in the evening and I was still in my office, Jack asked me to tell her Pierre was in a meeting and would call her back as soon as he was free. It was a favour Jack had asked and, since my own grandfather had been a legendary philanderer, I thought I understood why.

Pierre and Jack had been founding members of the Sordsmen's Club, a men's group that met once a month for lavish lunches in upscale restaurants. Members took turns making up the guest list. Women guests were welcome but wives were not. It was understood that each woman could, if she wished, spend extra time with a man who had been at the lunch, not necessarily the one who brought her, though I am told few ever did. I gather it was very elegant and a great deal of fun for all, but when I told Jack I had been invited by Pierre, he sternly forbade it. Definitely not the place, he said, for a vice president of M&S.†

Not surprisingly, having been born in Dawson, Pierre loved Robert Service poems about the "men who moil for gold," and the women they loved.

> There are strange things done in the midnight sun
> By the men who moil for gold;
> The Arctic trails have their secret tales
> That would make your blood run cold; . . .

---

* *Front Page Challenge* panellist.

† It's hard to remember the succession of titles or the reasons for my rapid rise to vice president, editor-in-chief, and member of the beleaguered board of M&S directors dealing with the cash crunches and worries about bank credit lines. Titles were cheap at M&S.

Pierre's reciting of the Sam McGee poem was the best version you could ever hope to hear. The stories he told, and the way he told them (in the books and on the screen) were vastly different from the stories kids had studied at school or heard from their parents. After Pierre, Jack said, Canada's history would never be dull again.

Sadly, he was wrong. Those schools that still bother to teach Canadian history have managed to return students to how it used to be written before Pierre, a bloodless version with cardboard figures and dull dates.

But back in the early 1970s it seemed as if we were at the beginning of a new era when our history would be exciting. Both *The National Dream* and its sequel *The Last Spike* were runaway bestsellers. Both were selections of the Book of the Month Club, thus adding about 40,000 copies to the first printings.

How Pierre Berton Is Responsible for My Marriage

E VERY YEAR THE challenge for Peter Taylor was to come up with new
ideas to promote Pierre's books. He created some of the craziest scenes
book reviewers and columnists had ever witnessed. One early example was
the massive cake with ten thousand candles intended to celebrate the ten-
thousand-copy first printing of Berton's *The Last Spike: The Great Railway
1881–1885* in 1971. It was wheeled in to Les Cavaliers on Church Street,
the only restaurant brave enough to risk the fire that would surely follow.

It took two fire extinguishers to put out the conflagration.

I have a photograph from the event, taken just before the fire. Pierre,
Peter Newman, and I are outfitted in period costume. The photo, appearing
in *Toronto Life*'s social column, prompted a recently divorced young lawyer
to phone and ask me for a date. Since we hadn't met before, he suggested
I talk to theatre critic Nathan Cohen, who would vouch that he was a fine
fellow. At the time M&S was courting Cohen, the most popular, wittiest
theatre reviewer in the country, trying to persuade him to write a book
about Canadian theatre. It was a strange call. Julian Porter, Cohen assured
me, was a likeable, good-looking, quasi-establishment figure—"quasi" because he chose to be—who could be trusted to keep his distance on a first
date. He had been a star of the Hart House debating team, had a fine legal
mind and, Cohen said, a quick wit.

It turned out to be much more than a date, but I couldn't have known that at the time. Julian seemed to be everything Cohen had promised and somewhat more. He was attractive, big, blue-eyed, with thick, silvery-brown hair and a firm but not bone-crushing handshake. He had the build of a football player. He had been school captain at UTS, a football player in high school, and a member of the Varsity Blues at university.

I didn't realize how nervous he was until we arrived at his chosen restaurant on Yorkville and he had some difficulty helping me out of my coat. Our date went steadily downhill after his preordered meal of pheasant in plum sauce arrived. As a rule, I disliked men who ordered meals for me and I have hated pheasant ever since a weekend in Scotland with my Scottish boyfriend in 1967. He had been quite charming but his family loved to shoot things. Spending most of the day with the "beaters," I managed to shoo some of the smarter pheasants in the opposite direction from where the men with guns waited for them to rise from the gorse and be blasted to smithereens. To top it off, the stupider pheasants, baked still full of buckshot, were served on pretty blue-and-white plates for supper.

Luckily Julian had also preordered the wine: a fine Montrachet, which came in a silver bucket of ice. Luckily because Julian, even more nervous after hearing about my Scottish experience, kicked over the bucket, the ice skedaddled across the floor, the wine spilled, and we fell in love.

His pedigree was, indeed, as establishment as Nathan Cohen had told me. His father had been chief justice of Ontario and minister of several portfolios in Leslie Frost's cabinet; his mother was the daughter of an admiral in the British navy. Julian was born in deepest Rosedale and could give a guided tour of the area, including who lived where and what they all did. But he was also fond of carnivals—he was Jimmy Conklin's lawyer—and took me for a ride on the then-highest roller coaster in North America. He had been lead counsel in a case defending art dealer Dorothy Cameron against obscenity charges over her 1965 erotic art exhibition *Eros 65*. The police had raided her gallery and seized several pieces of art deemed to be obscene. We still own one of those pieces: a large black-and-white of two nude women by Robert Markle.

He told me he had stammered when he was a child. As head boy at UTS, his job included reading out the list of boys in attendance. Those whose names started with sibilants never made the list.

He was a reader. He usually had two or three books on the go at the same time, and in 1971 he had been reading Raymond Chandler, Dante's *Inferno*, Kingsley Amis's *Lucky Jim*, and one of the James Bond books. He had been a young tour guide and talked about art and artists with great passion and knowledge. He still does. Like all the people I have loved, he is a terrific storyteller.

He had already been married to the daughter of another scion of the Toronto establishment (her father was senator, politician, former cabinet minister, and Tory leadership contestant Wallace McCutcheon) and was divorced with two children, so I felt reassured that he wouldn't want to marry again. I had no interest in marriage. His two daughters, just four and eight at the time, viewed me with overt suspicion. They had not been keen on the divorce and were still hoping that their parents would be reconciled one day. We would travel to various small-town Conklin carnivals, the girls sitting in the back in stony silence until it was late, when four-year-old Jessica would climb to the front seat to sleep on my lap. Suse, the eight-year old, preferred to sleep in the back.

I contrived to be less absorbed in my work than usual.

After the fire, the rest of Pierre's author tour was a resounding success. It featured Winnipeg goldeyes, New Brunswick fiddleheads, and wild blackberry pie, plus Last Spike cocktails—champagne, Curaçao, and orange bitters—served at breakfasts of buckwheat pancakes and maple syrup to bleary-eyed media types across the country.

There were massive lineups outside stores where Pierre was signing his books. At Bolen's in Victoria he managed to sign more than four hundred copies of *The Last Spike* before they ran out of books. Independent bookstores across the country (and there were many of them in the seventies) featured both history books in their windows, and the bookstore chains placed massive orders that they backed with advertising at their own expense. Today the one remaining bookstore chain tends to look for advertising dollars from publishers who want their books to sell.

*   *   *

WHEN JULIAN CALLED to ask whether I would accompany him on a trip to France, I didn't even think before I said yes. While he was representing Canada at the UNESCO Copyright Convention, I walked about Paris trying to come to terms with my staying in Canada for the rest of my life. We drove south from the city, meandered along the Gorges du Tarn, and got to know each other. By the time we reached Moissac, it seemed inconceivable that we would return to our previous lives.

Julian and I were married in January 1972, a few months after we first met. Alfons's brother, Fritz, who lived in Canada, kindly volunteered to walk me down the aisle. Julian's mother, who had hoped he would come to his senses before marrying a Hungarian, seemed to have resigned herself to the occasion. Our wedding photographer was Toronto boulevardier John Reeves, who talked almost incessantly while he took his black-and-white pictures and reassured me—because I needed reassurance—that marriages were not necessarily forever. There was a moment when I called Qantas to check flight departures for Sydney—in case I needed a quick getaway—but my mother, who had endured three weddings of her own, said I could always go to Australia later if this didn't work out.

Marriages in our family had not been particularly fortunate. Except for my grandfather's, they made no one happy and didn't last. My grandfather's lasted only because my grandmother Therese had been determined not to notice Vili's philandering. Vili had warned me that marriages rarely worked for women. His own mother, Jolan, could read and write in four languages, including Greek and Latin, but in her time, young ladies had few choices. "In the nineteenth century, it was pinafores and piano lessons and waiting for the right man to come along," he had told me. "You, on the other hand, you have a choice. Don't bother with marriage."

At the reception, Jack presented us with a massive goblet full of contraceptives, in case I was so thoughtless and uncaring about M&S that I planned to have children. Fritz's wife, who had been kind enough to host the reception, a lady with a private school background, was as horrified as my mother-in-law was at the crudeness of Jack's gift.

Aviva and Irving Layton gave us a Greek silver cake-slicer I still cherish, and Irving presented me with a poem called "For Anna":

You wanted the perfect setting
for your old world beauty postwar Hungarian
a downtown Toronto bar sleazy
with young whores pimps smalltime racketeers . . .

I have it framed in my office. It is a wonderful poem to reread during bad times.

Despite my sense that adopting a man's name deleted a woman's self, I changed my name to Porter with a great sigh of relief. I owed no allegiance to the name Szigethy, and Porter was so much easier to pronounce.

Julian's two daughters were both at the wedding, and though they were not thrilled with the new arrangements, they looked brave, hopeful, and quite splendid in the green velvet dresses Julian's mother had sewn for the ceremony. They would spend weekends with us for the next many years, at least until their new stepfather sent Suse to a Colorado boarding school. Jessica, who was shy in public, among family had a natural ability to charm and to put on one-person shows with tumbling, impersonations, and funny voices.

She is now an actor, a writer, and a macrobiotic chef. Suse became a counsellor, a teacher, and eventually a school principal.

I had met their mother, Susan McCutcheon, shortly before the wedding. She was polite and friendly, though puzzled by my decision to marry Julian. The divorce, she told me, had been her idea. Despite her negative assessment of my brand new husband, I liked her enough that I subsequently invited her to all our family get-togethers.

We moved into an apartment on Walmer Road, where my big piles of manuscripts could occupy our dining room table and the floor next to my side of the bed. Julian rarely brought his legal briefs home.

1972, a Year to Remember

THAT YEAR TURNED out to be extraordinary for publishing as well. Three of Pierre's books, *The National Dream*, *The Last Spike*, and *The Great Railway Illustrated*—a short text from both books, with pictures—were on bestseller lists at the same time. Back when Pierre first proposed the illustrated version, I was quite certain it couldn't work, especially following so close to the release dates of the originals, but I was wrong.

An eight-part CBC series based on *The National Dream* was in production. After it aired, the three books went on to sell more than 175,000 copies each. Those sales and Pierre's ongoing roles on TV, in newspapers, and on radio counterbalanced the fact that not all reviewers loved Pierre's versions of history. The Berton extravaganza continued unabated.

The year 1972 also saw M&S's publication of Sylvia Fraser's first novel, *Pandora*. I first met Sylvia at somebody else's launch party. I don't recall whose book it was but I do recall a large non-smoking house with a veranda and several doors that allowed people to go outside to smoke. Back then, I still smoked about a pack a day and found that smoking provided me with an excuse to take a break from a crowd. Smoking was also a fine occupation for my hands when I was nervous, and our launch parties tended to make me nervous.

Sylvia was on the veranda, talking to someone and looking beautiful. She was slender, with a small waist, but she filled out her soft, light-blue silky dress, her hair was soft and blond, her eyes very blue, her hands animated, her nails long and red. (Later I discovered that she used to chew her nails and wore fake, acrylic glue-ons.)

I had just finished reading the manuscript of *Pandora* and couldn't wait to tell her how riveting I had found it, how I had never read anything remotely like it, and how excited I was that we would be publishing it. *Pandora* is the story of a little girl in a wartime Canadian town. The minutely portrayed accoutrements of that era were as riveting as the writing itself. It's a story you are pulled into, then dragged along to witness both the young heroine's golden-curled innocence and the brutality that overtakes her.

That's what I started to tell her when she stopped me in mid-sentence and stared at me with barely disguised fury. The next moment she was in tears, running to Jack McClelland and demanding to know why he had betrayed her confidence. He had promised not to show the manuscript to anyone until she had done another draft. Jack, deflecting her accusations, denied that he had given it to me. Knowing Jack, I shouldn't have been baffled. A generous explanation of his slip-up is that he forgot his promise when he gave me the manuscript, but it is more likely that he had been hoping for a spectacular cat-fight between two blondes.

Sylvia and I didn't speak for months, a state of affairs that could have continued longer had Julian and I not bumped into her and her lawyer husband, Russell, on our 1972 honeymoon in Barbados. We were all gravely underdressed in bathing suits with nowhere to hide past sins, so we became friends.

We travelled around the island, drank lots of dark and stormies, discovered a shared delight in jumping on trampolines (mostly Julian), and gossiping about other writers, editors, and Jack, of course. Both Russell and Sylvia were funny, warm, engaging, and adventurous.

Harold Town had drawn the soft, gentle image of the young girl for the cover of *Pandora*. He offered to sell the original to Jack or to me but neither of us could afford the price. Russell bought it as a gift for Sylvia and it still hangs, framed, in her King Street apartment. Much later Harold lambasted me into buying one of his bugs-in-machinery series that I have hidden in our basement, hoping someone one day will need such a painting.

In addition to the Bertons and *Pandora*, M&S published *A Whale for the Killing*, one of Farley Mowat's saddest books, the story of a stranded whale he tried to save and send back to sea. It was harassed, shot, and killed by Newfoundlanders, thus ending Farley's love affair with the island. And probably theirs with him. Once again, Farley was surrounded by controversy.

And in 1972 Mordecai Richler returned to Canada from London. Jack introduced us (again) at a garden party at their home in Quebec. Mordecai was rumpled and at his acerbic best. Florence Richler was gracious and effervescent in a pink-and-blue dress. Brian Moore and his wife, Jean, old friends of the Richlers, were there. Brian and I had a long conversation about *Catholics*, a novel I had loved, and a much shorter one about *The Revolution Script*, which I had not liked. I could not understand why he had written it.

I had first met Mordecai in 1970. He had asked what I thought of the manuscript of *St. Urbain's Horseman*. We were in the Park Plaza Roof Lounge, and I was on my third drink (he drank Macallan). He listened to my extravagant praise and the very few suggestions I made, which, of course, he ignored. *St. Urbain's Horseman* won the Governor General's Award in 1971. In the Richlers' garden a year later, Mordecai talked about the grand award ceremony and the hilarious notion of someone in Canada standing in for the Queen.

While it wasn't evident at the time, the most notable book of 1972 was Margaret Atwood's *Survival: A Thematic Guide to Canadian Literature*, published by the House of Anansi.* It became the most-discussed book of the decade about Canadian writing and is still taught and debated at universities. It focused on the themes and ideas that had been central to Canadian fiction and poetry. Oddly, given how the book changed the conversation about Canadian literature, it grew out of a need to raise money

---

* Margaret wrote that Dennis Lee's editorial skills were indispensable for the book.

for the House of Anansi. Jim Polk, to whom Margaret was married at the time, told me that the manuscript began with twelve people typing feverishly in the August heat, drinking wine and exchanging thoughts, before Margaret pulled it all together into a book.

The first printing was an optimistic 4,000 copies.

Survival has now sold more than 150,000 copies—a phenomenal number for a book of literary criticism.* Of course it was not only literary commentary, it was a tribute to the wellspring of Canadian literature, a handbook that allowed readers to feel a sense of belonging, even pride in the culture their country had produced. Though it was criticized for its focus on survival as the central theme of Canadian literature, even its detractors had to admit that it was a powerful analysis and one that could draw in many of our most important literary works.

It was, in short, the perfect book for its time.

As Pierre Berton noted, with reference to his railway books, "the nation is bound together by its creative artists and not by parallel lines of rusting steel."

Two other major events defined 1972. The federal election in October was humbling for the Trudeau Liberals and for Canada's "philosopher king": in *Maclean's* Peter Newman called it "his fall from grace." Trudeau had campaigned confidently in T-shirt and jeans, but far fewer Canadians had voted for him. He was now in a minority government situation. The election was rather cheering for Julian, who had been rooting for Robert Stanfield. A lifelong Tory, he had worked on the Stanfield campaign and believed that Stanfield would have been a great prime minister. Sadly for Julian, and maybe for the country, he never got that chance.

And, of course, 1972 was the year Canada won the Canada-Russia hockey series. The whole country exploded in exultation at Paul Henderson's leg-

---

* Northrop Frye's *The Bush Garden: Essays on the Canadian Imagination* was published in 1971. It was much talked about in bookish circles, but it had modest sales. Northrop Frye had been one of Margaret Atwood's professors at the University of Toronto.

endary winning goal. Jack commissioned Jack Ludwig,* a novelist, journalist, teacher, and, ever since his Winnipeg childhood, passionate hockey lover to follow our team. He was there "when Ken Dryden took off on a rink-long dash that ended with him draped over Henderson," and for the triumphant roaring of "O Canada" with not a dry eye in the arena. Nor in Toronto where we watched the game. I still remember how everyone stood and sang. There was no longer any doubt that I had become a Canadian.

THE MOST IMPORTANT day of 1972 for me, though, was Boxing Day, when my daughter Catherine was born and forever changed my life. Having children tends to put everything else into perspective, particularly publishing.

My mother was our first visitor. She came from New Zealand, wanting to see her first grandchild and trying to determine the priorities of her own life. Sylvia Fraser was our second visitor, and though Sylvia remarked that the baby looked way too pink and much too small, she was willing to take on the responsibilities—if that's what they were—of godmother. Earle Birney sent the baby this short verse:

Welcome, welcome Catherine Porter,
Lovely momma's lovely dorter,
Looks just like her
Only shorter.

Jack arrived at the hospital with a large box of manuscripts in lieu of more traditional baby gifts and told me I would have plenty of time now to catch up on my reading. As an added bonus, he was willing to grant me a full four weeks of vacation time.

---

* My favourite Ludwig novel is *A Woman of Her Age*, published in 1973. I got to know Jack much better during the editing of that book and I liked almost everything about him. He was brave and uncompromising, despite the constant pain from his polio-afflicted leg.

For the Love of Words

I HAD MET Earle Birney during my first year at M&S. He was a tall, spindly, white-bearded figure with a strong resemblance to Don Quixote. I love the Harold Town drawing of Earle for the Purdy book that never happened. Earle was best known for his long narrative poem "David," a fact that he resented and liked in about equal measure. Poetry was only one of his passions. He had the astonishing ability to speak Old and Middle English. I had battled at university with Sir Gawain and Beowulf, but for Earle they were poetry, as was the unfiltered Chaucer. He was a traveller, a novelist, a teacher, a professor of literature, a mountain climber, a collector of memories and of remarkable women. I had met only three of them— all unusually attractive and accomplished. I knew only two well: Wailan Low, the great love of Earle's late years, and briefly my mother. Earle had courted my mother in 1969 and 1970, when she was visiting Canada from New Zealand. He even wrote her some fine, rather suggestive poems.

I found a couple of them in a drawer of her memorabilia, where she keeps photographs of her parents and her grandchildren (my children); letters from her father, Vili; miserable letters I wrote her when I was in the Sacred Heart Convent; and a few of my Hungarian poems. There is a particularly fine poem Earle wrote on Galiano Island where he appears to be missing her. There is another one he called "The Moon of Pooh Chi," celebrating the "melting of ice" and birds that invented special songs for my mother's benefit. Her nickname, the one that stuck from her early childhood, was Puci, pronounced a bit like Pooh Chi.

She was (thank God) not interested in a serious relationship with Earle. It would have been disastrous.

Earle and Wailan could not have been less similar physically. He was nearing seventy, painfully thin; she was short, cheerful, dark-haired, and more than forty years his junior. They moved into an apartment together on Balliol Avenue, Toronto, in 1973 when Wailan started her legal studies.

Earle's most tender love poems, such as this, are to or about Wailan.

. . . when warm winds come
she will move
all her body
in a tremble of light . . .

I hired John Newlove at M&S without so much as an interview because he had been recommended by both Earle and Al Purdy. I had read some of John's poetry, which was great, but had no idea whether he would be a good editor. He turned out to be a fine editor of both poetry and non-fiction, but he descended into rages when he drank too much. He often seemed on the verge of quitting or just erupting in anger and despair at the world. I was never quite sure whether his anger was aimed at the manuscripts sprawled across his desk, his experiences as a labourer or social worker in Western Canada (he fulminated about both), or me for bothering him in his office.

Among his most loathed editorial tasks was dealing with Earle Birney. Earle, if he felt slighted by Jack or M&S's lack of attention to his manuscripts, and by the scant presence of his books in bookstores he visited, was given to temper tantrums—in writing.

Earle's most frequent grudge during the years I worked there was "mac-stew," as he called us collectively, and, in particular, Jack. They had started sparring as long ago as 1949 when Jack had to convince Earle that army language, absolutely right for the men he too had fought beside, was not going to be possible in print. The censor would not allow him to publish *Turvey*. In the end, Earle had reluctantly changed words like *cocksucker*, *shit*, and *fuck*.

They used to exchange violent, mutually abusive letters that did not have to pass through the censor. This is one from the M&S Archives: "Dear Jack: Jesus fucking Christ, what in fucking hell are you up to? I haven't heard a goddamn word from you for six long bloody weeks and I want an explanation . . ."

Jack replied, pretending to be his own secretary, that he was "utterly revolted" by the language.

Earle responded thus: "Dear Jack: I am furious! If I can't write to my own fucking publisher in any form I wish, then I'll find a new goddamn publisher. Stuff the whole fucking thing up your ass . . ."

Earle fumed about the terms of his contracts or the delay in receiving them, about the lack of sufficient books at his readings, and about typos in his printed books. All these failings he blamed on Jack's preoccupation with saving the company—or selling it.

One prevailing rule of the book business, Jack taught me, is that an author will very rarely find his/her book in a store he/she visits and there will never be enough copies at a reading, unless nobody shows up—and that too will be your fault. Another is that no book is published without typos.

Sometime in the seventies Earle got into a legal spat with fellow poet Dorothy Livesay, who had written that his "David" poem had recorded the real death, or possible murder, of a friend. Julian agreed to represent him, but Jack refused to engage in the suit.

On several occasions, after listening to his tirades about my boss, I left Earle and Wailan's apartment in a fury. Somewhere in the M&S archives at McMaster there is a copy of one of his letters of apology. We had become reasonably good friends by then, and I remained a fan of his writing and of his conversation.

Earle had a lifetime of memories and old resentments to share. His best stories include his travels by freighter in the 1930s; his meetings with Leon Trotsky in Mexico; his partying with Frida Kahlo and Diego Rivera; his disillusion with the Fourth International; his visits with fellow poet and novelist Malcolm Lowry in a British Columbia cabin Lowry shared with his second wife, writer Margerie Bonner; his time as personnel officer in the Canadian Army; and his battles with fellow academics at the University of British Columbia. He had lived an extraordinary life and remembered all of it right up until he was hospitalized in 1994. After Key Porter published Sam Solecki's *Imagining Canadian Literature: The Letters of Jack McClelland* in 1998, Sam and I discussed publishing a similar volume of the letters of Earle Birney. I am still sorry I decided not to go ahead with the book. It would be a valuable addition to our literature, but I was worried about the shaky state of the book market.

Meetings with the Messiah

WHEN AL PURDY first met Irving Layton, he thought Layton was "so full of shit he couldn't make up his mind from which end it would exit . . . paradoxically, Layton was also genuine." Purdy admitted his comments may have been tinged with envy both of the parade of women who adored Irving and of the publicity Irving never failed to generate.

I felt it was a privilege to know him.

When I reread "The Bull Calf," I am still amazed by the sheer force of Irving's voice, and its utter sadness.

> The thing could barely stand. Yet taken
> from his mother and the barn smells
> he still impressed with his pride,
> with the promise of sovereignty in the way
> his head moved to take us in.
> The fierce sunlight tugging the maize from the ground
> licked at his shapely flanks.
> He was too young for all that pride.
> I thought of the deposed Richard II.
> "No money in bull calves," Freeman had said.
> The visiting clergyman rubbed the nostrils

now snuffing pathetically at the windless day.

"A pity," he sighed.

My gaze slipped off his hat toward the empty sky

that circled over the black knot of men,

over us and the calf waiting for the first blow.

Layton had such a commanding presence and sonorous voice that everyone fell into a reverential silence when he recited his poems. Everyone did not include Harold Town, who protested at one of Sylvia Fraser's parties that he would do a public drawing if Layton insisted on a public reading. Layton, undeterred, read "A Wild Peculiar Joy" and ignored Harold's heckling. I was relieved he didn't read the poem about the old Greek woman's orifices.

Layton was wide, short, square-shouldered, barrel-chested, somewhat hairy, usually tanned, with a bit of a belly that increased in girth during the decades that I knew him. He had bushy eyebrows, a slightly hooked nose, and longish grey hair that made him look like an Old Testament prophet. He often wore a large silver medallion hanging from a chain around his neck. It reminded me of Scott Symons's medallion.

He maintained that, just like the Messiah, he was born circumcised. On March 12, 1912, Jews came from far and wide to the tiny town of Târgu Neamţ to witness the miracle of little Israel Pincu Lazarovitch's penis. His grandmother had died young, he told me, because she had made a deal with God to trade her own life for that of his mother.

In search of a better life, his family emigrated to Canada and settled in Montreal's St. Urbain Street neighbourhood. Irving Layton, all agreed, was a better name for a Canadian poet than Israel Lazarovitch.

He told sad and hilarious tales about his father, the scholarly, frail, religious, rather distant man, and his mother, who railed against fate, and the horse-manure-throwing gentiles who messed up the alleyway in front of her small shop. His moving poem, "The Death of Moishe Lazarovitch," commemorates both his father and his mother.

Irving learned to use his fists in territorial wars between street gangs on Montreal's St. Elizabeth Street—the area where Jack Rabinovitch and

Mordecai Richler also grew up.* His friends had nicknames like Cross-Eyed George and Benny the Beanpole, and they fought like their lives depended on winning—which they sometimes did. He played handball in the same gymnasium where Jack Rabinovitch played a couple of decades later. Jack, Irving, and Mordecai all went to Baron Byng High School, and studied Latin and algebra.

I used to visit Irving and Aviva Layton in their book-lined house in Toronto. Aviva, small, tanned, vivacious, rivetingly pretty, had been with Irving for a number of years by then. They spent most summers on Lesbos, a Greek island, hence the tans. They were loud and affectionate. She often quieted him when he indulged in some of his verbal pyrotechnics, complaining about Canada's coldness, its refusal to talk about sex, or its unwillingness to be its best self.

Their young son David would sit at the table or perch on the arm of his father's or his mother's chair as his father declaimed. Though he tried a variety of methods, the boy was usually unsuccessful in attracting their attention. He hovered around Aviva, shouted and swore, tried to grab her as she walked past, but nothing seemed to work. The adults continued their conversations, Irving read his poems, Aviva produced more wine and food, and David shrank into aggrieved silence.

I remember sitting at their dining room table, when Irving talked of "Shakespeare, Milton, and I" all sharing the need to reach deep into the hearts of men. Of course he knew his Shakespeare and Milton, but also Keats, Spinoza, David Lewis and Canadian socialism, A. M. Klein, Louis Dudek, Maxim Gorky, Heinrich Heine, Jane Austen, Paul Celan, Nietzsche, and Nadezhda Mandelstam. His conversation ranged over a multitude of topics, including the Bible, Hitler, boxing, politics, Greek civilization, US elections, Vietnam, Roman emperors, the Soviet Union, Marxism, fascism, fads, fetishes, Anglo-Saxon puritanism, and, of course, sex and anti-Semitism. He told me that in the 1960s there were still places in the Laurentians that proudly displayed signs declaring No Dogs or Jews

---

* Much later, Jack Rabinovitch founded the Giller Prize.

Allowed. Anti-Semitism may have been outlawed but it was alive and well under the veneer of civility.

Irving was surprisingly pro-American. He supported the US war in Vietnam. Most people I knew were fiercely opposed to the 1970 War Measures Act. Barbara Frum, for example, believed it was inimical to Pierre Trudeau's own sense of a "just society." Irving, on the other hand, supported the suspension of civil liberties in Quebec.

Like Purdy and Birney, he was generous with younger poets, introduced them to his publishers, gave them advice about poetry and their love lives. Leonard Cohen was his lifelong protégé. Aviva used to say jokingly that she had married Leonard, not Irving (though, in fact, she never formally married Irving). The three of them had gone to a jewellery store to select a ring, but since Irving didn't have enough cash, Leonard purchased the ring and slipped it onto Aviva's finger.

Leonard loved Irving. He often travelled to conferences and readings with Irving, listened intently when Irving read his poetry. At an International Festival of Authors event honouring Irving on his eightieth birthday, Cohen made a surprise appearance. He mentioned the theological implications of Irving having been born circumcised. Embellishing the version I had first heard from Irving, he said, "Rabbis and doctors of law came from many miles around to visit Irving Layton in his crib and to look between his legs at that which was not there."

BECAUSE JACK PERSISTED in denying that he had editorial talents, I took the lead in discussing Layton's work with him. It wasn't easy. I had arrived at M&S just in time for *The Collected Poems of Irving Layton*. It weighed in at more than a thousand pages and we debated, poem by poem, about two hundred of them. I insisted that there was a limit to how many pages the book could have; he argued that a "collected" had to collect all his best work and that all the poems here were, indeed, his best. I was afraid the collection would diminish rather than burnish his image—and I knew Irving was insecure about reviews. While I thought he was brilliant, courageous, and passionate, some of the poems were quite dreadful, others were merely flawed. It was on that subject we parted ways.

Still, there is this wonderful poem "There Were No Signs," in *The Collected*:

By walking I found out
Where I was going.
By intensely hating, how to love.
By loving, whom and what to love.
By grieving, how to laugh from the belly.
Out of infirmity, I have built strength.
Out of untruth, truth.
From hypocrisy, I wove directness.
Almost now I know who I am.
Almost I have the boldness to be that man.
Another step
And I shall be where I started from.

When it was published, the volume still had six hundred pages. It was accorded a few measured reviews, but many suggested that Layton lacked a critical sense. It didn't sell as well as Irving's shorter collections that rarely sold fewer than three thousand copies. However, he credited *The Collected* with his Italian nomination for the Nobel Prize. He was celebrated by Italian poetry lovers.

Irving felt so beholden to his translator, Amleto Lorenzini, that he talked Jack into publishing Lorenzini's *Assyrian Sculpture in the British Museum*—a fascinating book, but it hardly fit into the M&S stable of Canadian literature, history, art, or politics.

A couple of years after *The Collected*, Irving retaliated with *The Uncollected Irving Layton*, the book with all the left-out poems and some additional ones he had written since. By then it was obvious that Irving would not be happy with only one new book a year. He demanded at least two despite my, I thought, convincing arguments that he would cut potential sales of each book in half. He ignored all efforts to weed out his weaker poems and raged at the notion that over-publishing was reducing his sales. If we resisted, he published elsewhere.

The year we published *The Collected*, we also published *Nail Polish*, a shorter book with a dreadful title and a vituperative introduction. Generally Irving used his introductions to launch unbridled attacks on his critics: "yahoos, sex-drained executives, pimps and poetasters." He let loose another torrent of vitriol in *Engagements: The Prose of Irving Layton*, which shouldn't have been published but was, a year or so later. The book, I thought, would harm Irving's reputation. But Jack believed in publishing authors, not books, and Layton was an author M&S published.

I was amazed at Aviva's willingness to overlook Irving's serial infidelities and not surprised that she fell for a lovestruck sheik in Morocco (while she entrusted David to Scott Symons and his then lover, Aaron) or that Irving took off with his student Harriet Bernstein. I am not sure of the order of these events, but in 1974 Julian and I visited Irving and Harriet in a small house in Niagara-on-the-Lake. Harriet was trying to reform Irving's lifelong habits of ignoring what happened around him when to observe those events did not suit him. Such events included the birth of children and the disorder that attended their arrival. While he loved the idea of his own virility and the pregnancies of women who loved him, he was more interested in the idea of fatherhood than in the children.

Eventually Harriet decamped with their baby daughter.

The poem that always brings me to tears is "Song for Naomi." Perhaps it's because I have daughters and have seen them running, carefree, through tall grass.

A Land of Poets

Irving Layton used to talk about Leonard Cohen with the pride of a father in the achievements of his own son. They wrote poems about and to each other. Several of Leonard's poems make reference to Irving or to one of Irving's poems. He regarded Irving as his "poetic master."

"I taught him how to dress, he taught me how to live forever," Leonard said. Irving's *The Swinging Flesh* and Leonard's *The Spice Box of Earth* had been launched at the same time in 1961. Both were sensations.

I read a lot of Cohen in the 1970s when Jack and I were engaged in a battle with Malcolm Ross, the editor of the New Canadian Library series, about including Cohen's novel *Beautiful Losers* in the New Canadian Library. In order to persuade Malcolm of the worthiness of the novel, I quoted what I assumed were persuasive literary passages over the phone to the progressively less and less polite Malcolm. The book had first been published in 1966, and Jack thought it was a literary bombshell. He wrote to Leonard: "It's wild and incredible and marvellously well written, and at the same time appalling, shocking, revolting, disgusting . . ."

I had found it difficult to read, its language overly florid, its characters hard to believe, but it does have some extraordinary writing, its lack of structure is mesmerizing once you decide not to care about structure, and it has what Malcolm found so distressing: very graphic sex.*

I didn't hear Leonard sing until about 1972. He was performing in Toronto and Jack had two seats close to the stage. Though he took up only a small portion of it, Leonard seemed to occupy the whole space, blue shirt, guitar, mic, and a spotlight. I don't remember all the songs, but I know he sang "Suzanne" and "Bird on a Wire." I was humming them for several weeks. Some days, I still do.

Jack seemed restless and harrumphed from time to time. When the show was over, he announced we were going backstage. In the small dressing room, he had barely introduced me before he launched into a speech about why Leonard was wasting his talent singing. His voice was shit but he was a great poet. His *Selected* had been a bestseller and had even won the Governor General's Award for Poetry.†

Leonard mainly nodded and smiled. Having first seen him on stage, I was surprised at how fragile he seemed. In the end he talked a bit about his new book, *The Energy of Slaves*, but I no longer recall what he said. The book was published the following year, but I didn't meet Leonard again till 1978.

JACK WAS CONVINCED that Canada was a land of poets. He believed that more poetry was written and read in Canada, per capita, than in any other country (and Edmonton, he thought, was our poetry capital). We certainly sold enough poetry books to support his theory.

The seventies saw Layton, Cohen, Atwood, Purdy, Birney, Ralph Gustafson, Raymond Souster, Doug Jones, Milton Acorn, George Bowering, and John Newlove attesting to that theory, and M&S was attracting some younger poets, Joe Rosenblatt and Susan Musgrave. *Storm Warnings*, Al

---

* *Beautiful Losers*, the book Malcolm Ross objected to ("The book turns my stomach. Quite literally, Jack!"), did finally find its way into the New Canadian Library in 1991 after Ross had retired and the stewardship of the series was taken over by David Staines.

† Leonard rejected the award.

Purdy's two volumes featuring the work of young poets, were successful and well reviewed. Musgrave's *The Impstone* and *A Man to Marry, A Man to Bury* got her the attention she deserved.

A plethora of new literary journals showcased Canadian poetry. Alongside the Writers' Union, there was the League of Canadian Poets (founded in 1966), where Purdy, A. J. M. Smith, and Earle Birney could support newer arrivals such as Dennis Lee,[*] Sid Marty, David McFadden, Gwendolyn MacEwen, Patrick Lane, Pier Giorgio Di Cicco, and Michael Ondaatje. I went to one of their meetings in Calgary, and tried to hawk poetry books from a hastily set-up table outside the hall. The poets bought one another's books and had them autographed. Purdy added to his large collection of other poets' signed books.

I didn't meet Michael Ondaatje till late 1978 or early 1979, when I was ready to leave the company. He had brought the manuscript of *There's a Trick with a Knife I'm Learning to Do: Poems 1963–1978*. He was lovely to look at, his strange blue eyes, the curly dark hair. Everyone wanted to see him. The editors ducked out of their warren and the salespeople walked down the corridor to the "reception" for a better view. What I remember about the poetry is the immediate, tactile, often abrupt, and wildly colourful imagery. And these lines from "Letters and Other Worlds":

My father's body was a town of fear
He was the only witness to its fear dance . . .

After reading Ondaatje's 1982 fictional memoir *Running in the Family*, I understood what the poem had already told me.

I STILL LOVE poetry but not with the questing urgency of my early years. Yet each year I listen to the Griffin Prize's short-listed poets read. Dionne

---

[*] I used to look for early versions of some of Dennis's poems, trying to understand why he changed them.

Brand's *Ossuaries* has taken up residence next to my bed, along with Al Purdy's *Naked with Summer in Your Mouth*, George Jonas's *Selected Poems*, Irving Layton's *Selected*, T. S. Eliot's *The Waste Land*, and a rich assortment of books I am reading or plan to read one day.

Scott Griffin created the prize in 2000 along with trustees Margaret Atwood and Michael Ondaatje. Scott seems to believe, as I do, that words can change the world. He is a most unusual businessman because, in addition to his founding and supporting an internationally lauded poetry prize, he pursues personal goals of derring-do, such as circumnavigating the globe in a sailboat, flying his aging Cessna 180 solo across the Atlantic and volunteering for the Flying Doctors Service of East Africa. *My Heart Is Africa: A Flying Adventure* is his account of the two years he spent working for the NGO.* He is a romantic, an adventurer, a storyteller, and a publisher: his Griffin Trust bought the House of Anansi in 2002.

---

* Every time I see Scott's rather regal wife, Krystine, I am reminded that this very accomplished woman accompanied her husband on his African adventure, crash-landed with him on an isolated island in Kenya, was arrested with him in Tanzania, slept on the ground, endured malaria, but stayed.

Peter's Establishment

WE FIRST MET over his manuscript for *Home Country*, an eclectic collection of his thoughts on people, places, and politics in Canada. Peter C. Newman was the editor of *Maclean's* magazine, then a monthly that he was planning to transform into a weekly. He believed *Maclean's* was part of the fabric of Canada, "a country that lies out there, magnificently unknowable" but ready to be known and written about. And he was just the man to do that.

He was slim, almost bald, with stunningly bushy eyebrows (in a hilarious parody of Newman's face, writer Alison Gordon compared them to "a pair of woolly caterpillars curled up for the winter on the egg of his forehead"), energetic, quite formal, serious though with a rare, infectious smile that made him seem many years younger and much more vulnerable than the self he otherwise presented. Even on hot days he dressed in a suit. He had begun life in Vienna and, to me, he still seemed quintessentially middle European. His parents were Czech Jews. He was ten years old when German tanks rolled into Czechoslovakia after British Prime Minister Neville Chamberlain's disastrous declaration that Britain wouldn't interfere in "a quarrel in a faraway country between people of whom we know nothing."

Peter's family came to Canada in 1940 as "immigrant farmers." They knew nothing about farming, but it was the only category of refugees Canada was willing to accept. For similar reasons, my mother had worked as a cleaning woman in a Polish hostel in Wellington, New Zealand. Like Peter, I had watched tanks roll into my country and, like Peter, I had seen the carnage in their wake. We had both come from old countries with more baggage, more regrets, and much more bloodshed than our adopted home. That helped create some common ground.

In 1944 Peter had been admitted to Upper Canada College as a "war guest" boarder, as I had been a "charity" boarder at the Sacred Heart Convent School. Neither of us was ecstatic about the experience, but we both learned English and Peter got to know several scions of Canada's power structure who would later grant him access to their inner circles.

I loved that he had worked, for a while, as assistant magician at Eaton's Toytown. I have had a soft spot for magicians ever since I watched my grandfather make coins disappear and pigeons fly out of his pockets.*

Peter didn't have time to come to East York, so we often had lunch at the elegant Courtyard Café on St. Thomas Street. We used to talk about Europe and Canada. He didn't drink. Given how much alcohol was consumed by most of our authors, I found it a welcome change. Unlike most people, he made no effort to fill long pauses in our conversations. I learned to sit with him and watch him eat sparingly but with great concentration.

I discovered that his wife, political journalist Christina Newman, who was researcher, fact-checker, and sometimes rewriter of Peter's prose, was not his first wife. I had met Christina at a couple of publishing parties and found her shy, but once engaged, she was voluble and exceptionally well-informed. Peter's first wife, to whom he was still paying alimony, was an Irish girl from County Antrim. As Peter said, and later wrote in his memoir *Here Be Dragons*, they had "had nothing in common but loneliness."

He kept a sailboat at the Royal Canadian Yacht Club and often invited

---

* Magic was also the basis for our friendship with Standard Broadcasting's Allan Slaight. Music lover, media mogul, philanthropist—Allan was the best card magician I ever met.

Julian and me for a few hours of sailing on Lake Ontario, the only time that I saw Peter really relaxed. Having volunteered for active duty back in 1947 and received his commission a few years later, Peter was still a reserve officer in the Canadian navy. He wore a sailor's cap that would become his trademark in years to come. A couple of times we were there for the RCYC "sailpast," a peculiar tradition that required us to stand still in a rolling, moving boat while Peter manoeuvred it into position to sail past "the commodore," a man in uniform on another boat, so they could salute each other.

Peter was a workaholic. In addition to conducting exhaustive interviews and research, writing his columns, and writing and promoting his books, he gave speeches for fees in the very impressive five-thousand-dollar-plus range. Peter had been editor-in-chief of the *Toronto Star* before *Maclean's*. His books had sold more than three-quarters of a million copies by the time he came to collect his best columns into *Home Country: People, Places and Power Politics*, published in 1973.

I had been reading him since I arrived in Canada. I admired his style, a gossipy, opinionated, minutiae-observant technique usually the purview of novelists. For example, he wrote of Richard Nixon: "in a small stillness of insight, I recognized a man so terrified . . . that he could barely keep himself under control." Or of the political magic of Pierre Elliott Trudeau: "a cool man in a hot world."

He wrote of his love affair with Canada, a brand of nationalism that did not manifest as anti-American, though he was in favour of placing restrictions on foreign investment before we were "reduced to minority shareholders in our own country." He was one of Jack's partners in the Committee for an Independent Canada. "As a nation," he wrote, "we are drowning in American dollars, American culture, American know-how, and the American dream."

We need our own dreams. I knew I had become a Canadian nationalist when I made this same argument in Ottawa to then Secretary of State (and Pierre Trudeau's friend) Gérard Pelletier and to Bill Davis when he was premier of Ontario. The choice, I said, is clear: either you want to have a nation or not. If you do, there are some sacrifices you have to make. One of those, I believe, is to take fewer American dollars and encourage, by whatever means are at your disposal, our own culture.

WHILE WE WERE discussing the various chapter headings for *Home Country*, Peter was already at work on his mega bestseller, *The Canadian Establishment, Volume One.* The original plan had been for Peter and Christina to write the book together, but their marriage broke apart while Peter was still conducting the interviews. He blamed their too-busy schedules and their youthful ambitions for the breakup.

His approach to his subjects was flattering and cajoling, on the surface, but in reality, very tough. He referred to it as his "take-no-prisoners" way of writing. "I grovelled to pry open the Canadian establishment's secrets but never told them mine."*

Most of the Establishment invited Peter into their homes and sat still for invasive interviews. Men like Bud McDougald, "the archetype of tycoon," Paul Desmarais, "head of the largest agglomeration of economic power in the hands of a French Canadian," E. P. Taylor, "the ultimate personification of riches gained and power wielded," the heads of the five banks, press lord Roy Thomson, investment guru Stephen Jarislowsky, Noranda's Alf Powis, Leo Kolber of Cemp Investments, shoe magnate Tom Bata, the Eatons, the Westons, and the Southams, those entitled men in corner offices, the men with resonant voices and "eyes of surpassing indifference"—astonishingly, they all talked to Peter.

Peter described them, their milieu, their schools, and their clubs, gave colourful examples of their manners and preoccupations, their valued possessions, even their families. Nelson Davis showed him his meteorite-paved driveway; Galen Weston told him about his father, the one-time baker who founded the Weston dynasty; Charles Rathgeb showed off his gold-and-leather bracelets, each one denoting his killing of one of the great animals (a lion, a leopard, an elephant). These were the men who really ran

---

* Peter wrote about the technique in *Here Be Dragons*, his memoir published in 2005.

Canada, the inbred, secretive, puritanical, iron-willed businessmen dedicated to preserving their status whatever the cost. They were heads of large corporations, big banks, or traditional family businesses. Peter made them all seem compellingly interesting.

The country had never seen a book like this, packed with detail, highly entertaining, a *real* inside look at the world of the very rich. Peter's style flowed with metaphors and long, rolling sentences. There was dialogue, personal observation, and some delightfully purple prose. Despite its girth and high retail price, the book flew out of bookstores at such a rate that we had to reprint almost as soon as the first 100,000 copies had been shipped. What else flew were threats of lawsuits. I read the letters to Julian over the phone, imagining that all of M&S's senior staff would end up in jail. As a libel lawyer who was used to litigation, Julian just laughed. Most of the thirty-seven letters were merely sabre-rattling, he said. Few if any of these men would want to go to court.

The only successful plaintiff, in the end, was Paul Desmarais of Power Corporation, who insisted on a rewrite of page 74. Rather than reprint the book, which we certainly couldn't afford to do, we took Julian's suggestion that we paste over the offending page in copies still in the warehouse and in those that could be found in stores. Desmarais accepted the proposal and most of us spent the weekend pasting. Of course this correction and the attendant publicity only served to promote the book.

Julian's proposal for avoiding costly litigation over the second book, *The Canadian Establishment, Volume Two: The Acquisitors*, was even more original. The judge had accepted his argument that we could not recall all the books already in stores and could not possibly reprint (he would have gone down in history as the judge who bankrupted M&S). We shipped black felt pens to all bookstores and libraries and encouraged them to black out a passage that had to do with a swimming pool and a chauffeur's uniform, that I won't risk repeating.

Unlike the men profiled in the first book, the "acquisitors" had acquired their wealth themselves. Many of them—Jimmy Pattison, Firp Taylor, Peter Bentley, Jack Poole, Smiling Jack Gallagher, George Cohon (McDonald's), Nelson Skalbania—were tireless in their pursuit. They enjoyed fortunes that allowed them to spend ten thousand dollars a day and have ultra-thin wives with a taste for the finest things money could buy.

It's interesting to view the two books from a distance of more than thirty years. Some fortunes have been spectacularly squandered. Some of the new breed of elite have joined the old in their private clubs and send their kids to the same schools. The tinge of *arriviste* no longer attaches itself to most of the newcomers—as long as they are still very rich. Much of the old money has remained in the hands of "the inheritors." The most colourful of them is, without a doubt, Conrad Black, who increased substantially the fortune he inherited.

AFTER HIS DIVORCE from Christina, Peter enjoyed the company of several enamoured women. I remember his wedding to the very beautiful Camilla Turner at a private ceremony at the Royal Canadian Yacht Club. She looked angelic with tiny white angel's breath flowers in her blond hair. Both Jack McClelland and Brian Mulroney gave speeches. The place was packed with Peter's admirers and I was thinking that, at last, Peter was going to be happy.

I was wrong. He didn't become happy until many years later, when he married Alvie, his fourth and last wife—"absolutely the last," he told me over scrambled eggs in 2016 in the King Edward Hotel's refurbished lobby restaurant. By then he had written thirty-five successful books; several had been made into TV series, and some of them had been published internationally. Even the Soviet Union had given *The Canadian Establishment* a keen reception.

Pierre Berton may have been the most successful journalist/non-fiction writer in Canada, but Peter was for many years the most talked about. Everyone had Peter Newman stories—his battles with Beland Honderich at the *Star*, his playing Stan Kenton while he wrote, the women who claimed he was the best lover they had ever had, his fellow writers who watched his every move and prided themselves in becoming Newmanophiles.

Julian tells the story of going to Newman's house in the Annex at four thirty in the morning to review legal issues and hearing Stan Kenton as soon as he opened the front door. At a party at journalist/activist June Call-wood's house, I overheard two women talking in great detail about Peter's talents in bed. Then there was the man who packed up his wife's clothes and dumped them on the street in front of Peter's office. He may have been the same guy who threatened to sue him for "alienation of affection."

Yet Peter still "hungered after the full banquet of recognition, money, access, and influence," all of which he already had but failed to recognize.* He wore his insecurity like a badge or a lapel pin, obvious to everyone who knew him. Though some of his books reveal bits of Peter Newman, he kept most of his secrets to himself, until his highly entertaining (Peter is always entertaining) memoir, *Here Be Dragons*.

---

* Peter C. Newman, *Here Be Dragons: Telling Tales of People, Passion and Power* (Toronto: McClelland & Stewart Ltd., 2004), 206.

A Northern Nation

W E ARE "A vast, half-frozen landscape in search of a country," according to Harold Town. But although we see ourselves as a Northern
people, few Canadians have ever ventured north of the tree line. As Farley
Mowat noted, few had any real interest in getting their "fat butts" up there
to see those vast half-frozen, open spaces for themselves. Maybe if more of
us ventured north, we would show more resolve to save what was left of
our Arctic for future generations.

Perhaps because Jack McClelland helped define what it was to be Canadian, M&S attracted a fair range of people with Arctic obsessions. I was
surprised to discover that most of them were immigrants or refugees.
Vienna-born George Swinton had travelled north for the first time in 1957
and had become obsessed with the region. A former intelligence officer in
the Canadian Army, now an art teacher, George believed his mission was
to bring Inuit art to a largely ignorant world. His *Sculpture of the Eskimo*,
in preparation in 1970, was one of them. Swinton was a large, highly entertaining presence in our offices, opinionated about everything including
book design, though as Frank Newfeld pointed out, his idea of design was
to cram more reproductions on a page than any book could reasonably
display. The irony of the fact that all three of us—George, Frank, and I—
were Central Europeans was not lost either on us or on other M&S staffers.

George was a prolific artist himself, an excellent draftsman, an imaginative colourist who could relate the work of Inuit artists to artists working in Paris and New York. I believe a couple of George's paintings are still in the National Gallery.

Herbert Schwarz, another immigrant from the lands the Hapsburgs once ruled, now lived in Tuktoyaktuk. He claimed to be the only doctor along the DEW Line (the US-Canadian line of defence stretching from Baffin Island to Alaska), which meant he had the longest medical practice in the world. He would tell me Arctic tales while sipping brandy from a hip flask he kept close. Even during our sweltering summer months, he usually wore a fur-trimmed parka. His *Windigo and Other Tales of the Ojibways* had been illustrated by Norval Morrisseau. He explained that these tales were first told him by Copper Thunderbird, a.k.a. Morrisseau, who had been born on the Sand Point Reserve in Northwestern Ontario and scooped up into a residential school. Drawing on the mythologies of his Anishinaabe people, Morrisseau created vibrant, colourful, mesmerizing paintings.[*]

Schwarz had enjoyed showing me Daphne Odjig's risqué illustrations for the book that was eventually published as *Tales from the Smokehouse*. The pictures made him giggle enthusiastically. What did I think they did up there during those long winter months? he asked. Much later, at Key Porter, we published *Odjig, the Art of Daphne Odjig 1985–2000* and in 1997 the retrospective *Norval Morrisseau: Travels to the House of Invention*, to coincide with an exhibition of his art.

In one of the Canada Council's second-floor meeting rooms there were two paintings by Morrisseau. They fairly dominated the room. Sometimes I found it impossible to focus on the discussions around the table[†] while facing them. They are not distracting; they are utterly absorbing.

---

[*] I wish I had bought one of the illustrations, but I was broke then, and when I offered to buy one of his paintings from the Kinsman Robinson Galleries in the 1990s, the prices were much, much higher.

[†] I served on the Board of the Canada Council for the Arts from 2008 till 2016.

Fred Bruemmer, whom I met for the first time in 1972, was born in Latvia and saw the Canadian Arctic for the first time while he was on assignment in Frobisher Bay (now Iqaluit) for *Weekend* magazine. He wrote of its rugged beauty, its haunting loneliness, its infinite space. "It has the vastness of the sea, the grandeur of a Bach fugue."* It was a love that stayed with him for the rest of his life. He spent at least six months of every year living with the Inuit.

His *Seasons of the Eskimo* was the first book we planned together. There would be five more before I left M&S, and another ten at Key Porter. I loved the times we spent together, Fred talking about the Arctic and coming up with new ideas to contain both his quiet enthusiasm for the place and his evocative photographs.

Apart from Farley Mowat, James Houston was Jack's favourite Arctic adventurer. Their affinity for each other may have come from shared experiences during the Second World War. Jim had fought with the Toronto Scottish Regiment. After the war, he was a civil administrator among the Inuit in the Eastern Arctic for fourteen years, painting, writing, and working for the federal government. He told fascinating stories about sharing meals of raw fish and raw seal liver—a delicacy—hunting walrus, building igloos, using Inuit-made sunglasses. When he came south again, he brought along not only his own sketches but also sculpture and prints by the people he had come to know. James organized the first Inuit art show in Montreal and helped set up the first commercial Inuit art co-operative on Baffin Island. He introduced the highly original work of Kenojuak Ashevak (creator of "Enchanted Owl"), Pitseolak Ashoona, and Kiakshuk to the art world. On behalf of the artists, he offered Inuit pieces for auctions in Rome, London, Paris and of course Toronto, Montreal, and Ottawa.

Jim would go on to spend several years as a master designer for Steuben Glass in New York. His works are breathtakingly beautiful pieces of seemingly solid glass with figures inside that appear to move as you turn them in the light. Sometimes one comes up for auction but I have never

---

* From the introduction to *Survival: A Refugee Life*.

found one I can afford. One of his most celebrated works is the seventy-foot *Aurora Borealis* sculpture for the Glenbow Museum.

He loved to tell a story about sitting in his Manhattan office one spring day as a huge flock of snow geese flew over the building. He left his urban comforts to follow them north, he claimed, not stopping until he reached the Arctic again. Manhattan may not be on the snow geese flight path, but it made for a great tale.

Despite his craggy features, his lantern jaw, I think James remained a kind of boy hero, keen to have new adventures. Seventeen of his children's books are still available, including the one published by Key Porter: *Whiteout*, the coming-of-age story of a rebellious seventeen-year-old city boy who goes to live on Baffin Island. One Houston story, *Spirit Wrestler*, is about a boy who becomes a shaman, though I would be surprised if the writer's presentation of Shoona and the white man who possesses truly magical powers would be acceptable today, when cultural appropriation is a sin.

I am still planning to go to the North, though so far I have only made it as far as Churchill, Manitoba, to see the polar bears.

The Best and the Brightest

J ACK ALWAYS CLAIMED that it was a privilege to work at M&S, and he was right. But he was also fortunate to have such brilliant editors and designers. I've already mentioned Jennifer Glossop, who edited Margaret Atwood and Marian Engel. Both Mordecai Richler and Margaret Laurence respected her keen eye and gentle manner, as did Peter Gzowski and George Swinton. The witty and accomplished Charis Wahl edited Rudy Wiebe, Michel Tremblay, and Hubert Aquin. Lily Miller, who among many books, edited Leonard Cohen's *Death of a Ladies' Man*, remained unperturbed by the usual M&S chaos. M&S editors were known for their ability to juggle multiple projects on a wide variety of subjects.

In later years I worked with Linda Pruessen, who edited fiction and non-fiction, children's books and young adult books, including those by Dennis Lee and Carol Matas. Barbara Berson edited Erika Ritter and Tim Wynveen at Key Porter and proved to be very patient when she edited *The Ghosts of Europe*, my third non-fiction book. The multi-talented (fiction, non-fiction, children's books, and canoe refurbishing) Susan Renouf edited Farley Mowat's later books. Phyllis Bruce developed her own imprint at two publishing houses. The imaginative Rosemary Shipton, known for her high standards and the many prizes won by authors she worked with, edited my *Kasztner's Train*. Linda McKnight, my first M&S hire, went from educational editor to managing editor, to president and publisher of M&S, then executive vice president and publisher of Macmillan, and finally became an agent. John Pearce edited my early mysteries and later, as my literary agent, continued to offer editorial advice.

Editors are a strange breed. Strong-willed yet exceptionally sensitive to other voices, devoted to their work yet uninterested in claiming credit, they rarely lay claim to fame. Ellen Seligman, as I've noted, was one of the very best. In just a few months after arriving at M&S, she developed an astonishingly assertive personality. She stubbornly refused to submit to M&S's relentless schedules: a manuscript was either ready for publication or it was not. In addition to Margaret Atwood, she also edited books by Michael Ondaatje, Jane Urquhart, Elizabeth Hay, Guy Vanderhaeghe, and David Bergen, to mention a few.

After I left M&S, Ellen and I would meet from time to time to talk and drink Chablis or Sancerre—she knew her wines—and talk about clothes, books, cooking, her health, my back, and gossip. I served on the PEN Canada board when Ellen was chair. It was then I learned to admire her steely determination in a way that had eluded me earlier.

Many M&S grads, whether in editorial, sales, or marketing, went on to long careers in publishing. Scott McIntyre, who had left M&S in 1969 to travel in Europe, returned to join Jim Douglas in Vancouver, at first as a fellow West Coast rep, then as a partner in Douglas & McIntyre, a highly respected publisher. D&M produced some of the most beautiful art books in the country, and Scott, never too shy to rejoice in his authors' successes, celebrated his fortieth anniversary as a publisher in 2011 with his usual aplomb and apparent self-confidence. Few of us knew of the financial struggle he was facing at the time. We have remained colleagues for more than forty years in the fraught fields of Canadian publishing politics—competitors for authors, once almost partners, and always friends.*

John Neale had been at M&S as sales manager under Peter Taylor. He was effervescent, imaginative, and very, very funny. Most days at the office

---

* Douglas & McIntyre published three of my books.

he was accompanied by his dog, a black lab he said he had picked up quite accidentally. He would later become chairman of Random House Canada. A less likely corporate man would have been impossible to imagine, yet his successors have admired him for his leadership in building a publishing powerhouse with outstanding financial results.

Patsy Aldana, who started Groundwood, a children's publisher in association with Douglas & McIntyre, has been a friend and occasional sparring partner. She has been honoured by the Writers' Union, by the Bologna Book Fair, and by the International Organization of Books for Young People. But my best memories of Patsy are of her in full flight decrying some injustice she has observed and will not accept quietly.

M&S was fortunate to have on staff some of the best book designers, including the legendary Frank Newfeld and the wildly inventive David Shaw, who designed many of M&S's poetry books and art books, including the two Roloff Beny tomes about Iran.* M&S book covers from the seventies are known for their bold, sometimes psychedelic designs.

I have had the privilege of knowing the best and the brightest book publishers of my generation. We survived on hope and promises. We argued and battled with governments, with successive ministers and deputies, with the bosses of the Canada Council and various provincial arts councils for recognition that what we did was of unique value to the country. It still is. Roy MacSkimming wrote in *The Perilous Trade: Publishing Canada's Writers* (2003) about the "junta," the small group of us who had been asked by the Association of Canadian Publishers to present our case to the government, to explain that without an independent press it would be very difficult for our voices to be heard and that, while our bestselling fiction would still travel the globe, our Canadian non-fiction would die or be relegated to personal blogs. That, like many of our battles of the 1980s and nineties, is worth refighting with every new generation.

---

* One of my favourite David Shaw designs is Max Braithwaite's hilarious *The Night We Stole the Mountie's Car*—winner of the 1971 Stephen Leacock Memorial Medal for Humour.

The Disinherited

I AM NOT sure what I was expecting next from Matt Cohen, but *The Disinherited* was certainly not it. I thought Matt, like most young writers, would draw on his own experience, that the novel would feature people like Matt and his friends, the women who had loved him, or whom he loved, the people who had inhabited the student/teacher/activist world of Toronto. Instead, *The Disinherited* belonged to a group of people so remote from Toronto, so far from downtown that I found it strange that they could exist in Matt's world.

They had sprung whole, he told me, from some part of him he hadn't known existed, as if the Thomas family and their friends and acquaintances had arrived fully alive, very demanding, as if all he had to do was to record their well-lived lives. It was as if he and his characters had been living in parallel universes, each unknown to the other. Most days, he thought, their world was far more convincing than his own. Take Richard Thomas, for example. He was as solid as an oak, sprung from the hard soil of Ontario's farmland, north of Kingston, where even now a man can barely eke out sustenance for a family, a man in love with an indifferent land. Or his passionate wife, Miranda, who harboured family secrets and hopes. I had imagined that the character Eric might have carried some of Matt's own dreams and sense of estrangement, but as Matt gave me pieces of the manuscript, I realized he too had sprung whole from Matt's imagination.

After *The Disinherited*, we published two more Kingston novels. Already then I was curious about Katherine Malone, Matt's sexiest heroine. But it would be years before Matt decided to come back to her and write *The Sweet Second Summer of Kitty Malone*.

"She wasn't ready to tell me her story," Matt explained. Or she hadn't lived it yet.

Matt and I became friends through the Salem manuscripts. It was a gradual process, and I don't know when we closed the distance between author and editor. I remember long walks, drinks in the Holiday Inn's bar, Matt's arriving at our home with a bag full of manuscripts and his playing tennis with Julian in Georgian Bay and failing to mention that he had once been an Ontario junior tennis champion.

Around 1978 I suggested a children's story and he came up with a most unusual one, *The Leaves of Louise*, an unfunny precursor to his series of funny children's books using the pseudonym Teddy Jam. They were all published by his partner Patsy Aldana's imprint, Groundwood.

Although Matt's books garnered some critical success, a few even appearing on bestseller lists, they did not become bestsellers. And the positive reviews were always accompanied by nasty attacks on Matt's prose style, his characters, his storytelling. A few critics surprisingly launched almost personal attacks on everything Matt felt was important in his writing.

I didn't succeed in talking Mordecai Richler into selecting one of Matt's books for the Book of the Month Club when Mordecai was a judge. As far as I could tell, he had never even read an entire Matt Cohen manuscript. But my tenacity impressed him sufficiently that we would go for drinks— usually at the Park Plaza Roof Lounge—though not even four or five Macallans could soften his heart.

When Matt and Mordecai finally met, they had nothing to talk about. They stood, largely in silence, ignoring each other.

Matt continued to write, though the books didn't make him a living. Nor, as Matt argued, did they change anyone's life, as philosopher George Grant had changed his. Matt was his own harshest critic.

To make ends meet, he ghosted other people's books. There were several of these strange partnerships, but the one I remember best is the autobiography of the young woman who may or may not have accidentally killed the Hollywood actor John Belushi. While suffering great pangs of grief over her ruined life and his death, she decided Matt would be her salvation, the man who would listen and forgive everything. "A kind of priest," Matt said, after a long night of listening and trying not to fall asleep. "I can't imagine how those guys do it. Priests. Day after day." He thought perhaps the fact that priests were encouraged to forget made it easier for them.

BECAUSE I WAS a European with the burden of the Holocaust in my mind, because we had now known each other long enough for me to ask, I had wanted Matt to tell me about growing up Jewish in this part of the world. He had never talked about being Jewish. His fiction didn't relate to his Jewish experience. His fictional people were farmer folk, Irish, Scots, English. His last book, *Typing, a Life in 26 Keys*, begins with this: "A Jew is a person in exile from nowhere. Or maybe that's a myth I like to believe because the truth is too oppressive." All four of his grandparents had escaped Russian pogroms, and all their children had been eager to escape the immigrant experience.

"Besides, with a name like Cohen," he once told me, "you don't have to advertise that you're a Jew. Only an idiot would miss the fact. And no, I haven't been escaping, I have been what I am." He didn't want to be a Jewish writer. He was simply a writer.

Matt had been planning to write a book about Joseph Roth, the Austrian Jewish writer dead since 1939, but he hadn't decided yet whether it would be a novel or a fictional biography, an inquiry into Roth's death. Though he had not been brought up to be Jewish, he felt a deep kinship with Roth based on their shared values as Jewish intellectuals. I know I was looking forward to reading more of the manuscript. It would have been a great book for Matt.

The Spanish Doctor opened another door for Matt, another set of imagined people to write about, and many brilliant books followed. Some of his best writing, I think, is in *Elizabeth and After*, published by Knopf. It won the Governor General's Award for Fiction in 1999, just a few weeks before he died.

There is this wonderful passage Dennis Lee read at a memorial for Matt:

> Mysteries begin with the body but sometimes the mystery is not death but love. There is so much to love. Cats. Bits of dust caught in the light. Colours. Unexpected waterfalls. And of course: the body. Warm skin on cool sheets. The blood's night hum. Summer heat seeping through damp moss. The raw smell of an oak tree opened in winter. A long-missed voice over the telephone. So much to love that life should be made out of loving, so many ways of loving that all stories should be love stories. This one is about a man and a woman.

For Matt, that special love was Patsy Aldana, and for the children they shared, including the ones she brought with her into their marriage.

The last time that I saw him we laughed more than we cried, shared memories, asked questions of each other we would not have asked before. As Matt said, when you are dying, nothing is personal. When we said good-bye, I told him I was sure he was going to live. I thought it was what he wanted to hear. Now, I'm not so sure.

The Greatest Gift

I THINK *THE Stone Angel* has one of the most wonderful opening lines of any novel: "Above the town, on the hill brow, the stone angel used to stand. I wonder if she stands there yet."

I had fallen in love with Margaret Laurence long before we met. My affection for her grew with the manuscript of what became *A Bird in the House*, a series of short stories based on her childhood and her family, set in her fictional Manawaka. I remember calling the sales director of her US publisher and going on and on about what a fabulous book it was going to be. The sales director (I don't remember his name) suggested that it would really help Margaret's sales to relocate Manawaka in the American Midwest. Not much difference, he had said, between Manitoba and, say, Minnesota or Wisconsin, and since Manawaka didn't exist, it could be anywhere. It's a credit to Margaret's sense of humour that she laughed when I told her.

She hated Toronto: she called it Vile Metropolis, or V.M. for short, though she had agreed to be writer-in-residence at Massey College for the 1969–70 academic year. It was when we first met. I think she may have persuaded herself that the college was not really Toronto. It had been designed by architect Ron Thom to look and feel separate, enclosed, quadrangled, peaceful. Its master then was the redoubtable Robertson Davies, whose novel *Fifth Business* was published by Macmillan in 1970, the same year that we published *A Bird in the House*.

During 1972 and '73 Margaret was deeply involved with her next novel, the one she said would be her last. She was editing and rewriting long before she was ready to show it to anyone else. *The Diviners* features Morag Gunn, a novelist living in rural Ontario who is trying to discover the meaning of the past, including her own, and thus the meaning of her life. One of the novel's most deeply felt themes is the possibility of gaining new vision from the terrible, colonial past that had almost destroyed our Indigenous peoples. Morag's sexual relationship with the Métis songwriter Jules seems to presage some form of understanding, in the same way that water divining relies on the deeply intuitive relationship between humans and the earth:

> The river was dark and shining, and the moon traced a wavering path across it. Morag sat cross-legged on the dock, listening to the hoarse prehistoric voices of the bull frogs. Somewhere far-off, thunder.
>
> Incredibly, unreasonably, a lightening of the heart.

I loved that manuscript!

Her editor at Knopf, Judith Jones, wrote a long, detailed set of notes on where she had to take the novel next and how and why. Jack McClelland agreed with most, not all, of her suggestions and added a few of his own.

Contrary to the myths he had spread about his own lack of interest in editorial matters, how he left that for others better qualified than himself, Jack was a very careful reader who managed, despite his improbable working methods, to dictate excellent editorial observations and notes. He worked late into the nights, drinking vodka, reading manuscripts, and dictating memos and letters. As the night wore on, his observations would become more repetitious and less measured. He would then give the tapes to Marge in the morning. "The drinks are the only things that keep me awake," Jack used to say. He was pleased that Marge could decipher most of what he had said. The fact that he rarely read his own letters (most were signed by Marge or declared themselves to be "dictated but not read") before they left his office, added to the risk he took in having them sent. His notes to Margaret were a good example of both his method and his editorial skills. But given how the letters were produced, I often had to explain to a befuddled Margaret what Jack had meant.

Margaret was insecure about her own abilities as a writer and, unlike some M&S stalwarts, took criticism very seriously. "I learned something important from Margaret about writers," Jack wrote in his later tribute to her accomplishments. It was "the anguish, the anxiety, that an author experiences while waiting for a judgment from the publisher—the kind of uncertainty that remained with Margaret long after she had become an established writer."

I used to go to Margaret's cottage, the "shack" she called it, near Peterborough on the Otonabee River, to explain what Jack had really meant with his most recent letter to her. I don't remember what the letters said, but they would have been typical Jack notes about something she had objected to where he thought she had been unreasonable. I still remember the small cottage, piles of paper in organized stacks, and the old typewriter she had to abandon to talk with me. The land—not exactly a lawn—slanted down to the water. There was a wooden bench and table, a dock, and a small rowboat that may not have been hers.

I didn't know her well then, but I knew Hagar, Rachel, Stacey, and now Morag. She seemed much like them: strong, brave, and already almost a friend. She was, then in her mid-forties, a strong, broad-hipped woman with short, greying hair; a pale, wide, open face with high cheekbones and dark, almond-shaped eyes; black-framed glasses; no makeup, a slight smile. She wore loose, shapeless, comfortable dresses, often beige with some pattern. She smoked so much the ashtrays were always full.

She would make tea and offer cookies. Her hands shook noticeably and her forefinger was tobacco-stained, as was mine, from too many Rothmans. Though I had managed to reduce my smoking while I was pregnant, I was now back to about a pack a day.*

She was interested in how I was doing and whether marriage agreed with my temperament. She had been married for a number of years and had two children, but marriage hadn't agreed with her. She had wanted to devote herself to writing. On the other hand, had she not married, she would not have been in Africa and would not, then, have been able to write the books she had written there. She felt her African experience had been vital to her as a writer. She said she loved having kids, something I once told her daughter Jocelyn, who gazed at me in disbelief. It is hard to be the child of a serious writer who is often distracted and unavailable when you feel you need her.

Though she tried, Margaret said, to spend time with her children when they came home from school, she found it difficult to stop in the middle of a passage or chapter that was finally coming together. She told me, "Writing for me is torture but I have to do it. And once I start, I don't slow down."

When she left her husband and moved to Elm Cottage in Buckinghamshire, north of London, *The Stone Angel*, she said, had been her most precious possession.

Late in the day, she would open a bottle of whisky or wine. We often talked about books and authors we had been reading. She loved Graham Greene, Sinclair Ross, W. O. Mitchell, Joyce Cary, Al Purdy's poems and Wole Soyinka and Chinua Achebe, whose books I had not read until she told me about them. She talked about her time in Pakistan, where she had loved the people.

It was Margaret who first told me the story of the brain surgeon who is seated next to a novelist at a dinner party and says, "You're a novelist? Strange, when I retire I plan to write a novel." And the novelist replies,

---

* I had started smoking in New Zealand, when I was trying to shock the Sacred Heart Convent nuns into expelling me. I didn't stop smoking until after my daughter Julia was born.

"What a coincidence! When I retire, I plan to take up brain surgery." I heard different versions of this later, often attributed to Margaret Atwood, but the one I remember best is Margaret Laurence's and how she laughed even before she finished telling it.

Though they fought and argued, Margaret adored Jack. She was always ready to forgive him. She hated author tours, radio and newspaper interviews, the whole wretched chore Jack had insisted she had to do to make people pick up one of her books. She loathed the limelight, but he had persuaded her to "make an ass of myself" in public. She had no desire to become a household name. Though she was willing to teach students who wanted to be writers, she was so shy she suffered stomach pains, shaking hands, and sweaty palms every time she had to face a class. As she kept telling me, she was "not a performer."

When *The Diviners* was published in 1974, M&S's publicity department organized a divining session, complete with two water diviners, on the grounds of the Ontario Science Centre. Margaret was to be the centrepiece of the event, but she chose, instead, to spend her time hiding behind the bushes and hoping that members of the press would either not find her or not recognize her if they did. I had a mickey of Scotch in my purse to keep her spirits up.

The Diviners won the Governor General's Award for Fiction, it had long and respectful reviews in Canada, the United States, the UK, and several other countries where it had been translated, but it aroused the ire of fanatics who found it "reeked of sordidness" and tried to have it banned in schools. One religious leader launched a letter-writing campaign. The Huron County School Board managed briefly to have the book banned in its schools.

The newly minted Writers' Union of Canada, the Canadian Library Association, the Canadian Booksellers Association, and the Ontario Secondary School Teachers' Federation all formed policies to combat censorship. Margaret herself, though she dreaded such occasions, defended her book by reading and speaking to packed halls. She had a strong moral sense. She couldn't understand how anyone could take her book for an immoral screed, let alone blasphemous and pornographic.

Jack's approach was to try to make light of the proposed book banning and suggest that the publicity could help sell more books. Though the ban was lifted, it's astonishing that there are still some school boards who do not list *The Diviners* on their recommended lists for libraries.

Later, when she was the main speaker at the Harbourfront Author series (started by Greg Gatenby, a graduate of the M&S slush piles), she was so terrified about being on stage—even after several glasses of wine I persuaded her to drink—that she asked my then six-year-old daughter Catherine to stand with her. She even encouraged Catherine to keep her balloon flying through the reading, hoping it would distract the audience from looking at her.

Jack had said he needed her presence on the M&S board after the Ontario government's 1970 bailout. Margaret thought that the whole thing was a waste and that Jack and I had choreographed each meeting before the board members arrived. She had strenuously objected to M&S's publishing Roloff Beny's books about Iran because of the brutality of the Shah's regime.

A couple of years later Jack cajoled her into attending the 1978 celebration of Canadian literature in Calgary. The pretext was Malcolm Ross's retirement from the editorship of the New Canadian Library, a big literary event to celebrate Canadian writers, the series, and Ross personally. The 1978 Calgary Conference on the Canadian Novel was to select the one hundred "great works of Canadian fiction," of which at least ninety were in our New Canadian Library series. Margaret found the whole idea repugnant. She recognized it for what it was: a thinly veiled publicity gimmick designed to sell more books. Jack was, as usual, shameless about anything that would increase sales. In the event, the one hundred "best" were selected through some kind of rigged ballot that even Ross, the supposed hero of the conference, found embarrassing.

Margaret wrote to Jack afterwards that while she enjoyed meeting other writers (Gabrielle Roy, Roger Lemelin), her opposition to anyone using the one hundred books list persisted. Jack was unrepentant. He replied (April 6, 1978) that he was delighted *The Stone Angel* was number one and that Gabrielle Roy's *The Tin Flute* was number two of the hundred. "I don't understand this bullshit," Jack wrote about her opposition to the conference. "I push this thing because it is good for the country." As far as he was concerned, what was good for M&S's writers was good for Canada.

I don't know how Jack talked Margaret into attending the 1982 Night of the 100 Authors, a fundraiser for the Writers' Development Trust.* I stood with her backstage, offering solace and whisky, neither of which succeeded in calming her anxiety about making another public appearance. As far as I recall, the only M&S author who didn't show up that night was Mordecai.

---

* The Trust was established in 1976 by Margaret Laurence, Margaret Atwood, Pierre Berton, Graeme Gibson, and David Young. It became the Writers' Trust some years later and is still going strong as I write this.

Escaping the City

I N HINDSIGHT, I am not sure whether the CNE or Charles Templeton was responsible for our building a cottage on an island in Georgian Bay.

Both Julian and I loved our work but sometimes it became too much and 1974 was one of those years. Julian was fighting a number of major legal battles; he was still involved with the Canadian Conference of the Arts; he had agreed to be on the board of the Canadian National Exhibition, and would be appointed chairman the next year. The Ex, as it was affectionately called, is an annual affair held at Exhibition Place in Toronto. It lasts eighteen days in August and attracts more than a million visitors. It's supposed to be all about agriculture and technology, but as far as I could tell, it was about a bunch of thrill rides including a massive roller coaster and a midway where smart operators tried to talk you into contests to win plush toys. That part of the Ex was run by Julian's client, Jimmy Conklin, and Julian loved to hang out there talking to the carnies, trying out the rides, eating hot dogs and burgers.

I have a photograph of Julian on the chair-swing ride with three-year-old Catherine and another feeding her a huge cream puff at one of the Ex's formal events. She loved the cream and the occasion but threw up in the men's room afterwards.

Jimmy had a private railway car on the grounds that he used while the Ex was on. We used to repair there in the evenings for more talk about more carnival events and food offerings. Gina Godfrey, Paul Godfrey's wife, attempted to teach me how to dress and to wear white gloves while pouring tea for the ladies—a relatively painless task usually performed by the CNE president's wife. Paul Godfrey, who was Metro Chairman, used to tell me how well he thought of Julian and how brilliant he would be as chairman. I have a hilarious photo of Julian with Paul in a horse-drawn cart, back when Paul had longish hair and a lantern jaw.

Julian hosted the annual opening events with celebrity guests like Bob Hope and the chief of the Clan Macmillan from the Scottish Highlands. Bob Hope failed to be even mildly entertaining, but Julian made up for it by giving one of his rousing luncheon speeches, complete with imitations of George Diefenbaker and Ontario premier Leslie Frost. The Macmillan event was grand, with the bands, the bagpipes, and the men in full regalia marching to salute our guest. The one small problem was that the chief had caught his kilt in the slats of the CNE's wooden folding chair and couldn't stand without taking the chair with him.*

IN 1974 I was overwhelmed by trying to manage M&S's massive publishing program and feeling guilty about not spending more time with my daughter and almost as much guilt about not paying more attention to the books. I had hired a live-in babysitter but I found myself racing home every few hours, in case she was not the right person. I had fifteen speeding tickets in two years and it was only my good luck and my obvious desperation that saved my driver's licence.

---

* By strange coincidence, the shooting party where I had decided to root for the pheasants had been at his estate near Perth, in Scotland. My erstwhile date for that day still lived on the estate.

On one of our frequent visits to Charles Templeton's very simple wooden cottage near Penetanguishene, I mentioned that what we needed was pretty much what he had, a cheap country getaway. Charles had just finished a book for M&S, a new biography of Jesus, using all four gospels and "rendering" them in modern English. Charles had been an evangelist with Billy Graham's Youth for Christ movement, exhorting the masses at rallies throughout the United States, Europe, Japan, and Canada to open their hearts to the Christian faith. Though he had left most of his faith behind somewhere, Charles still believed that Jesus had been an extraordinary man.

Now he was writing what he viewed as a "potboiler," a thriller about the kidnapping of the US president. I used to read his drafts, while Julian listened to music and Catherine played with some wooden figurines Charles had. We would sit at his dining room table with drawings of the places he had used for the setting of the novel and go over the plots and characters. He had examined streets, security response teams, and armoured cars, and had invented the scenario as if he were, personally, in charge of the kidnapping.

Charles was erudite, engaging, witty, charismatic, and self-perceptive. He had intense eyes and a tiny, thin-lipped smile that questioned his own seriousness. He had theories and stories about everything: politicians, businessmen, God, novelists, humourists, inventors. He had invented a system for transporting oil from the Far North—but there were no takers; it was too costly to produce. He invented a coil filter for cigarettes that kept tar away from the smoker. Tobacco companies didn't see the need for it, then. I think Charles's best invention was a teddy bear with a self-warming belly that was eventually trademarked and manufactured as TeddyWarm by Mattel. Unfortunately, even that did not become a big hit. Luckily, the potboilers made up for it. *The Kidnapping of the President* would be a national bestseller in 1975.

He talked of the sense of isolation that Georgian Bay gave him, with its perfect view of the lake through the big picture windows and, stretching behind the house, a large tract of land where you could still see foxes and deer. He offered to look for a place for us, close enough to him that we could come by often, but not so close that we felt hemmed in.

Julian bought a small Hunt, an energetic snub-nosed boat with an inboard motor and a tiny cabin, where we could sleep curled up but not lying flat. Baby Catherine would snooze between us when she felt like snoozing, which was not very often. We scouted for cottages for sale in Georgian Bay, but as we had put all our savings into our Moore Park house, we didn't have enough money.

Charles came to the rescue when he purchased a piece of land he thought we would like on an island across the bay from his place. It was not expensive and he was in no hurry to be repaid. We bought an inexpensive prefab to put up on what we used to call Charles's plot. Before the plywood walls went up, we spent nights on the pressed recycled wood platform and heated Catherine's milk over kerosene. We bathed in the lake. It was heaven.

My mother arrived from New Zealand that year and managed to withhold her initial opinion of our island refuge. She immediately became friends with both Charles and his wife, Madeleine. Her marriage to Alfons was not working once she discovered that he had an affair, but I didn't think she would be planning to stay with us. We had always had a complicated relationship. She was too young—only nineteen—when I was born, there was a war, a long siege, and my father had vanished. After she clambered out of the cellars of the burned-out Buda castle where the family had taken refuge during the bombardment, there was nothing to eat and nowhere to live. My mother had moved into my grandparents' still-standing house on the Buda side of the Danube, but they couldn't keep the house under the Communist government's rules about what a single family was allowed to have. We moved to an apartment in Pest that everyone hated. My mother found work as a surveyor of roads and railways with the occasional bridge thrown in for variety. I stayed with my grandfather, who had lost everything but seemed to delight in telling me stories. I saw a bit of my mother when she was on vacation, but on those occasions she liked to go on dates. She was very pretty and smart. Everyone loved her company and, as usual, there was little room for me in her life. I had assumed her marriage to Alfons would keep her happy, but it didn't.

She decided to stay in Canada. Dudley Witney helped move her belongings into an apartment a few blocks south of our home. In short order, she started work as a town planner for a company on Eglinton Avenue.

That Great, Always Recognizable Voice

Barbara Frum was more than a national celebrity; she was a sort of national friend whom everyone recognized. Most people felt as though they knew her personally. It was that familiar, slightly husky, inquisitive, often amused voice most of us cherished. I hesitate to say she was an icon because I know she would have hated that. Once a fellow writer at a conference referred to her as a "national monument" and Barbara collapsed in uncontrollable laughter. "And crumbling," she said.

When we first met, she had just started as co-host of CBC radio's broad-ranging current affairs show, *As It Happens*. We were at the house she shared with her husband, Murray, two young children, a huge collection of African art, and a dog. It was 1971. The topic of conversation was Quebec, particularly Pierre Trudeau's invocation of the War Measures Act the year before. Shocking as the kidnapping of James Cross and the kidnapping and murder of Quebec cabinet minister Pierre Laporte had been, Trudeau's suspension of civil liberties and mass arrests in Quebec were an unjustifiably excessive response, a far cry from his "just society" ideals.

There were about a dozen people in the room, including June Callwood, Bill (Trent) Frayne, and, as always, Murray. Both Julian and June were directors of the Civil Liberties Association. Everyone thought the government had overstepped its limits, that the people of Canada had not been consulted on such draconian actions as the summary arrest of hundreds of Quebecers. Trudeau's facile characterization of his critics as "bleeding hearts" and his warning, "Just watch me," added fuel to the fire of protests.

Being a lawyer, Julian questioned the legality of the mass arrests. There had been no "apprehended insurrection," no excuse for Trudeau's actions. Julian had been in the same history class as Barbara; they knew their Canadian history; they had known each other for twenty years or so. She often called him about upcoming interviews, seeking points of law that would be relevant to her questions.

Barbara asked the tough questions no one else asked and she reached people no one else reached. She used to joke about calling the Pope through the Vatican switchboard and asking him about the latest scandals in Rome. She interviewed Sandra Good, roommate of the woman who tried to assassinate President Ford, an FBI agent who had operated in Canada, the Maharishi Mahesh Yogi fresh from his launch of the Age of Enlightenment, and Dr. Alex Comfort, the "love guru." She covered Watergate (1972) from the beginning. She talked with PLO spokesman Shafiq al-Hout and once reached the British ambassador during a mob attack on his embassy. She remained calm while questioning the abusive Harold Ballard about the fate of his perpetually losing Toronto Maple Leafs, and in one of the show's light segments, she questioned the Cookie Monster and the spaghetti-eating champion of the world. Famous for breaking news, the show itself frequently became the news.

Barbara was diagnosed with leukemia in 1974. She was thirty-six years old and at a high point in her career. When she told her co-workers about her diagnosis, it was a mark of their affection and respect for her that not one of them ever told anyone else. She hadn't wanted the maudlin commiseration of strangers, nor special treatment. Those of her friends who knew never spoke about it, though we all watched the evening shows with anxiety and watched her at our dinners and parties with concern. It was as if denial would render it untrue. As the years went by and she was still alive, we became bolder and more confident.

She was determined to live what was left of her life on her own terms and not as an invalid. Most important, she didn't want her children to know. She didn't want her relationship with them changed in any way or their choices to be influenced by her illness. The person she talked with most often during the dreadful first few months after her diagnosis was June Callwood. June was a great listener, and that was what Barbara needed the most: someone to listen to her grief and outrage.

My friendship with Barbara grew closer when we worked on her book, *As It Happened*. I organized transcripts of past interviews with common themes into piles on her dining room table. Each pile would form the basis of a chapter. We chucked some because they would soon become dated, added others she thought would stand the test of time, and then Barbara set about writing the connecting passages, commentaries, and introductions that made the book into the bestseller it became.

Her children, David and Linda, would drift in and out of the room, commenting on the process, discussing topics of the day, or just asking whether they could do something or go somewhere. I was always impressed by Barbara's way with her children: loving, respectful of their opinions, listening, arguing when she disagreed with them. They often joined guests at the Frums' big round dinner table, when David* would seize the opportunity to try out his new ideas on Bob Fulford and Geraldine Sherman, or June Callwood and Trent Frayne, William Thorsell (the new editor of *The Globe and Mail*), Federal Deputy Minister Allan Gottlieb (and eventually Canada's ambassador to the United States) and his wife, humourist writer Sondra, the CBC's Peter and Eva Herrndorf, various politicians, businessmen, intellectuals, and us.

The great M&S publicity machine had fun sending Barbara on a cross-Canada tour because there was not a radio or TV station or newspaper or book-signing venue that didn't want her. The tour had to be arranged in chunks to fit her busy schedule, but everyone was thrilled to

---

* David Frum would grow up to be a journalist, political commentator, speechwriter for George W. Bush, and fierce critic of the Trump administration.

meet her. Everyone, that is, except the silly radio interviewer who hadn't read the book and launched into a series of highly personal questions. Barbara retaliated with "dead air": silence, as the man babbled to fill the time. She called to ask me once whether anyone at all slated to interview her had bothered to read the book, a question many authors ask. I had to confess that, if past history was any indication, they hadn't bothered, but at least, in her case, most of them would have listened to *As It Happens*.

Emboldened by her survival, we had begun to toast the coming year again at our New Year's Eve dinner parties. I long to repeat one of those warm, laughter-filled New Year's dinners with Barbara and Murray, sometimes with her mother, Florence, and with Bob Fulford, Geraldine Sherman, and many of our shared friends. We all brought potluck contributions to the meal, told stories, debated politics, talked of our children as they grew up. And there was that memorable night in 1983 when Murray danced on the table, celebrating that Barbara was still with us.

Their home seemed always to be under construction—furniture moved, paintings and sculptures assumed new places. Murray believed that it was impossible to appreciate a work of art if you became too used to it. He moved art and furniture around to make sure you would see it again. In addition to African art, they had been collecting American and Canadian artists. They added Oceanic art and art deco furniture. Over the years most of the spaces in their home became occupied by art, and they knew the story of each piece and why and when they had acquired it.* New elements were added to the existing building, rooms were enlarged, the patio expanded, the garden took on a whole new life with paths and new plants, a gazebo was added, then a waterfall.

Barbara's approach to their living space was exactly the opposite to mine. I had done almost no decorating. Our garden looked dismal even at the height of summer. New plants I bought tended to wither as soon as they focused on me. Barbara suggested various improvements, including a wooden platform to extend into the ravine behind our house. I loved the

---

* Today many of the African pieces are in the Art Gallery of Ontario.

idea but fell short of the execution. She also gave me a single dark-green plant she had pulled out of the ground in her garden as we walked by. She thought it would work well in front of our place in Georgian Bay, where not much had ever grown. It turned out to be an aggressive ground cover that killed most of the local plants, even the poison ivy, and still flourishes more than thirty years later.

Marian's Way

W HEN SHE WANTED to talk with me about something, Marian Engel
preferred to come to our home, as did many M&S authors, rather
than take the long drive to Hollinger Road. She was usually gentle and
kind but assumed a tough, no-nonsense pose when in company. The effort
often required her to have a large drink to fuel her courage. At one of our
book launch parties she took a strip off Attorney General Roy McMurtry
over the divorce laws (unfair to women); at another, she challenged one of
Julian's lawyer friends on how lawyers handled rape cases (not well).

She often had two cigarettes going at the same time.

She was asked once whether she wrote women's books. She answered:
"I hate hearing them referred to as women's books because it makes me
think of women's magazines of the old kind—women without brains. I
don't write for that kind of woman." But at least the novelists she admired,
such as Gabrielle Roy and Margaret Laurence, were no longer referred to
as "lady novelists."

Marian felt perpetually under-appreciated. Reviews were at best am-
bivalent and at worst unpleasant.

In 1975 she separated from her husband, Howard, a CBC producer
and later author of the Benny Cooperman series of private eye mysteries. Benny, the unkempt Jewish gumshoe who lives in Grantham and eats

chopped-egg sandwiches, became a fixture on our bookshelves. I still have them all.

I suggested to Marian that she might like to contribute something to a book of Canadian ghost stories. She said she couldn't do that, but she did offer us a really strange short manuscript about a woman who has a very passionate, though not entirely satisfying, affair with a bear. It was an unusual, often quite funny, and rather disturbing story, but also a literary tour de force. Its original shorter version had been destined for the Writers' Union fundraising book of pornography, based loosely on *Naked Came the Stranger*, the 1969 American literary hoax written by twenty-four journalists.

The Union, being impecunious, had numerous fundraisers, but the only one I remember is the All-Star Eclectic Typewriter Review, where Jack McClelland, with cape and fangs, danced across the stage as Jack the Knife, five women with wigs and beards appeared as the Farley Mowat Dancers, and Berton belted out "The Shooting of Dan McGrew."

I sent copies of the manuscript to people I thought might say something positive about it and most of them did. Margaret Laurence, Adele Wiseman, and Margaret Atwood (she had read the earlier version as well) loved it. Irving Layton thought it was brilliant. When I asked Jennifer Glossop, then M&S's most senior editor, to take it on, I was worried that she would find the sex too graphic or too offensive. In a long memo dated November 25, 1975, I suggested a plain white, classy front cover, nothing garish, several quotes praising the novel, and the line "a novel that may shock . . ." Jennifer wasn't shocked, finished editing the manuscript in three weeks, and the resulting book, *Bear*, became a huge success. It was hailed as a new kind of Canadian book by critics and fellow writers. Roy MacSkimming gave it a rave in the *Star*. It won the 1976 Governor General's Award for Fiction.

Interesting to recall that the jury for that year was composed of Mordecai Richler, Margaret Atwood, and Alice Munro. Atwood and Munro, like Margaret Laurence, had always been very supportive of other Canadian writers; Mordecai had not. He seemed quite dismissive of the idea of a national literature. And even if there was one, he had no desire to belong to it. Although he liked some Canadian works—Morley Callaghan's short stories and Robertson Davies's novels, for example—his literary heroes were not Canadian. They were American, like Saul Bellow and Philip Roth, or English, like Kingsley Amis and Muriel Spark, great writers who had written funny and emotionally strong books. He thought the greatest writer of our time was Evelyn Waugh. Mordecai had derided cultural frontiers in art as a "patriotic production." Having been in Quebec during the FLQ incidents of 1964, he had seen the burning of Canadian flags. If that was patriotism, he said, he wanted none of it.

He didn't believe in special treatment for writers. He was damned if he would admire a book because its author was Canadian. But he did like *Bear.*

A Whole Lot Larger than Life

F OR ABOUT TWO decades Roloff Beny was Canada's most famous photographer. He had a reputation for stunning visual effects, spectacular architecture, and lush, operatic scenery, photographs that seemed like Renaissance paintings. He was a perfectionist, often spending a whole day on one image, making sure it was exactly as he imagined it should be.

He was born Wilfred Roy Beny in Medicine Hat, Alberta, and his father still called him Wilf. After a stint of art classes at Banff and later at the University of Iowa, he changed his name and, progressively, his appearance. By the time I met him, he was flamboyantly gay, wore flashy furs and form-fitting suede or leather trousers, leather vests, and beads. Strangely, he seemed to attract older women who thought him romantic and irresistibly entertaining. Several of them even insisted on helping to fund his travels. Signy Eaton of Eaton Department Stores was certainly one of them, as was Peggy Guggenheim, and Lorraine Monk, empress of the National Film Board's Still Division, which had funded *To Every Thing There Is a Season*, was another. Published for the 1967 centennial, this stunning book had been a monumental success. An exhibition entitled *A Visual Odyssey, 1958–1968: Roloff Beny* opened in the Observation Gallery of the new Toronto-Dominion Centre in 1971. His prints and early paintings were acquired by galleries and art museums.

Despite his success here, Roloff said he found Canada restrictive and visually uninspiring. He preferred Rome, where he bought the top two floors of a beautiful late-nineteenth-century building on Tiber Terrace in Trastevere. You could see the Tiber through the windows. Part of the ceiling had a Roman-style mural. Though most of the statuary was imitation, the apartment had the appearance of a Roman villa. Roloff's books and hundreds of his photographs were arranged on a long, low table. There was a roof garden or terrace with an elegant arrangement of terracotta vases, a pale-ochre changing room, a small dipping pool, a couple of chaise longues, and an assortment of potted plants. There were numerous exuberant visitors, expensively dressed women, Roman friends of Roloff's, and at least once, Pierre Elliott Trudeau with an entourage of civil servants. His housekeeper offered drinks in Venetian glasses and there was fruit on Venetian platters.

I was there for several days, helping to put together our presentation of Roloff's books on ancient Persia and, later, on Iran, both commissioned by the Shah and the Shahbanu of Iran.

Jack saw *Persia, Bridge of Turquoise* as an opportunity to break into the exclusive circle of international art book publishers and as a chance to sell a lot of books to the Iranian royals and hangers-on. There was a one-page "message" from Her Imperial Majesty Farah Pahlavi, the Shahbanu, and an essay by Seyyed Hossein Nasr, head of the Imperial Iranian Academy of Philosophy.*

The slides were magnificently colourful: markets, mosques, the ruins of palaces, lush vegetation, awe-inspiring winterscapes. Roloff saw the work as "an austerely spiritual yet sensual feat that is Persia," and we would have the honour of producing the book for the world market. His previous big international books, *India, Island Ceylon, In Italy*, and *Rajasthan*, had all been produced by the prestigious art books publisher Thames & Hudson. This one was going to be ours.

When I travelled from Rome to Toronto with Roloff, the page layouts,

---

* He is now at George Washington University.

the cover concepts, the massive mock-up, and the slides, my chief job became to not lose any of the pieces and to convince customs that they were of no value. Naturally, I also carried Roloff's suitcases, his papers, and his camera case, and followed a few steps behind him, as befitted my lesser status. I had no trouble with customs because I was so exhausted I told them they could keep the whole lot, if they really wished to, I didn't care, so they laughed and let me keep everything. Roloff was not so lucky. What with his fur jacket and small purse, he was a natural target. They demanded to know the value of the delicate plaster cast for a Roman head he carried much too carefully, and when he insisted (several times) that it had no value, that it was a gift from an Italian admirer, one of the customs guys dropped it, then apologized, but since it was of no value . . . Roloff wept all the way to his hotel.

His next book, *Iran, Elements of Destiny*, was to be an even more lavish production, an overt puff piece about Iran under the Pahlavi dynasty. Jack had been utterly charmed by the Shahbanu, "the most beautiful woman I have ever seen on or off the silver screen." He was impressed by the glamour, the sheer glitter of the Peacock Throne, by the reception he and Roloff were accorded, and by being part of a world he had never entered before.

We took a mock-up to Frankfurt (it weighed about twenty pounds) and I lugged it around to publishers of high-quality illustrated books. By the time the fair was over, we had managed to share at least some of the horrendous costs of the colour separations, the printing and binding, and, of course, all the extras Roloff insisted would make the book worthy of its subject. Thames & Hudson agreed to take a few thousand, as did most of the publishers who had taken Roloff's previous books. When I first presented our mock-up to Eva Neurath, the doyenne of Thames & Hudson and an almost ethereal presence at that messy international book fair, she inquired, her soft voice rising, why on earth Jack McClelland had decided to become an international art books publisher and did he know what he was getting into.

There would be specially dyed endpapers (in a design borrowed from a glazed tile and stucco pattern at the entrance to the tomb of a Sufi "saint"), silkscreening, thick dyed paper with gatefolds for the text and black-and-whites and the best available opaque paper for the colour. It was to be printed by Italy's top printing house, Mondadori, which softened the blow of their exorbitant price by taking a small edition in Italian for themselves.

For Jack, that was just the icing on the cake. He was convinced that the business deal with the Shah and Shahbanu of Iran would bring in enough cash to save M&S. He was wrong, of course, but I am sure not even he could have foreseen the precipitous fall of the Pahlavi dynasty.

IN EARLY 1977, prior to Jack's next visit to Tehran, we spent a few days in Rome to prepare the royal presentation. We ate in a local restaurant, where Roloff was greeted with great fanfare and given the best table with a view of the square and the Tiber. Jack paid for Roloff's lunches, dinners with his friends, and even his electricity bill. I spent most of my time in the basement, in a kind of darkroom the landlord had provided. I was selecting photographs for the mock-up of *Iran.*

All the participating publishers had been invited to Tehran for some grand receptions, a tour, and long luxury hotel stays. My friend Ken Webb, whose company was in charge of the binding, still talks about that visit as the most extraordinary time of his fifty years in the book business. He also remembers the spectacular reception at the Canadian Embassy, hosted by Ken Taylor, our ambassador who later saved the US embassy staff after the Ayatollah took over.

In the end I didn't go to Tehran because I was pregnant and we didn't think it was a look that would appeal to the Iranians.

Jack called after a few days to warn that he might not be back for a while, if at all. He spent most of his time waiting for an audience in a palace where the book was no longer of vital importance. Negotiations took even longer. He thought he might end up swearing at the heavy-set, fully armed men with dark glasses whose job included making sure that guests behaved.

I think the only reason he survived was that the Shah and his well-armed men had more important matters to contend with than a pissed publisher yelling obscenities at microphones embedded in the walls. Iran was Jack's first visit to a country where surveillance was normal.*

Roloff, himself, had been at his outrageous best in Iran, demanding spectacular accommodation for his cameras and himself, cursing the Shah's notorious secret service, and complaining to the Shahbanu if something was not to his liking. On the occasion of Empress Farah Pahlavi's birthday, he had presented her with a photograph of himself naked except for some tropical fruit covering his genitals. Jack had been sure Roloff would be executed, but strangely, that did not happen. Perhaps Iran's pre-Revolution society was far more tolerant of gay men than the religious rule that followed.

Margaret Laurence, who had joined the M&S board only because Jack begged her to do so, was horrified that M&S was publishing *Persia, Bridge of Turquoise*, but at least that was a celebration of Persia past. *Iran, Elements of Destiny*, a "paean of praise to the vision of the Pahlavi dynasty," was inexcusable. She spoke passionately about the Shah's brutal tyrannical regime and the violence of SAVAK, his internal security force. The experience of opposing Jack in public pained her so much, she was shaking all over, but she persisted. M&S directors' meetings were now mired not only in sorrow about our financial situation but also in outrage over Jack's desire to make up our shortfall from his deal with the Pahlavis. In the end, Margaret resigned from the board, as did Farley Mowat. Much as we needed the money, I found it hard to be supportive of a project that celebrated a regime as repressive as the Shah's. But since he was determined to proceed, I urged Jack to collect the money for the books in stages, starting with when he signed the agreement and ending when the books went on press.

Sadly, neither *Persia* nor *Iran* made money for M&S: *Persia* because of Roloff's ongoing demands to improve the quality of the paper, the binding, the colour separations (it was the most beautiful book M&S ever pro-

---

* Julian had done much the same during our 1973 visit to Hungary when he shouted at presumed microphones in our room in Budapest's Gellert Hotel. It was Julian's first trip behind the Iron Curtain.

duced); *Iran* because the Shah's rule was overthrown in 1978. He and his family were forced to flee by the time the Arabic edition had been air-freighted to Tehran. The Ayatollah Ruhollah Khomeini was not interested in meeting the exiled Shah's obligations. M&S lost about $350,000. It was a huge amount at a time when the firm was already in the red. Jack was so distraught that though I had been very tempted, I managed not to say anything like "I told you so."

ROLOFF'S NEXT ADVENTURE was to be Egypt. He had outlined a grand book on the beauties of the country—its past, present, and future, the pyramids, the dam—and President Sadat was sufficiently interested in funding the project that he invited both Roloff and Jack to lunch in his presidential retreat. Though I had never wished the president of Egypt any harm, I was relieved when his assassination prevented yet one more of Roloff's wildly unrealistic projects from costing M&S another fortune.

Roloff died in the marble bathtub of his Trastevere apartment in 1984. Though the Rome police declared it was death by natural causes, Jack remained unconvinced. There had been too many people partying and staying over in Roloff's apartment, too many of them had keys to get in unobserved, and Roloff, by then, had begun to seem more like a target for ruthless opportunists and less like the great artist he had aspired to be.

I recently looked at Roloff's *People: Legends in Life and Art,* published posthumously by his friend Mitchell Crites. It features such luminaries as Elizabeth Taylor, John Huston, Ezra Pound, Leontyne Price, Rudolf Nureyev, and Margot Fonteyn. There are a couple of superb portraits of Peggy Guggenheim, taken at her elegant palazzo in Venice where Roloff had been a frequent guest. The book, I believe, refutes critics' charge that Roloff didn't know how to photograph people. These surprisingly intimate images, including the one of Noel Coward on the cover, display his unerring eye as well as his affection for his subjects.

The Establishment Man

I LIKED HIM from the moment we met in early 1976. Amazingly, that was right after I read his 1,530-page manuscript (not including the notes) on Maurice Duplessis, once premier of and certainly the most powerful man in Quebec. Barely thirty-two years old, Conrad Black already had the deportment of a corporate man. He was immaculately dressed in a pin-striped suit that looked as though it had been especially crafted for his six-foot, broad-shouldered frame. His dark curly hair had a perfect part.

I was impressed by his dexterity in turning his master's thesis into a book that was, for all its unwieldy length, readable and interesting. He spoke both English and French with a nineteenth-century bravado that would have been admirable in an ambassador. Barely out of university, he had bought *The Sherbrooke Record* with a couple of partners and said he planned to expand his media holdings.

Our introductory lunch with Jack to discuss *Duplessis* was a disaster. Jack drank a lot, Conrad did not. Jack talked of economic nationalism and the Canadian business elite's greed and self-interest, its easy sale of the country's assets to the Americans. Conrad, self-confident and loquacious, was already a member of that elite. When he suggested that the solution to Canada's Quebec separatism problem might be for the nation to merge with the United States, Jack was outraged. Conrad tried to explain that he had not been seriously promoting such a merger; he was merely pointing out that the Americans would take a much tougher stance with a breakaway state than English Canada had taken with a province that wanted to leave Confederation. We, the rest of Canada, must stop trying to appease Quebec by acceding to its unreasonable demands. Still, Jack departed in high dudgeon, leaving Conrad and me to finish the wine and discuss publishing his book. The main topic then and later in my office was how to diminish the sheer size of the manuscript. He agreed to some proposed cuts but resisted others, and the manuscript was still way too long when it went to production.

During that year, I got to know Conrad better. I was impressed with his feats of memory. He could describe historic battles in detail, knew the name of every ship in the Spanish Armada, and talked about Bismarck, Disraeli, and Cromwell as if he had recently dined with them. His portrayal of US presidents and Canadian prime ministers was memorable and often acerbic. As Peter Newman said, "He could recite anything he had ever read and mimic almost anyone he had ever heard."

JULIAN AND I hosted a modest book launch at our home and invited Isabel and John Bassett, formerly part owner of *The Toronto Telegram*, and journalist Peter Worthington with his wife Yvonne Crittenden, book reviewer for the *Toronto Sun*. John at that time owned Baton Broadcasting and was part owner of CFTO-TV, later CTV. We were frequent guests at their Rosedale home.*

A couple of years earlier, John had closed his newspaper and sold its subscription lists to the triumvirate that started the brand new *Toronto Sun*. Peter Worthington, its editor, was one of the owners. The book launch turned into a long evening with memorable speeches, toasts to Conrad's success, and jokes about the Tories' chances at the next election.

---

* Isabel, Yvonne, and I were all second wives. Divorce was still anathema among the Rosedale set but not at the Bassetts' table. Isabel's *The Parlour Rebellion* was published by M&S.

Most of the reviews of *Duplessis* were excellent—in part, I think, because none of the reviewers knew as much about the subject as Conrad did and most of them were astonished by his erudition. Sales in English Canada surpassed our expectations, and it was a bestseller in Quebec. That Conrad could engage in discussions and debates in French was a happy surprise for the Quebec media. The 1978 CBC/RadioCanada television miniseries based on Conrad's book drew sizable audiences.

Eventually Jack and Conrad settled their differences, but Jack remained suspicious of Conrad's views about Canada.

WHEN PETER NEWMAN decided to write a whole book about him, Conrad was only thirty-seven. I confess that I tried to dissuade Peter from writing it. It was too soon, I argued. Conrad had a long way to go before he reached his full potential both in business and in life. Peter countered that Conrad was the quintessential establishment figure and would form a perfect part of his Canadian Establishment series.

We were both right. Conrad did go on to lead a storied life well beyond the 1982 publication of *The Establishment Man* but the book was, as Peter predicted, a bestseller. Conrad was already famous for having completed his takeover of one of Canada's most significant financial empires, the Argus Corporation, thus increasing his fortune twenty-fold. Argus had been founded in 1945 by E. P. Taylor, with minority partners Bud McDougald, Wallace McCutcheon,* and Eric Phillips—all portrayed in *The Canadian Establishment.* Its assets included Dominion Stores, Hollinger Mines, Domtar, Standard Broadcasting, and Massey Ferguson. A photograph of its pillared and porticoed headquarters at 10 Toronto Street was featured on the cover of Peter's *The Canadian Establishment.*

---

* Wallace McCutcheon had been Julian's father-in-law while Julian was married to his first wife, Susan. Julian had worked on Wallace's election campaign. Susan and I became friends after we met and I was delighted to be able to share her and Julian's children with her. They grew up to be two remarkable women.

The Establishment Man was launched on a passenger ferry moored in Toronto's harbour. There were several speeches and free booze for the media. Everyone except Conrad wore casual clothes, and a couple of the over-refreshed media members jumped or fell overboard. It was one of the last big-budget M&S launch parties I attended. The interest-free loan of $961,000 had been used up long ago, and additional loans had now run the company's debt to the province to $2.9 million. Jack's many efforts to find outside investors had failed, the Iran adventure ate up what little was left in M&S's coffers, and Jack's deep unhappiness cast a shadow over everything he said.

By then, of course, I had left the company.

Vili Racz, my extraordinary grandfather and the storyteller of my childhood, in his First World War uniform.

On the catwalk modelling a dressing gown for a New Zealand department store—one of the many jobs I took to support myself through university.

My grandmother Therese, my mother's dog, and me in our old house in Budapest, just before we were moved to a small apartment on the other side of the Danube.

Margaret Atwood in 1969, around the time we first met.

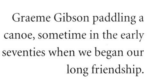

Graeme Gibson paddling a canoe, sometime in the early seventies when we began our long friendship.

Between Peter C. Newman (*left*) and Pierre Berton at a McClelland & Stewart event for authors and booksellers.

Artist Harold Town outside the Art Gallery of Ontario in 1969, around the time we were assembling his book, *Drawings*.

One of my first jobs at McClelland & Stewart was to print, collect, and box copies of Scott Symons's controversial *Civic Square*. Here he is in 1979.

Al Purdy at his A–frame on Roblin Lake, in Prince Edward County.

The young novelist Matt Cohen at about the time we first met. We remained friends for more than thirty years.

Julian and me on our snowy wedding day.

Sylvia Fraser with her goddaughter, my daughter Catherine, in 1973.

My mother, Maria (Puci), in 1986, as beautiful as she was when we left Hungary.

The magnificent Irving Layton with Isabel Bassett at one of our many book launch parties.

With my two daughters, Catherine and Julia.

The remarkable Earle Birney—
poet, teacher, mountain climber,
adventurer, lover, novelist.

Jack McClelland in his usual pose at the office: feet on desk, cigarette in hand, phone at the ready.

Laughing with
Mordecai Richler
at a McClelland &
Stewart party.

Farley Mowat, the ultimate storyteller.

Margaret Trudeau at around the time Seal Books published her bestselling memoir, *Consequences*.

Aritha van Herk and Jack McClelland (*centre*) on a platform in front of her giant $50,000 cheque for winning the inaugural Seal Books First Novel Award for her novel *Judith* in 1978.

At a Seal Books party with
Bantam Books' Alun Davies.

With John Irwin, publisher of *Hidden
Agenda*, and Janet Turnbull at the subway station in Toronto where my first
mystery begins.

I first met the legendary Leonard Cohen
in 1972, when he was not yet a legend.

The Uneasy Balancing Act

WE STARTED 1977 with long meetings in New York and Toronto, hammering out the details of a new venture Jack imagined would add considerable cash to the M&S coffers. We were discussing a joint venture with Bantam's president Oscar Dystel and editorial director Marc Jaffe. It—the new venture—would be publishing inexpensive mass-market paperbacks written by Canadian authors. Jack was certain that the key to profitability was having direct access to supermarket and convenience store racks, where casual browsers could pick up books. He had tried to market a cheap paperback line in the 1960s but found that those racks were controlled by mass-market wholesalers with big bucks and needed an endless supply of new "product." His efforts were defeated not only by a requirement to pay for rack space and the need to constantly resupply books, but by a system where unsold books were destroyed, rather than returned for possible resale. The stores would simply tear the covers off the books, as proof they were unsold, and return them to the publishers for full credit. This worked relatively well for publishers who were printing millions of books at a fraction of the cost Jack incurred for much smaller print runs.* Big multinational publishers

---

* The more you manufacture, the lower the cost for each unit. That's the way it is with socks. That's the way it is with books.

such as Bantam were the most successful. M&S, on its own, hadn't a chance. Hence, the creation of our joint venture, McClelland-Bantam Limited, publisher of Seal books. Both Jack and I were to be on the board with Dystel and Jaffe.

Jack was sure that with Dystel and Jaffe he had found the right formula. Not only did they know how to sell a lot of cheap books, they were likeable, entertaining guys with flair: Dystel, the scrappy businessman, and Jaffe, the patrician expert in commercial fiction.

Dystel had grown up the hard way in the Bronx, pioneering publishing paperbacks in uniform inexpensive formats, beating the competition to such multimillion-copy bonanzas as Peter Benchley's *Jaws*, Judith Krantz's *Scruples*, and James Herriot's *All Creatures Great and Small*—a book that spawned an entire series of Herriot titles. Jacqueline Susann's *Valley of the Dolls* alone had sold more than 8 million copies. Marc Jaffe, the Harvard grad, deserved credit for millions more, including books by J. D. Salinger, William Styron, William Peter Blatty, and Louis L'Amour. In 1971 alone, Bantam sold 10 million copies of Blatty's *The Exorcist*.

"We'll have the best of two worlds," Jack announced. And for a while, it looked as though we did. Dystel and Jaffe supported Jack's newest make-waves-for-young-writers venture, the Seal First Novel Contest, agreed to publish the winners and add more Canadian books to their US lists, hosted us to dinners in fine restaurants, and expressed nothing but joy at the prospect of increased Canadian sales. I was appointed to the McClelland-Bantam Board and ran our end of Seal as a sideline to my M&S job. For the first couple of years, Seals were M&S bestsellers: Peter Newman's *The Canadian Establishment*, Margaret Atwood's *Lady Oracle*, Brian Moore's *The Doctor's Wife*, some Farley Mowat titles, and of course Charles Templeton's *The Kidnapping of the President* and *Act of God*.

MY DAUGHTER JULIA was born in July 1977. In a moment of unbridled generosity and, possibly, with an eye to legislation regarding maternity or parental leave, Jack gave me five weeks off. And once again, a child of mine was celebrated in verse, this time by noted poet A. J. M. Smith:

Dear Julia Porter, happy child,
born of a lovely mother, worthy sire,
I wish you all things joyful, all high-styled.
I build a sacrificial fire
of fragrant cedar to make my wishes
magic spells. May all your hours
and days be gentle and delicious—
with love and laughter filled, sunshine and flowers.

But I knew there wouldn't be many "joyful" days for me at M&S.

Most of the staff were women, which was the case for all publishing houses, but few were in management positions. Having babies was frowned upon and asking for raises when a woman was at the age of having babies was detrimental to promotions. Women, of course, earned much less than men.* Jack maintained he had hired more women not because they were cheaper but because he had "discovered that women are generally more efficient." I still have a copy of Jack's hand-written memo to me explaining why my salary would stay at ten thousand a year, about thirty per cent lower than that of senior male employees. Even John Neale, who had started as sales manager after a couple of years as M&S sales rep in Ontario, was earning more. I was pissed off and let Jack know it, but I didn't quit, at least not then.† I loved working at M&S. It seemed like the perfect job: being paid to read, to comment on interesting manuscripts, to spend time with extraordinary people. I wasn't angry at Peter and John; they were part of a delightful, usually inseparable trio, including John's black lab, and my low income was not their fault. It was Jack's.

By this time I was both running M&S's publishing program of more than a hundred books a year and involved with Seal Books. There were many meetings in New York, book fairs in Frankfurt and London, the

---

* In 1981 women working full-time were still earning about fifty-four per cent of what men earned.

† From Jack's unpublished and incomplete autobiography.

American Booksellers' Association's annual affairs in a variety of cities, sales conferences, and seemingly endless editorial and marketing meetings. In addition there were long discussions with Charles Templeton, Richard Rohmer, Matt Cohen, Margaret Laurence,* Peter Newman, Farley Mowat, Marian Engel, Birney, Purdy, Layton, Pierre and Elsa, of course, and many other authors on our unwieldy M&S lists. The creation of the fifty-thousand-dollar Seal Books First Novel Award added an extra bit of excitement to our lives, but now the reading of the hundreds of manuscripts submitted for the prize deprived me of whatever sleep a new mother is able to snatch between late-night feedings. Seal's partners in the award, Andre Deutsch in the UK and Bantam Books in the United States, had agreed to publish and promote the winners. Selecting the short list and arguing with Andre Deutsch and Marc Jaffe about the eventual winner took nerves of steel, which I lacked that year.

I remember one long, tempestuous debate with Andre over the possibility that W. P. Kinsella's *Shoeless Joe* might win the First Novel Award. Andre said trying to sell that book in the UK would be akin to our promoting a novel about an imaginary cricket team in North America.† It was an argument I couldn't win.

Jack's assessment that being M&S's editor-in-chief was more than a full-time job was correct. I had been working about ten to twelve hours a day, and now, with two children, I tried to get home early enough to read a few stories to Catherine, walk about with Julia till she nodded off, put them to bed, and then start reading manuscripts. I rarely slept more than four hours. My big white take-home bags expanded on Fridays for extra reading time on weekends.

For several months I tried to convince myself that I could manage everything. Jack encouraged me to imagine it could be done. He even

---

* *The Olden Days Coat.*

† *Shoeless Joe* went on to become an international bestseller (though not in the UK). It was the basis of the very successful movie *Field of Dreams*, starring the young Kevin Costner.

offered to have Catherine do her drawings in his office while I ran meetings in the boardroom, and a couple of times he took Julia in her portable bassinet and stashed her under his windows while I ran off to do presentations to major accounts. Since Julia was still nursing, I used to pump milk in the women's washroom. Once, when I was in Imperial Oil's boardroom, trying to talk them into sponsoring a big new Canada book, I noticed that all the men had stopped looking at me and were staring fixedly at my end of the glossy table. I had misjudged the time and milk was pooling rapidly between my elbows.

I didn't finish my sales pitch, I just ran.

I was a seventies feminist. I believed that women could do it all, but I was losing focus, wore the same clothes most days, seldom washed my hair, and began to lose my sense of humour. In a *Saturday Night* article Bob Fulford asserted that the major event of the 1970s was "the triumph of feminism." At the beginning of that decade, I would have agreed with him. The sixties had included the sexual revolution, the birth control pill, and a general feeling that now everything would be possible for women. Yet at the end of the seventies, I was too exhausted to feel any sense of triumph. Our hiring a new charming German babysitter did little to assuage my constant anxiety.

Once when Marian Engel was coming back from a TV interview, she told me that the other woman on the show had had her hair done, looked svelte in a tight black sweater, wore very high heels, and had perfect makeup that didn't run under the strobe lights. Marian was hot and sweaty after a sleepless night with her twins, her hair was damp, she wore something beige she had pulled on in a hurry, and she had not noticed the baby vomit down both shoulders where she had burped the babies—two at once. In addition to taking care of the twins, she was busy advocating for the Public Lending Right for authors, was involved with the Writers' Union, whose early meetings were often held at the Engels' Brunswick Avenue home, was a member of a couple of book prize committees, and carried on lively correspondence with Hugh MacLennan, Timothy Findley, Margaret Laurence, and several other writers. Her home was a cluttered confusion of books, dishes, letters, baby bottles, and notes spilling over the edges of tables and rearranging themselves on the carpet.

Our home, I told Marian, had taken on the Marian Engel look with mountains of manuscripts spilling onto the floor, Catherine drawing on piles of unanswered mail, Julia on my lap as I read, and Julian picking his way through the debris of my working life. He rarely came home before nightfall. He was busy with one of the accused on what the newspapers referred to as "the dredging case," involving alleged bid rigging for tenders in a number of harbours. The case grew to encompass most of the large dredging companies in Canada. The two-year criminal trial started in 1977, the year Julia was born. During the examination of witnesses and the trail itself, Julian would invite some of the leading counsel to dinner—a great opportunity to work on my cooking skills.

I had learned to cook from my grandmother, who was also learning to cook after we moved to the apartment in Pest. Before the war, she used to have a cook, a maid, a spacious house, and a gardener. By the time I was ten, I could make soups, eggs à la russe, and crepes.

Julian's co-counsel turned out to be appreciative eaters. But I was usually too tired to eat myself.

Intermission

WE TOOK BABY Julia to Georgian Bay when she was only a couple of weeks old. Our prefab was finished; we had running water and, amazingly, even electricity. Catherine was already a swimmer, and she loved the lake. That summer Julian's stint as president of the Ex ended, so I didn't have to appear on site wearing "appropriate" clothing and didn't have to make polite conversation or pour tea for the ladies.

The Hunt was still in good shape—it's on its last breaths now—and Julian used to drive it at great speed across the lake to Charles's cottage. Catherine called him Uncle Chawas and loved exploring all the gadgets at his home, while Charles explained how everything worked. Charles was then putting the finishing touches to his most successful book, *Act of God*. He was under no illusion that these books were literature or that they had staying power; he thought they were entertainments, in the same way that some of Graham Greene's books were entertainments. He plotted them much as he might have planned a complicated puzzle.

He was so determined that the story be plausible and the settings authentic that he had gone to the Vatican, managed to gain entry to the Pope's apartments, and visited all of Israel's Christian Holy sites. I thought that this attention to minutiae was supposed to distract him from the hard truth that his Christian faith had failed, that he no longer believed in God.

It was a great relief for him when the manuscript was finished and he no longer had to grapple with its dark centre.

US rights to *Act of God* were auctioned for $200,000, a large amount in the late 1970s. Bantam Books' Marc Jaffe had been the successful bidder, ensuring that Charles would get excellent treatment on both sides of the border. Charles and I were feted at the Westbury Hotel by a coterie of senior Bantam people. There was a sumptuous dinner with very expensive wines, since Charles professed to know a lot about wine.

Despite the nasty reviews, the personal attacks on "a failed evangelist," and persistent interview questions about Charles's early days with preacher Billy Graham, the book sold well in both the United States and Canada.

AMONG MY MOST bizarre memories of 1977 is Irving Layton's sixty-fifth birthday party at Casa Loma, the fairy-tale castle in the middle of Toronto. There were elaborate preparations. Jack, Sylvia Fraser, Aviva, and I had several secret meetings to plan what was to be a surprise for Irving. Julian was tasked with delivering the unsuspecting Irving to the venue. He had persuaded Irving that an Ontario government minister wanted to consult him on some matter of policy—the sort of flattering pretext Irving found irresistible. It's astonishing that none of the more than a hundred invited guests breathed a word about the event. Irving was genuinely astounded and not immediately pleased when Julian ushered him in through the massive oak doors to be greeted by people shrieking "Happy birthday!" But he quickly warmed to the occasion.

There was music and there were speeches, including a long encomium from Moses Znaimer, whom Irving had taught at Herzliah School in Montreal. Irving, Moses said, had convinced his class that only poets and poetry mattered. The rest of the world was useless. Moses ended his speech with "Irving, you have ruined my life. Because of you I feel worthless." After the speeches, a giant cardboard cake was wheeled in. Sylvia Fraser, in a backless red dress, leapt out of its white centre and everyone sang "Happy Birthday."

Moses had come with a camera crew, who recorded the entire over-the-top evening, so I assume there is a film of it somewhere. I wonder if it includes some footage of the rather lonely figure of young David Layton,* lost in the crowd, trying to figure out how he fitted into the picture of general conviviality.

Another strange memory of that year and the next is reading bits of Leonard Cohen's new, unnamed manuscript. He had been sending in parts of what he sometimes referred to as *My Life in Art*, a title he mercifully abandoned. The manuscript was rank with disappointment, bitterness, and desperation. Part of the desperation, as I wrote to Jack, was Cohen's apparent fear that he had little or nothing left to say, that he was no longer a lover and not yet a priest. He wrote of impending death and the embarrassment of having so few ideas. He kept adding to the manuscript and changing some of the prose and the poems, though the tone of bitterness and anger stayed. In one memorable passage he wrote: "Death to this book or fuck this book and fuck this marriage. Fuck the twenty-six letters of my cowardice. Fuck you for breaking the mirror and throwing the eyebrow tweezers out the window . . ."

Now and then he still referred to the manuscript as *My Life in Art*, and though I know he worked on it for several years, it felt like something he had dashed off in a moment of fury. The lyrical poems like "All Summer Long" were easy to overlook in the thicket of anger and loss. I thought *Death of a Ladies' Man* was an infinitely better title for what he wanted to say. Jack hated it, but we set type and designed alternative cover treatments. Leonard always had his own ideas for covers and wanted to see the options.

We were in Montreal for the new Montreal International Book Fair, an event Jack had imagined would bring together publishers, writers, agents, and booksellers from all over the world.† He had rented a suite of rooms

---

* David Layton wrote his own book about his improbable childhood, *Motion Sickness*. In spite of its tough though affectionate portrayal of his mother, Aviva gave the book her wholehearted support.

† He had been one of its founders, and though the fair has changed some over the years, it is still an annual event, now called Salon du Livre de Montréal.

alongside the pool, so that bookish partygoers could recover in the water after too much smoke and too many drinks.

Cohen had not wanted to be part of the scene, so we sat on the carpet in the corridor outside the suite and looked at covers, paper samples, and pages with different type treatments. He was very quiet, sombre really, as he examined each cardboard-backed design, then picked one with a few adjustments. Looking at the book today, I think it is the perfect jacket for this deeply unhappy work: creamy brown with old-fashioned black type and a gold-embossed drawing of two intertwined figures, a winged man and an equally winged (though somewhat squashed) woman, purporting to represent the spiritual union of the two sexes. It's a reproduction of a woodcut in the 1550 *Rosarium Philosophorum*.

By 1978 Cohen had become an international celebrity. Hundreds of thousands turned out for his concerts, and the voice Jack had thought was a handicap had become his trademark. Though the book was still an expression of misery, it sold reasonably well and continues to sell still. The critics were harder on it than they had been on his previous books, and even the well-meaning took exception to the inexplicable prose commentary he had added to the poems.

I WAS HAPPY that Aritha van Herk's *Judith* won the inaugural Seal Books First Novel Award in 1978. She was the right kind of writer to become an international star. She was only twenty-five years old and as feisty as her heroine. It was also the right kind of book: an unusual setting (an Alberta pig farm) and a fine literary style. I loved the novel, Jack loved the book and the chance to present the award in a way that would attract maximum attention. Peter Taylor created a giant cheque that hung high on a billboard outside Place Bonaventure so as to provide cameras with a good view both of the presentation and of Jack and Aritha balancing precariously over the attending groups of critics and usually (but not on this occasion) jaded media types. There were publishing offers from around the world.

*   *   *

ONE OF THE last books I worked on at M&S was *Landmarks of Canadian Art*, edited by Peter Mellen, whose Group of Seven book had been my education in Canadian art. *Landmarks* was also an outsized, expensive art book with 150 reproductions. Every work was chosen by our specially appointed panel of experts, "each one in the forefront of his or her area of specialization." As it happened, however, it was a group of warring individualists, each with a different idea of what was great Canadian art.

The one notable exception to the wars was Jean Sutherland Boggs, former director of the National Gallery of Canada, and Harvard University professor of fine arts. Though she was tough and opinionated, she was also a peacemaker and an enthusiast. She may also have been somewhat preoccupied because she was about to run the Philadelphia Museum of Art, and she wanted the selection settled before she started her new job. Long before then, I'd decided that I couldn't do it all when it came to publishing—at least not well enough to make sense of my days and nights.

I told Jack I would quit as soon as he found a replacement. Instead, he wrote me a long letter (September 14, 1978) suggesting a number of scenarios for my future. His preferred option was for me to take over running Seal Books (its corporate name was McClelland-Bantam Limited). While I pondered the options, I would certainly stay both on its board and on the M&S board.

Talking about Feminism

A YOUNG WOMAN at a recent social event asked whether I was a feminist. I could tell from the slight sneer with which she endowed the
word where she stood on this subject. Never one to back away from a fight,
I told her that I have always considered women to be equal to men in both
intellect and ability.

The Communist control of Hungarian society made it vital that women
worked. My mother was a surveyor, outdoors all winter and summer, away
from home for weeks at a time. Her sister Leah was a truck driver. In New
Zealand, women were still expected to be at home, though in the countryside they helped run the family sheep farms. My mother, of course, continued to work, but once she got her qualifications confirmed, she was in an
office, practicing town planning.

The late sixties didn't offer equal opportunities for women. Certain
professions and courses of study were off the table, and even in the same
jobs, women were paid less than men. I resented being paid less than my
male colleagues not only at M&S but also at both Cassell's and Collier
Macmillan. I knew it was unfair but I thought I could live with it, if I
was doing something I loved. There were few women in management
positions, fewer on corporate boards, and some of us engaged the issues
head-on through expressing our ideas openly.

By the seventies, of course, Betty Friedan's *The Feminine Mystique* was part of our history, as was Germaine Greer's militantly anti-male *The Female Eunuch*. Most women, unlike Greer, did not feel we had to hate men to be feminists. Margaret Laurence was a feminist. She publicly supported the Canadian Abortion Rights League, believing that women should have the choice whether to carry a child to term. She believed that women were about equal to men in most respects, except when they were superior. Still, she liked and sometimes loved men.

In *Dropped Threads: What We Aren't Told*, an anthology of women's writing edited by Carol Shields and Marjorie Anderson, there is an essay by Margaret Atwood that captures the era of "garter belts and panty girdles" when there were things that were not openly discussed. "Abortion. Incest. Lesbians. Masturbation. Female orgasm. Menopause. Impotence. Anger . . ." We've come a long way since then. "I remember a grand fermentation of ideas," she wrote. "Language was being changed. Territory was being claimed. The unsaid was being said." She taught a new course at York University called Canadian Women Writers.

In her essay "Writing the Male Character," delivered as the 1982 Hagey lecture at the University of Waterloo, Atwood spoke of what civilization might be without the contributions of men: "No electric floor polishers, no neutron bomb, no Freudian psychology . . ." In her usual ironic tone, she went on to say that "they're fun to play Scrabble with and handy for eating leftovers." For the novelist, whose work features male characters, there is the challenge of writing about some men who are "good" but not "weak," men who are not "rapists and murderers, child molesters, warmongers, sadists, power-hungry, callous, domineering, pompous, foolish or immoral, though I am sure we will all agree that such men do exist."

On *This Country in the Morning*, Marjorie Harris carved out a women's segment of at least twenty minutes each week to talk about equal pay, equal rights, and even daycare. All my friends were feminists. Marjorie, Sylvia Fraser, Geraldine Sherman, Barbara Frum (though she protested once that the women's movement was primarily middle-class, for women who could afford the luxury of self-discovery), Margaret Laurence, Margaret Atwood, Marian Engel, Doris Anderson, Isabel Bassett, Yvonne Worthington, and of course, the extraordinary June Callwood.

June was the most polished, least pretentious writer ever to have been hired by *Maclean's*. Even Peter Gzowski, who was a tough competitor, admitted that he never lost his admiration for June's brilliant way with words. She was witty, irreverent, sharp but forgiving. She dressed in pastels. She seemed to have a year-round tan; long, thin legs, usually in slingbacks; blond, flighty hair; and a big smile. She was a seventies feminist, a social activist determined to reach the consciences of people too involved with their own lives to care about others. She dealt with homelessness, drug addiction, AIDS, women, children, and the law. She wrote thousands of magazine and newspaper articles, twenty books, and ghosted a host more, for Barbara Walters, Dr. Charles Mayo, and Otto Preminger among others. She was also a devilishly daring glider pilot—a skill she learned in her late sixties and continued to perfect till she was in her eighties.

We were friends for more than thirty years. We talked a lot, laughed a lot, and tried to make sense of each other's passionate engagements. June's were usually more exhausting and often less rewarding than mine.

BOB FULFORD WAS right in his *Saturday Night* article in that by the mid-seventies feminism was no longer a fringe movement. There were more women in senior management. We had gained new rights. Some companies wanted to appear progressive by hiring women to serve on corporate boards. But it was slow progress. It was not until the late seventies that I had my first invitations to join corporate boards. In seemingly quick succession, I served on the boards of M&S, M&S-Bantam, Imperial Life, Maritime Life, Peoples' Jewellers, Doubleday, Alliance Communications, TVO, Ryerson, York University, the Empire Company, Hollinger, and a bunch of charitable foundation boards where at last I wasn't the only woman. I was appointed to boards because the time was right and, to all appearances, I was a business executive. I had a ringside seat for the take-over of some companies, the struggles for succession in others, the family feuds, and one bankruptcy.

A lot has happened for women since the seventies. Did we, as some women today argue, adopt patriarchal goals? Did we emulate men in our power suits, striving to sit at boardroom tables and in parliamentary offices? We probably did. Certainly the shoulder pads of my blue and yellow suits were a far cry from my old miniskirt outfits, but it was a step that gave women choices. (One photo of me on the cover of a business magazine wearing a yellow suit with seriously padded shoulders made me look like a stuffed canary.) Did white women own the feminism of the sixties and seventies? It seemed that way, but then white men owned the political and business power. We did not, intentionally, exclude women of colour. Doris and June, Sylvia and Margaret did invite them in and some of the time we were successful. But only some of the time. It's so rewarding today to see a multiplicity of women of all backgrounds finding their own voices and telling their own stories.

That I became president of a wonderful publishing company—Key Porter Books—in the early 1980s was in large part due to the changes other women had fought for. So, in answer to the young woman's question about whether I am a feminist, hell, yes, I have always been a feminist and it is time to celebrate our own. But that assessment itself brands me as a second wave feminist. The third wave, as its many advocates declare, is upon us now, and it assumes that previous waves were defeatist, that we bought in to the male mystique. Naomi Wolf's *The Beauty Myth: How Images of Beauty Are Used Against Women* argues that we are still emotionally and physically tortured by our need to look beautiful. The assumption is that our achievements have been "manipulated by those hostile to feminist causes." She is right, of course, but myths are tough to get rid of and this one has been around for so long, we barely notice the ads and commercials that feed on our insecurities and perpetuate its existence. Still, I am hopeful. We have come a long way, but there is still a long way to go. Each generation of women must find its own way, and my daughters' generation, and the generation that was born after theirs, is, I am happy to see, redefining feminism and its central issues. It will be up to them to decide where the #MeToo movement will take us. The time is right for naming and shaming perpetrators of sexual aggression, though I fear that some men have been publicly lynched without due process and I resist the push to seeing women as hapless victims. We are much better and stronger than that.

Rebel Daughter

WRITER AND ACTIVIST Doris Anderson was on the front lines of all our battles for equal rights.

The illegitimate daughter of a rooming house keeper and an itinerant tenant, Doris had grown up in her mother's rooming house in Calgary, where she learned a great deal about taking care of herself: no one else was doing the job.* When she decided she wanted to go to university, her high school teacher told her it would be better if she allowed boys with lower marks to go ahead of her: girls ended up marrying and didn't need degrees.

Doris was stubborn. She went to university.

Eventually she became the editor of *Chatelaine*, a women's magazine, during the 1960s and most of the seventies. In addition to the usual women's magazine content, like cooking, baking, decorating, and perfect housewifing, she ran articles on abortion, rape, women's choice not to have children, and violence in the home, stories of women juggling family and career and on being "successfully single." We had come from *I Love Lucy* and *Father Knows Best* to *The Mary Tyler Moore Show* and *Charlie's Angels*. Doris's editorials on pay equity, child care, custody arrangements,

---

* Key Porter published Doris's aptly named autobiography, *Rebel Daughter*, in 1996.

and women's sexual fulfillment were discussed, disputed, applauded—depending on who you were. I was in the applause section.

In 1967 Doris served on the Royal Commission on the Status of Women in Canada. Its 167 recommendations on such matters as equal pay for work of equal value, maternity leave, daycare, birth control, family law, and pensions were hardly revolutionary, though they caused considerable debate both in and out of Parliament. It was not until 1969 that Dr. Henry Morgenthaler opened the first abortion clinic in Canada. His clinic was soon raided by police and he was charged with performing illegal abortions. The Criminal Code prohibited abortions unless the woman could prove to a panel of doctors—usually all male—that the pregnancy would threaten her life or that it was the result of incest or rape. In 1988 the Supreme Court of Canada effectively legalized abortion and confirmed a woman's right to make decisions about her own body. Yet abortion remains a contentious issue both here and in the United States, where some states still do their best to prevent access to the procedure.

Doris had an impressive grasp of a range of ideas, and she always knew she could bring an audience along, even if they disagreed with her at the beginning. She spoke with a wonderful western drawl; she was statuesque, tall, broad-beamed, confident. Her magazine was like herself, outspoken, no nonsense, tell it as it is. Doris knew how to lean in long before Sheryl Sandberg's *Lean In: Women, Work and the Will to Lead* became a bestseller.

We used to have lunch at various Toronto eateries and discuss issues of our time and how our lives were still affected by perceptions of suitable roles for women. The only woman in a senior management role in book publishing in the 1960s was Gladys Neale of Macmillan. She had worked her way up with dogged determination to become one of the best educational publishers in Canada.*

In addition to running *Chatelaine*, Maclean Hunter's most successful magazine, Doris managed a household with three rambunctious boys and

---

* Francess Halpenny didn't become associate director of the University of Toronto Press until 1979.

a very busy husband, a lawyer with a serious interest in politics. On summer evenings we were often at their Rosedale home, where the boys took turns leaping from the roof into the pool amid great whooping shouts of joy and derring-do. Doris, though she growled her disapproval, was proud of her sons and remained calm in her role as host and mother.

Under her stewardship, *Chatelaine* doubled its circulation, yet when Doris applied for the job of publisher, she was denied. The job went to a less-experienced insider—a man with similarities to the character "Laughing Horse" in her novel *Rough Layout*, which featured a woman not unlike herself running a magazine, not unlike *Chatelaine*. It was one of the last novels I signed when I was at M&S. Doris used to joke that I chose to resign rather than face a potential lawsuit.

When she applied to be editor of *Maclean's*, she was, again, deemed unworthy by the boys' club that owned the magazine. One of those men told her that she simply couldn't represent the company publicly. *Maclean's* was losing more than a million dollars a year, yet management wouldn't trust a woman who had run a profitable magazine with fixing its flagship monthly.

Doris resigned from *Chatelaine* in 1977. That was about the same time as her marriage began to unravel. She used to talk to me about weighing her options. What would be more difficult: staying in a broken marriage or becoming a single mother? It took a few months of thinking and debating with herself before she decided to end her marriage. Peter, her oldest, was in high school and stayed with his father, while Doris took a long camper trip with the other two boys in Europe.

For a while after the trip, she experimented with staying at home and writing, but she had too much energy to remain sedentary. Besides, she was determined to keep fighting for women's rights, even if she no longer had *Chatelaine*'s platform. She had championed the need for more women in politics and now, when the opportunity presented itself, she grabbed it.*
She ran for the Liberal Party in Eglinton and lost.

---

* By 1984 there were six women in the cabinet, including Barbara McDougall, Minister of State for Finance, and Pat Carney, Minister of Energy, Mines, and Resources

Afterwards, still licking her wounds, she accepted the post of chair for the Canadian Advisory Council on the Status of Women. Although Doris had been a lifelong Liberal, many of her staunchest supporters turned out to be Tories. Inevitably, she crossed swords with Lloyd Axworthy, an influential Liberal member of parliament. He seemed to be under the impression that Doris could be persuaded to toe the party line. Needless to say, he was wrong. When he pushed the executive, over Doris's objections, to cancel a national meeting to discover what women wanted from the new Charter of Rights, Doris and a small group of women organized a non-governmental ad hoc conference that drew thirteen hundred women from across the country. None of them was paid. In the end, Section 28 of the Charter stated simply that men and women are equal under the law. That may not seem like such a revolutionary gain by today's standards, but up until 1982 such recognition had eluded us.

I was not the only friend who advised Doris not to accept the ungenerous offer of the presidency of the National Action Committee on the Status of Women. It didn't pay. Its members were chosen from two hundred organizations, representing 3.5 million women, with a myriad of issues. At the time its members were battling it out over a range of issues, including whether homemakers should be allowed to join the Canada Pension Plan. They had approached Doris because she had become a celebrity and, as she told me, nobody else would take the job.

Yet the job was, in some ways, the right choice for Doris. It gave her a close connection with women across the country and, eventually, around the world. She could not have written her 1991 book, *The Unfinished Revolution*, had she not been with NAC. She could rely on her reputation and connections to reach women around the world and provide a significant overview of the status of women in twelve countries. The book tackles some of the tough issues—daycare, the workforce, safety, violence against

---

and later, Minister of International Trade, a post she held when Canada negotiated the Free Trade Agreement with the United States. Key Porter published her memoir, *Trade Secrets*, in 2000.

women, availability of jobs—and it examines how far women had come in their own countries since their mothers were their age.

I am ending this chapter the way Doris ended her *Rebel Daughter*:

If women had more say in how the world is run, we wouldn't be worrying about the next quarter's profit picture, or whether Moody's is going to award us an A++ rating. Our priorities would be more focused and practical than that: we would be thinking of nothing less than the future of the planet. . . . Isn't it time women stopped holding up half the sky and began making at least half the decisions right down here on earth?

In Search of My Father

IN 1975 I had received an astonishing phone call from a man who claimed he knew my father.

I must admit that I have understated my efforts to find my father. I wrote him long letters when I was growing up in Budapest and gave them to Vili to post to wherever he thought my father resided. My mother had stopped looking for him after she served her time in jail for attempting to leave the country to join him in Austria. Incarcerated in the Sacred Heart Convent school, I had visions of being rescued by my recalcitrant father, who had, so far, failed to appear. The convent would offer him a grand opportunity to redeem himself, I thought. I wrote heart-rending letters and long heroic poems to him and tried to send them via my aunt Leah, who said she knew where he was. She said she had promised not to tell me.

My other aunt, Sari, mentioned once that my father had moved to Australia. When I was working two jobs and going to university, I saved up enough to hire a private detective to track him down. I am not sure he tried very hard, though he reported that a Hungarian immigrant called Szigethy had changed his name to Spencer and lived in Perth, Australia. Then he told me that Spencer had left with his family for the United States. He said he had no more information and my money ran out.

The man who called me at M&S said he had seen an article about me in

The Globe and Mail and made the connection. The article had mentioned my pre-Porter name. The caller claimed he knew a man who had used the same name once. Naturally, I was wary.

"He used to be István Szigethy, but he has changed his name to Steven Spencer and he lives in Winnipeg," the man informed me. Steven Spencer had married a Hungarian woman with two children, whom he had adopted. He had been a social worker. He was charming and had many friends. He was a patron of the Winnipeg arts scene. He and his wife were passionate bridge players. The man knew this from personal experience. He and his wife had played bridge with the Spencers. He gave me a Winnipeg phone number.

I think I called at least four times before I found my voice. He denied all knowledge of a daughter, all knowledge of Hungary, my mother, his time in the Gulag. He claimed he was born here, in Canada. He made this claim with a heavy Hungarian accent, not so different from how my grandfather sounded after twenty years of trying to learn English.

I hung up.

But I did tell Jack McClelland the story one evening over drinks at the Fort Garry bar. Since we were already in Winnipeg, Jack seized the opportunity and, pretending he was a stringer for *Time* magazine, phoned Mr. Spencer. Jack said he was writing a story about his daughter, Anna, and wished to interview him.

My father—because Mr. Spencer really was my father—reluctantly consented. Jack drove me to the apartment building but decided to leave me on my own for the occasion. That was how I met my father for the first time since he ruined my Christmas in 1949 by appearing in a greatcoat at our door in Budapest just as my presents were likely to be opened.

He seemed quite ordinary, as was his apartment, with the photographs of his wife and two children, the rug, the coffee table, the TV set. Everything was ordinary, except the fact that he now conceded he remembered a small girl who was said to be his daughter.

He told me a long story about having been too afraid of Vili to stay in touch, too afraid even to send money once he had found a job in Australia. He did not want to talk about his time in the Gulag but told me how he had met his current wife and her children in an Austrian refugee camp in Salzburg. Oddly enough, it was the same refugee camp where my mother and I stayed before we were shipped off to New Zealand.

I visited him again a few years later when he was already dying of Parkinson's. His wife had placed a large photograph of me on top of his TV set. "He is very proud of you," she told me. She encouraged me to take him for a walk in the park across from their apartment. He talked about my mother as I pushed him in his wheelchair and how pretty she had been and how young when they met during the war. He talked about Vili, who had seemed all-powerful to him, as Vili had seemed to me, but for him, my grandfather was a dangerous, threatening presence, not the benevolent storyteller of my childhood.

When I told my mother that I had met him, she was surprised that he had finally acknowledged me. A few weeks before my phone call, she had found out where he was and phoned him. She said he showed no interest in seeing either of us again. That was the first time she mentioned that she knew he had fathered another child, a boy, in the Gulag. The mother was one of the villagers who lived near the labour camp. Some of them had been kind to the inmates, gave them bits of bread and potatoes, though they didn't have much themselves. In my father's case, one of them had given him a bit of love. When we met for the last time, I didn't ask him about his son. Years later I learned that he had been in Vorkuta Gulag, the labour camp I featured in my novel *The Appraisal.* One day, maybe, I shall visit Vorkuta and try to find my half-brother.

I had wanted my father to meet his granddaughter Catherine at least once before he died. In hindsight, I am glad it didn't work out. She would have retained a memory of an old, dying man who was a complete stranger to both of us.

MY BELOVED GRANDFATHER Vili Racz died on July 18, 1976. We had talked a couple of weeks before his death, when he was trying to decide whether to go into hospital for an operation or stay and wait for death at home. I cried during most of our conversation. He tried to keep my spirits up by saying that he would not allow a little thing like cancer to beat him. In hindsight, of course, I should have flown down to Australia to be with him, but I kept putting it off and then it was too late.

The night he died, our windows rattled and one of our doors slammed shut in the wind. I wondered whether he had been saying goodbye.

PART TWO

No Rose Garden

Looking for a New Gig

D URING MY BRIEF but determined attempt at homemaking in 1978,
I tried to immerse myself in what I considered domestic tasks, like
gourmet cooking, baking, knitting, and decorating. As the only changes
we had made to our house since we bought it had been the shiny new
wallpaper with cheerfully cavorting blue and pink elephants in the children's bedroom, there was a great deal of scope for my activities: the living
room's pale-beige flocked wallpaper, for example, the heavy yellow drapes,
the plush grey wall-to-wall carpeting. I replaced the two single beds in
Suse and Jessica's bedroom (Julian claimed the originals were from the
Salvation Army), and we removed old shelving to build bookcases for our
thousands of books. Odd, Julian thought, that neither of us had objected
earlier to leftovers from the previous owners. A magazine story about our
hosting book launches at home refers to our house as dog-friendly but
quite devoid of style.

The truth is we were both so busy, we hadn't noticed. Now I was creating merciless havoc in our formerly peaceful spaces. I consulted (briefly) a
decorator who suggested a coffee table covered with reptile skin (ignored
that advice), had someone dispose of the grey broadloom, stripped the
wallpaper, repainted the walls, bought several pieces of furniture and a
new dog we called Lilo in honour of my aunt Leah (nicknamed Lilo), who

had been the beauty of my family. Journalist Allan Fotheringham wrote later that our home was "decorated by dogs."

It was around that time that I first noticed a pink-dressing-gowned, pink-slippered ghost in our dark basement. I had been on the point of dismissing the apparition as a postpartum mental twitch when Sylvia Fraser asked me if we had a tenant downstairs with a separate entrance. Then Catherine complained of a lady in the basement where I had hidden her birthday presents. Ruth Fraser, who stayed with us during a visit to Toronto in the mid-1980s, may have been the last to see her. Then the pink lady vanished with as little notice as had presaged her arrival. She may have been displeased with my redecorating. Or we were all delusional. In any event, I stopped revamping the house.

Nothing came of my knitting beyond a very long, brown-and-blue-striped scarf, as ugly as the orange sweater I had knitted for my mother when I was at the Sacred Heart Convent in Wanganui. The nuns believed that the way to deal with girls was to keep them busy, and knitting and crocheting were high on their list of activities. Once I had learned enough English to protest, they were inclined to let me read comic books instead. They were worried about my background as a child revolutionary, and I made sure they would continue to worry by looking very fierce. I have kept a few scary photographs of myself in school uniform.

At the cottage, I subjected Geraldine Sherman and Bob Fulford to my experiments in cooking. They would arrive with their two young daughters, who became friends with Catherine and Julia. I have a wonderful photograph of Bob and Geraldine sitting in the back of our boat, reading sections of *The New York Times.* They were both, essentially, city people, but they proved to be amazingly adaptable. Geraldine, who was a feature and short-story writer, book reviewer, and radio producer, was also a dab hand at fishing. Who knew?

Jack Batten and Marjorie Harris turned out to be fearless boaters. Jack had been friends with Bob since his early days at *Maclean's.* He was a jock with a passion for hockey, jazz, movies, and tennis, a former lawyer who had no desire to practice law, and a freelance writer who could make any subject interesting. He has now written about forty books, but back then he was merely at number five. Marjorie Harris had worked in art galleries and at the CBC, and freelanced for *Chatelaine*. She took (what I thought odd at the time) a strange interest in our Georgian Bay vegetation and rocks. As it turned out, she became a gardening maven with a huge following of would-be green-thumbers. The Georgian Bay rocks she collected along the shore were to be a feature of her much-photographed garden. But back then, she didn't talk much about gardens. We sat on the dock dreaming up ideas for books that would sell, such as *Historic Canada, Toronto: City of Neighbourhoods*, and *Farewell to the 70s*, all of which appeared later.

Peter Worthington and Yvonne Crittenden visited less often, because their Jack Russell terriers had taken an instant dislike to Lilo. They felt the same way about our long-haired dachshunds who succeeded the ill-fated vizsla.

Margaret Atwood and Graeme Gibson visited occasionally, paddling to the back of the island to see the osprey nest and the big rock where the snapping turtles sunned themselves.

We, in turn, often visited Charles and Madeleine Templeton in their imposing new house built over the ruins of an old railway hotel. Charles had designed it himself. It required brand new furniture to go with the grey stone and glass, and the stylish Madeleine had been happy to oblige. She had spent years in Paris, looked like an Ingres portrait, and spoke softly with a French accent. We happily took their discards.*

Charles's stories about his life as an evangelist, a political candidate (never successful, though a couple of times he came close), a journalist, cartoonist, inventor, editor, playwright, and television and radio interviewer were fascinating. He was still very fond of Billy Graham, spiritual adviser to various US presidents and a bevy of congressmen, but they no longer talked about faith. He had gossipy stories from his time as a television producer and interviewer (of, among others, Evelyn Waugh and Rebecca West).

---

* We still have the worn brown-and-beige couch Charles donated to our unfinished living room and the trundle beds we used when we were his guests.

Since Charles co-hosted *Dialogue** with Pierre Berton on CFRB radio, the Bertons too were frequent visitors. Pierre and Charles could debate any topic vociferously, even when they agreed with each other. Afterwards, we would take the Bertons around the lake in our boat to cool off, while Charles got back to his writing.

IT TOOK LESS than a couple of months for me to recognize that I was completely bored. It took even less time for Julian to come to the same conclusion because I had begun to take an unhealthy interest in the law. He had been hired by James Leslie Bennett, former RCMP officer and one-time head of Canadian counterintelligence, now living in Australia, to sue Ian Adams and Gage Publishing over Adams's novel *S: Portrait of a Spy: RCMP Intelligence—The Inside Story.* Peter Worthington had brought the book to Julian's attention, pointing to similarities not only between S and Bennett, but also between himself and a character called Hazlitt. Hazlitt is the editor of a right-of-centre tabloid "claiming to represent the working people's interests," as was Peter. S, a KGB mole used as a double agent by the CIA, is investigated by his own team and cleared only because he has some damaging evidence against members of the Canadian intelligence service. Julian intended to fiercely defend James Bennett's reputation. I, on the other hand, supported Ian Adams, the writer. In fact, he was a writer we had published at M&S. Worse, other writers, including many of my friends, aligned themselves with his defence when the judge demanded that he reveal his sources. There was even a fundraising drive to pay Adams's legal fees.

In the end, Bennett settled out of court.

It was one of the few times that Julian and I were firmly embedded on opposing sides of an issue. Very likely the true test of a good relationship is

---

* They did more than four thousand *Dialogue* sessions before the program was cut in 1983.

when two people passionately disagree on something but continue to dine, laugh, and live together.

In early 1978 Peter Worthington hired Julian to defend him against the charge of violating the Official Secrets Act. RCMP officers descended on the *Toronto Sun*'s offices and demanded to see the "leaked" documents. The case was seen as a test of the freedom of the press in Canada, and it was good to see my various friends of all political persuasions cheer Julian when the case against his client was dismissed.

WHILE I PONDERED Jack's proposal that I run Seal, I decided to consider other options.

Before I was married, I was often invited over by David (the English expat) and his friend, Alan Edmonds. Edmonds, another English expat, ex-Fleet Street journalist, would later became a most unlikely, dishevelled television success with his quirky interviews for CTV's *Live It Up*. Alan invited me to do a screen test interview for *Live It Up*. I had to go into a variety store on King Street East and pretend to purchase some item I neither needed nor wanted and engage in a bit of banter with the merchant. There were at least four takes, the store owner becoming less and less cooperative each time and finally asking whether he could go home now. I had no difficulty turning down Alan's job offer.

I thought about calling Moses Znaimer, now head honcho at Citytv, but he was in the middle of negotiations with new partners—first Multiple Media, then CHUM—and gossip had him grumpy and combative.

Then I thought I would apply for work at CBC Radio, because I loved the CBC. I had been a keen listener to *This Country in the Morning* under its various hosts, but particularly Peter Gzowski, because he loved to interview authors and he offered them lots of airtime to promote themselves. Unlike most radio and TV hosts, Peter actually read the books, listened to the authors, and tailored his follow-up questions to what they said. Listeners were keen to share their feelings and ideas with Peter. It was as if he were a personal friend, a confidant, someone who would love to come by for a piece of cake and a story or two on a rainy afternoon. I used to drive M&S authors to his interviews and keep them coffeed and entertained so they would not be too nervous. But when I talked with Peter, I didn't know how to introduce the subject of a job.

At one of the Frums' frequent parties that often spilled onto their patio and into the garden, I approached Barbara Frum's producer, Mark Staro-wicz, and the head of CBC radio and television's current affairs program-ming, Peter Herrndorf. Neither of them seemed to know what to do with my question about a job at the CBC, but both of them were eager to talk about M&S authors and about M&S's relatively new venture with Bantam Books. The CBC was soon to air a television series based on Peter New-man's *The Canadian Establishment* books, and they were both interested in Peter's progress with the *Bronfman Dynasty.*

Then they wanted to discuss the Seal First Novel Award and how the next prize would be presented. Was there a way of topping the Aritha van Herk performance?

Julian had been at university with Adrienne Clarkson, who was then co-hosting *The Fifth Estate*, but I didn't know her well enough to ask whether she thought I could be a plausible candidate for a CBC job. I got to know her better later when she was Ontario's Agent General in France. We rented a house near their summer place in Provence and stayed with her and John Ralston Saul in Paris. But by then I was back in the book business.

I REMEMBER TAKING a long walk through the Mount Pleasant Ceme-tery with Julia in her stroller, Catherine running ahead and back, making whooshing noises and lifting her arms like the wings of an airplane. It was a few months before Christmas of 1978 and Catherine was very excited about the potential for "amazing" gifts.

I thought about how much I missed the excitement of new manu-scripts, the hours I spent with writers discussing their work, the delight of holding a printed and bound book when it arrived. I even loved the smell of freshly printed pages. I still do. Who was I kidding? As Jack had foretold, I was hooked on books.

In January 1979, I accepted the appointment to become Seal's president and publisher. According to Jack, it was to be a two-days-a-week kind of job, leaving me plenty of time for children. Seal's offices were in a dull 1950s building about five minutes' walk from our home and practically adjacent to my daughters' school.

Soon after I moved into my new office, Bill Deverell won the second Seal Award, for *Needles.* Jack and Peter Taylor decided it would be fun to deliver the fifty thousand dollars in cash, and I had the honour of presenting him with his unwieldy reward. Bill, a BC criminal lawyer with impeccable courtroom credentials, was equal to the task of hamming it up for the audience. There is a photo of Jack, Bantam's Alun Davies, Bill, and myself, ill at ease but grinning in very dated outfits. Mine is a horrid long poufy skirt and matching top.

Needles was a natural for the paperback market we had hoped to conquer, a fast-paced page-turner, perfect for the commercial fiction market. But even Bill was somewhat stunned when Taylor's team delivered hypodermic needles with each press kit. The book was set in the international drug trade, starring a sympathetic protagonist with a heroin habit. Bill, who had been counsel in a thousand trials, including about thirty for murder, was magnificent on tour. This was, we thought, a great way to attract more commercial fiction writers with flair.

Sealing

M Y DAY-TO-DAY CONTACT at Bantam was the dapper Welshman Alun Davies, their designated hitter for all international markets. Alun was charming, argumentative, always well-informed about the world's book markets and about who was doing what to whom and why, including the sexual proclivities of employees from London to Sydney, from New York to New Delhi. He had once worked in Canada for Longman's and thought he had a good grounding in what Canadians wanted to read. As a Welshman living all over the world, he thought nationalism, particularly that of the cultural kind, was a passing fad.

When I agreed to take over Seal in 1979, Alun was in Australia. Later, when I met Bantamites from Australia and the UK, I discovered that their Alun problems were pretty much the same as mine: he tended to know more about what they were doing than they did. In fact, I liked him rather more than many of them seemed to. Alun, I thought, had shown remarkable resilience when dealing with the Lucy Maud Montgomery estate's implacable lawyer, Marian Hebb, and with Kevin Sullivan Productions's *Anne of Green Gables* series.* But he had a penchant for countermanding my de-

---

* By coincidence, in 2003 Julian defended Marian Hebb when Sullivan Entertainment sued her and the Montgomery estate for libel.

cisions, sometimes as if by accident, other times after long perorations on how certain kinds of books (Matt Cohen's, for example) never worked in mass market paperback. To illustrate a point, he would cite examples from other countries. I discovered from colleagues in those other countries that he did pretty much the same there, using Canadian examples. They sometimes called him "the wily Welshman."

In an effort to find those elusive commercial fiction writers (we were thinking of Blatty, Benchley, and L'Amour), we thought Richard Rohmer was an ideal candidate. His first novel, *Ultimatum*, had been at the top of the bestseller lists. Plus, he was a war hero. He had flown 135 missions and taken part in D-Day. As a young fighter pilot on a field mission during the invasion, he had reported seeing Field Marshall Rommel in a German staff car. Headquarters sent a Spitfire to strafe the car, thus wounding one of the Germans' top commandants. He was now a lawyer, an honorary lieutenant general of the Canadian Armed Forces, chief of the Canadian Reserves, honorary adviser to the Canadian Defence Staff, an advocate of culture, former chair of the Royal Commission on Book Publishing, a Conservative political insider, and a recipient of numerous honours and awards, including Commander of the Order of Military Merit. He was tailor-made for the M&S-Bantam promotion machine.

However, his potboilers, *Exxonoration*, *Exodus/UK*, *Separation*, and so on, were short-lived, despite Bantam's marketing moxie. Richard didn't care about style. He wanted to get his stories told and his ideas out. The writing (hasty, since he dictated the novels) and the characters (wooden) were of little interest to him.*

I remember Richard coming to my office one day to tell me that he had analyzed bestsellers and now realized that his books needed to have more sex scenes. Since he had no idea how to write them, he wanted me to refer

---

* Among the Rohmer oeuvre that the indefatigable Jennifer Glossop edited was the unfortunately titled *Balls*, which made everyone snicker rather than consider Richard's prescient warnings about the growing reliance on fossil fuels and the possibility of a US grab for Canada's natural resources.

him to some well-written sex in other books that he could use as a guide. Seriously.

We experimented with thrillers like Ian Slater's *Firespill* and Leo Heaps's *The Quebec Plot* and several exceptional mysteries by L. R. Wright,* who had won the Edgar Award for *The Suspect*.

I also tried historical fiction by commissioning a series called *The Canadians* that promised a "gripping saga of the conquest of a continent," as well as the ensuing "consuming loves and raging hates, fierce loyalties and unyielding vows of revenge." The books sported what we thought were stirring titles, like *Bloodbrothers*, *Patriots*, and *Birthright*. Because they sold well, author Robert Wall, who had five children and a not-too-well-paid teaching job at a university, kept them coming at the rate of about one a year.

I had failed to persuade George Jonas and Barbara Amiel to come to Seal with their *By Persons Unknown*, about a famous murder case in Ontario, but George did give me the chance to publish his novel *Final Decree*, a thoughtful exploration of a simple immigrant's deterioration in the "new world." It was not, however, in any sense commercial.

Looking back, I suspect that neither Jack nor I had the right instincts for commercial fiction. With literary fiction, even if it sells fewer than five thousand copies (the number Jack thought we should be able to sell of Matt Cohen's and Adele Wiseman's novels), you have the satisfaction of a book of lasting value. With commercial fiction, more often than not, you have published something with only a few months of shelf life.

Since Jack and I wanted to increase the number of new Seal books, I had to reach outside the M&S lists.

I THOUGHT I would finally have a chance of attracting W. O. Mitchell. I already knew him from Banff, where he had been friendly, and I enjoyed

---

* L. R.'s nickname was Bunny. Her mysteries are being reissued by Felony & Mayhem Press.

our talks about his retinue of young Canadian writers. He was magnificent when he had an audience, a natural storyteller with a plethora of tales, some of which found their way into his books, while others did not. I was particularly fond of the one—true or not—about Joe Clark, long before his brief stint as prime minister of Canada, sitting in an outdoor crapper while W. O. and other pranksters tied the wooden shack to a pickup truck and towed it away, leaving the déshabillé Joe and the toilet behind.

W. O. would never publish with M&S while Farley Mowat was one of our stars because he and Farley had not been on speaking terms for de-cades. W. O. believed that he had helped the young Mowat get published both in Canada and the United States and that his good deed was rewarded by Farley's "churlish" denial that such help had existed.* In a *Saturday Night* article, Farley had accused Bill of rejecting his stories that would later be-come *The Desperate People* and advising him to write simple boy-meets-girl romances. In the 1981 NFB film *In Search of Farley Mowat*, Farley repeated the accusation. I don't know what really happened but I suspect that, as with most things in life, there is more than one version of the truth.

I was then and still am an avid fan of the way W. O. talks his way into readers' hearts with just a few words early in his stories and never lets go. Of all his books, my favourite is *How I Spent My Summer Holidays*, the compelling, terrifying tale of a young boy robbed of his childhood.

We bought paperback rights to five of his books—*Jake and the Kid*, *Who Has Seen the Wind*, *The Kite*, *The Vanishing Point*, and *How I Spent My Summer Holidays*—from his hardcover publishers, Macmillan. The ad-vance of $125,000 seemed like a lot at the time, but it turned out to have been a good investment. Mitchell barely needed promotion. At sixty-seven, he was at the pinnacle of his career both as a writer and as a performer. He gave readings to packed houses across the country, his white hair flying, his voice rising and falling as the story required, enjoying the applause, getting ready for the next tale.

---

* While W.O. was fiction editor of *Maclean's*, he also helped Alice Munro, Alistair MacLeod, and Ernest Buckler, among others.

Sometimes when he was in Toronto, he would drop by our home, pour himself a drink, and settle into a living room armchair, stretching out his long legs, leaning his head back, telling stories. My kids loved them, as did his wife, Merna, who had heard them all before but still enjoyed these occasions to listen again. His voice had such range, from a whisper to a high pitch to a gravelly rant, that I could hear it from outside even before opening our front door.

I experimented with non-fiction, to see if we could establish a non-fiction line without buying the rights from another publisher. *Jimmy: An Autobiography* was such an experiment. Convincing Bantam that Jim Pattison was a "big name" had not been easy, but I got lucky when Bob Hope called him "a sort of Lee Iacocca with frostbite." They certainly knew Iacocca.

Most people west of the Rockies knew Jimmy by reputation. Thousands shopped in his Overwaitea stores, travelled on his ferries, listened to his radio stations; hundreds of thousands knew of his Ripley Entertainment and had heard of his modest early start as a used-car salesman. *Jimmy*, ghosted by journalist Paul Grescoe, was beautifully written and had a great golden cover with Jimmy grinning while he adjusts his bow tie.

It's interesting to see how often interviewers asked him when, having achieved all that success, he was going to retire. He had not given the matter a single thought. Nor had he done so ten or so years later when I visited him in his Vancouver office. He was still a man in a hurry. His impressive collection of photographs covering one whole wall was still missing a few presidents, prime ministers, and corporate kings. To mark the occasion of showing me his city's skyline, he played some tunes on his trumpet. He seemed ageless and tireless. You can watch a 2015 video of Jimmy playing "Happy Birthday to You" at the hundredth anniversary of his Overwaitea Food Group.

He stayed married to the woman he had fallen in love with more than sixty years before, and though he may have been the richest man in Canada, he lived in the house they had bought when they first became parents. He saw no reason to change.

We spent a weekend once on his yacht, *Nova Spirit*, cruising along the

BC coast. There was never a quiet moment. Jimmy loved to hear good conversation and tried to engage his guests in a variety of activities. I suggested he should try "writing" his own book, one giving business advice to future generations, and I made the mistake of mentioning that he might be retiring soon. He looked at me with concern about my sanity: going strong at eighty-four or so, he was excited about some new venture, pleased with the expansion of his Ripley's franchise, and looking forward to another trip to Walmart's head office in Bentonville, Arkansas. He liked the way the Waltons operated. I wonder whether he still does.

I asked Gordon Pinsent, writer of the original *Rowdyman*, to turn his successful CBC television Christmas special, *A Gift to Last*, into a novel. He was an accomplished performer, charming, erudite, a fine writer, a delight to watch and listen to, but my God, did he ever find it difficult to finish that book. Alun Davies started suggesting that we should just cancel the contract rather than keep postponing publication. In the end, though, Gordon did deliver and the book was, of course, a national bestseller.

The Challenge of Being Julian

I N APRIL 1979, Julian, a busy partner in the firm of Porter and Posluns and already on the Stratford Festival's board, was elected chairman of the Toronto Transit Commission. I don't think he realized that both boards faced crisis and that he would be spending more time dealing with them than he could spare from the law. Other than daily complaints from subway and bus—the Avenue Road route!—passengers, many of whose comments were delivered directly to our home, the TTC was manageable. Stratford, not so much. The day of Julian's first annual general meeting, actor/director Richard Monette shouted "You pig" at the retiring president of the board, a foretaste of interesting times to come.*

Martin Knelman, theatre and movie critic, cultural commentator, and gossipy wit, would write about the turmoil in *The Stratford Tempest*, a 1982 book that recounts the events after Julian's appointment to head the search committee for a suitable artistic director. Suitable, at a time of simmering Canadian nationalism, meant Canadian. Lloyd Axworthy, minister of immigration, Mavor Moore, head of the Canada Council, legendary actors

---

* Monette himself would be artistic director of the Stratford Festival from 1994 till 2007, and he was unfailingly polite to Julian every time they met.

Martha Henry, Hume Cronyn, and William Hutt were all involved in the melee. Julian, always a quick study, decided that the only feasible option was the inspiring, well-qualified, but mercurial John Hirsch.

Hirsch lived a couple of blocks from our house in Moore Park. He was suspicious of Stratford's approach because he felt he had been snubbed and insulted by them in the past. Despite that history, Hirsch was flawlessly cordial at their first meeting. Julian took me along for some subsequent meetings because Hirsch too was born in Hungary and, by strange coincidence, had also become a Canadian nationalist. Lean, hirsute, reserved, with a soft Hungarian accent, he offered wine and pretzels but not a hint of being inclined to consider the Stratford position. He believed in nurturing and promoting Canadian talent, not at the expense of excellence but at the expense of the colonial mentality that, he believed, still reigned supreme on Stratford's board. Julian was so eager to break through Hirsch's resistance that he overstepped his board mandate and actually offered Hirsch the position, with details to be worked out later. I think they both rather enjoyed the media storm that followed, but it took all of Julian's powers of persuasion to calm the board.

In spite of that kerfuffle, Hirsch took the job. He liked the challenge of Stratford at a time when he knew every move he made was going to be scrutinized and, if possible, debunked by his opponents. As Julian had predicted somewhat unconvincingly, the 1981 season was a huge success, due as much to Muriel Sherrin, whom Hirsch imported from CBC drama, as to Hirsch's own genius. Brian Bedford, Richard Monette, Len Cariou—already stars on stage—added the glamour, as did Nicholas Pennell and Fiona Reid.

We attended most of the openings, and Julian settled the board down to enjoy the shows. He loves theatre, Shakespeare in particular. He can recite bits of dialogue and soliloquies with as much verve as an actor. The courtroom, where he still did most of his acting, is itself a stage where opposing counsel fight with words before an audience. Julian loved jury trials. I think Hirsch recognized in him a fellow thespian.

I met festival founder Tom Patterson on one of our Stratford trips. He was keen to reminisce about the early days of the festival, the efforts to persuade the town to allow a festival each summer, his time with Tyrone Guthrie and Alec Guinness. Without their extraordinary talent and the support of the British theatre community—not just the actors, but the experienced costume crew, the dancers, and the stage managers—Patterson felt the festival would never have happened. His memoir, *First Stage: The Making of the Stratford Festival*, ghosted by Allan Gould, should be required reading for Stratford's annual new arrivals, both the talent and the board.

As for me, I remember Tom every time we are in the Tom Patterson Theatre. The town of Stratford has justified his dream. No longer the failed small town he left behind when he went to fight in the Second World War, it is a major international attraction, site of an inspiring theatrical extravaganza that drew an audience of half a million in 2017. There are plans now for a new Patterson Theatre building. I think Tom would be pleased.

Sylvia's Magic

S YLVIA FRASER HAUNTS these pages and will, no doubt, continue to be part of my story for as long as my story lasts. She is a novelist, a journalist, an activist and, as June Callwood was, an occasional ghostwriter.

After our honeymoon in Barbados, Sylvia and Russell shared two more magical holidays with us, one in Bermuda, where we hired scooters, explored small, hard-to-find beaches and the Fourways Inn, and one in Haiti, where we stayed far above the Tonton Macoute–infested city and woke to birdsong.*

Jack's insistence that M&S authors take part in over-the-top publicity gambits reached insane proportions when it came to the 1980 launch of Sylvia's *The Emperor's Virgin*. Jack and Sylvia donned togas with gold-leaf crowns and attempted to ride in a kind of gilded chariot drawn by two surprised horses down Yonge Street to the launch party, where she was to be attended by scantily clad young men posing as slaves. Jack was in his element as the emperor, but Sylvia was supremely uncomfortable and ex-

---

* It is hard to imagine such an idyllic holiday now, after the devastating earthquake and seeing photos my daughter Catherine brought back from her reporting about the catastrophe for the *Toronto Star*.

ceptionally cold. The whole affair had been meticulously planned by Peter Taylor to coincide with the Ides of March, a dangerous time in Shakespeare's Rome and an unpredictable one in Toronto. A snowstorm put an end to the chariot ride, and my intrepid friends completed the journey on foot.*

I had been an early reader of *The Candy Factory*, a book that, like *The Emperor's Virgin*, is still disturbing in its intensity. I sent Sylvia long, detailed memos about its structure, characters, and symbolism, and we spent long nights drinking chocolate liqueur while discussing every aspect of the manuscript.† When he was presenting it at the M&S sales conference, Jack talked about Sylvia's heightened sensibility. Her perceptions of reality and of the inner lives of people were sharp, exacting, searingly honest.

Berlin Solstice, her fifth novel, was another dark, compelling book set in the grimmest days of the Third Reich. The violence in this novel, perhaps more than in her previous books, foreshadows what she was finally forced to face about the violence in her own childhood. Her perfect marriage would become one of the victims of her desperate struggle to confront that evil.

"I rarely use the word 'brilliant.' I use it now, with respect, about this novel," wrote Margaret Laurence. "I'd give my left tit to have written *Berlin Solstice*," wrote Irving Layton in July 1984: "having a sharp eye for selecting the apt metaphor and revealing detail, she keeps her prose elegant, crisp, and energetic. . . . Even the dullest and the most self-complacent philistine will find it impossible not to be moved."

It was on one of those preternaturally bright days well known to people who live in or near the Rockies that Sylvia found out her father was dying. We were at the students' pay phone, a very public spot under one of the Banff Centre's buildings. Her mother had just told her the news. It was as

---

* I know Sylvia hates this story and the way it keeps reappearing online, but I just couldn't resist.

† There is a five-page memo to Sylvia from me, dated May 29, 1974, in the M&S fonds at McMaster University.

if the bottom had fallen out of Sylvia's world. She was shaking and gagging and unable to talk. I thought at first that it was the shock of a parent's dying, but it wasn't. It was the horror of her slowly dawning recognition that her father had abused her as a very young child. It would take some years before she fully confronted that truth. As she describes the experience in *My Father's House: A Memoir of Incest and of Healing*, "When my father died, he came alive for me. A door opened, like a hole cut in the air. It yawned before me, offering release . . ." For Sylvia, it was the beginning of a journey that would reveal the source of her nightmares and allow her long-buried child-self to emerge and reveal itself. She had buried this "other self" deep in her subconscious so she could live a near-normal life.

In 1984, having disposed of her worldly possessions, she moved to California for two years to write *My Father's House.* The full impact of her remembering the sexual abuse that had devastated her childhood was such that Sylvia had to disappear for some months to try to deal with the pain. But she always stayed in touch and I always knew where she was and, mostly, what was happening in her life. The memoir is, like all of Sylvia's books, unflinchingly honest, horrifying in its details. Since publication in 1987, the book has become a classic. It is taught in some university courses and remains enormously helpful for others who have endured childhood abuse.

A magazine profile once described Sylvia as "intrepid." She has travelled down the dark passages of her own past. She also travelled alone into Egypt, India, and South America. She was the first person I knew who had tried ayahuasca—not once but eight times—in the Amazon jungle under the guidance of a shaman. She had gone on this journey of psychic exploration to discover something about the universe and maybe to draw its healing power to herself. As usual, Sylvia abjured all notions of safety. She prefers to fly without a safety net. One Sylvia Fraser book, *The Rope in the Water: A Pilgrimage to India*, tends to find itself on my bedside table and I still dip into it to remind myself that there may be some magic left in our industrialized world.

We meet and talk often and, as with all friendships, there are usually some quite banal things to talk about, things like future dinners or movies we both wish to see or wish we hadn't seen, but I know that under her cheerful good humour, there is a depth of knowledge and understanding of human nature that I can draw on, if I need to. Sometimes, with a close friend, it is easy to forget what attracted you to them in the first place. With Sylvia, that's never been an issue. That's why I remind myself never to take her for granted.

Trying to Heal the World
with Graeme and John and Monte

THE MOST SATISFYING manuscript I read during my early Seal years was Graeme Gibson's *Perpetual Motion*. Determined to include it in Seal's list, I promoted it to M&S.

Graeme and I had some strange conversations about why Jack had not offered to publish Graeme's first book, *Five Legs*. Graeme's theory was Jack's literary tastes did not include innovative writing. My theory, at the time, was that M&S had simply misplaced the manuscript and when it was discovered at the bottom of the slush pile, Jack was too embarrassed to admit it. When I asked Jack about it, he claimed he had not read the manuscript; he could hardly keep track of all submissions.

By the time the book was published by Anansi in 1969, Dennis Lee had spent months working with Graeme to make sure that it was the best it could be. "He forced me to think more clearly about my intentions, about the implications of my work, than I had previously thought possible," recalled Graeme about Dennis's editing.

We used to go to an uninspiring restaurant on St. Clair Avenue, across from Seal's equally uninspiring office, and talk about writing and writers, about the Writers' Union and its aims, about why Graeme had co-founded the Writers' Development Trust, and his determination to broaden its mandate. He had been a close friend of Scott Symons at a time when Scott

needed friends, but Graeme severed their relationship after Scott's poi-
sonous attacks against women writers, particularly Alice Munro, Marian
Engel, and Margaret Atwood, in the 1977 *West Coast Review*. He was a
friend of Matt Cohen's and interested in Matt's travels in Europe and the
direction Matt's new novels would take.

I am not sure what led us into a discussion of Joseph Roth, but I know
he was astonished that I hadn't read *The Radetzky March*, and he gave me
a copy of the book. Roth had been a citizen of the Hapsburg Empire in its
dying days, a journalist, novelist, essayist, with an uncanny prediction of
the future as he surveyed the crumbling empire. Years later, when I met
the last almost-emperor-king, Otto von Hapsburg, in Pocking, a suburb of
Munich, I discovered that he too was a Roth fan.

Perpetual Motion was the story of a man so obsessed with the invention
and building of a perpetual motion machine that he destroys everything
else that could lend his life meaning. The setting is nineteenth-century
Ontario but the scope of the novel is man's single-minded fascination with
machines and industry to the exclusion of nature and humanity. It was an
ambitious work that I have returned to from time to time during the years
since because the book's message and its anti-hero's overweening determination seem like a parable for our times.

Reviews were mixed. A number of the usual reviewers had no idea what
to make of the book. Some gave it a pass, a few attacked it for being dense,
Bob Fulford panned it, but those who liked it made up for the others.
Graeme and I had become friends along the way. He is generous, warm, a
great storyteller. I remember him at our cottage, sitting hunched over in
the bunk room our children shared, singing "Greenland Whale Fisheries"
to help them go to sleep. An odd choice, I thought, but it worked.

When he finished writing his next book, *Gentleman Death*, Graeme's
most moving, saddest, yet most humourous book, he told me he would
not write fiction again. He had now said all that he wished to say about the
human condition, about creativity, the absurdities of aging, the futility of
writing fiction in a world gone crazy, and about mortality. He felt no desire
to say more.

In chapter 10 of *Gentleman Death*, Graeme's protagonist writes an average of two hundred words a day. "But here's the point, in the time it takes me to find my two hundred words over a hundred species of plants and animals become extinct. In case you're interested, that's thirty-six thousand a year . . . It's a sickening thought."

It was Graeme who introduced me to John Livingston, whose *One Cosmic Instant: A Natural History of Human Arrogance* we published at M&S. John explained the title: "one cosmic instant," assuming a twenty-four-hour clock representing the time of the earth's existence, is the approximate time of man. Yet—and that was the point of the book—humanity has wrought such devastation on the earth that we will end by destroying it. Our unbridled greed and hubris have led us to believe that we are the sole owners of our cosmos, above all the other life forms which we domesticate or kill in our rush to propagate our own species. As a result we destroy nature and, eventually, ourselves. I did not need convincing. I had seen the plastic, the oil slicks, the dead fish in the ocean and in Lake Huron.

Later at Key Porter, my next publishing adventure, we published his *Rogue Primate: An Exploration of Human Domestication.* The *Toronto Star*'s reviewer said that "if you buy only one book this decade let it be *Rogue Primate*." It won the Governor General's Award for Non-Fiction.

Graeme, an early supporter of the World Wildlife Fund, also introduced me to Monte Hummel, its executive director. His very modest office was also on St. Clair Avenue. Monte looked like a sixties hippie—long hair, faded jeans, colourful shirt, sandals—and he was utterly committed to conservation of life on earth. He talked very fast, almost breathlessly, of the need to preserve small life-sustaining organisms essential to the ecosystem. But it was the large animals that potential funders of WWF found attractive, which was why I suggested a book about polar bears and other Arctic wildlife. It was the first of many books we published as fundraisers for World Wildlife.

I became a member of the WWF board and supported Monte's vision for more than twenty years. In time, Key Porter would be known worldwide for its books about the environment.

The First Lady

W HEN WE FIRST met in 1980, Margaret Trudeau was stunningly
beautiful, in her mid-twenties, too young to be the mother of three
little children, and much too young to be the wife of Canada's prime minister. Pierre Trudeau, despite all his dashing ways, was thirty years older
and unable to share in her sense of fun, her lightness of being a former
"flower child." That thirty-year age difference was one of the factors in
their publicly failing marriage, but only one. Her resistance to the coddled,
formulaic existence expected of the wife of a prime minister, his highly intellectual approach to problem-solving, her desire to be free of constraints,
her insensitivity to embarrassment, his natural superiority to those he regarded as intellectually less capable (most people) than he was, his frequent
long absences, and his unrelenting work schedule all contributed to their
breakup. Margaret's first memoir, *Beyond Reason* (Grosset & Dunlap), did
not help the situation. Her US promotion tour, with interviews on *Phil
Donahue* and Merv Griffin's talk show, her star treatment—appearing with
actresses Liv Ullman and Hermione Gingold—and all the questions about
her secret lover added to her notoriety.

But here she was in my office with chapters of a new book and there
I was thinking it would be an easy sale. Even Alun Davies, who had been
optimistic that I would settle for maybe one new book a month, had no

doubt that Margaret Trudeau's memoir would be a bestseller. She was front-page news wherever she went. Washington was scandalized when she wore a short dress to a White House state dinner; in Venezuela she sang an impromptu accolade to the country's first lady; in Mexico she gave a passionate speech—uninvited—about women's rights. *People* magazine ran a feature on her "Manhattan escapade," which turned into a plea for freedom. She made the covers of *Look, Time, People,* and *Maclean's* ("The Margaret Factor" and "Margaret and the Rolling Stones").

She was angry at her situation and she felt let down; her sense of having been wronged was reason enough for a second book. Hadn't she been a big part of Pierre's first election campaign? She felt she had "humanized" him. She had made him seem less of the cool intellectual and more like the charming father of cute children, the romantic husband of a beautiful wife. But by the 1979 election, she was no longer at his side.

The manuscript itself was not nearly as salacious as the public expected, but it did mention Margaret cavorting with the Rolling Stones, her appearances at New York's Studio 54, her wild "freedom trips" to jet-set parties in New York and London, and her usually swift returns because she desperately missed her children.

Consequences also revealed her affairs and her addiction to drugs and to the limelight. She was drawn to Hollywood, thrilled with meeting the stars, with giving in to Jack Nicholson's irresistible "sneering charm." She dined with Ryan O'Neal in a Polynesian restaurant in Beverly Hills and thought she had fallen in love, only to become disillusioned with O'Neal's inexhaustible self-regard. She accepted an invitation from a Peruvian race-car driver to visit South America while Pierre was in the thick of an election campaign. Her every move brought out the paparazzi. She had come to share the view, widely held by the media, that her presence would only detract from Pierre's chances of reelection.

In a moving passage, Margaret wrote about wanting to destroy Joyce Wieland's colourful quilt *Reason Over Passion,* hanging on a wall in the prime minister's residence. Its message was a reflection of one of Pierre's sayings, one that had become absolutely hateful to her.

Later we talked about the coincidence of our both having Christmas babies—Justin and Sacha Trudeau were both born on December 25, and both my stepdaughter Jessica and Catherine were born on December 26*—and about her ambition to become a photographer. I thought she was talented, troubled, insecure, and undisciplined, too anxious to stay still, always wanting to be on the move. I liked her courage and her honesty, her refusal to take either herself or her position as wife of the prime minister seriously. Sometimes she left one of her little boys at our house for a few hours while she visited friends in Toronto. He was a charming child with a minor problem around toilet training but he was not a bawler and we got along fine.

After Joe Clark's short-lived occupation of 24 Sussex Drive as prime minister, Pierre handily won the 1980 election and Margaret returned to Ottawa. She took pains to acknowledge Pierre's affectionate bond with their three boys, their shared values of honesty and loyalty, and the way all three boys adapted to the separation.

At the end of *Consequences*, Margaret also became more thoughtful. She wrote of her regrets for having "robbed Pierre of his dignity at various stages of our life together," and she acknowledged her own failings, her need for an audience, her romantic delusions, and her "outbursts of despair." She relished the time she spent with the children, then nine, seven, and five, the "warm cocoon of happiness" she helped build for them.

I had no idea then that she would be diagnosed with bipolar disorder, but in hindsight, all the symptoms were there, I just hadn't recognized them. Once when I visited her in the Ottawa house she shared with her second husband, Fried Kemper, the other Margaret greeted me at the door. She was depressed, almost immobilized, seemingly trapped in a vortex of what she called her "tunnel of darkness." It was not until 1998, when her son Michel was killed in an avalanche in BC, that Margaret was finally diagnosed and could get the help she needed. In her third memoir, *Changing My Mind*, she wrote about facing her demons. It had been, she said when

---

* We usually celebrate their birthdays together and they both hate having birthdays so close to Christmas.

we met in Saanich, BC, during the summer of 2010, an excruciatingly painful book to write but one that had helped her and was going to help others with mental illness.

If the tearfully applauding audience at the Sunshine Coast Festival was any indication, her message has been welcomed, as has her presence at the side of her eldest son, Prime Minister Justin Trudeau.

Michael's World

E ARLY IN 1980 my mother lost her job when the firm where she had worked as a draftsman was sold to a larger firm and the company sought what they called economies of scale. After some weeks of contemplating her future, she decided to take a few years off and volunteered to help look after Catherine and Julia. We agreed that this would give us a chance to travel without anxiety about a babysitter. By and large, we had been lucky with babysitters, but not always, and I was plagued with guilt every time I left on another business trip.

Julian and I signed up for a Butterfield & Robinson cruise up (not down) the Nile with a group of friends, including George and Martha Butterfield, pioneers of luxury travel, Peter Worthington, his wife Yvonne, Bill Graham,* and his wife Cathy. We could afford to join them because Julian had had a good year in law, including a famous obscenity case about Monty Python's *The Life of Brian*, and we could leave the kids in my mother's care.

It was a slow, peaceable journey that took us back some three thousand years to a time when the pharaohs ruled the known world and had the

---

* Bill Graham had been a friend of Julian's since law school. He would become Canada's foreign minister in the Chrétien administration.

power to command armies of slaves to build monumental structures to remind them of death. There is nothing quite like walking through the ruins of an ancient civilization, in some ways not unlike our own, to put your life into perspective. Shelley's "Ozymandias" ("king of kings / look upon my works ye mighty and despair") had helped me when I was struggling with English during my last year of university in Christchurch (earning a meagre living in a stamps shop, attending school at night). I was then still very much a Hungarian refugee, dropped into a foreign land, trying to figure out how to exist. What saved me was reading poems and stories that offered a more universal experience. Now, on this floating hotel, out of my ordinary existence, I was drawn back into the appeal of stories, some of which I had read before, some of which were new, and many not yet written. I knew I wanted to be back in publishing, not the limited Seal kind I had just signed up for, but publishing the way Jack had first taught me—the only way I knew—where you publish authors, not just books, and certainly not "units," as the Bantam boys used to refer to books at sales conferences.

When we returned to Canada, I decided to talk to Michael de Pencier (Julian had known him since the University of Toronto, and Michael and his wife, Honor, were the only friends from Julian's former marriage who attended our wedding) about publishing books, and Michael, a magazine publisher, seemed mildly interested. He confessed that he had once asked Jack how long it would take him to learn the business and Jack had said about ten or fifteen years. Michael assumed that he was joking!

Michael was old Ontario, a philosophy grad, entrepreneur, always on the lookout for new ideas that either could be fun to develop or could make a lot of money, or both. He was slim and sporty (an effortlessly good tennis player, a nimble hockey player, and a competitive golfer), with longish hair, and judging by his choice of clothes, proudly colourblind. Honor used to set out his socks in the evening so he would not leave home wearing different colours.

He had bought *Toronto Life*, then a dull, money-losing magazine, for a dollar and the assumption of its debts. His journalist-broadcaster friend Peter Gzowski anted up the last five thousand dollars and recommended

John Macfarlane,* fresh from *Maclean's* and not yet thirty years old, as editor. Both Peter and John admired Milton Glazer and Clay Felker's brash, stylish *New York Magazine*, and Macfarlane proceeded to remake *Toronto Life* into the kind of lively city magazine that Glazer and Felker would have run in Toronto.

Michael added *Key to Toronto* and a few others: *Keys, Quill and Quire, OWL* and *Chickadee, Fashion Magazine*, and *Canadian Art* (with Maclean Hunter as fifty per cent partner). He would buy a piece of *Canadian Business* and later *Canadian Geographic* (in partnership with the Royal Canadian Geographic Society), *Wedding Bells*, and a bunch of other magazines I have quite forgotten. By the 1980s the company was the largest private magazine publisher in Canada.

Michael's partner in various ventures, including Key and a small book publishing company, Greey de Pencier Books, was Phil Greey, who was also old Ontario, but with real estate holdings including the downtown buildings now inhabited by their various enterprises. Phil and Michael had initially set up in a tiny rented office on University Avenue, buying, fixing, and selling trade magazines, such as a monthly dog lovers' magazine, a curling magazine, and *The Apartment Owner*. Now, they were running a highly successful enterprise.

Phil took little interest in the day-to-day. He was busy acquiring and refurbishing old buildings on Front Street, The Esplanade, and Church Street. He was an unusual landlord, easy about collecting rent and always ready for a friendly chat. What he may have lacked in attention to detail, such as cleanliness of his rental spaces, he made up for in good humour and a casual attitude to landlording. His tenants trusted him and would not have left even if something cheaper were offered.

Bantam's office on St. Clair Avenue was arid and modern, with no sense

---

* John Macfarlane and I had first met at M&S when he and legendary athlete Bruce Kidd were proposing to write a book about "the death of hockey." It was published by New Press with, as John told me, "disastrous results," since Canadian hockey proved, in 1972, to be far from dead.

of excitement about books, just a few guys running the Canadian operation, often unexpected visits from Alun Davies, and salesmen dropping in
to pick up samples. The Seal office was one narrow, dreary white-painted
room. Michael's Front Street offices were full of creative people, lots of
talk, books everywhere, magazine covers on the walls, big windows, sunshine, and bars and restaurants on the streets below. Visiting those offices
was stimulating. There was always someone to talk to, and Michael usually
had some project on the go he wanted to discuss.

Coincidentally, the Front Street entrance to Key was not far from the
Royal York Hotel, where I had started my Canadian life. The lonely Newfoundland lad who had asked me for bus fare home was still in the small
triangular park I would pass on my way to the subway. But now I felt completely at home. The St. Lawrence Market's fresh food stalls were a block
away, as was the bar Coasters,* where Marjorie Harris and I would sit at a
small table near the windows, drink wine, and make lists of book ideas. If
I was going to start building a publishing company, I was going to need
some books.

The challenge was enormous. There would be no proven authors to
submit new manuscripts, no backlist that could generate income while I
figured out how to make a name for myself as a book publisher. On the
other hand, there would be no warehouse full of unsold books. No crip-
pling debt. It would be a fresh start, and Canada was bursting with talented
writers looking for a new home.

That year Jack, always inventive and desperate for new ways to raise
money, came up with an idea for getting rid of his cash-absorbing ware-
housed books: he was going to bypass the booksellers and have a giant
warehouse sale. The booksellers hated it, but many of them understood.

I volunteered for the checkout counter.

---

* Coasters was also Peter Taylor's and John Neale's usual watering hole. Peter, after
leaving M&S, had gone to work for the Toronto Star Syndicate, and John had gone on
to work for Doubleday. Neither of them ever lost his boyish charm.

Finding the Key

O N DAYS WHEN not much was happening at Seal, I began to hang around in Michael's downtown offices, using a spare desk he had offered. My window faced the famed Gooderham (also known as the Flatiron) building, a historic site with an extraordinary mural by Derek Michael Besant on its wide west end. There is a stunning photograph of the mural in André Kertész's book* that we produced a couple of years later.

The offices were a warren of loosely connected spaces stretching a block south to The Esplanade and, as I traversed them I discovered a wealth of creative enterprises and extraordinary talent. *Toronto Life* was on the second floor, at the Front Street side. By the time I started to spend more time

---

* *André Kertész: A Lifetime of Perception* was produced in 1982 to coincide with the opening of an exhibition of his photographs. André, who was another Hungarian expat and a famous artist, would phone me frequently to complain about his life, his dealers, and his sense that time was passing him by, that his kind of photography was no longer valued.

there than at Seal, John Macfarlane* had been succeeded by Don Obe as editor. Don had been at *Maclean's*, *The Canadian* (a weekend supplement launched by the *Toronto Star* and Southam Press in 1965), the *Vancouver Sun*, and *The Toronto Telegram*. He was a soft-spoken, small man with a rounded back and a large sense of humour, a character right out of Damon Runyon or W. P. Kinsella. He had the most unruly eyebrows of anyone I knew, and that includes Peter C. Newman. His moustache was an old-fashioned "tell" that often betrayed his response to a question before he spoke. He was catcher on the *Toronto Life* "boys' baseball" team, and while he couldn't throw worth a damn, he excelled at scowling into submission any opponent trying to steal a base. Of course he smoked too much and may have drunk too much, but he loved talking about writing and writers and knew how to make an interesting magazine. I envied the students he taught at Ryerson's journalism classes.

Marq de Villiers, a former reporter, feature writer, and Moscow correspondent for *The Toronto Telegram*, was executive editor. He was an Afrikaner with a virulent dislike for the apartheid policies of his former country. We shared an interest in the Soviet Union and its Gulag prison system.

Years later I would persuade Marq to write a book for Key Porter called *Into Africa: A Journey through the Ancient Empires*. It required a lot of travel—on the cheap, because we didn't have much money. Sheila Hirtle, his wife and a fellow journalist, did the research for nothing. It's a brilliant book that sheds light on little-known pieces of history, the vanished empires of the African continent, their rulers who traded with the Egyptians and the Romans, and the few remnants of their times. Murray Frum, a collector of African art, thought it the best book on the subject.

---

* In 1988 John Macfarlane partnered with Jan Walter and Gary Ross to form the publisher Macfarlane, Walter & Ross (Stevie Cameron's *On the Take* was a notable release). He continued to have a storied career in magazines and journalism, including a second stint at *Toronto Life* from 1992 to 2007, and as editor and co-publisher of *The Walrus* 2008–2014.

About halfway between Front Street and The Esplanade, after several narrow corridors and stairs, was CB Media, publisher of *Canadian Business* magazine. It was a joint venture of its editor Sandy Ross, Michael de Pencier, and politician-diplomat-historian Roy MacLaren.* Unlike other business magazines, Sandy's *Canadian Business* was entertaining as well as informative. An experienced journalist—the *Vancouver Sun*, *Maclean's*, CBC's *This Hour Has Seven Days*, the *Toronto Star*—with a keen sense of humour and a Vancouverite's healthy disrespect for old Bay Street money, Sandy loved entrepreneurs, enjoyed their gossip, and followed their successes and failures, some of which he recorded in his book *The Risk Takers.*[†]

Sandy's windowless office featured piles of manuscripts, most of them on the floor, and a vintage pinball machine. He was boyish, in a 1960s sort of way, with old-fashioned round glasses obscured by floppy dark hair, always a lit cigarette, ash on his jacket, and a perpetually messy desk. His conversation flitted from subject to subject, idea to idea, with only a tenuous connection among them. He was constantly in motion, fingers tapping, eyes shifting. He bit his nails, wrote lists of items to remember, and left trails of his discarded notes wherever he went. He played drums in a jazz band and was fired, reluctantly, by his bandmates for speeding ahead of the music. A number of talented young women were crazy in love with him. We may have become friends in part because I wasn't.

About a year later, Peggy (Margaret) Wente, later columnist with *The*

---

* Roy had been a Liberal member of Parliament and spent twelve years in the Canadian foreign service with postings in Saigon, Prague, and at the United Nations. In 1978 he published *Canadians on the Nile, 1882–1898*.

† Sandy—like Pierre Berton, Peter Worthington, Earle Birney, Helen Hutchinson, John Turner, Joe Schlesinger, and Allan Fotheringham—had worked for the University of British Columbia's *The Ubyssey*. Joe Schlesinger would go on to a long career in television and journalism. John Turner was finance minister in Pierre Trudeau's cabinet and, briefly, prime minister of Canada. Helen Hutchinson became anchor of *W5* and *Canada AM*. Publishing may not be a profitable business, but where else can you spend time with such extraordinary people?

Globe and Mail, took over the editor's chair. Hired by Sandy, she was the first woman editor of a business magazine in Canada, and maybe in the entire English-speaking world. Sandy moved to Calgary to launch *Energy*, an offshoot of *Canadian Business*, which seemed to have run into Albertan resistance. Perhaps the fact that it came out of Toronto was a problem, though Sandy didn't think so. He was bristling with ideas and usually in exceptionally good cheer during our long lunches on The Esplanade. He barely touched his food as he gesticulated his way into new strategies that could, maybe, work. Sadly, in the end he had to recommend they suspend publication of *Energy*.

Key's art director and all-around guru was Ken Rodmell. He had trained under Toronto's legendary graphic designer Allan Fleming, perhaps best known then for creating the CN logo and designing *Canada: Year of the Land*, the bestselling Centennial book.[*] Ken had been art director at *The Canadian* when Harry Bruce[†]—one of the best writers in Canada—was editor. Balding and sturdy, Ken walked about eight kilometres to work every day from Moore Park, wearing his trademark running shoes, blue jeans, and all-weather-and-occasions jacket. He, too, played in a jazz band and on the "boys' baseball" team. Ken was viewed as preternaturally wise. Sometimes you had to wait for him to tell you what he thought of a particular idea, but it was worth the wait. He was generally right.

Michael Rea was the accountant or CFO—Key was not much on titles. Already an environmentalist (later he became COO of the Nature Conservancy), Rea tended to be conservative about new ways to spend money, and he too was usually right.

---

[*] Fleming was a genius at typography, advertising, and magazine design (he had been art director at *Maclean's*), and creative director at the University of Toronto Press. He designed stamps and logos (for the Ontario Science Centre, for example) and posters. It would have been difficult to walk down a major street in Toronto in the late sixties without seeing some of his handiwork.

[†] Harry's *Down Home: Notes of a Maritime Son* is one of Key Porter's best books, and the book Jonathan Webb is proudest to have edited for us.

Annabel Slaight ran Greey de Pencier Books, *Architecture Canada*, and a few other small magazines, but she was looking for something she could really get excited about. That turned out to be children's magazines. She and Mary Anne Brinckman, an old friend of Michael's, took over the *Young Naturalist*, a children's magazine owned by the Young Naturalist Foundation, and turned it into *OWL*, a colourful, fun magazine for kids aged eight to twelve.

Mary Anne, who was beautiful in a languid, French sort of way, and Annabel, who was intense and very persuasive, headed across the country to raise money and build circulation. The trip worked beyond our expectations. I know, because for many years I was on their board. Circulation grew, grandparents subscribed, and *OWL* spun off *Chickadee* for the younger kids, books, videos, French language and Italian editions, and a television series on TVO. I have a few stills from an early show with my daughter Catherine investigating giant bubbles with Dr. Zed.

Annabel, Mary Anne, and I spent long evenings that stretched into early mornings, sitting on the floor of the Brinckmans' Rosedale home, drinking wine and dreaming up new ways of presenting information to kids and of attracting investors to a Canadian nature magazine. In 1985 Phyllis Yaffe, a former executive director of the Association of Canadian Publishers, took over as the operating boss of what had become OWL Communications.*

There were so many bright young people in those shabby, interconnected offices, so much talk about opportunities, a general sense that something exciting might be just around the corner, why not meet it halfway. Michael, supposedly at the hub of all that activity, had a small office in what seemed like a passageway to the lavatories.

He had the strange notion that if you invite bright people to inhabit

---

* Later she moved on to Alliance Communications, where we met again while I was on the Alliance board. She led the team to win the television licences for Showcase and History Television. When Atlantis bought control of Alliance, she was appointed CEO of Alliance Atlantis and oversaw the company's worldwide operations. As I write this, Phyllis has assumed the role of Canada's consul general in New York.

your space, they will eventually produce bright ideas, a few of which may even be good for business.

It was obvious that Key had the creative energy, the imagination, and the potential to launch a terrific book company.

FOR THE FIRST few months at Key, I shared an office with Peter Gzowski. Neither of us was paid. There was a shoulder-high divider between his area and mine and Peter delighted in pretending it was a French pissoir, with himself peering over the top with the faraway look of a man taking a leak. He was generally good-humoured, with occasional lapses into general gloom and flagrant self-pity.

Peter was a three-pack-a-day smoker with brown-framed, drooping glasses, short beard, floppy hair, and a pock-marked, sallow complexion. He was an atrociously bad dresser. He wore sweaters with holes and shirts that popped out of his belts. There was not a word of exaggeration in the very funny story he wrote about his clothes habits for *Canadian Living*.

He regretted his decision to host *90 Minutes Live*. He thought he should have known that, unlike Barbara Frum and Adrienne Clarkson, he was not cut out for television. He had seemed exactly how he had felt on camera: ill at ease and almost embarrassed. It was the only complete failure on an ever-steeper upward climb: the youngest managing editor of *Maclean's*, editor of the *Star Weekly*, a competitive jock, a quick, perceptive writer with a flare for minute observation, a CBC star.

When M&S commissioned Peter to write the story of two young people who survived a plane crash only to face horrifying pain, hunger, and the prospect of cannibalism, I was surprised he accepted. It was not the kind of story I imagined he would like to write, but I was wrong about that. He was, as he saw it, "between gigs" and seemed to enjoy writing as a reporter, without expressing opinions of his own. *The Sacrament* was published in 1980.

Most of the time our shared office resembled a day in the London fog, which I didn't mind though I began to develop watery eyes and occasionally had to go outside for a breath of air. I had been a one-pack-a-day person since I left the convent but cut the habit after Julia was born, and now did not seem like a good time to start again.

Peter desperately wanted to be back at the CBC and I kept reassuring him that they would call, but each day that they did not he lost more confidence. Meanwhile he kept writing for *Canadian Living*. He won a National Magazine Award for his 1981 profile of Wayne Gretzky and started to write *The Game of Our Lives*, about his own love of hockey and about Wayne Gretzky and the Edmonton Oilers.

A couple of times Peter took me to Woodbine. He loved the races and knew something about a few of the horses and trainers. He won and lost a few times, but betting wasn't why he went. It was at Woodbine where he first met Gillian Howard, the woman he finally settled down with for the rest of his life. She was warm, affectionate, funny, and thoughtful, a perfect partner for Peter.

Now and then we would go down to one of the restaurants or bars along The Esplanade or on lower Church Street and he would test book ideas on me, such as a biography of his great-great-grandfather Sir Casimir Gzowski, a rather romantic figure who was born into Polish nobility and emigrated to Canada after the Russian invasion of Poland. An engineer, soldier, businessman, and statesman, he had overseen the building of our roads, bridges, and railway lines during the nineteenth century. Peter was proud of the Gzowski name. He explained that for a few years during his childhood he had lost it when his mother had married a man called Brown who had insisted that Peter should take his name. Fortunately, he changed his name back to Gzowski before he graduated from university.

Peter was as take-no-prisoners competitive on the golf course as he had been when angling for jobs he wanted. His home course was at The Briars on Jackson Point, Ontario, but he played many of the courses in Canada and a few elsewhere. The PGI, or Peter Gzowski Annual Invitational Golf Tournament has now raised, I am told, about fourteen million dollars for literacy.

Of course the CBC did finally call and Peter did go back to radio in 1982, to host *Morningside*. Though 1982 was the year we launched Key Porter Books, I didn't offer a book contract to Peter (much as I would have liked to publish his memoir and a book about his grandfather), because Jack and I had agreed that I would not poach M&S authors. Peter Gzowski was an M&S author.

By 1987 *Morningside* had more than a million listeners. Peter's gravelly voice, his enthusiasms, his delight when discussing someone's prize pumpkin or a new novel with Mordecai Richler have become legendary. Then there were the political pundit segments, the lively letters to the show (such as for the "duke and the fork" question, when hundreds of people chimed in*), the memorable meals, the light verse, the "torrent" (Peter called it) of short stories, and of course the personal reports from across the country.

For the next fifteen years, an interview on *Morningside* meant a noticeable jump in book sales. I remember driving our first authors to the CBC for their chance to talk with Peter on the air. His producer invited me on his show when my second novel, *Mortal Sins* (yes, I would become a writer as well), was published. He was confident and charming, shifting with surprising ease from topic to topic in a broad-ranging interview, but he made sure that the title of my novel was mentioned every few minutes.

He produced several *Morningside Papers* spinoffs, won a ton of awards and appointments, and had he lived long enough, he might even have won the competition he thought he had with Bob Fulford for the most honorary degrees. We miss him.

---

* Who said, "Keep your fork, Duke, there's pie," and where was it said?

Farewell to the Seventies

M Y CHANCE TO be a bright young person at Key came initially with a trip to Texas to see whether the owners of the *Where* magazine chain might be interested in a merger or, better still, a buyout. We already had a few *Key to* magazines in Canada, so why not expand? The Texans were interested, or at least happily surprised, but it took them a very long time to come to terms. That first meeting—they were stunned to meet a woman representing a potential business partner—was followed by another when Michael de Pencier and I went to Dallas together. This time they took us more seriously. By then Key had bought their fifteen-magazine chain and Michael was exploring a new venture of television in hotel rooms with them. Michael was the perfect acquisitor: patient, friendly, laid-back, willing to negotiate, making deals on a handshake. Key became the chief purveyor of content for *Where*s in most major cities in North America, a thick, flashy *Where* in London, one in Paris, and one in New York.

Another time, Michael asked me to meet with a potential investor in *Where Budapest*, a fellow Hungarian who lived in a very posh part of London. Although I took his aged dachshund for a geriatric pee stroll, he was not yet willing to invest in a Budapest franchise. Eventually, though, he did. A few years later, Michael would be running a forty-two-city (six were franchised) magazine chain.

But long before then, we had set up Quintus Press to produce a limited-edition book on the work of artist Christopher Pratt. The project had been suggested by Christopher's dealer, Mira Godard. We approached art expert David Silcox to write an appreciation of Pratt's work.* Ken Rodmell designed a magnificent book with soft and inviting paper, lovingly reproduced paintings, a trimmed canvas slipcase, and a handmade, signed, and numbered Pratt silkscreen print in each copy. Three hundred copies, priced at $2,100 each, sold out so quickly that Michael wondered why anyone would be discouraged by the book business.

Marjorie Harris and I produced a few door-stoppers for other publishers, the best of which is a book we dreamt up in Georgian Bay, *Farewell to the 70s: A Canadian Salute to a Confusing Decade.* It's an enjoyable romp in the company of some of that era's memorably entertaining characters and writers. Sandra Gwyn, Ottawa insider, wrote about Pierre Elliott Trudeau: "Our Style Was the Man Himself." Peter C. Newman wrote that our new history began in the seventies. Bob Fulford contributed "Seventies-Speak" ("impact" as a verb, "the bottom line," "getting it on," and other gems I hope will vanish in time). Environmentalist, bike-riding Toronto mayor John Sewell wrote about the city. Filmmaker Fil Fraser, who was then married to my friend Ruth (now Bertelsen), wrote about the "best years" of Western Canada. Actor-director Donald Shebib and Bob Fulford's movie critic pseudonym, Marshall Delaney, wrote about Canadian feature films. The *Toronto Sun*'s Joan Sutton wrote about love; comedian, actor, director Don Harron about preoccupations; and psychiatrist Dr. Ned Shorter about sex in the seventies. John Eaton (yes, Eaton's was still alive then) wrote about retail. Parliamentarian Judy LaMarsh wrote about women in the news, and Doris Anderson wrote about women in society.

As befits a door-stopper, the book was full of photos and cartoons of

---

* Silcox, the leading authority on Harold Town's work and on the life and work of David Milne, is the author of *Painting Place: The Life and Work of David B. Milne* and the sumptuous art book *David Milne: An Introduction to His Life and Art.* For twelve years he was president of Sotheby's Canada.

the era. We featured Paul Henderson's winning goal from the 1972 Canada-Russia series, Alberta Premier Peter Lougheed at the Calgary Stampede, Bob Stanfield dropping the ball, Joe Clark celebrating his 1979 victory, René Lévesque chain-smoking, Pierre Trudeau at the height of Trudeaumania and at his storybook wedding to Margaret.

On the back flap there are glamorous photos of Marjorie with curls and me wearing Gloria Steinem glasses. *Farewell* was published in 1979, and it's still fun to read—even if you didn't live through the seventies. Canadians were a lot more hopeful and effervescent then, or perhaps that was just how Marjorie and I saw them and ourselves.

BY THE END of my first decade in Canada, I felt I belonged here. I no longer saw myself as an immigrant, and my frequent visits to Bantam had cured me of any notion that it would be fun to work in New York. It had been a heady time to be in Canadian publishing. Our writers and our poets had become well-known; some were even celebrities. And there were great new voices. Michael Ondaatje, for example, had published six poetry collections before the end of the decade, and Alistair MacLeod's first book of poetic, inspired stories, *The Lost Salt Gift of Blood*, was published by M&S in 1976. Lorna Crozier's first three poetry collections appeared before the end of the decade, as did six of Pier Giorgio Di Cicco's. Many of Al Purdy's young poets had come into their own.

The International Festival of Authors opened its doors in 1974. It quickly became the place to hear and meet writers. Robertson Davies, Margaret Laurence, Hugh MacLennan, Al Purdy, and Farley Mowat all read there during the festival's first years. Greg Gatenby, the amiable M&S slush-pile king, became its first, usually charming but sometimes cantankerous, artistic director, a commanding figure who could bring in authors from anywhere in the world.

Publishing houses sprang up like weeds across the country. Stan Bevington's Coach House Press, started in Toronto in 1965, was printing beautiful books. Douglas & McIntyre in Vancouver published its first title in 1971. Thistledown Press was born in Saskatchewan in 1975. The prestigious Porcupine's Quill published its first title in 1975. Breakwater Books opened its doors in St. John's, Newfoundland, in 1973. The House of Anansi, that brave experiment by two editors, and New Press, once almost a protest movement, were becoming the establishment.* Canadian books had grown to occupy more than a quarter of retail space in bookstores. At the Frankfurt Book Fair, publishers from all over the world were coming to us to ask what new Canadian writers had been discovered. They were eager to buy "options," to purchase without even reading the manuscripts. Ten years earlier, we had never heard of options.

Literary agents too were no longer a rarity. In the early seventies, agenting in Canada was a genteel kind of business, usually practiced by softspoken, highly intelligent women. New Yorker Nancy Colbert, later joined by her husband and fellow New Yorker, television producer Stan Colbert, set up her agency in 1976. By the end of the decade, there were a few more agents. Beverley Slopen, an M&S graduate, almost drifted into agenting (she was helping Morley Torgov with his manuscript) while still writing for *Time* magazine and working for the Book of the Month Club. By 2017 she represented more than a hundred writers. Lucinda Vardey and Denise Bukowski started in the early 1980s. Jan Whitford, whose authors included Booker Prize–winner Yann Martel and Giller winners Bonnie Burnard and M. G. Vassanji, joined Vardey at the end of the eighties. Dean Cooke, a Seal survivor, followed in 1992. Bruce Westwood, who by 2017 ruled over a bevy of other agents representing more than four hundred writers, started in 1995. Anne McDermid founded the McDermid agency in 1996.

The seventies were a great time for the theatre too. There were new plays by Judith Thomson, Erika Ritter (Key Porter would later publish her *The Hidden Life of Humans*), Michel Tremblay, and David Fennario (his *Balconville* debuted at the Centaur in 1979). John MacLachlan Gray and Eric Peterson's *Billy Bishop Goes to War* filled theatres across the country, as did Linda Griffiths's *Maggie and Pierre*. Bill Glassco opened the Tarragon

---

* For a more complete list see Roy MacSkimming's *The Perilous Trade: Publishing Canada's Writers* (McClelland & Stewart, 2003).

Theatre in 1971 to feature Canadian plays. I was thrilled to be invited to join the board.

On one of my many forays to the American Booksellers' Association's annual fair, Marc Jaffe took me over to the Random House booth and presented me to its owner, Si Newhouse. We shook hands and stood around, neither of us quite sure what we were supposed to be talking about, until Marc mentioned that I was a fine publisher in Canada but would do even better in New York. Newhouse seemed unimpressed, but a few days later I had a phone call asking me what my conditions would be for moving to New York.

I could not think of any.

By the end of the seventies I was not only a Canadian nationalist but the married mother of two and stepmother of another two children.

I was here to stay.

Taking a Leap in the Dark

I RESIGNED FROM the M&S Board in July 1982. With his customary aplomb, Jack wished me luck: "There is little left to add except to say that I love you dearly but that is hardly news." We agreed that when I started a publishing company, I would not take any M&S authors unless they had already left his firm and that I would stay out of fiction publishing, at least for a few years. He had decided to appoint his long-time colleague Linda McKnight president and to devote his own time to solving M&S's financial problems.

Key Porter Books, a partnership between Michael de Pencier and me, was launched in the fall of that year with what became a number one best-seller: *Malice in Blunderland: or How the Grits Stole Christmas*, by veteran columnist Allan Fotheringham. Allan was already a friend. We had met shortly after I wrote him a note suggesting that, as with most good journalists, there was "a book in him." He was so surprised by that suggestion that he came to Toronto and allowed me to buy him lunch at the Inn on the Park's Café de l'Auberge, more stately than the Bistro, where I usually ate with M&S authors, but I wanted to make the occasion formal enough to impress. This was in 1977, when I was on my way out of M&S. Allan, who had expected a stern woman of what they used to call a "certain age," as befits an august publishing firm's editor-in-chief, wondered whether I was an assistant sent along to excuse a busy boss lady.

Because he had such a huge presence in the media, I had expected a much larger man. I assumed he would be cut from the Pierre Berton cloth. Several publications featured his photos above his columns, but they were mere mug shots: a round, pugnacious face, brownish hair, no neck, eyes staring defiantly at the observer. He was the "emperor" of the back page of *Maclean's* and national columnist for the Southam chain of newspapers, known for his irreverent wit, his disregard for conventional wisdom, hatred of hypocrisy, and caustic views on politicians of all parties. He was one of the Parliamentary Press Gallery boys (the "boys" included one gal, the courageous westerner Marjorie Nichols, who was, at age twenty-three, the first woman in the Ottawa Press Gallery).

He talked about his birthplace, Hearn, Saskatchewan (one of his usual lines: "People from Hearn are called Hernias"; and another: "It's a village so small we all had to take turns being the village idiot"), and about *The Ubyssey*, the UBC student paper that produced so many professional writers. He said he lived mostly in Vancouver, had an intense dislike of Toronto, and abhorred Ottawa, where he also had an apartment: "the city that fun forgot" or "ennui on the Rideau" as he billed our capital city.

Peter Newman, he claimed, had "invented" him when he hired Allan to write a national column for *Maclean's* from Vancouver. It was a shock for the rest of *Maclean's* staffers to learn that he was going to cover national politics from BC. It was even more of a shock that Fotheringham became the most-read columnist in the magazine.

Allan's initial surprise at my youth was followed by his shock at discovering that I was very pregnant and needed a bit of help from the waiters to extricate myself from the armchair.

Because he was busy covering news stories and flying around on the "People's Republic Airline" (Air Canada), he didn't get around to writing a book until early 1982, when Key Porter began. Allan claimed afterward that he barely glanced at the contract and had no idea what Key Porter was, though he did know that I was his publisher because I locked him up in Jack Batten's house for the four weeks (my deadline) it took him to write the book. Jack had gone on vacation while he and Marjorie Harris were sorting out their short-lived marital differences, so the house was available to rent.

It was a great way to isolate Allan from the temptations of Toronto. By the time Jack and Marjorie patched things up, the manuscript was finished.

Most days I took him nourishment and copies of his past columns I thought he'd find inspiring. Some of the columns, slightly altered, found their way into the book, but none of his readers minded. Allan was a master of the short, perfect description, the witty put-down, an inventor of words and phrases that became part of the language used by other journalists and fans. Such as "The thread that unites the country is the distaste for the Natural Governing Party, alias the Liberals." Or this description of Premier Brian Peckford: "shirty, prickly, with eyes that dart like dark cherries plugged into an electric guitar." Or "René Lévesque himself, the world's greatest advertisement for lung cancer, a tiny man in a grubby raincoat with a paster-downer hairstyle" Or: "Montreal is the only Canadian city with 4 a.m. traffic jams." Or his affectionate description of British Columbia as "Lotusland," even while he maintained a home there and people stopped him in the street to greet their hometown hero.* Walking into the Hotel Vancouver, he was hailed by the doorman with "Good afternoon, Dr. Foth" and some witty bit from one of his columns.

We had our first sales conference at home in our dining room. Tom Best, who was a sales rep with book distributors Stanton MacDougall at the time, remembered our two dachshunds barking through much of the presentation.

Malice in Blunderland began with "Someone, God knows, has to save the country" and ended with the judgment that Pierre Trudeau was, after all, "a dilettante."

It was an instant bestseller. Allan toured from coast to coast, signing books, haranguing interviewers, making his fans laugh and ask for more. It was hardly surprising that there were six more books and that every one of them followed the first book to the bestseller lists. He was feared and

---

* In its 2011 congratulations to the City of Vancouver on its 125th birthday, *The Globe and Mail* listed the ten most influential people in its life. The list included both entrepreneur Jimmy Pattison and Allan Fotheringham.

loved in about equal measure. I remember eating lunch with him in Ottawa's Chateau Laurier and watching in amazement as senior politicians, even those he had maligned in his columns, marched up to his table to engage him in discussion about the day's events in the House of Commons. Since he was fond of elucidating puzzling political situations for his readers, Allan too began to refer to himself as "Dr. Foth." Prime Minister Jean Chrétien, famously, would call him "Mr. Fuckingham."

Meanwhile he replaced panellist Gordon Sinclair on *Front Page Challenge*, adding one more occupation to his list of financially rewarding pursuits. He was, then and for many years to come, Canada's highest-earning columnist. He insisted on mentioning this fact at every opportunity where journalists gathered, thus ensuring their everlasting envy. But even among them, he had his admirers.

IT WAS IN the Hotel Vancouver's bar that Allan introduced me to Jack Webster, "the Oatmeal Savage," a tough-talking, Glasgow-bred radio and television talk-show host such as the country had never seen. He had been a major in the British army and would talk to anyone, no matter how "high and mighty." He didn't care about etiquette, which had stood him in good stead in 1963 when he negotiated with the RCMP and guards on behalf of prisoners in the notorious New Westminster federal pen. He had managed to procure the release of the hostages and gain promises of more humane treatment for the inmates.

Webster didn't engage in pleasantries, even with Shirley MacLaine (though she claimed he was cuddly), or Prime Ministers Jean Chrétien and Pierre Trudeau. But as I got to know him, I realized he did have an emotional side. He was devastated by a decision he had made years ago when he had allowed doctors to perform what he thought was a minor brain surgery on his depressed wife. Instead of becoming cheerful, she became an invalid for the rest of her life. Her depression, he now realized, was the result of the loss of their first child, conceived before they married and given up for adoption, as had been the custom in 1940s Britain. Now Webster was obsessed with wanting to find that daughter.

When we went to his hideaway on Saltspring Island, he played bullfrog to my kids' butterflies in the swimming pool (you had to be there!) and later serenaded them with a wild assortment of songs. He accompanied himself on his small self-playing piano programmed with his songs. The one I still remember is his broad rendition of "Oh but it's hard to be humble when you're perfect in every way . . ."

In the end, he did find his "love child" and they managed to build a relationship before Webster died.

ONCE CATHERINE AND I drove to Chilliwack, where Foth had attended secondary school, for the annual harvest party, and Allan taught my daughter how to milk a cow, something neither of us imagined he had ever done. We met his mother, who painted lovely flower pictures, and his stepfather, who was a dedicated gardener. Like Webster, Foth had his soft side.

MALICE IN BLUNDERLAND put Key Porter on the publishing map. It was irreverent, perceptive, politically astute, and prepared the way for a whole slew of books on Canadian politics and politicians, most of which shot straight up the bestseller lists. They attracted national publicity and several letters from major law firms.

Allan Fotheringham was followed by journalist and troublemaker Claire Hoy; Val Sears, who gave us *Hello Sweetheart, Get Me Rewrite*; Red Tory and political insider Eddie Goodman with *Life of the Party*; political pundit Charlie Lynch; Maude Barlow on how our politicians had given away the country; and Donald Ripley on the down-and-dirty game of politics Down East.*

In Vines, a dark wine bar on Wellington Street, we persuaded journalist Stevie Cameron to write *Ottawa Inside Out*, the backrooms-and-bedrooms

---

* *Bagman* was published in 1993 after arduous and very lengthy discussions with Julian about libel.

story of what really went on in political Ottawa under the Mulroneys. There was, indeed, a large, curious audience for books about politics in Canada. That ever-elusive book buyer "the general public" was interested in its country and the issues and events that influenced its daily life.

In 1982 the media saw us as the scrappy new kids on the block, and that was the year our scrappy lawyer, Julian, made the Eaton Centre remove the festive red ribbons from Michael Snow's *Canada Geese*, an art installation in the centre's great hall, on the grounds that Snow's rights had been infringed. Julian had also been retained by businessman Norris Walker to sue CTV for libel over an eighteen-minute item on *W5* accusing Walker Brothers of being dangerous polluters. Julian relishes jury trials. I attended his forty-five-minute address to the jury, a spectacular performance, Julian pleading, shouting, ending with "Won't you . . ." his voice quivering, "Won't you," descending into tears, "Won't you let Norris Walker die with his name cleared of this infamy?"

The jury awarded Norris Walker the largest damages in Canadian legal history at the time. Jack Batten wrote about the case eloquently in his bestseller *Judges.**

We had a lot to celebrate at our annual New Year's dinner with the Frums. Catherine had just turned ten and she was starting to make new friends at school. (She had been bullied the previous year, an experience she later wrote about as columnist in the *Toronto Star*.) Julia had entered kindergarten without anxiety, insisting that I let her walk to Deer Park School with her friends. *The Journal*, the CBC's new evening news program, was launched in 1982, eight years after Barbara's leukemia diagnosis, and she was as brilliant on television as she had been on radio. After the first season, she became the program's sole host. She loved the work. The stress and late nights didn't bother her. Co-workers thought of her as a sort of den mother with time for everyone who needed time, small, thoughtful gifts for special occasions, sandwiches if the day went too long. Her dog,

---

* The decision was appealed and a new trial was ordered because the Court of Appeal determined the damages were too large.

Diva, who accompanied her to work, became everyone's pet, even those who otherwise loathed dogs.

When their daughter Linda was graduating from McGill, Barbara and Murray took us to dinner at Johnny Arena's upscale eatery, Winston's, to discuss ideas for her career prospects. Linda, Barbara was convinced, would be a writer. She had been editor and writer at the *McGill News Magazine*. Barbara knew her daughter had the talent, the tenacity, the opinions, the aptitude for research required (though I doubt she imagined Linda would be a senator one day). I suggested a book about Canadian universities from the students' point of view. Barbara loved it but insisted I not tell Linda how the idea came about. She didn't want her to know that her mother was concerned about her future.

When Linda graduated, I commissioned her to research and write what became *Linda Frum's Guide to Canadian Universities*, another of Key Porter's early successes.

Inviting the World to Love Canada

U NLIKE JACK, I enjoyed going to Frankfurt's giant annual book market for publishers. It is the size of several football fields laid side by
side and layered one over another in several halls. It's noisy, smells of spicy
sausage, sauerkraut, wet socks (it usually rains during the fair), sweat, anxiety, and fear. Each year there are the "big books" that everyone talks about
and the quiet future bestsellers that no one mentions. Back in the eighties
and nineties, and even in the mid-seventies, every publishing house worth
mentioning and every literary agent worthy of the designation would be at
the fair, displaying wares and ready to make deals.* We all arrived hopeful
and some of us scurried home carrying the burden of failure. Able to speak
five languages reasonably well, I enjoyed the company of publishers from
other countries, many of whom became lifelong friends.

Key Porter's first employee, Lorraine Durham, came with me to help
sell our book ideas. She had great instincts for what would make saleable
books, she had the necessary editorial skills, was well organized—I had

---

* In 1997 I wrote a mystery set at the Frankfurt Book Fair. *The Bookfair Murders* was
that year one of "the books of the fair." It was later made into a very forgettable TV
movie.

always lacked a talent for tidiness—and, as Julian used to say, "she could charm the birds out of the trees." I had found Lorraine at Key. She was about twenty-five years old, six feet tall, with blond hair, the figure of a fashion model, and a smile that could melt the hearts of even the toughest German and Japanese book buyers. The Australians nicknamed her "Petal" for her instant blush when confronted by Aussie humour.

ONE OF MY Frankfurt friends, Jürgen Braunschweiger of the regrettably named Reich Verlag, invited me to join a loosely knit organization called Motovun, named after a small medieval town on top of a conical hill on Yugoslavia's Istrian Peninsula. At least, the last time I saw it, there was still a Yugoslavia for it to belong to.

We were all encouraged to bring our plans for illustrated books, our husbands, wives, and children. Catherine and Julia came a couple of times, and Julian once. Bato Tomašević, the elegant Motovun president during the years I attended, was born in Montenegro but viewed himself as resolutely Yugoslav and tried to bring together publishers from both sides of the Iron Curtain at a time when the Cold War was still frigid and the two sides rarely met.* Bato was president of Revija, a Belgrade publishing house.

There were also publishers from Denmark, China, Bulgaria, West Germany, Italy, Yugoslavia of course, Finland, France, Norway, Sweden, Poland, the UK, the United States, and one Canadian, me. Some of the original members, including Jürgen, had bought and renovated houses in the village. One of the annual meetings was held on a ship sailing from Dubrovnik to Venice. Both Catherine and my mother—she was complimented by all on her startling green eyes—came that time.

Today Motovun is in Croatia and the house where we used to meet has been confiscated by the government. Bato, who had dreamt of a peaceful

---

* Bato's book *Life and Death in the Balkans* is a fascinating memoir, now published in twelve languages.

country undivided by racial strife and long memories of past battles won and lost, had the distinction of being condemned to death by *both* Croatia and Serbia. The sentence had less to do with his publishing and more with his having been head of Yugoslav television before the country descended into violence and ethnic cleansing.[*]

An exceptionally pretty Canada book was suggested by Jürgen and endorsed by the Italian Automobile Club for its book club. I consulted Ken Lefolii, freshly arrived at Key after Michael bought a small "what's on" magazine called *Toronto Calendar*, which Ken had been running. Now he became one of the group of bright people around those offices, a guy with a lot of ideas and not much to do.

Ken Lefolii had been the hero of the legendary 1964 *Maclean's* magazine mass walkout that saw most of the great names in Canadian journalism—Peter Gzowski, Harry Bruce, Bob Fulford, and Ken himself—resign en masse in the wake of his firing. It had been a point of principle: no editorial interference by management. Ken talked Jack Batten, who was a copy editor at the time, out of joining the others. Instead, he persuaded the new editor, his replacement, to promote Jack to writer—a job in which he has thrived ever since. "I thank Ken practically every time I see him," Jack says.

Peter Gzowski and Ken remained friends. Natural storytellers, they sparked off each other, they made everyone laugh. They also shared a passion for horses and racing, buying a yearling together for ten thousand dollars, a princely sum for two writers. They had hoped to make a fortune when it was sold. It hadn't worked out that way. As Peter recalled, Johnny Canuck, the horse, had "lacked heart." As did the wooden yawl they also bought together. It sank.

I asked Bob Fulford to write the text for our soon-to-be beautiful Canada book. The photographs came from one of the National Film Board Still Division's favourite sons, John de Visser, who had photographed every part of Canada. He was willing to go back and reshoot anything we felt needed an update.

---

[*] The Motovun Group still meets but in other countries.

Ken and I assembled and edited the book. I do not recall much about the process except that we laughed a lot and drank a lot of wine at various eateries along Church and Front Streets, while coming up with captions that didn't repeat other captions. It's not surprising that after my immersion in nationalism, the title would be *Canada: A Celebration.*

The book was published in ten countries in twelve languages, including Serbo-Croatian, and was still more or less in print when I last looked on Amazon. It spawned a line of illustrated books that we published over the years. In fact, it was such a success that at our traditional Key Porter Friday afternoon pub times, we all vied for the silliest illustrated book ideas to which we could append "a celebration" or "a tribute." But *Canada: A Celebration* also proved that books about our country could sell internationally and open new doors for Canadian photographers and writers.

It was an exciting prospect.

Dudley and Malak

As I mentioned, Dudley Witney and I became friends through his M&S books. After *The Barn*, I had commissioned *The Lighthouse* (Alan Edmonds* and I wrote the text) and *Summer Places* with *The New Yorker*'s illustrious Brendan Gill. I have no idea how Dudley had talked Brendan into writing the text, let alone spending a great deal of time roughing it in Canada's cottage country. His natural habitats were New York and East Hampton. Born in Hartford, Connecticut, a Yale graduate, a film and theatre critic, a "Talk of the Town" feature writer, an architecture critic, an attendee at formal parties with celebrities, he had been writing for *The New Yorker* for more than forty years. He was a patrician presence, tall, thin, with an aristocratic nose and a seemingly inexhaustible store of anecdotes, hilarious and embarrassing stories about people like Dorothy Parker, Buster Keaton, Eleanor Roosevelt, George Plimpton, Georges Simenon, and Man Ray. He was also the author of some fifteen books and an admirer of Frank Lloyd Wright, whose buildings he delighted in showing me in New York.

What could have hooked Brendan was the architecture of grand old summer places in the United States—the Biltmore House, Boldt Castle, for

---

* Yes, the same Alan Edmonds who had starred in *Live It Up*.

example—rather than our prefab in Georgian Bay. But he didn't complain about the rain, the food, or the narrow bunk beds. Dudley and Brendan became inseparable friends. Dudley was the only outsider at Brendan Gill's eightieth birthday party and perhaps the last to talk with Brendan about his dying.

DUDLEY'S NEW BOOK was going to be about ranches. He had cajoled historian and journalist Moira Johnston, with six previous books to her credit, to write the text. Moira, I thought, had been a little bit in love with him, a fate she would have shared with several other talented women of his acquaintance.

Dudley was an unusual man, comfortable anywhere, so long as he liked the company—even when that company was his own. He had spent years living out of a single suitcase, spending nights in friends' homes or in his car. When he decided to photograph ranches, he drove his ancient Russian Lada throughout the US heartland, where no one had ever seen a Russian car before and few had ever met an Englishman, let alone one with a passion for ranching. He was a hit with the ranchers, as he had been with cottagers, farmers, and lighthouse keepers. He had a mischievous sense of humour and, while he took his work seriously, he was unable to take himself seriously. He became friends with people he found interesting and a few who were almost as unusual as Dudley himself. He spent a lot of time with artist and philanthropist Nelje Doubleday (yes, that Doubleday family) in Wyoming, with novelist Marian Engel in Toronto, with the great bird artist Fenwick Lansdowne in BC, and with us and our daughters in Georgian Bay.

The Ranch: Portrait of a Surviving Dream was designed by Ken Rodmell and edited by Ramsay Derry, a former editor of Robertson Davies, in Key's cluttered boardroom over coffee and beer, but mostly long discussions about life. Ken, Ramsay, and Dudley were all happy philosophers.

When we were about halfway, Ken prepared a mock-up of the first hundred or so pages—much as M&S had done for *The Barn* and Roloff Beny's *Persia*—and I flew to New York and Boston to see if we could sell US publishers on joining our print run. In the end we presold so many copies to

Doubleday that they paid for our entire printing. I remember taking the same presentation to Woodward's in Vancouver and talking them into taking a chance on a book I feared would be ignored by the Eastern media.

Later we commissioned Dudley to produce *Railway Country: Across Canada by Train* and *An American Journey by Rail.* And last, my personal favourite Witney book, *The Moorlands of England,* the book that took Dudley home to his first love: the landscape that had also inspired the Brontë sisters.

Having established a bit of a base and a reputation, we found it easy to publish Malak Karsh's *Canada: The Land That Shapes Us*; *The Northwest Passage* with Ed Struzik and Mike Beedell; Freeman Patterson's *The Last Wilderness: Images of the Canadian Wild*;* Dudley Witney's *Canada: Railway Country* and *An American Journey by Rail*; and Fred Bruemmer's *The Arctic World.* Foreign publishers loved our big illustrated books and bought them in large enough numbers that we felt shielded from the unpredictability of the Canadian market.

Even at home, we became known for photographic books. We commissioned Malak Karsh to produce books about Ottawa and the Parliament buildings. Malak was Yousuf Karsh's less famous but no less talented brother; his images of Ottawa make it seem like a city where you would actually want to live. In the spring he would lie among the tulips to get the best views of the flowers. In the winter he photographed skaters on the Rideau Canal. At eighty-three he was still climbing scaffolding to get close to the Parliament buildings' gargoyles.

Born in Armenia, bearing the burden of memories that defy Turkish denials of the genocide, Malak was inordinately proud of his adopted country. I remember his induction in the Order of Canada and the celebration that followed in the Senate chamber. "I have had the chance to portray the magnificence of Canada, and something of the indomitable spirit of the people who are fortunate enough to inhabit it," he said. I knew how he felt.

---

* Our first printing was 30,000 copies, a significant number even in 1990.

Our Spanking New Premises

THE OFFICES WE moved into after we had outgrown our squatting privileges at Key were on the corner of Church Street and The Esplanade, at the far end of Phil Greey's block and directly above Brandy's, a noisy hangout for young men and women looking to hook up after work. The smell wafting upstairs was of stale beer, barbecue sauce, and cheese. The building had been a warehouse, the floors were uneven, and our chairs would roll down the length of the passageway to the stairs if you didn't plant your feet firmly enough. The rattan window blinds had long since stopped functioning and hung at half mast. The wallpaper in the boardroom was a sort of Arabian pattern of blue and gold, and there were two or three fake garish-green dusty palm trees left over from a movie company that had used the premises before us.

There were a lot of mice, a few small rats in the early evenings, and roaches that had been living there for a long time and had no intention of leaving. Once, while most of us were in the boardroom, a ceiling panel fell down, bringing with it a nest of mice, roaches, and a dead bird. Luckily, the rest of the office had no panelling, only the original wooden planks that held up the floor above. We could hear every footstep and some of the conversations from the fourth floor. Having spent a decade at M&S's Hollinger Road offices, I felt right at home in our shabby surroundings. I was excited to be starting a new publishing company, a bit like an acrobat might feel, flying without a net, doing exactly what I loved to do.

We had a tiny but versatile staff. Lorraine Durham was our first editor. Our first sales manager was Peter Waldock, former president of Penguin Books Canada, who happened to be between jobs. He was well-informed when it came to motivating book buyers. His only problem was that he had put his back out lifting boxes and most days he was proposing new sales approaches while lying on the floor alongside two offices, being too tall to occupy only one doorway.*

Peter was succeeded by Tom Best, scion of the famous printing Bests. I used to travel to Frankfurt with his dad, who always wore a rosebud in his lapel and managed to look elegant even after the eight-hour flight. Tom was charming, lively, and amazingly combustible. When he left, we gave him a brass gavel he could use for whacking the table for emphasis, rather than damaging his hands. He went on to be VP sales at HarperCollins.†

My first secretary-assistant was Gloria Goodman, who had been recommended by Judge Rosalie Abella's office and proved that judges' offices could be hilariously funny. She kept me organized and laughing through most of our first tenuous years. Once when I had a German author in my office, she goose-stepped outside my door in an uncanny imitation of John Cleese in *Faulty Towers*.

Robert Wilkie, formerly of M&S, managed production and our finances and insisted that each of our new manuscript acquisitions had to have a "profit & loss" form attached, showing our expectations—however unrealistic—of the book. He was also an expert proofreader (he'd started as a hot metal typesetter in Edinburgh). Jonathan Webb, editor and former

---

* Peter has recently retired from his successful wholesaling company, North 49 Books.

† Tom now runs First Book Canada.

co-winner of the Seal First Novel Award, was an early employee, as was the estimable Krystyna Ross, managing production and design.[*]

TED ALLAN USED to say the place had character. He would frequently bring his own lunch while we talked in my office. He would settle between the half-broken springs of my Goodwill discard couch, seemingly undaunted by the bar below's aromas. He still had his neatly trimmed Van Dyke beard, the quick smile, the fast movements of the hands as he explained or remonstrated, but his shoulders had begun to stoop and he was no longer interested in going to the restaurants on Church Street. "Doctor's orders," he said, as he opened the plastic container of his meagre lunch.

It was during those long conversations that he told me about the women in his life. He could never atone for taking his beloved sister to an insane asylum. He talked of his affairs with novelist Doris Lessing, a few other writers and actresses, and his one true love, Gerda Taro. They had met during the Spanish Civil War.

On a bright, sunny day in July 1937, Gerda and Ted went to witness a battle near Brunete, west of Madrid. General Walter of the Republican Thirty-Fifth Division had ordered them to leave, but they didn't. Gerda was taking pictures as bombs exploded all around them; she photographed planes strafing retreating soldiers, and kept taking pictures, ignoring the bullets and flying rocks, as men were blown to pieces. Ted pleaded with her, but Gerda wouldn't listen. They finally jumped on the running board of a car. Moments later, a tank veered into the side of their vehicle, throwing Gerda and Ted into a ditch.

Gerda died at dawn the next day.

Ted never recovered.

---

[*] Jonathan moved on to M&S and a distinguished career as an author. Krys has spent some thirty years in senior positions in the book business, including CEO of eBound, Canada.

*   *   *

ACTOR HUME CRONYN visited only once but everyone wanted to see him and hear his famous voice talking about his magical Ontario childhood, his wife and fellow actor, Jessica Tandy, and the plays they had both been in on Broadway. Our subsequent meetings were all in the New York apartment he shared with Jessica, who frequently corrected his memories. Despite his charm and self-deprecating humour, Hume was every bit the star and he knew it. Years later, he finished writing his memoir, *A Terrible Liar.* The title, he explained, was his reference to the role memory plays in a memoir. There was going to be a second volume but Hume got busy with television and, I believe, the film *The Pelican Brief.*

Toronto Star columnist Gary Lautens* used to drop in on his way to work, just to see how we were getting on. In the early nineties we published a collection of his funniest columns: *Peace, Mrs. Packard and the Meaning of Life.*

Eric Wright would come by and chat with anyone in the so-called reception area, then walk down to my office past the dusty rubber plants to share some snippets of gossip. Eric was chairman of the English department and dean of arts at Ryerson College (now University) for a number of years and he used to bring chunks of his first Charlie Salter mystery manuscript to board meetings when both he and I served on the Ryerson board. Once I had been so engrossed in the manuscript of *The Night the Gods Smiled* that I inadvertently voted against one of my own motions.

Eric's mysteries won numerous awards but my personal choice of all his books is the memoir that reads like the best fiction, *Always Give a Penny to a Blind Man.* He was soft-spoken and loathed all forms of pretension. His *Moody's Tale* is a deliciously funny take on pretensions. He had retained some of the humour that got his impoverished working-class family through the worst of times. Out of the ten children, he was the only one who succeeded in getting an education.

---

* Gary wrote the bestsellers *Take My Family . . . Please!* and *How Pierre and I Saved the Civilized World.*

Explorer Joe MacInnis showed his underwater slides in the boardroom and former prime minister Joe Clark wrote much of his book, *A Nation Too Good to Lose*, in the office next to mine. At lunchtime he would ask if someone was interested in joining him at the small coffee and sandwich place on the corner of Front and Church Street. Joe was often accompanied by Livio Copetti, the number two guy in our two-person accounting department. When people recognized him, Joe responded with a small smile. None of the hand-waving bravado of other politicians. Once when a woman at the food counter said to him, "You know, you look like Joe Clark," he replied, "I know, it's a burden I have to bear."

Despite the dust and the noise, the mice and the roaches, there was some magic in those offices: Freeman Patterson, philosopher-artist from New Brunswick, with his soft voice and his sets of magical photographs, ready to show us the beauty you could capture; Dudley Witney on my couch talking about the drama of the moors; and Fred Bruemmer talking about his love of the Arctic. Fred wrote about "its rugged beauty, its haunting loneliness, its infinite space. It has the vastness of the sea, the grandeur of a Bach fugue. The Inuit call it 'Nunatsiaq,' the 'beautiful land' and it became my second home." He would write more than a thousand magazine articles and several books about the Arctic and its people.

Fred was, essentially, a shy man who had not been interested in revelations about himself. He hated promotion tours and invasive questions. Yet he was a mesmerizing storyteller. His wife, Maud, once told me about the wonder-filled, happy stories he used to create for his kids—a miraculous feat given his own childhood traumas. The stories, she thought, had brought him close to them, despite his long absences. It took time and persistence for me to talk him into writing *Survival: A Refugee Life*, a memoir that deals with the sadness and deprivation of his early years, his time as a slave labourer in a Soviet camp, the starvation, disease, the mistreatment. He and his sister had been forced to dig their parents' grave. Only fifteen years old, shrivelled, emaciated, but determined to live, Fred made his way to Canada. He learned English (he already spoke six other languages), journalism, and photography while working several back-breaking menial jobs.

The Inuit called him "Amarak," the wolf, lone wolf, because he liked to go for long, icy walks by himself. He spent six months of the year in the Arctic, sharing igloos and tents with the locals, tagging along on their hunts, eating the food he was offered, learning about their culture, the animals who shared their land.

He was about sixty then. He had undergone a high-risk heart transplant operation in Montreal, and his new, young heart was struggling with his aging body. He told me he would, finally, write "that book"—if he lived.

KEY PORTER RAN on an extremely tight budget. Staff, in the early days, often had more than one job. Trying to save a salary, we installed a telephone answering system that could direct calls to the few extensions we had. Then I got this letter from Farley Mowat:

"To the President (if there is a live one, and I begin to doubt it): I have had it with your fucking phone system. Please post a notice that if anyone wants to hear my voice, they will have to call me. . . . I swear I will never again endure the inane babble of your goddamn machines."

After that, we hired a part-time receptionist who was willing to work for next to nothing in order to be involved in publishing, and Farley decided to come to Key Porter for his next book. One of our early volunteer receptionist-proofreaders, Marion Garner, later became publisher of Vintage Canada.

I hired Susan Renouf for the first time in those early years. I had met her father, the legendary Harold Renouf, when we were both on the Imperial Life board, where I had learned to watch his every small movement because Harold always knew when someone was concealing something. He told me that his daughter was moving to Toronto and could be interested in a job in publishing. She came to us as our first junior editor and remained with Key Porter in a variety of jobs, ending in president. She would leave from time to time to have babies or to try her hand at a different firm, but she tended to return. We have remained friends through it all.

1984

WHILE THERE HAD been perilous times before, Jack McClelland nominated 1984 as the worst year in his life. M&S had, quite simply, run out of money. The bankers were concerned about the debt, printers had stopped delivering books unless they were paid in advance, and authors were agitating about royalties. On annual sales of about $10 million, the cumulative debt had risen to $5 million. Had the Ontario government not stepped in with a $2.5 million aid package, the firm would have gone into an irreversible tailspin. That Jack was able to secure an additional million from friends, many of whom were writers (including Margaret Atwood, Pierre Berton, Farley Mowat, Peter Newman) and one property developer: Avie Bennett, should have given him reason to celebrate. It hadn't. He had hated asking friends to invest in a firm with such a terrible financial record. He described his efforts to sell shares in the company as akin to selling shares in his own wife. Every day, he dosed himself with alcohol to endure those calls. By the end of the process, he had concluded he had become an alcoholic.

While his hardy group of employees opened bottles of sparkling wine in the warehouse to celebrate the cash infusion, Jack brooded at home in Kleinberg. He claimed he had an abscessed tooth, but when he called me, all he would say was that he was utterly depressed. While grateful for the support, even the good wishes from competing publishers, he didn't think he could carry on much longer. The industry he had loved was now a very different beast from the one he had entered in the 1950s. This is how Farley summed it up, at the time: "There is no long-term cure. Eventually, everything will be owned by the conglomerates and run by accountants."

Farley was right, but that time hadn't arrived yet. In 1984 there were still a lot of independent bookstores and there were still three book-buying chains, and the 1970s enthusiasm for starting new publishing ventures hadn't evaporated. Michael and I were confident enough in Key Porter's ability to thrive that we purchased the list and inventory of Fleet Books, an imprint of Van Nostrand Reinhold, owned by the Thomson organization.*

Fleet had a smallish Canadian non-fiction backlist we thought we needed for a bit of stability while we continued to publish books that made headlines. The acquisition meant that we could also hire Phyllis Bruce, who had overseen the Fleet list. She is a superb editor with the kind of equanimity that made our chaotic new venture seem manageable.

With her boxes of books and contracts, Phyllis had initially moved to the Key office I once shared with Peter Gzowski. Her desk was hidden behind a bookcase so my visitors would be surprised when she emerged. It was a great arrangement because Phyllis could comment on book projects and conversations without having to leave her desk. Within the year, she would move to our new offices on The Esplanade with a view of the parking garage.

Canoeist Bill Mason and photographer Freeman Patterson were the stars of the Fleet list. Bill's *Path of the Paddle* was a classic, and he was already working on *Song of the Paddle*. He was a naturalist, conservationist, and filmmaker produced by the National Film Board: his *Paddle to the Sea* had been nominated Best Short Film in the 1968 Academy Awards. His *Cry of the Wild*, the most moving film about wolves I have ever seen, should

---

* The vendor, oddly enough, was the Ontario government, since it had precipitated the bankruptcy of Clarke Irwin by cancelling its guarantee of Clarke Irwin's operating bank loan, right after the sale of Fleet/VNR to Bill Clarke.

be required viewing for all schoolchildren, in case they are learning to be hunters.

Patterson was Canada's most successful nature photographer, but he was more than that. For him photographing nature was a form of religious experience. He had a master's degree in divinity; his thesis was "Still Photography as a Medium of Religious Expression." He had once been dean of religious studies at Alberta College and was one of the National Film Board Still Photography Division's busiest artists. The NFB's Lorraine Monk featured his work in her big photography collections. His *Photography and the Art of Seeing* was already a classic teaching text for would-be photographers, and Freeman organized photography courses all over the world. His students were so inspired by him that many returned for more sessions. I was amazed to learn that even his *Namaqualand: Garden of the Gods*, the book that was in mid-production when we took over Fleet, would find a ready market. Two South African publishers vied with two British publishers for the right to sell it in South Africa.

Freeman's series *Photography for the Joy of It*, *Photography and the Art of Seeing*, *Photography of Natural Things*, *Photographing the World Around You*, and later, *Photo Impressionism* all found ready markets, as did his sumptuous coffee-table books, *Portraits of Earth* and *The Last Wilderness* (which he edited for us). He always strives to connect the natural world with what the human eye is capable of seeing. He maintains that photography is, essentially, a right-brain, instinctive activity, but only after you master the left-brain craft that allows you "to stop thinking" and just do.

Every one of Freeman Patterson's books was a Key Porter event. We would meet with him in our badly lit boardroom to discuss his vision for the book, his reasons for wanting to present it, and his hopes for its audience. Afterwards, we would go to one of the bars to celebrate.

After Phyllis left to start her own imprint at HarperCollins, Clare McKeon took over the care and handling of Freeman's work. Clare, who had worked with me at M&S (Linda McKnight believes she was my second hire), joined Key Porter in the early nineties as our managing editor. Both Freeman and Clare were Maritimers, she from Cape Breton, he from Shampers Bluff, New Brunswick. She admired both his talent and his ideas and was a fierce advocate of his books. She told our sales force that Freeman was a visionary genius.

His photographs do, indeed, lead one to that conclusion. My only experience of working with Freeman had not seemed like work. I went to his home in Shampers Bluff to discuss new book ideas, but instead we ended up going for a long ride on his motorbike, both of us wearing his leather chaps, helmets, and visors, while he talked, as much to the wind as to me, about the inspiration for his work. When we returned to the house, he showed me several hundred photographs that recorded the life of his garden.

Freeman's next book was called *The Garden*.

Journalists and Politicians

N O PUBLISHER CAN be good at every genre and, as I had learned from the best of them, if you spread yourself too thin, you will accumulate too many unsold books. You have to mark your territory.

After Allan Fotheringham launched us into politics, we knew that there was a large, curious audience for books about what went on in the backrooms of the nation. That ever-elusive book-buyer, "the general public," was interested in issues and events that influenced the buyer's daily life. And people loved gossip. Stevie Cameron's *Ottawa Inside Out* was filled with it. Claire Hoy's *Friends in High Places: Politics and Patronage in the Mulroney Government* catalogued the most egregious scandals of the Mulroney government: Tunagate, the sinking of a cabinet minister, Sinclair Stevens, Mila Mulroney's renovation bills, and the cronies who had the inside track to the PMO. Brian Mulroney was enraged by Hoy's allegations, though there was nothing he could hang a lawsuit on. Adding insult to injury, Julian, a fellow Tory, had made sure that we were legally safe.* In a later unguarded interview with Peter Newman, Mulroney alleged that he

---

* Julian did a great deal to keep us safe and relatively calm during both the M&S and the Key Porter years.

would have appointed Julian chief justice but for that "unfortunate" Hoy book. Luckily, Julian didn't take that comment seriously.

I remember some of the legal threats we received, and that few of them ever made their way to trial. Saskatchewan politician Colin Thatcher* served notice of legal action over a quickie mass-market book by journalist Heather Bird that suggested he had his wife killed (he was serving time for that offence in an Alberta jail). There were lawsuits by the two men hired by Mr. Buxbaum† to dispose of his wife (they were in jail for that offence); by the Scientologists over *The Bare-Faced Messiah*; and by coroner Morton Shulman over allegations in Ken Lefolii's *Claims: Adventures in the Gold Trade*. I had a tendency to panic when I saw writs arrive, whereas Julian thought writs were just a way of scaring publishers into cancelling books. They shouldn't work, and with us, they rarely did. We lost in our bid for an early release of the book about the Buxbaum killers but won against the Scientologists. We backed down when threatened by Morton Shulman because Julian advised we would not have the necessary funds for a prolonged court case.

I approached Vancouver *Province* columnist Allen Garr to write about British Columbia premier Bill Bennett, "the kind of leader," Garr wrote, "who makes people feel comfortable about their prejudices." *Tough Guy* got national coverage and even Jack Webster congratulated us on the success of the book. Bill Bennett was a great deal less enthusiastic, but at least he didn't sue.

I HAD MET Premier Peter Lougheed through Julian's Conservative Party connections and spent several days, both in Edmonton and in Toronto, trying to persuade him to write a memoir. He was a brilliant politician, a tactician with charm, persuasive, tough, perceptive, and almost always

---

* *Not Above the Law*, by Heather Bird.

† *Conspiracy to Murder: The Trial of Helmuth Buxbaum*, also by Heather Bird.

ready to listen to other opinions. He was an attractive combination of modesty and bravado. He had played football with the Edmonton Eskimos, had been to Harvard, and had the debating skills and sharp mind of a business school graduate. He enjoyed the limelight, though not the presence of his minders; he was embarrassed by the adulation of Albertans but missed it when it was no longer there.

Progressive Conservatives had ousted Alberta's Social Credit, after thirty-six years of uninterrupted rule, in 1971. He had become premier on a wave of Western self-confidence and desire for change. He set up the Alberta Heritage Trust Fund to try to "ensure the prosperity of the future generations of Albertans."

Contrary to Toronto's suspicions, Peter was not a Western separatist, but he fought for Alberta's place at the negotiating table where energy was discussed. "The blue-eyed sheik of Alberta," as he was called by Southam Press's Charlie Lynch, did not invent the slogan "Let the Eastern bastards freeze in the dark," though I suspect he was amused by seeing it on Albertan bumper stickers. He promoted provincial powers without wishing to destroy the federal system. In that, he was not much different from other premiers I have known. He viewed his tactics as fair in light of the federal grab for Alberta's resources.

When Robert Stanfield gave up on the leadership of the national Progressive Conservatives, Peter could have seized the opportunity. Despite his lack of French, newspaper surveys declared him to be the clear favourite. After a lot of thinking and discussion with various advisers, including Dalton Camp and Julian, he decided he could not win against Pierre Trudeau. He was probably right about that.

The Lougheed Legacy had started life as Peter Lougheed's memoir, ghosted by David Wood, but Peter decided that the person who wrote the book should take all the credit. David Wood had earned his stripes not only in media and public relations but also as the older man who had befriended Peter when he was just a young lawyer. Peter had trusted David with his secrets but, in the end, despite its access to the backrooms, the book lacked emotional insights that no amount of cajoling could elicit from David.

When I was working on the manuscript, Peter drove me to the airport a couple of times. I think walking on the red carpet to a movie premiere with the star would have been rather like my experience walking with the premier of Alberta at the Edmonton airport. People shouted, cheered, called his name, and Peter waved and shouted back, as if greeting old friends. Years later, when he was no longer premier, we walked along a Calgary street and I looked at passersby, but now there were few cheers. Though Peter continued to serve on many corporate boards after he left politics, he was no longer the emblem of Alberta's ambitions.

Looking for Trouble

B IG JOHN, AS most people called John Bassett, former newspaper publisher, was a Hearstian figure, loose-limbed, wide-shouldered, handsome with a toothy smile and a large handshake. He had been a tennis
champion, but when his knees started to give him trouble, he hired tennis
pros to partner with him for doubles games that Julian and I had no hope
of winning. Nor did Peter Worthington and Yvonne Crittenden, though we
all enjoyed losing on the courts at the Bassetts' impressive Caledon home.

Some years we would dine in the great hall while a chamber orchestra
played at the top of the grand staircase. Isabel was an attentive and welcoming hostess; John was ebullient and edgy, wanting to debate and argue
about obscure British history, long-forgotten wars, and the politics of the
day. John had been an unsuccessful candidate for the Progressive Conservatives in two elections, once in Quebec and once in Ontario. Julian had
worked in both federal and provincial elections, and Ontario premier Bill
Davis had been trying to persuade him to run for Parliament.

Peter was thinking about announcing his candidacy for the nomination of the Progressive Conservative Party in a Toronto by-election. He
was outspoken, opinionated, charming, and looked remarkably like Har-
rison Ford in the later *Star Wars* movies. The roles he had played were
as swashbuckling as Ford's, except that Peter's were real and genuinely

life-threatening. His father, Major-General Worthington, "Worthy" or "Fighting Frank" to all who knew him, had fought in the First World War. Peter had been an air gunner in the Second World War and had fought with the Princess Patricias in the Korean War. As a correspondent for *The Toronto Telegram*, he'd reported on wars, coups, and revolutions in the Congo, Iraq, Algeria, Angola, Lebanon, New Guinea, Biafra, Israel-Egypt, and Vietnam.

Peter had a gift for being on the cusp of history. He had interviewed Iraq's Sandhurst-trained Brigadier Abdel Karim Kassem, and he was there when King Faisal's uncle, Crown Prince Abd al-Ilah, refused to surrender and his whole family, including the children, was massacred. He had met one of the world's "most durable monarchs," King Hussein of Jordan, over Coca-Cola and coffee. Alone in Gamal Abdul Nasser's study, he interviewed Egypt's strongman for about three hours. Nasser joked about cartoons of himself in the British papers. When Peter mentioned Israeli fears about being driven into the sea, Nasser just laughed. "That's just Arab rhetoric," he told Peter.

He interviewed the Dalai Lama, India's Nehru, both Mobutu and Lumumba in the Congo, and a very drunk Soviet spy, Kim Philby, in a bar in Beirut. Once he was trapped in a firefight between the French Foreign Legion and the Front de Libération Nationale in Algeria. Astonishingly, you can see Peter in the famous photograph taken by a news photographer at the moment Jack Ruby gunned down Lee Harvey Oswald in 1963. Peter helped and supported Igor Gouzenko, the man who first revealed the extent of Soviet spying in Canada and was disbelieved by many. Peter believed him, and Peter was right. He also interviewed Gouzenko and wrote the story.

When Peter was stationed in the USSR for *The Toronto Telegram*, Olga, the intriguing, seemingly eccentric, but pretty wife of a senior Soviet KGB man, asked for his help to defect. Though he was initially suspicious that Olga was a double agent, Peter found a way with the help of James Leslie Bennett, then head of Canadian counterintelligence (he would later sue writer Ian Adams), and after a few narrow escapes, the pair reached Canada, where Olga settled and managed to eke out a living, mostly from Peter and Yvonne.

Not surprisingly, Peter's favourite poet was Rudyard Kipling.

I had been trying to persuade him to write a book since the seventies. Having heard all these stories, wouldn't everyone? But he was too busy to write a memoir and he thought he still had a lot of life to live. He had launched the *Toronto Sun* in 1972, with two other former *Telegram* staffers, Don Hunt and Donald Creighton. They had the advantage of the *Telegram*'s subscriber list from John Bassett and a bit of money they had scraped together. Eddie Goodman—political insider, founder of the law firm Goodman and Goodman, and another Bassett friend—had been the first outside investor to put his money on the table.

With Peter as the *Sun*'s editor, the new tabloid was irrepressibly feisty, innovative, entertaining, irreverent, and outspoken. While it drew attention for its "Sunshine Girls," it also championed democracy. "Democracy is valued most by those who have lost it," Peter wrote. When many liberal idealists continued to see the USSR through rose-coloured glasses, the *Sun* remained deeply suspicious of the Soviet Union. It also challenged Pierre Trudeau's sympathies for Fidel Castro and Mao Zedong.

In 1978, after his first triple-bypass surgery, Peter hired journalist Barbara Amiel to replace him as editor. Barbara, then still married to George Jonas, with whom she had co-authored *By Persons Unknown: The Strange Death of Christine Demeter*, was a columnist at *Maclean's* and a very glamorous woman about town. Peter continued as a columnist.

He resigned from the *Sun*'s board of directors in 1982, when they voted (unanimously, except for Peter) to sell the tabloid to Maclean Hunter. He assumed that the paper would lose its independence and become dull. He thought that success had already made it less than it should and could have been. It would no longer be breaking stories, no longer strutting its opinions across the front page as it had done during the first years.

Surely he would, at last, be ready to write that book.

But no, he tried to get the federal Progressive Conservative nomination in Broadview-Greenwood, and when he was blocked from that, he ran as an independent. He lost to the NDP,* giving my book yet another chance

---

* I suspect Joe Clark's Tories gave a sigh of relief as Peter was never going to be a silent backbencher.

to be completed. I have kept two of Peter's campaign posters and one five-foot-high photo of him, taken when he climbed to Mount Everest's base camp after his second coronary bypass.

We published *Looking for Trouble* in 1984. To my surprise, while Peter was on his publicity tour for the memoir, he was fired by the paper he had helped start. He thought he could be critical of the *Sun* when it deserved criticism. As it turned out, he couldn't.

Of course, we issued a new edition of *Looking for Trouble*, featuring Peter's dismissal and its aftermath.

Eventually, when tempers cooled, Peter returned to the *Sun* as a columnist, filing his stories well ahead of the deadlines, and filing at least twice as many as he was paid for. Being Peter, he couldn't resist what he called "the boy scout stuff," so he took off for Angola to write about the fighting, to Eritrea to see the war of independence for himself, and to witness a few incidental skirmishes along the way.

Peter's last column was published on May 14, 2013. This is how it began:

If you are reading this, I am dead.

How's that for a lead?
Guarantees you read on, at least for a bit.

I've Always Told Stories

M Y MOTHER, MY aunts, my grandfather, and his mother and grand-mother all told stories. Some of them were even true. I still remember the awesome tales about dragons, magic trees, and fearless princesses my mother told me when we were in jail.

My grandfather Vili, like many good Hungarians during Communist times, had also spent time in jail. He used to tell me long, historical stories set in past centuries, starring members of our family who seemed to be more interested in brandishing swords than in writing, but he believed their stories lived on in the telling. I had always sensed that the time would come when I would write about him and his strange tales—that book was *The Storyteller*—but in the early eighties, I was not yet ready to deal with my grandfather's tales. His death was too recent.

Instead I wrote a murder mystery, set in the book business, starring a Canadian journalist and her childhood friend, a publishing executive in New York. It was territory I knew well and one I enjoyed skewering. The two leads were loosely based on people I knew, as were some of the dead bodies whose demises were investigated by my team of unlikely detectives.

I had so much fun writing the book that I had quite forgotten one of the basics of mystery writing: you have to know, in advance, who the culprit is, so you can tie up the loose ends in the end. I was close to four hundred pages when I realized that no one in the book could possibly have been responsible for all the murders. Ken Lefolii read the manuscript, and while he enjoyed the writing, he noted that it was important I should present a plausible killer and plant hints throughout. Mystery lovers did not like some new character sprung on them at the last minute. They needed a chance to guess who had "done it." I had to go back to the beginning and rewrite the entire manuscript! The lesson I learned was that the author always had to be in on the secrets, even if she chose not to show her hand.

After I had rewritten it, John Irwin published *Hidden Agenda* in 1985, another wretched year for Jack at M&S, but he sent me an enormous bouquet of flowers, even though he suspected that at least one of the victims was based on him. My editor, John Pearce, was able to sell rights in some fifteen countries. I was presented with two copies of the Japanese edition at the Frankfurt Book Fair.

When I began to write my second mystery, *Mortal Sins*, I knew who had done the deed and why. That made the process less exciting for me, since I knew where the story was going, but it was easier not to have to guess what the end would be.

Both mysteries feature a journalist and a book publisher. The journalist is a little like Marjorie Harris. I even used Marjorie's Annex neighbourhood street in Toronto. The character is also a little like me. I used bits of my own life, such as the scene where Judith sits on the floor between her two children's beds, making sure they are breathing.

The publisher, Marsha, is a little like Carole Baron of Dell-Delacorte and a little like I might have been, had I accepted Marc Jaffe's suggestion and moved to New York. I admired Carole because she fought hard for her authors and never backed down even when her bosses insisted she should stop being pushy. Marsha attends the kinds of sales conferences I went to in New York when I was with Seal. She works in corporate offices not unlike Bantam's and tries to persuade her tougher-minded colleagues on Fifth Avenue (yes, that's where Bantam's head office was) that books are more than just "units" and the author is more than just one of the "elements" that make a saleable "product."

My Candidate

I SHOULD NOT have been surprised when Julian told me, over a Sunday lunch with the kids, that he wanted to be a provincial candidate in our Ontario riding in 1985. I knew Julian had been involved in party politics since he was a child. His dad, a lifelong Tory, had served in nine Ontario portfolios, including Minister of Education, Treasurer, and Attorney General. Premier Leslie Frost had been a regular visitor at the Porter home on Pine Hill in Rosedale. Julian had been on Wallace McCutcheon's 1963 campaign team and was with him at the 1967 leadership convention when McCutcheon lost to Robert Stanfield. Apart from shared Conservative sympathies, Wallace was, at the time, also Julian's father-in-law.

In 1968 Julian had handled the advertising for Bob Stanfield's hopeless campaign against Pierre Trudeau's Liberals. He travelled across the country with Stanfield and managed (not very well, he thought) the Leadership Debate anchored by Charles Templeton. The country was wild about Trudeau. Crowds followed wherever he went. Stanfield's strengths—thoughtfulness, stability, consideration for others—did not have a chance. Julian used to tell stories about Stanfield's good humour, his self-deprecating wit no matter how discouraging the situation. Once, when the small plane had just made a hazardous landing somewhere in the Maritimes, Stanfield asked,

"Have I spoken here before?" When he was told yes, he said, "In that case, I hope you rented a small hall."

During the mid-1970s Julian was one of Peter Lougheed's speechwriters, a late-night drinking companion of former premier John Robarts, and later an occasional member of Premier Davis's famous breakfast club at the Park Plaza Hotel.

Julian was, no doubt, the reason why Key Porter was chosen to publish the big blue Ontario sesquicentennial book in 1984. I have a photograph from the launch: Bill Davis and me, sitting side by side but looking in opposite directions. He is very handsome and I seem very uneasy. In another photograph, likely taken at the same event, a grinning Brian Mulroney is holding up *Ontario* so that the camera can record his delight with the book. He dedicated it to me "with admiration and warm wishes." Three years later, when we published Claire Hoy's *Friends in High Places*, he would not have held up any book published by Key Porter.

In 1984 Julian seemed to spend more time on the phone with Bill Davis, Peter Lougheed, and Dalton Camp—not at the same time—than usual, and he did mention that he thought if he didn't run now, he never would. Dalton was the ultimate Conservative Party insider. He had helped John Diefenbaker win the 1957 federal election against Lester Pearson and ten years later manoeuvred the end of the Diefenbaker era by insisting that party leaders had to be subject to the membership's vote. At the ensuing leadership review, an outraged Diefenbaker was denied another automatic term as leader.*

Dalton then switched to provincial politics in Ontario. He and his brother-in-law Norman Atkins were part of the Big Blue Machine that had managed four elections for the provincial Conservatives and won them all. Dalton and Bill Davis, Julian told me, thought that he should take a chance now, but I was so busy with publishing that I was astonished when he asked me to join him at the nomination meeting.

---

* Dalton remained, forever after, a pariah in Conservative territory west of Toronto, and even in Toronto he was regarded with suspicion.

It was a grand occasion with band music and balloons in the Royal York's Canadian Room, Julian looking impressive in a charcoal-grey suit and me smiling fixedly at everyone who came by. He was thrilled with winning the nomination and fairly confident that he would do well in the elections. Though I had watched Jeanne Lougheed be pleasant and charming, laugh at the right times, and look solemn when called upon, I didn't know how political wives were supposed to behave.

Once he was declared the Progressive Conservative Party's candidate for our riding of St. David in Toronto, he got organized. By then Bill Davis had left his party with the dubious gift of one of the most divisive issues of the day in Ontario: publicly funded education at Catholic schools. The Anglican bishop had Julian stand in his living room while he delivered a verbal assault that my husband thought lasted a full three minutes. Undeterred, Julian made stirring speeches, jogged along all the area's streets from house to house and from apartment to apartment, including in the Jamestown area south of Bloor Street, where residents seemed to have more existential concerns than who would win the next election. Catherine, Jessica, and Julia posed with us for photographs, our journalist friends wrote flattering columns, while we tried to imagine how our lives would change if he won. It was not a comforting picture.

Our friends in the media wrote glowing columns about Julian. Margaret Atwood mentioned his "integrity," Roy Peterson drew a flattering picture of him roller skating in Vancouver's Stanley Park, Fotheringham called him "a heavy," and Bob Fulford weighed in with praise for "the sort of man who makes the room he enters a better place to be." June Callwood said, "I would trust him with my life." Peter Lougheed sent an encouraging note: "The first twenty years are the hardest."

"Julian Porter for St. David" signs went up on lawns; brochures and posters were distributed. We wore our Julian Porter buttons.

Then, on the first weekend of April 1985, there was a terrorist threat in Toronto: a self-styled Armenian Army threatened to blow up the subway system to draw attention to the Armenians suffering under Turkish rule. The police made the deeply unpopular decision to shut down fifty-nine kilometres of track. Despite my lack of enthusiasm for the stunt, Julian, chair of the Toronto Transit Commission, decided to ride the trains during the rush hour. Fortunately, the bomb threat turned out to be a hoax.

On April 19, we hosted a dinner for Peter and Jeanne Lougheed, and everybody came. There were politicians (both federal and provincial), novelists, journalists, broadcasters, moguls, artists, and Susan, Julian's first wife, and her brothers. The press sent photographers and gossip columnists.

By election day, May 2, 1985, the provincial Conservative Party had enjoyed forty-two years in office. It would have been a proud record even for Albania, Julian said, trying to be philosophical about his loss to Liberal lawyer Ian Scott. We held hands on the way to Ian's victory party central, they said all the right words to each other, hugged, and that was the end of Julian's political ambitions and of the PCs' uninterrupted rule in Ontario.

Julian called his six major clients, including the College of Physicians and Surgeons, and told them he would never run for political office again. We went to Rome for a week, stayed in the Teatro di Pompei on Campo de Fiori, Julian's favourite small hotel, enjoyed the outdoor market noises in the mornings while drinking our lattes, then walked to Julian's favourite churches to see his favourite frescoes, ate in his favourite restaurants near Piazza Navona, and absolutely did not talk about politics. Always a choice after-dinner and book launch party speaker, Julian now added Pierre Trudeau and Bob Stanfield to his John Diefenbaker and Robert Kennedy impressions.

I returned to my office and commissioned a bunch of political books, including Larry Zolf's *Survival of the Fattest: An Irreverent View of the Senate** and Eddie Goodman's *Life of the Party*, which was launched in that fusty old Tory hangout, the Albany Club. Everybody who was anybody in the Conservative world came—some of them just to look themselves up in the index, others to take home a signed book.

---

* Larry had the endearing habit of phoning late in the day to read me long passages in his manuscript to make sure I would find them funny when presented with the complete work. One person who did not find them funny was Senator Anne Cools, who sued us both for libel and won.

The Right Honourable Jean

IN 1984, WATCHING on CBC television as Jean Chrétien was defeated at the Liberal Convention, I thought he was the classiest, least affected man in the Ottawa Civic Centre that day. I was with a roomful of Conservatives, all of whom were keen to know who would succeed Trudeau, but no one expected to become teary after Chrétien conceded. He was magnificent in defeat.

Instinct told me that thousands of people would want to read a book from this man. I was also sure he would make a comeback. I wrote him on November 7, telling him as much and promising that the book would sell more than 100,000 copies. By the time I finished writing the letter, I knew how we were going to achieve that target. I mentioned Key's magazines, saying that we had published Allan Fotheringham and Peter Worthington. Though he didn't like either of them, Fotheringham because of his pesky wit and Worthington because he was a right-wing Tory, at least Chrétien would have heard that both books were bestsellers.

I promised him simultaneous French and English publication, a cross-Canada promotion tour, and a big Montreal launch. During my many trips to Montreal and to the Frankfurt Book Fair, I had become friends with several Quebec publishers. One of them would surely take a chance with a Chrétien memoir. He was a native son of Shawinigan, he had grown up in Quebec, and he had made a huge—though disliked by many—name for himself when campaigning on behalf of the 1980 referendum on sovereignty for Quebec. He was a patriot, one who was willing to go to any lengths to save the country he loved.

Fortunately, I was not the only person who was persuaded of Chrétien's appeal. Ron Graham, political journalist and author of *One-Eyed Kings*, had the same idea, and he was interested in helping Chrétien write his book. His 1981 *Saturday Night* profile "Jean Chrétien and the Politics of Patriotism" was balanced and thoroughly researched. He agreed to write the book if we could sign a contract.

I first met Jean Chrétien in his Lang Michener law office in downtown Toronto. I was surprised that "*le p'tit gars de Shawinigan*" ("the little guy from Shawinigan") was over six feet tall, athletic, highly intelligent in both official languages, and without most of the linguistic foibles that had characterized his popular speeches. He had studied law at Laval and had run his own law firm in Shawinigan before entering politics at age twenty-nine on Lester Pearson's team. One of nineteen children (ten of whom did not survive infancy), he had had to fight for everything he achieved. His family had always been Liberal, anti-clerical, anti-establishment. Though he always had the support of his parents, nothing came easily. He had overcome what many viewed as a handicap—partial paralysis of his face—and had to learn English quickly in order to fit in with his peers in Parliament.

He had held seven portfolios, run and won his seat in two elections, and was Trudeau's front man in Quebec, tasked with keeping the country together despite René Lévesque's extraordinary appeal to those who liked the idea of being *maîtres chez nous*. I had watched him, as had many of us, on May 20, the night of the 1980 Quebec Referendum: he was exhausted, his voice was hoarse, his shirt soaking wet, but he was still forceful and convincing.

Chrétien had been at the centre of the battle to patriate the Canadian Constitution, and though he had crossed swords with Peter Lougheed over the National Energy Program (an effort by the federal government to redistribute Alberta's oil revenues to the rest of the country), he had persuaded Peter to support the Constitution in 1982. To everyone's surprise, and despite John Turner's newsletters criticizing his performance, he had successfully managed the Finance portfolio. I do not think the relationship with Turner ever recovered from what Chrétien felt was a betrayal. He once told me that the biggest mistake young politicians make is that of blind trust. The warring between the two men never entirely subsided.

Based on a short description of the proposed book, my friend Pierre Lespérance of Les Éditions de l'Homme guaranteed the French edition would appear at the same time as the English, if we would send each chapter as it arrived. Pierre owned the biggest publishing business in Quebec, Sogides,* with Éditions de l'Homme as one of its several imprints. Pierre was an impressive presence at book fairs, a big outspoken guy, not given to flattering government officials, even when they distributed impressive subsidies.

CHRÉTIEN LIKED RON Graham's essay sufficiently to agree that he would do the talking and Ron would do the writing. After we signed the contracts, I asked him to come to our office to meet the staff. I walked with him down Bay Street, across King, and down Church Street to The Esplanade. It was a cool day but his jacket was unbuttoned and he wore no overcoat. He walked fast, almost at a jog, now and then stopping to shake hands, waving to people who called out to him, shouting his responses in both English and French, while I struggled in my heels to keep up with him.

Phyllis Bruce, who later edited the manuscript, remembers his arrival at our decrepit boardroom, the plastic plants and the ceiling both shedding dust. He asked for a beer, took off his jacket, rolled up his sleeves, and told our small group what he wanted to say in the book and why he was writing it. He talked about the country with the same conviction I had seen on television when he fought for a united Canada.

He won them over immediately.

---

* Pierre sold Sogides to Québecor in 2005 and left the company in 2013, thus depriving the publishing world of one of its most interesting and colourful figures.

Pierre Lespérance's translators went to work on each chapter as it arrived by courier from Key Porter.

We launched the French edition first—*Dans la Fosse aux Lions*—at Montreal's Grand Hotel with both French and English press and about another twelve hundred well-wishers in attendance. Pierre Trudeau gave a speech about Chrétien and I spoke about the book. Chrétien's own speech was short and oddly self-deprecating. I had been so nervous about my French, which has usually been serviceable if not brilliant, that I quite forgot to worry that Trudeau knew I had published one of Margaret's unflattering books.

I needn't have worried. He was impeccably polite and offered to have coffee with me afterwards. He said he wanted to learn more about the publishing business, about Hungarians in Canada, about my own background. He was charming and focused, equally witty in both French and English, and not once did he mention Margaret or *Consequences*.

Allan Fotheringham wrote about the subsequent Toronto launch of *Straight from the Heart*: "Most anyone who is anyone is here—politicos, literary types, social wall-climbers, all the shovers and makers." About eight hundred people showed up to cheer, drink warm wine, and buy signed books. Fotheringham intuitively recognized the occasion as the launch of Chrétien's leadership of the Liberal Party. The throngs who came to hear him characterized the whole publicity tour. He was in his element and the crowds loved him.

The book sold more than 200,000 copies in English and maybe half that in French. Chrétien, whenever we talked, wanted to know the numbers and what all those quasi-intellectuals (that would have included Trudeau's circle of friends and advisers) and the Bay Street gurus (people like John Turner) thought of the sales. Years later, when the Trudeau memoir (called simply *Memoirs* by M&S) was published, he was always keen to hear how he had outsold "the Boss."

I used to visit Chrétien in his office across from Parliament Hill, hoping to persuade him of the importance of supporting Canadian cultural institutions, particularly Canadian publishers. Most of the time he listened but was busy with his own agenda, such as who would lead the Liberals in Quebec, or what the likely outcome of a by-election was, or what the Albertans were thinking. Sometimes we talked about his writing another book, once he retired. This one, he joked, would be called *Straight through the Heart* because it would finally settle scores with all those who had backstabbed him during his days on the Hill. I expect one of the people who might have suffered heart problems had Chrétien ever written that book was Paul Martin.

On the heels of our overwhelming success with *Straight from the Heart*, Key Porter won the "Publisher of the Year Award" from the Canadian Booksellers Association.

The End of an Era

I N HIS UNFINISHED autobiography called *My Rose Garden*, Jack Mc-Clelland wrote of his utter exhaustion after 1984. The cash injection he had worked so hard for was not going to be enough. His latest warehouse sale of M&S inventory had been a disappointment: only about $600,000 worth of books, valued at about $3 million, were sold. He simply didn't have the heart for it any longer. His decision to hand over the day-to-day running of the business to Linda McKnight had not freed him, nor could he stop interfering with her efforts to control costs or maximize income.

I reread a memo Jack wrote to Linda, outlining a strategy for publishing new poetry. He proposed a kind of subscription book club under the direction of M&S's poetry editor, Dennis Lee. It was to be called "the Dennis Lee Editions Club" and its membership was to be garnered through mailings, direct sale by poets, and promotion to university departments teaching Canadian literature. What with the banking problems the firm was facing, this would have been just the kind of seven-page memo to drive Linda, a very sensible person with an excellent grasp on how publishing worked, crazy.

Somewhere in the midst of that dreadful time, he proposed that we merge our operations, that Key Porter invest half a million dollars in a joint enterprise and we take over the managing of M&S's banking obligations. He would remain chairman and I would be chief executive. Much as I loved Jack and M&S, we declined. Michael and I knew that, in practice, we would have been running a gauntlet of bankers demanding repayment of their loans. We would have had to invest at least another $1 million to settle them down. Michael told Jack we simply didn't have enough money. Perhaps he could wait a couple of years?

Then came Jack's showdown with Linda over the licensing of some M&S books to Seal for what Linda considered derisory amounts. Since Jack owned controlling interest in Seal, he was also in a conflict of interest. Jack saw the deal as a source of fast cash for M&S. Linda suggested that Jack let her run the company, since she was president, and recuse himself as chairman emeritus. When Jack rejected her proposal, she considered her own position untenable and resigned. Her resignation made all the papers, including five consecutive front-page stories in *The Globe and Mail*, leaving Jack to explain to the public, the authors, and his investors what he had in mind when he instructed M&S's president to make the deal with Seal's publisher, Janet Turnbull.*

When Jack called me, outraged about the negative publicity, I found it difficult to sympathize. Having appointed Linda to fix M&S, he gave her no chance to do so. He still wanted to call the shots. He told me that nobody understood that selling paperback rights was not a sale but a short-term lease, that the books would still belong to M&S when the leases ran out. His banking situation, he said, now was almost beyond rescue. He could not, absolutely could not, face another showdown. He suggested that we buy M&S outright: "Get the albatross off my back," he begged. Key Porter's

---

* It was while working for Seal that Janet first met John Irving, the famed American novelist (*The World According to Garp*, *The Hotel New Hampshire*, and many more to come). They married after a whirlwind romance. I remember the wedding at Bishop Strachan School chapel (her alma mater), with Robertson Davies reading the lesson, and the reception at the Badminton and Racquet Club, where John recited a Yeats poem. I had a chance to talk with one of my literary heroes, E. L. Doctorow, and Farley Mowat danced with my fifteen-year-old daughter Catherine.

directors—Michael de Pencier, Murray Frum, Julian, Michael Rea, former banker David Lewis—spent days trying to find ways to raise the money. Michael suggested that we could have M&S declared a national treasure and raise the money to keep it whole. That approach, Jack responded, would take longer than he could accept. What with the hyenas snapping at his heels, his authors needing constant reassurance, the press—God, he hated *The Globe and Mail*—looking for more nasty stories, and, of course, the booze, he could not hold out much longer.

A week or so later, he called again to tell me that he had finally made up his mind. He would sell M&S to Avie Bennett. Bennett already had some shares, since he had been in the $1 million investment group. He was a real estate guy, Jack said, with a yen to do something cultural, and would I please meet with him and tell him how the book business worked. He sent me packages of current M&S financials, inventory, staff, and his assorted memos. I should make the business sound rosy and play up the part about how many interesting, talented, and famous people you meet when you are a publisher. My task, Jack said, was to help close the deal.

MY FIRST IMPRESSION of Avie was that he had scant interest in publishing but did like the idea of spending time with celebrated authors. His wife, he told me, had a passion for serious literature and had always read voraciously. She would want a role in the selection of titles.* Later, in an interview, he said he thought he had bought M&S so he could have lunch with people like Margaret Atwood. An eminently good reason, I thought, as long as you had enough money to indulge yourself.

Avie and I sat and talked in various Front Street and Church Street eateries, drinking coffee, going over inventory numbers, individual staff positions, profit-and-loss statements by season and by book, royalties and advances against royalties, and how publishing decisions were made. Most of the time he wore a bemused expression, as if all this was detail he didn't

---

* She never did become involved in the business.

need to know. Now and then, to prove he had been listening, he would ask good questions, such as why keep stock of books that hadn't sold more than two copies in a whole year.

In 1985 Avie bought Jack's shares in M&S (but not Seal) for $1 million, paid out over ten years. He paid off all the minority shareholders and ploughed a further $1 million into the business. Given his reputation—he had always paid his debts and had even repaid his father's and uncle's debts after they went bankrupt—bankers had no qualms about extending loans. M&S had, I imagined, a chance to thrive again. Jack agreed to stay on in an undefined role for five years.

The *Toronto Star* ran a picture of the two smiling men, side by side behind an array of microphones and cameras. Avie seems happy and a bit shy, Jack looks as if he is about to start weeping. In the Getty Images photo from the same press conference, he is not even hiding the tears. Nor was I hiding mine. None of the celebratory speeches, the delighted authors I had known while working with Jack, made me feel better. It was the end of an era and all I felt was grief. I knew that Jack, though he said he was relieved he no longer carried the burden of the business, was bereft.

Avie moved M&S downtown to a new building he owned on University Avenue. Though his attachment to that dreadful building on Hollinger Road defied logic, Jack felt as if everything he had worked so hard to preserve was being upended. He complained that his office was too small and that it was next to the toilets. He held the phone up so I could hear the flushing (I couldn't) that, he insisted, interfered with his thinking. If he kept his door open, he could tell who was struggling with diarrhea and who had prostate problems.

People who used to work for him were now seeking advice or approval from Avie. Worse, some of "his" authors were beginning to warm to Avie, who had, they believed, saved M&S.

After about fourteen months of trying to exist in Avie's shadow, Jack called it quits. It was painful but he realized that staying would kill him. I was not surprised when he told me it was over. M&S was now someone else's bailiwick.

For a while Jack experimented with being a literary agent. His long-time secretary, Marge Hodgeman, and his daughter Sarah helped with the day-to-day. But he confided that agenting made him feel like a procurer, a "john." He hated soliciting money for authors rather than offering them money. He had never quite recovered from the time Peter Newman's "Hudson's Bay"* book went to Viking/Penguin in the UK. M&S's offer to publish with a $50,000 advance had at first seemed acceptable, but Newman became intent on an international audience and, with it, a vastly bigger advance. Peter's lawyer/agent, Michael Levine, was sent to tell Jack that the figure was $500,000; without it, the book would not be published. Jack was furious, and let Levine know it, but said that if anyone would pay such an amount, he would not stand in the way. With the legal path cleared, Levine showed the proposal to Viking/Penguin's publisher, Peter Mayer, who indeed offered $500,000 for world rights. Jack put a brave face on it, writing to Michael Levine on November 30, 1982 that "It is done, sealed, I am no longer Peter Newman's publisher in Canada." Still, Peter had been with Jack for all his previous bestsellers, and the departure had really stung.

I used to meet Jack in the garage of his Avenue Road apartment building: there was no smoking inside. We would be standing near the automatic doors, Jack chain-smoking and regretting that he couldn't even offer me a drink. His wife, Elizabeth, had turfed all his bottles. He had it on good authority, he told me once, that Avie had lost $2 million on M&S already. "And everyone said I was a bad businessman? Compared to Avie? I was a genius. I never lost a million in one year." Later he told me that Peter Newman told him that Avie had lost $12 million in his "first seven years as the owner.... However, buying M&S had forced him to sell his shopping malls at the peak of the market, and overall he had ended up further ahead than he might have otherwise."†

At a funeral we both attended, a cheerful woman approached Jack as we headed for the exit. "Didn't you used to be Jack McClelland?" she asked.

"I don't think so," muttered Jack.

---

* *Company of Adventurers* was published by Penguin in 1985, *Caesars of the Wilderness* (*Company of Adventurers Volume II*) in 1987; *Empire of the Bay* was published in 1989.

† Jack was going to mention this in the epilogue of his memoir, *My Rose Garden*.

Saying Goodbye to Margaret

M ARGARET LAURENCE WROTE this about Jack in 1986:

> I first met J. G. in 1959, when he had accepted my first novel, *This Side Jordan.* He visited Vancouver, where I then lived, and I was very young and frightened until I met him, when I knew that here was someone who really knew how to read. Our association has gone on since then. We have differed in viewpoints, and have exchanged many an angry and witty letter and have always somehow made up, because basically we were on the same side. I used to call him, for years, ironically, "Boss," an irony that we both appreciated.

It's dated Lakefield, the year she asked if I could bring "the Boss" for a visit. We knew that Margaret was gravely ill and that her health would not improve, so I picked up Jack downtown and headed to Highway 401.

All the way east to Lakefield, Jack drank vodka and talked about Margaret, about Gabrielle Roy, and Farley and Pierre, Margaret Atwood, James Houston, and even Roloff Beny and why he had risked his friendship with Margaret to publish those Iran books. He talked about how impossible the business of book publishing had become, and he talked about what rude awakening Avie would face as the years went on and his funds dwindled.

Margaret was welcoming as always, delighted to see us. We sat at her table, talking and drinking till late into the evening. Wanting to give them privacy, I came and went, looking at framed photographs, some taken by her son David, whose talents she was so keen to extol. It was a clear, shadowless day even with the sad winter trees in the gathering dusk and her small plants by the window that caught what was left of the sun. She talked about how difficult it had always been to write. That *The Diviners*, she had known from the beginning, was to be her last book because she had said in it all she had ever wanted to say. That she had been fortunate in her friends. She mentioned Adele Wiseman, whom she had known for decades and who had been to Lakefield recently, and Al Purdy, who had been a close friend, though they rarely saw each other.

Neither she nor Al had mentioned to me that they had corresponded since about 1965. The book of their letters reveals a great deal about their thoughts and feelings about the process of writing. In a 1967 letter, for example, she tells him about "trying to transform the ordinary, and I have never yet tried to transform anything quite *this* ordinary. . . . So many things have got chucked out in the process—the whole thing is a matter of paring down to the bone, of shedding gimmicks, even of shedding many explanations."* And Al, writing about Rilke and poetry, observed: "Emotion, rationality both must be fused in natural language."†

I thought, at the time, of her speech four years earlier to the Trent University Philosophy Society on the subject "My Final Hour of Life." She did not know then that she would be diagnosed with inoperable cancer. I clipped the excerpt from *The Globe and Mail* and have it still. It is light, funny, and nakedly honest. She spoke of not being a believer in "famous last words," how she had found King Lear's words, "Prithee, undo this button" infinitely more moving than highflown rhetoric. I know those words have always made me tearful no matter when or where or how often I have

---

* *Margaret Laurence–Al Purdy: A Friendship in Letters*, edited by John Lennox, McClelland & Stewart, 1993.

† Ditto. In a June 6, 1974 letter.

seen *King Lear.* She spoke of her desire to be a citizen, as well as a writer, a mother, a friend, while learning the profession of writing.

We all embraced and no one cried when we left. I kept my tears in check till we were back in the car. Jack was a long way from sober and keen to stop for another drink to dull his pain—the vodka was finished. He urged me to drive to Port Hope because Farley could always be counted on to have some liquor. The Mowats' house was dark, as one might expect at 1 a.m. but Jack was not about to give up. He threw stones at Farley's window, the one in his separate study, facing the garden, until Farley opened it and shouted something obscene to discourage kids. Not being a kid, Jack was delighted.

Jack and Farley stayed up and drank most of the night.

MARGARET COMMITTED SUICIDE on January 5, 1987. She didn't want her family and friends to endure the long goodbye. On hearing the news, I thought of the unforgettable Dylan Thomas lines she had put on the frontispiece of *Stone Angel.* She had decided instead "to go gentle into that good night."

This is the beginning of Jack's tribute to Margaret:

Margaret Laurence was probably the greatest gift to the literary community that Canada has ever known—not only through writing, but through her sheer presence—her caring, compassion, support of other writers, her deep love of all things that we value most. She was a friend. I loved her . . .

In his own farewell poem, "For Margaret," Al Purdy wrote

. . . this silly irrelevance of mine
is a refusal to think of her dead
(only parenthetically DEAD)
remembering how alive
she lit up the rooms she occupied

like flowers do sometimes and the sun always
in a way visible only to friends
and she had nothing else.

The country should have declared a day of national mourning and all flags, wherever they were, should have been lowered to mark her passing.

Imagining Canadian Literature

ONE OF THE conditions of the sale of M&S to Avie Bennett had been that Jack could not compete with his own firm; he was not to write or edit any books except those commissioned or signed by M&S. When he got an offer from HarperCollins to edit a couple of anthologies, Avie told him he couldn't do so unless he wished to break their agreement. That would mean, Jack told me, that he would not be paid the balance of the $1 million. In a letter to HarperCollins, he wrote that Avie considered even anthologies to be in breach of their agreement. In a short letter to Key Porter's Phyllis Bruce on October 2, 1989, Jack explained that "the stakes are too high and it ain't bloody well worth it" to put the balance of his payments for M&S at risk.

Jack now realized that, although it had almost killed him, he still loved the business. He felt he had been involved in something vital: the publication of significant creative artists at a time when Canada came into its own in the literary world. All his close friends had been writers, and without them, he didn't know how to be. He was in mourning.

I had been trying to talk him into writing a memoir. He would have all his papers to rely on for memories, and his daughters and Elizabeth would help. At one point he consulted former M&S editor Lily Miller about a few pieces he had prepared but not finished.

I offered $50,000 for his autobiography, but he thought he would see if he could get more from someone else. His title, *My Rose Garden*, harks back to an often told Jack fable: It's a lovely, sunny evening, the birds are singing, no clouds in the sky; you decide to take a walk in your pretty garden; along the path the air is perfumed with roses. Suddenly you step on a rake. That, in a nutshell, is book publishing.

We talked a lot at our home in Toronto and at the McClellands' Muskoka cottage, planning chapters, trying to shape the story. He found it hard to focus. The vodka failed to fill the void of no longer being Jack, the publisher. Elizabeth's efforts to hide the liquor failed, as did his voluntary stint at the Addiction Research Centre, then at Bellwood. He resisted the tone of forced piety, the references to "higher power or divine guidance."* It was, he thought, boring, and the staff indulged in quasi-religious prattle. He found it about as beneficial to him "as Christian Science and about as logical." He called me after Bellwood to tell me that he had been sorely tempted to lead a resistance movement of the "inmates"; that he disagreed with the centre's conclusion that he was an "arrogant cynic." If he had been a cynic, he would not have been able to run a publishing company for so many years, as publishing requires huge doses of optimism.

Though he still had friends, he felt lonely. He and Elizabeth spent some winter months in Florida so he could swim in the mornings and try to work on the book in the afternoons. We met there for coffee (not drinks). He was tanned and much fitter than the exhausted Jack I had known over the past few years. But when I told him the sun and the water were obviously good for him, he warned me never to believe the obvious. "I usually look better when I am seriously ailing," he said. "Actually, I am near death." Jack was a bit of a hypochondriac and tended to develop symptoms of diseases he heard or read about, but in this case he was probably right. Not long after our meeting he fell into the pool and would have drowned had it not been for a pair of observant young women who happened to see him fall.

---

* From Jack's notes on the Bellwood experience.

He told me later that he didn't think Avie would allow him to publish the autobiography with another publisher. But, he said, he had offered Avie a choice: if he insisted it must be published by M&S, Jack would write atrociously nasty things about Avie; if he let him "off the hook," Jack wouldn't even mention Avie's name. "You will publish a book that you will hate or you will not publish a book that will have no hard references to you," he told Avie.

I don't know whether this story is true, but it sounds like Jack.

He never finished the memoir, though there are pieces of it languishing in the McMaster University Archives.

Instead, some years later, Key Porter published *Imagining Canadian Literature: The Selected Letters of Jack McClelland*, edited by Sam Solecki. The book captures his tone and his extraordinary ability to be a friend, an editor, confidant, and tireless supporter of his authors. He wrote long, emotional letters to each of them, responding to their needs, worries, concerns. He had even agreed to tell an author's wife that her marriage had failed when her husband, the author, could not bring himself to do it.

In a verse letter Leonard Cohen told Jack:

You were the
real prime minister of Canada. You still
are. And even though it's all gone down
the tubes, the country that *you* govern
will never fall apart.

The Doubleday Gamble

THE DICTIONARY DEFINES *hubris* as excessive self-confidence, and that would pretty much define my reasons for thinking that a deal with the gigantic German publisher Bertelsmann would be a good idea. When they first approached me in 1986, I imagined that their Canadian acquisition, Doubleday, would partner with Key Porter, that it would warehouse, ship, and sell our books at a fraction of what it cost us to do all that ourselves. Plus, given Doubleday's heft in the marketplace, we would be offered better deals for advertising, more bookstore shelves, more reviews . . . In hindsight, of course, that was not only hubris, it was downright silly.

This is how events unfolded. In its effort to put more of the Canadian book market into Canadian hands—at the time, about seventy per cent of that industry was foreign-owned—the federal government, through our suave minister of communications, Marcel Masse, had come up with a new national policy. The "Baie Comeau" policy, as it was called, declared that it was "essential that there be a strong book publishing and distribution industry owned and controlled by Canadians." Hence, every time one multinational publisher bought another one that had a Canadian subsidiary, the publisher had to offer controlling interest in the subsidiary to Canadians. The policy was based on the reasonable assumption that it is good for Canada to have its own publishing industry.

After Bertelsmann, a US$2.4 billion German media conglomerate, bought the prestigious American company Doubleday, which had a Canadian subsidiary, I had a call from Alun Davies, the irrepressible, gossip-loving Welshman who now ran the entity known as Bantam Doubleday Dell International. Would I be interested in becoming Doubleday's Canadian partner? I was both flattered and intrigued.

Bantam Doubleday Dell's chief honcho, Alberto Vitale, who could have given Marcel Masse lessons in suave, came to our home with Alun Davies. I had met Alberto at Frankfurt and London book fairs and American Booksellers' Association (now BEA) events. He was short, Italian, with a big smile and small twinkly eyes behind black-framed glasses. He was considered smart but an outsider by most of New York's publishing princes, but I had always enjoyed his company. He had been a financial wizard at Olivetti, then at the Agnelli family holding company, before he came to America. He was convinced that publishing was tough and that no amount of talent could win in this business without strong financial backing. You had to keep the wolves from the door or your company would vanish. The 1980s were the time of mergers and takeovers in the publishing business. The weak would be swallowed up by the strong. Old-world companies would become imprints in larger companies. Bertelsmann had the kind of money Alberto needed to succeed.

When our negotiations on how I would borrow most of the money to buy fifty-one per cent of Doubleday Canada and what would happen to Key Porter Books began to stall, Alberto suggested a short break and a walk outside.

It was winter. Our path was covered by heavy, wet snow. Alberto grabbed a shovel and cleared the way in about five minutes. He was practically dancing with the shovel, skipping along in his tasselled loafers, looking like a kid with a new toy. When he returned, he was flushed, wiping the condensation from his glasses. "Well?" he asked.

He assured me that we would work out the details of their role with sales and distribution of Key Porter books, and I agreed to the deal, including borrowing most of the money from Bertelsmann itself. Somehow I imagined that I could manage both companies and even finish the novel I had been writing.

The next couple of years turned out to be chaotic. I ran between the two offices, trying to remember what had been left unresolved and where.

Doubleday's offices and warehouse were in an old brick building on Bond Street in downtown Toronto. There was one floor for book clubs and one for publishing. The warehouse was on the lowest floor, with shelves for outgoing packages and a giant machine they called Jaws whose function was to chew up every returned book, even those in pristine condition. Simpler and more economical this way, Alberto had explained when I protested that many of the destroyed books had been reordered by bookstores.

My intrepid assistant Gloria Goodman remembers how each of us clutched huge white canvas bags full of paper and manuscripts and drove up to Bond Street from The Esplanade for two and a half days each week, unpacked, made calls, handed out memos, attended meetings, emptied our in-baskets into the same canvas bags, and headed back to Key Porter. The joke going around Key Porter was that no publishing decisions were made by us before midnight.

On the plus side, I managed to persuade Bertelsmann that we needed more Canadian selections in their seven book clubs, especially the Literary Guild, the Doubleday Book Club, the Mystery Guild, and the History Book Club. I hired Susan Renouf to be editorial director of the book clubs, and we bought Canadian books to supplement or replace some of the American selections. We made Canadian titles main selections (that would mean around 15,000 additional sales for the authors); we bundled packages of three or more Canadian classics into a selection; and we took chances on new writers. It was not only good for Canada, it was profitable business and, Susan Renouf believes, could have grown into an alternative to Amazon, had Bertelsmann not been so wedded to what it had been doing for so many years. As it is, those book clubs have all vanished in Canada and the United States.

I hired John Pearce,[*] who had been editor-in-chief at the now defunct Clarke Irwin, to be editor-in-chief of Doubleday Canada. He managed

---

[*] John was also the editor of my first two novels, *Hidden Agenda* and *Mortal Sins*, and he is now my agent.

a growing list of some fine books, including Sylvia Fraser's *My Father's House*; Doris Anderson's *The Unfinished Revolution*, which Doris described as "a labour of love"; Lawrence Martin's *Breaking with History*; along with books by Joy Fielding, Charlotte Vale Allen, and Paul Quarrington.

At the Frankfurt Book Fair, John and I bought the Canadian rights to publish several books by one of my beloved mystery writers, Ruth Rendell. I still remember the excitement around the Hessischer Hof bar the night we concluded the deal.

During the preceding decades, UK and US publishers both considered Canada to be part of their territory. They sometimes fought over who would "have" Canada, but we were never a deal-breaker. Very few of us were able to persuade literary agents in other countries that Canada was, in fact, a country and that their authors would benefit from being published rather than just distributed here. Louise Dennys of Lester & Orpen Dennys was another Canadian publisher battling for the right to license Canadian rights. With her literary taste, tenacity, and lovely British accent, she had managed to hive off rights for such luminaries as Italo Calvino, Ian McEwan, and P. D. James.

At the time of the Rendell purchase, Century Hutchinson's Anthony Cheetham had held her Canadian rights. He expected to see the arrangement continue, though Ruth was receiving a fraction of the money she got when her agent sold Canada as a separate country. It was at least seven years before Anthony* spoke to me again. I am still reading Ruth Rendell and have mourned her death with all her other fans.

I am not sure why Michael de Pencier agreed to my splitting my time between our venture and Doubleday, though I assume the notion of co-operating with a large multinational seemed tempting initially. But he was also preoccupied with growing Key—I was on his board then—and in 1987 he was distracted by a debilitating lawsuit.

---

* Anthony Cheetham is another publishing legend. In addition to starting Century Hutchinson, he also founded Abacus, Orion, Macdonald Futura, Quercus, and most recently, Zeus—a great name for a publishing house, especially one run by Anthony.

The prominent Reichmann family sued *Toronto Life* magazine for $101 million (until then, the biggest amount ever asked for in a Canadian libel suit) over an article by Elaine Dewar entitled "The Mysterious Reichmanns: The Untold Story." At the time, the Reichmanns' Olympia and York was the largest real estate development company in the world. Julian was *Toronto Life*'s lawyer and, like me, a director of Key Publishers, *Toronto Life*'s owners.

The case stretched into two years with endless meetings, discoveries, and misery for Michael. I still can't reveal the nature of the final settlement, except that it was painful for all of us.

DESPITE OUR FREQUENT commiserations, I was still surprised when Jack called in January 1987 to say that he wanted to sell us his fifty-one per cent of Seal Books. He argued that since he no longer ran M&S, it was pointless to have Seal. Plus, since Avie had assumed he would be offered Seal, Jack was eager to deny him the pleasure. I needed time to think. I was already busy with two companies, had two young daughters and a busy husband, and was a member of a number of corporate boards.

Julian and I went to Switzerland that winter at director Norman Jewison's invitation (we had become friends while I was trying to persuade Norman to write a book). Our daughters skied with Norman's much older children, Julian took on the mountain with Norman, and after a few disastrous attempts to ski, I walked along the paths skirting the ski hills, thinking about the future.

On the way home, I decided to give Seal another try. At the time I thought that if my relationship with Bertelsmann was going to work (sort of) for Doubleday, perhaps it would also work for Seal. The purchase of Seal was quick, since Jack wasn't looking for much money and Alberto was, indeed, keen for Key Porter to acquire majority shares.

We moved Seal's small office to the Doubleday building on Bond Street and I hired Dean Cooke to be publisher. Dean had worked at Doubleday before, and I assumed he would fit in easily. In a year or so, however, this formerly cheerful and charming man became strangely morose. He had difficulty navigating a path between Alun Davies and me. Both of us seemed to think we were in charge, and we frequently made contradictory decisions. Several times Alun cancelled contracts I had negotiated, and almost as often, I ignored his objections.

Any illusions I had retained that there would be an advantage to Key Porter from the affiliation with Doubleday vanished near the end of my first two years. Alberto explained that he saw no reason for Doubleday to take on Key Porter's sales, and anyway, they were going to close the Canadian warehouse. It was much, much cheaper to ship everything from Chicago. I couldn't argue with this premise for the US books on the list, and he couldn't understand why Canadian books should be any different. But I found the notion of shipping Canadian books from a Canadian printer to a US warehouse to be shipped back to Canada unacceptable. For him, it was a simple matter of mathematics—as simple as his patient explanation proving that it was cheaper to destroy and reprint, if needed, than to select, store, and ship.

It was interesting to meet the Bertelsmann men. In particular, I remember the rather wizened Reinhard Mohn, a former lieutenant in Rommel's Afrika Korps, whose family firm prospered printing propaganda for the Nazis but collapsed at the end of the war. By 1986 Mohn had rebuilt the company and grew it into a giant conglomerate. Peter Olson, Bertelsmann's chief honcho in the United States, had an office in a separate building from the rest of the company. He managed to sound both conspiratorial and obsequious about Bertelsmann's US ambitions. He spoke several languages, including German and Russian. The company already published more than two thousand new titles a year, and Peter was tasked with significantly increasing its twenty per cent market share. He was ruthless but not ruthless enough to achieve the numbers until after he had negotiated the purchase of Random House. I would love to have overheard his negotiations with Alberto Vitale. In a 2008 article, *The New York Times* billed Olson the enigmatic "godfather of Random House," but later that year, his time as CEO of the merged companies was up.

Marcus Wilhelm, the fun-loving book club numbers man, had been sent to Canada for a test run before he was to go to the United States to guarantee Bertelsmann's market dominance. At heart a young rebel, despite his family's conservative connections, Marcus was delighted with the growth that the Canadian selections brought, and he loved the attention of Canadian publishers. But he had greater ambitions than whatever Bond Street could provide.

I had observed the preening "Bertelsmen"—they were all guys—in Paris, New York, London, and their headquarters in Gütersloh, but their best performance was always at the Frankfurt Book Fair. Dinners in their grand hotel suites and parades along the crowded aisles established their reputation, as did the colossal sums they were willing to pay for what they considered lead books or lead opportunities. I had the chance to file in with the rest of the international staff to the big annual, guarded Bertelsmann party, the party everyone who was anyone in the publishing world wanted to attend.

From *Mortal Sins* to *The Bookfair Murders*

M OST OF US never get over our childhoods. While I had acquired Canadian citizenship and a fully formed Canadian identity, those Hungarian phantoms continued to haunt me. My experiences with the Communist criminal justice system, what I had seen of the '56 Revolution, my memory of the young Russian soldier who died while I was holding his hand, as much as my grandfather's stories have remained part of who I am. There was no room for those memories in my publishing life, or in the life I had built with Julian and our children, though there was one strange event when Catherine was eight years old.

She had started to sleepwalk. Most nights I would find her wandering along the passageway to the stairs, or trying to open the back door toward the ravine. Julian and I read up on the dangers of waking someone when she or he was sleepwalking; instead we walked with her, making calming noises, and trying to gently steer her back to her bed.

After a few months of sleepless nights, I made an appointment with a child psychiatrist. He was a big, soft-spoken guy with a sunny disposition. Catherine, apprehensive, sat on my lap and watched him intently. About five minutes after we settled in, he got a pile of white paper and an assortment of colouring pencils and told her he would love it if she would draw him some pictures. She got down on the carpet and began to draw. As she was attacking the sheets of paper, he began to ask me about my childhood. He was particularly interested in the times I spent in jail, about the mangled bodies I had seen on the streets of Budapest, and how my mother and I had managed to escape. I kept telling him that the reason we had come was Catherine's sleepwalking.

An hour later, he told me our session was over, took Catherine's drawings, and complimented her on her choice of colours and her compositions. "Let me know if you have any more problems," he said to me.

"Is this it for today?" I asked.

"This should be the end of it," he said. "You have a very sensitive daughter. And don't forget she listens even when you are not talking."

He was right and Catherine never sleepwalked again.

The reason I tell this story is that I had assumed my childhood memories had receded over the years in New Zealand and Canada. They hadn't and they had a strange way of showing up. There is a mysterious, malevolent figure in *Hidden Agenda* who is probably Hungarian, and the central figure in *Mortal Sins* is clearly Hungarian, hiding a terrible secret under a false identity in Canada. The novel turns on how far he and his family are willing to go to hide his true identity and how he had come by it. Both books are also satirical inside stories of the publishing world in Canada, the United States, and Europe.

With my third mystery, *The Bookfair Murders*, I had a chance to make fun of that Grand Guignol of book events, the annual Bertelsmann party at the Intercontinental Hotel during the Frankfurt International Book Fair. There were five hundred carefully selected guests. The picture I presented with the Bertelsmann wives at one end of the room, and the mistresses at the other, was only a little bit fictional. They actually mingled at the packed buffet tables. The novel's central story of an author continuing to write her novels after her death because the company publishing her can't afford to let her be buried was then a bit unusual, but true. Nowadays, the bestselling dead keep producing their books, unapologetically, and the public keeps buying them, as long as they are pretty much the same as the previous books.

I have kept one of the giant red banners List Verlag, German publishers of *The Bookfair Murders*, displayed over the wide avenue leading to the convention grounds: *Mord auf der Buchmesse: Nur List kennt der Tater* (Murder at the Bookfair: Only List knows who did it). It's now the backdrop to one end of our tennis court in Georgian Bay and does a grand job of keeping the wind out.

I dedicated *The Bookfair Murders* to my eclectic group of book fair friends, a.k.a. the Quasimodo dinner group. It included British agent extraordinaire Clare Alexander, Penguin Australia's Bob Sessions, Transworld's Patrick Janson-Smith, Workman's Carolan Workman, St. Martins's Tom Dunne, and the inimitable, brilliant wit Les Pockell. Though we were scattered all over the world, we had all grown up in the book business. Frankfurt was our annual reunion. The dinner had one unbreakable tradition. Bob Sessions, at some point, would stand up and tell a long, hilarious, shaggy dog version of a Quasimodo joke. We all knew it so well, we'd call out our beloved turning points or howl with outrage if Bob left out a bit.

It was Les Pockell who, having spent several years in Japan working for Kodansha, was able to initiate me into interpreting Japanese reactions to seeing book projects. They ranged from the mild "very interesting," meaning "no thank you," to the more determined "hmm, very, very interesting," meaning "stop showing me this piece of Western trash," and the final "hmm," meaning "I would sooner die than waste one more minute looking at this dreck." "One more thing," he instructed. "Do try to look shorter."

Les's invaluable advice saved Key Porter's Polly Manguel and me a great deal of time during selling trips to Japan. One day in Tokyo, there was an earthquake during Polly's rather spirited presentation. The table and our chairs moved, the chandelier swung, the windows rattled, and Polly and I followed our hosts' example in pretending not to notice. She mentioned later that it would have been an ignominious way to die.

Polly, who was with Key Porter for a number of years, was a funny and brilliant salesperson. On our international travels we always shared rooms to save money, laughed a lot, listened to each other's phone calls, and bought each other wine when we felt discouraged or wanted to celebrate. Polly had been married to writer Alberto Manguel. They divorced when he announced that he was gay. Polly liked to talk to all three of their children every day, timing her calls so that they would be home from school.

TO MY ASTONISHMENT, Catherine announced in 1989 that she wanted to be presented as a debutante at the Helicon Ball in Toronto. Not everyone has heard of the Helicon Ball, and if you are neither a dignitary nor Hungarian, chances are you would not have been invited. It is a somewhat anachronistic old-world ball with long gowns for the women, dinner jackets or traditional Hungarian evening wear for the gents. There is an introductory dance called *palotas*, performed by energetic young people in colourful embroidered costumes. As far as I could determine, Catherine's interest in things Hungarian was negligible. She spoke five or six words of the language, hated the couple of times I tried to interest her in Hungarian school (they did folk dancing), and when I took my two daughters to Hungary, she was eager to get home to her friends. Hardly surprising, since she was about eleven at the time, and one of the highlights of my childhood, tiny Lake Balaton, was a huge disappointment after Lake Huron and Lake Ontario.

But now she was seventeen and determined. Julian took waltzing lessons from an abrasive German woman who thought he lacked talent for dancing. Catherine looked spectacular in her white, layered lace gown (I wish we had kept it). I have a photograph of her practicing her curtsy for her presentation to Lieutenant-Governor Lincoln Alexander, her father grinning sheepishly at her side.

As the psychiatrist said, Catherine had listened even when she seemed not to be listening—and even when I wasn't talking.

Five Years of Struggle to Come to Terms
with an Illusion

WHEN MARCUS WILHELM was moved to the United States to take over the American Doubleday book clubs, he was replaced by a numbers man from Bertelsmann's head office in Gütersloh with no interest in the clubs' Canadian selections. Commitments that had been made in the United States were to be honoured in Canada, even when the books seemed quite unsuitable to our audiences. Every Canadian selection was a battle, and the bundles of Canadian classics that Susan Renouf had introduced into the program no longer fit the systems Bertelsmann had developed.

I remember meeting for breakfast in Frankfurt with international book club boss Dr. Walter Gerstgrasser, who informed me that, while deviations for each country were acceptable, overall direction had to come from the men (yes, they were all men) who had developed the clubs and had grown them to more than 25 million members worldwide. It was Gerstgrasser who introduced me to Karsten Dietrich, in charge of France Loisirs, the French club, Bertelsmann's most successful book club enterprise at the time. Karsten was sympathetic to what I had been trying to do in Canada, but he told me the kinds of changes would be viewed more favourably by the bosses if I was working for the book clubs full-time. It turned out that there was no love lost between the clubs and the publishing divisions.*

I used to visit Alberto in New York: he rarely came to Canada. Our discussions about Doubleday Canada were cordial but infrequent. The 1980s recession had been tough on the booktrade both sides of the border. He reminded me that the real value of Doubleday Canada was in its right to sell books produced in the United States, and as long as those sales continued to be at least ten per cent of the American market, there would be few problems. Canadian books were a negligible part of their overall income, but as long as they didn't lose much money, there was no harm in them. He said he thought it had been wise that I had hung on to Key Porter. At least it was something I could have real influence over. That could never be the case with Doubleday. As for the Canadian government's protectionist policies, he believed that phase would pass. Canada needed American investment and increased trade with the United States. He saw no sense in nationalism—not even of the benign Canadian variety.

Alberto had little interest in individual authors. He was a businessman. His job—and it was a big job—was to steer the company right in troubled waters and make sure everyone did their work for the benefit of the corporation.

I am not sure how the partnership lasted five years. I was constantly exhausted, worried, beleaguered by too many demands and looking for a way out of my multiple roles. My usually laid-back staff was complaining. No one understood why certain books would be published by Key Porter and others by Doubleday. I had lost track of where Seal fit into the overall plan. Or whether there was even an overall plan. My original idea of Doubleday's performing sales and warehousing functions for Key Porter had gone down the drain and I now realized that there was never going to be an independent Doubleday Canada. As far as Bertelsmann was con-

---

* It was only in Canada, and only because of the government's policies on takeovers, that the clubs and the publishing division produced combined year-end financial statements. The whole exercise drove the Bertelsmen crazy.

cerned, all parts of the puzzle had always been intended to fit into the large Bertelsmann group—publishing on one side, book clubs on the other. I knew I had to get out of the partnership.

Bantam Doubleday Dell and I parted ways reasonably amicably when I invoked the "buy-sell" clause in our original agreement. I am not sure which one of us was more relieved, Alberto or me. We managed to remain cordial, though mutually suspicious. From time to time I visited him in his swish New York offices. Occasionally he still invited me to lunch. As did Marcus Wilhelm, who had taken over all of Bertelsmann's US book clubs but complained that the fun had gone out of the mail-order business as well as his own life. The pressure was unrelenting and the top honchos were unwilling to admit that there were crucial differences between the Bertelsmann model for book clubs and how American buyers operate.

After the end of my Doubleday adventure, we also sold Key Porter's shares in Seal Books to Bantam Doubleday Dell. When I was asked why, I answered that I gave up on it for the same reason I had given up skiing. It wasn't going to get any better.* "It hadn't worked for Jack and it wasn't going to work for me." Bantam's administrative overhead charges, their destruction of all returns and unsold books, their approach to write-downs was never going to work for a small, nominally independent company such as Seal. "Nominally" is, indeed, how it felt when Bertelsmann decided to exercise their option to buy our shares. There was no chance that we could bid competitively in the terms of the buy-sell agreement we had signed when Key Porter bought the majority of Seal shares.

After all that struggle, it was a relief to return to Key Porter full-time. Even the dusty overhead beams looked good.

Alberto Vitale had been appointed president of Random House in 1989. He was given a much larger office with a much better view and an expense account that had no difficulty stretching to expensive lunches at

---

* Roy MacSkimming quotes this in *The Perilous Trade: Publishing Canada's Writers* (McClelland & Stewart, 2003).

the Four Seasons Restaurant's inner sanctum, where waiters were eager to usher him to what I assumed was now his usual table.

The last time I saw Alun Davies, he had retired, but he still knew all the gossip about everyone important in the book business. He let me take his small white dog for a walk in a nearby park.

Saving the World, One Book at a Time

EVER SINCE MY mid-teens, I have been an environmentalist. It started with too many imported rabbits and the clear-cut, eroding mountainsides in New Zealand. Then, in 1965, my stepsister Ines and I sailed from Sydney, Australia, to Naples, Italy. There were islands of floating plastic debris, the stench of dead fish, and as we entered the Indian Ocean, oil slicks. Years later, I listened to the Indigenous people in Haida Gwaii off the coast of British Columbia talk about their success in stopping the forestry companies' clear-cuts. I wrote an article about "the ghosts of Haida Gwaii" for *The Globe and Mail.* In the Pacific Ocean there had been mounds of cans, bits of netting, and plastic bottles rolling in with the waves. I had been on the board of the Young Naturalist Foundation with Mary Anne Brinckman and Annabel Slaight, working out ways to engage kids in the battle to save what would soon be their own world.

In Georgian Bay, clams have been replaced by zebra mussels. Our shoreline is often lined with soapsuds, and the carp that used to mate at the back of the island every spring are gone. I believe John Livingston's thesis that we are on the verge of destroying our own planet. And I believed Farley Mowat when he told me we were, ourselves, on the path to extinction. Both John and Farley blamed our own, all-too-human greed.

Ever since I first met Monte Hummel, I had been eager to support the

World Wildlife Fund. Monte and I planned books both as fundraisers and to focus attention on the need to preserve what we still had of the natural world. In the early days we spent hours plotting approaches to corporations for funding and to governments to set aside protected areas for wildlife. Monte was a great advocate. He had an unfailing memory for the facts, the numbers, the spaces—"You can't save species without saving spaces"—where we still had a chance to make a difference. There was one memorable telephone meeting with a Progressive Conservative federal minister who didn't even listen to our full pitch before he said, "You've got it, Monte."

After *Arctic Wildlife* and *Polar Bears*, Key Porter published WWF's *Endangered Spaces: The Future of Canada's Wilderness*, a call for action to preserve Canada's natural heritage. It set out a plan to claim 39 million hectares of land for parks and wilderness areas, including Wapusk south of Churchill for polar bears, Ivvavik in the Yukon for caribou, grasslands for prairie wildlife in Saskatchewan, South Moresby for marine species. Our petition collected more than a million signatures. It was a monumental effort, in part organized and paid for by Glen Davis, millionaire son of Nelson Davis of *Canadian Establishment* fame.

Glen was a naturalist, an explorer of wilderness areas, a big, ruddy-faced man who enjoyed canoeing with friends, and wearing Mountain Equipment Co-op clothes, Tilley hats, and red sweatbands, drinking beer, and eating burgers. He lacked every kind of pretension and had little use for his fortune, except for what good it could do. There was not much he didn't know about endangered spaces and species. We used to meet at Biagio's on King Street, and later with Monte and WWF staff in the Granite Brewery at Eglinton and Mount Pleasant. That was where we planned the caribou book, published by Dundurn after I had left Key Porter.*

Glen was consistently kind. Knowing that environmentalists made little money, he used to buy Elizabeth May's formal outfits for meetings with

---

* *Caribou and the North: A Shared Future*, by Monte Hummel and Justina C. Ray, 2008.

government functionaries. Elizabeth, later the Green Party leader, was then executive director of the Sierra Club. I was very fortunate to have known Glen.*

We published Elizabeth's *At the Cutting Edge: The Crisis in Canada's Forests*, survived two lawsuits launched by forestry companies, and continued to take our chances with her *How to Save the World in Your Spare Time*. Elizabeth is both a passionate advocate and a witty companion who always makes a distinction between the seriousness of her subject and her own rather modest Cape Breton self. We used to joke about retiring to Nova Scotia, a couple of addled old ladies with not much to do but read books and lecture the locals on how life used to be. Nova Scotia, we both believed, is more tolerant of addled old ladies than other parts of Canada. It's a joke—or was it a plan?—I also shared with Susan Renouf, who hails from Nova Scotia and has more reason than I have for being in love with the place.

SINCE JACK WAS no longer part of M&S, and Farley Mowat felt no loyalty to Avie Bennett, he decided to publish with Key Porter. In the past, we had weathered many publishing storms together, travelled together on a few of M&S's mad promotional tours, and shared concerns for Jack's health and well-being. Publishing Farley has remained one of my best memories of this crazy business, and I still cherish some of his late books: *My Father's Son*, for example, *Born Naked*, and *High Latitudes*. His ferocity had not softened during the years since the publication of his first book—*People of the Deer*—at M&S.

As Margaret Atwood wrote in her introduction to *High Latitudes*: "His rage can be Swiftian, his humour Puckish, but his compassion for creatures great and small has been consistent. . . . The fact that he's grinning

---

* Sadly, my friend Glen was murdered for his money in the World Wildlife's underground parking garage on May 18, 2007. I never pass by that place without feeling unutterably sad.

like a goat should fool no one: he has always been a deeply serious and intensely committed writer."

Though Farley tried to dissuade me because he didn't think it would sell, we reissued *Sea of Slaughter*. Much of the horror it records has been superseded by worse horrors inflicted on the oceans, but it remains a must-read for everyone who cares about our world and wants, against all odds, to change the way people behave. I had hoped to persuade high school libraries to order copies and teachers to recommend it to students. Farley didn't think that would work: educators stay away from real issues and in the end the book would not make a jot of difference. He was right on both counts.

Farley championed our publishing Paul Watson's *Ocean Warrior, My Battle to End the Illegal Slaughter on the High Seas*. Watson, a former Greenpeacer (founded in 1971, Greenpeace champions the environment), had created the Sea Shepherd Conservation Society, a group dedicated to preserving marine life. They had scuttled whaling ships, chased foreign fishing boats out of Canadian waters, stopped sealers killing baby seals on ice floes, and during the filming of the documentary *Sharkwater*, attacked the crew of a fishing boat illegally shark-finning.

Dealing with the peripatetic author, who styled himself Captain Watson, was challenging. However, his short visits dressed in full imitation (I assume) leather to the Key Porter offices were sufficiently exciting to make up for the difficulties. Later Captain Watson starred in the TV series based on his life.

I called R. D. Lawrence, Charlie Russell, and Fred Bruemmer and told them Key Porter was committed to publishing books about nature, wildlife, and the environment.

R. D.—I never called him by whatever his forename was—had become a conservation teacher after surviving both the Spanish Civil War and the Second World War. Like Farley, he had become disillusioned with humankind. He lived on a large piece of land in Haliburton County where he maintained a wolf pack. We commissioned him to write several books, including *Trail of the Wolf, The Shark, The Natural History of Canada*, and *In Praise of Wolves*, and to edit a series about wildlife for young readers.

A passionate advocate for the conservation of spaces where animals could thrive, he believed that our governments were only interested in managing wildlife for the sake of a minority: hunters. Ontario was still approving the poisoning of wolves, and it had opened provincial parks to hunting at a time when most indigenous wolf species were endangered.

Charlie Russell's first encounter with the white Kermode bears was on Princess Royal Island, in northwestern British Columbia. He was working on a film and became fascinated with one young bear in particular. It was playful, curious, and not in the least afraid of humans. Bears on this island had not had much exposure to our own murderous species. Charlie was the son of Andy Russell, wilderness guide, author, and photographer, so Charlie had already encountered bears, but none like this one. He ate, fished, and even wrestled with the young bear. His book, *Spirit Bear: Encounters with the White Bear of the Western Rainforest*, came out of this experience. Like R. D., he believed that there was much more revenue—if financial returns were to be the only measure—from bear viewing than from bear hunting. Fortunately, Princess Royal Island has been classified by the World Wildlife Fund and Environment Canada as part of a protected area.[*]

We commissioned Fred Bruemmer to write and provide photographs for several books, most of them about the Arctic, where Fred felt completely at home. He was a child of the Second World War, one of two hundred survivors out of more than two thousand inmates in a slave labour camp. The Inuit, like Fred himself, were survivors in a harsh environment that allowed for no missteps. Fred's *The Arctic World* is, I think, one of the most spectacular books we ever published. It presents the Arctic not as a remote, hostile, empty, and lethal environment but as a place full of the most diverse life. The book draws on all of Fred's talents: perceptive nature

---

[*] Charlie went on to spend eight years in Kamchatka, trying to convince people that grizzlies were worth preserving. He built a relationship of mutual trust with the bears, but reading his book about the experience convinced me that it is fatal for bears to befriend humans.

photographer, journalist, researcher, and storyteller, as well as a lover of the Arctic peoples.

The most beautiful marine conservation book we published was Joe MacInnis's *Saving the Oceans*. Few people know as much about the oceans as Joe. An explorer, a scientist, a medical doctor, a diver—the first scientist to dive under the ice at the North Pole—he had launched the Deep Diver submersible that can provide accommodation four hundred feet underwater. He was on the team that found the *Titanic* and was one of the first to see the remains of the *Edmund Fitzgerald* after its forty years in Lake Huron. Astonishingly energetic, fast-talking, finishing a few of my slower sentences, Joe had not slowed down after hundreds of dives and as many adventures.

I presented slides and mocked-up pages from our illustrated books at the Frankfurt Book Fair. The plyboard dividers of our booth were usually festooned with large colour photos of wolves, grizzlies, polar bears, narwhal, moose, puffins, songbirds, seabirds, owls, eagles, and seals.* Our idea was that wandering publishers and booksellers would stop and want to see more. We were particularly successful at attracting German and Dutch publishers, none of whom had seen much wildlife before. We added books about rivers and mountains, salmon, sharks, and whales. We commissioned a book on Canada's National Parks and, despite our failed efforts to sell it at national parks kiosks, managed to make it a bestseller.

Along the way, we became one of the foremost environmental publishers in the world, and as we surveyed the stands at the Frankfurt International Book Fair and at the American Booksellers' Association's annual events, no one else seemed to rival our commitment. Even Sierra Club Books in San Francisco bought our books and were happy to come back for more.

---

* Many of the books were edited by Michael Mouland, who went on to work for Firefly Books after Key Porter. Jonathan Webb edited the bird books, most of which were written and photographed by amateur birder John (Jack) Mackenzie, who was a friend of Michael de Pencier and a professional in the financial business.

Margaret Laurence, anxious about my introduction, and Catherine focusing on her balloon, on the podium during the Authors at Harbourfront series.

Barbara Frum at the CBC, interviewing someone for *As It Happens*.

A young Conrad Black (*left*) sharing a laugh with Prime Minister Joe Clark.

The redoubtable journalist and advocate Doris Anderson in her office at *Chatelaine*.

Peter Worthington's election button. He ran for the Conservatives in the 1984 general election.

Michael de Pencier, John Honderich, Peter Gzowski, and Honor de Pencier at a Peter Gzowski Annual Invitational (PGI) golf tournament in the 1990s.

With McClelland & Stewart president Linda McKnight (*left*) and literary agents Bella Pomer and Lucinda Vardey (*right*).

With Lorraine Durham (*left*) and Annabel Slaight in the makeshift Key Porter booth at a Canadian booksellers' convention.

My close friend and renowned photographer Dudley Witney, in 1995.

Alberta Premier Peter Lougheed and writer David Wood at the launch of *The Lougheed Legacy*.

The irrepressible Gloria Goodman with a larger-than-life picture of me at the launch of my second novel, *Mortal Sins*.

Prime Minister Brian Mulroney holds a copy of *Ontario*, our big sesquicentennial book, in 1984.

Jean Chrétien at the podium in our home celebrating the English language publication of his soon-to-be mega bestseller, *Straight from the Heart.*

Journalist Allan Fotheringham at a cover shoot for his book *Birds of a Feather*, published by Key Porter in 1989. The bird kept nipping at his ear during the shoot, but we got this great photo out of it—and it was hilarious to watch.

Jack McClelland announcing the sale of McClelland & Stewart to Avie Bennett (*right*) in 1985.

Author and photographer Fred Bruemmer, whose books and images form a lasting legacy of the Arctic.

Filmmaker Norman Jewison at one of our dinner parties, with Margaret Atwood in the background.

Author Basil Johnston at the Native Arts Festival in Owen Sound, 2005.

My friend, the multi-talented, urbane CBC producer, brilliant writer, and all around wit, George Jonas.

The unstoppable journalist, author, and activist June Callwood.

With Scott McIntyre of Douglas & McIntyre at a Giller Prize gala.

With Peter Munk at the launch of *Kasztner's Train*.

With my dear friend Jack
Rabinovitch at a Giller Prize gala.

In Budapest in 2005, when I was visiting as part of a CBC documentary commemorating
the fiftieth anniversary of the Hungarian Revolution.

From time to time, Douglas & McIntyre's Greystone Books* presented a challenge with Candace Savage's books—*Pelicans, Eagles, Wolves, Grizzly Bears, Wild Cats*—but it was, overall, a friendly contest.† Scott McIntyre and I were both graduates of M&S and are still close, even though we have both left the trenches of the book biz.

My favourite of all those conservation books remains *Wintergreen*. It's Monte Hummel's personal story of his relationship with and affection for the 270 acres of land around Loon Lake where his cabin hides. It has been his sanctuary, a kind of spiritual wellspring, "a safe harbour that makes no unwelcome demands," that has inspired his work. Monte believes that most of us have been to such places and can, if we decide it's sufficiently important to do so, contribute to the conservation of our natural world. In Canada, a significant portion of that land is in private hands.

---

* Greystone, with Rob Sanders as publisher, is now an independent affiliated with the Heritage Group and with the David Suzuki Institute.

† Candace Savage was tough competition. She is the author of more than twenty books and the winner of several writing awards, including the Hilary Weston Writers' Trust Non-Fiction Prize for *A Geography of Blood*.

Growing Pains

A FTER A TUMULTUOUS but exciting decade, I was still imagining that we could expand Key Porter Books. In 1991 we had an opportunity to acquire the inventory and contracts of publisher Lester & Orpen Dennys, a prestigious literary house run by Malcolm Lester and Louise Dennys. The strange saga of that acquisition began with Christopher Ondaatje, Michael Ondaatje's older brother. He was a member of Julian's investment club, the Canyon Club, a group of fifteen seemingly macho guys who invested a small (about two thousand dollars each) amount in a fund that the money-making wizard members could spin into enough gold to provide food and wine for the group in fine restaurants and occasional trips with wives to warm places in the winter or golfing destinations in the summer. I was one of the wives.* Christopher was one of the dross-into-gold spinners. Tall and spindly with a sharp-edged nose, he had an intense look when he was interested in something. There is a striking portrait of him in London's National Portrait Gallery, donated by the man himself. When he wasn't interested in what you were saying, he just walked away.

---

* Strangely, several wives took up religion: a few became Protestant pastors, others Catholic philosophers who argued for the admission of women into the priesthood.

On those Canyon Club trips, Christopher often discussed publishing with me, including how he had built Pagurian, his tiny book publishing venture, into a profitable corporation with assets of more than $300 million and growing. He also talked about his childhood in Sri Lanka (then Ceylon) and the English private school he had to leave when his family lost its fortune. He talked of his alcoholic father, an almost mythic figure who, though loved and revered by both his sons, had managed to drink away their inheritance.

When the family's funds withered, Christopher and Michael's mother moved to London to escape the scandal. She made ends meet by running a boarding house. Christopher came to Canada determined to reverse his father's legacy. He had represented Canada in the four-man bobsled team at the 1964 Olympics, but that was not the only kind of success he sought. He co-founded Loewen, Ondaatje, McCutcheon with two other Canyon members: Charles Loewen and Julian's former brother-in-law, Fred McCutcheon. The firm specialized in research-based investment banking and, while Charles did most of the heavy lifting, Christopher was its swashbuckling financial genius.

Not surprising then that Christopher's hero was the adventurer-writer Richard Burton. He had a portrait of Burton in his dining room, and his plans for the future, he told me, included following in Burton's footsteps.*
Why he had wanted to buy a small literary publishing house was mystifying. L&OD had famously published (in Canada) Italo Calvino, Kazuo Ishiguro, Ian McEwan, P. D. James, Don DeLillo, Graham Greene, Martin Amis, as well as Joy Kogawa, Sandra Birdsell, Josef Skvorecky, Alberto Manguel, to mention a few. They also had a prestigious history list with books like *The Illustrated History of Canada* and Irving Abella and Harold Troper's *None Is Too Many*. But that could not have been the reason Pagurian bought L&OD. A few industry insiders thought he wanted to have

---

* His 1996 book, *Sindh Revisited: A Journey in the Footsteps of Captain Sir Richard Francis Burton 1842–1849, the Indian Years* is fascinating not only for what it reveals about Burton but also for what it reveals about Christopher.

his own book published by a respected house; others guessed that he was impressed with Louise's British literary credentials, including the fact that she was Graham Greene's niece.

It was easier to see how Malcolm and Louise walked into the deal. They had cash-flow problems of the type most publishers encounter when they hold too much inventory. Plus they had been charmed (who wouldn't be?) when Christopher had flown them to Bermuda and given them the royal Christopher treatment. I still remember the late summer day in 1988, in the Roof Lounge of the Park Plaza, when Christopher and Louise announced the deal to the press.

The honeymoon lasted only a few months. Christopher sold Pagurian to Hees, a holding company controlled in a hugely complicated way by Peter Bronfman and Jack Cockwell. He then moved to the UK, where he became known as a prominent philanthropist and was awarded a CBE.

Tim Price, chairman of Hees, said the firm had no desire to run a publishing house. Having concluded that publishing was "a very difficult business," they decided to shut it down. That move would save them the cost of paying outstanding debts.

In 1991 we acquired what was left of L&OD in a series of negotiations that were as tough as they were baffling, given what an infinitesimal portion of Hees's holdings—it had grown to about $500 million by then and L&OD's gross income was less than $1 million—were involved. I once asked Peter Bronfman when we both served on the Alliance Board why his group had taken such a rough stand on this company, when they could have been generous or waited until they found someone to buy it as a going concern. He told me that while he, personally, had been sympathetic—he said he liked Malcolm—he had agreed long ago to stay out of all Hees corporate decisions. That approach may have been a colossal mistake for several reasons, but those belong in another book.

A good question at the time would have been why I thought it was a good idea to buy the L&OD assets. There are two answers: first, because I thought we needed variety in our backlist. A strong backlist, I had learned at M&S, would give us ballast for years when we couldn't get the bestsellers we needed. Jack had always reasoned that the backlist was his company's real strength and he had taught me most of what I knew about the business. The second reason was my admiration for what Malcolm and Louise had built. Our deal with Hees guaranteed that all L&OD authors would be paid their outstanding royalties. Then Key Porter could ensure that their books would continue to have a life. Most of the authors were willing to sign on with us, though some of them would not commit to future titles.

One of the most valuable projects we acquired was *The Story of Canada* by Janet Lunn and Christopher Moore, illustrated by Alan Daniels, a project that Phyllis Bruce, with infinite patience, nursed to completion. I remember her trying desperately to urge Daniels to deliver the last of his spectacular drawings.

The book won all the awards available for Canadian children's books and went into several printings and editions. Janet was shy, thoughtful, and not keen to do the kind of publicity that we had planned for her, but she went, accepting most of her appointments with grace. She also agreed to edit our *Canadian Children's Treasury*, a big illustrated book that, like *The Story of Canada*, went through many printings—about one hundred thousand copies sold when I last looked. For it was also another foray into the door-to-door sales market we had entered with our first big Canada book, *Canada: A Celebration*. There were, then, several unusual characters running operations that sold books through large offices, leaving a sample book with the receptionist and returning to deliver the books bought and collect the money.

We reissued most of the L&OD novels, including Kazuo Ishiguro's Booker winner *The Remains of the Day*, Joseph Skvorecky's *The Engineer of Human Souls*, and one of Graham Greene's least successful books, *Monsieur Quixote*. Taking over their list felt like dressing in someone else's Sunday best, but it was satisfying to see the books thrive, and we designed a new L&OD imprint for the international fiction list in honour of the little company that disappeared. We added new titles by Norman Levine, Sylvia Fraser, and Matt Cohen.

Louise, Malcolm, and I had long meetings and a few lunches at Biagio's to try to find a way for them to join us, but the discussions faltered (we didn't have enough money) and Louise accepted an offer from Knopf Canada, an imprint of Random House, to become its publisher. Some L&OD authors followed her. I was not unsympathetic, but a few of the departures were painful.*

P. D. James, for example. I had been a P. D. James fan since I read her first Adam Dalgliesh mystery, *Cover Her Face*, and I had hoped that her three mysteries could be the beginning of a KP mystery line. We met in her agent Elaine Greene's quite charming London office decorated with photographs of authors, shelves of books, and a low table heaped high with manuscripts. Elaine offered tea and was impeccably polite but equally emphatic in her determination that the mysteries, together with new books Phyllis (the *P* in P. D.) was going to write, would go to Louise. Their relationship, she argued, was important to Phyllis and she simply could not begin with someone new. Though the agent agreed that our contracts were binding, she said that as a publisher who cared about authors, I should let her client go. To add a nice touch to the general moral suasion, she said she had read and enjoyed *Hidden Agenda*.

I agreed reluctantly and remained P. D.'s constant fan, reading each of her books as it came along.

---

* Louise Dennys went on to publish some extraordinary books, including Yann Martel's *The Life of Pi*, John Irving's *Last Night in Twisted River* and *Avenue of Mysteries*, and several P. D. James and Alberto Manguel titles.

New Challenges

IN 1992, AFTER I disengaged from Bertelsmann, I hired Susan Renouf (formerly of Key Porter, later at Doubleday Book Clubs) as KP's editor-in-chief. This move was not unlike Jack's hiring of me some twenty years earlier: going through tough times needed fresh thinking. Perhaps because Susan had, by then, two growing children and a third one still to come, she had a passion for children's books. She started kpk, a children's line, with a series of classics retold for children, for example, Tim Wynne-Jones's *The Hunchback of Notre Dame*, illustrated by Bill Slavin. Tim's novel, *Odd's End*, had been an early winner of the Seal First Novel Award, and he has gone on to be one of Canada's most beloved YA novelists. *The Hunchback* was sold to Orchard Books at Bologna, the world's most enjoyable book fair. Several foreign language publishers partnered with us for his *Dracula*, illustrated by Laszlo Gal. Laszlo, who had been a famous illustrator and graphic designer in Hungary, had settled in Toronto after the '56 Revolution. His art was dark, brooding, very detailed and painterly. In another century, I think, Laszlo would have been painting murals in cathedrals and palaces.

Later Susan added, among others, *The Last Straw*, a wonderful Christmas story by Fredrick Thury and Vlasta van Kampen, Thomas King's

Coyote Sings to the Moon (illustrated by Johnny Wales),* and my grandchildren's beloved *The Deep Cold River Story* by Tabatha Southey, who became a popular columnist at *The Globe and Mail* and *Maclean's*. Susan also commissioned my daughter Julia and Patricia Pearsall to produce *Before I Say Goodnight*, with royalties going to the Make-A-Wish Foundation. Julia had been working with children living with blood-related illnesses. She went on to work for the Hole in the Wall Camps, Right To Play, and Jays Care. She has an uncanny ability to empathize with kids in pain.

Since we had taken on L&OD, we were now publishing fiction. We started with Tim Wynveen's *Angel Falls* (winner of the Commonwealth Prize), and Trezza Azzopardi's *The Hiding Place* (short-listed for the Booker), Joan Barfoot's witty yet profoundly moving novels *Getting over Edgar* and *Critical Injuries*, Erika Ritter's *Hidden Life of Humans*, and Sylvia Fraser's *The Ancestral Suitcase*.

IN 1992 WE launched Lester Publishing with Malcolm Lester. I had always admired his talent and I knew that he would add a new perspective to our list.

From the beginning, Key Porter had been the little company that could do what other companies could not. We were nationalistic, opportunistic, and by the 1990s stable, having managed the three legs of our finances: local books with subjects of interest to the Canadian public, international books tailor-made for the world, and books designed for non-returnable sales, such as the door-to-door market, mass-market merchants, and Costco and Price Clubs. Malcolm was going to bring a different, more erudite, more scholarly perspective.

Lester Publishing's first books would help define the company: new

---

* Two more Coyote books followed, all edited by Linda Pruessen. I had been a Thomas King fan since I'd read *Green Grass, Running Water*, and I was really happy that he won the BC Writers' Award for *The Inconvenient Indian* in 2012, the year I was on the jury.

editions of *The Illustrated History of Canada*, civil liberties champion Alan Borovoy's *Uncivil Disobedience*, George Jonas's aptly named *Politically Incorrect*, and reissues of Irving Abella and Harold Troper's *None Is Too Many* and Modris Eksteins's *Rites of Spring*. Some were books about the history of the country; others tackled political and moral issues that I cared about.

The Illustrated History of Canada was the first comprehensive, one-volume illustrated history of the country, written by leading historians yet readable, featuring hundreds of engravings, cartoons, and photographs.

Alan Borovoy's book about civil disobedience and its consequences is still relevant today as neo-Nazis and black-balaclava'd groups fight it out with each other and police. Borovoy himself was charming, persuasive, and even funny when recounting his tales of "a democratic agitator."

I was friends with George Jonas and had published him at Seal. While we often disagreed, his was a voice I understood.

The reissue of *None Is Too Many* was particularly significant for me. As far back as I remember, I had been a student of Holocaust history, because the country of my birth had joined Nazi Germany early in the Second World War and more than half a million of its Jewish citizens had been murdered in Auschwitz Birkenau. It was a story I first heard from my grandfather, who had saved a few people by hiding them in our cellar.* Years later I returned to this terrible subject with the writing of *Kasztner's Train*. The story haunts me still.

None Is Too Many shattered the myth of Canada as a kind, accepting country. It has, according to its authors, "arguably, the worst record of any Western country in trying to save the doomed Jews of Europe." The authors have a deep and broad knowledge of the persecution of Jews.

I had known both Irving and Rosalie Abella for some years. A member of the Supreme Court, Justice Abella, Rosie to her friends, is the most interesting, serious, funny, committed judge in the country. She is also an affectionate, brilliant, thoughtful friend and a hilariously eclectic collector

---

* Had he known his name would be among the "Righteous" in Jerusalem, he would have been appalled. He was ashamed he hadn't done more.

of memorabilia. The child of Holocaust survivors, she has great respect for life and the rights of ordinary Canadians. Her father, a Jew, had to stand at the back of the classroom in Krakow to study law. Rosie is determined that no one should ever be singled out for punishment because of race, colour, religion, or sex. Irving has been the love of her life.

We reissued June Callwood's moving book *Twelve Weeks in Spring*. It describes how a group of people helped nurse a friend who was dying of cancer. When Sylvia Fraser asked June whether she could foresee a time when she herself would need or want such help, June snorted. "Would you want your friends to spoon-feed you and empty your bedpan?"*

When June herself was first diagnosed with inoperable cancer, her first reaction was delight that her illness could be used as a fundraiser. "Don't worry," she told Sylvia, "this will work out for everybody."

MODRIS EKSTEINS'S BRILLIANT *Rites of Spring: The Great War and the Birth of the Modern Age* is a highly original cultural history of the first half of the twentieth century—from Stravinsky's revolutionary ballet to Hitler's death. Meeting Modris was one of the bonus moments of being part of Lester Publishing.

Later, Key Porter published his evocative *Walking Since Daybreak*, a manuscript I understood viscerally. The subtitle is *A Story of Eastern Europe, World War II, and the Heart of Our Century*. Its opening lines are unforgettable: "Shattered cities. Smoldering ovens. Stacked corpses. Steeples like cigar stubs. Such are the images of Europe in 1945, images of a civilization in ruins."

The city of my birth had become such a place during the 1945 siege of Budapest, when the Soviet armies encircled and bombarded the civilian population. The German army blew up its historic bridges, and roaming gangs of Arrow Cross men murdered Jewish citizens. I was a baby in a cellar during that time, but I heard the stories, and as afterwards we endured

---

* See Sylvia Fraser's essay "Hurricane June," *Toronto Life*, 2005.

a Communist dictatorship under Soviet occupation, the ruins of prewar Budapest were left untended during my Hungarian childhood.

Modris, too, returned to the country of his birth. After many years of absence, he found his sojourn in Latvia "fraught with emotion."

As Modris had been fascinated by the turbulent tales of his family, so had I been fascinated with my own family's distant past in Transylvania and in southern Hungary, now part of Serbia. My grandfather had been a hussar in the Austro-Hungarian army during the First World War, the one that ended with the Treaty of Trianon. As he never tired of saying, that treaty had been victors' justice. It had cut off more than half of our country, including the part where my family had thrived for centuries.

Walking Since Daybreak won the Writers' Trust Non-Fiction Prize in 1999. My own quasi-non-fiction book, *The Storyteller: Memory, Secrets, Magic and Lies*, appeared a year later. It was a story I had been writing in my head for most of my life, but I think reading Modris's story helped me decide where to end the tale.

Basil Johnston's Ojibway Heritage

CANADA HAD ITS own tortured history. When I read the published findings of the Truth and Reconciliation Commission, my mind went back to my friend Basil Johnston and all that he managed to teach me during the years that we knew each other.

We first met in 1975 when he was working at the Royal Ontario Museum's Ethnography Department. He delighted in showing me the rooms where his "finds" were housed. Those days he used to dress quite formally in grey pants and jacket, but as time went on, he started to wear a traditional embroidered vest and an elaborate string-tie pin that looked like a silver wheel. We often went across the street to the Roof Lounge of the Park Plaza Hotel, and Basil would tell me stories about life for the Anishinaabe, bits of history, legends, the sources of the legends. He'd talk about his friends and about his own funny escapades before he was captured by "the system."

Basil was only ten when he was taken to the residential school in Spanish, Ontario. More like a threat than a place name, Spanish had loomed large in the imaginations of children on reserves. Teachers and sometimes parents would threaten that if kids didn't behave, they would end up in Spanish. Basil's little sister, only four years old, was taken along by the dreaded "Indian agent" only because the man needed to complete his form—the one that called for two children from the same family. She was too young to understand what was happening, and Basil was just old enough not to explain.

Located 130 kilometres west of Sudbury and 200 kilometres from Sault Ste. Marie, Spanish was a no-industry town, half emptied by the Great Depression, relying for its subsistence and entertainment on the St. Peter Claver school, where the children put on performances of baseball, hockey, and plays selected by the Jesuit priests.

For Basil and the other boys, aged four to sixteen, "the school" meant "reformatory, penitentiary, hunger, exile, dungeon, whippings, kicks and slaps." It's the life Basil recounted with both humour and sadness in his childhood memoir, *Indian School Days*.

The priests, who ran that school and other schools like it in Canada, assumed that "Indian culture was inferior." One boasted that "not a word of Indian is heard from our boys after six months. This was achieved through strict discipline and rigorous punishment."

In addition to strict discipline and hard work, the purpose of the school was to foster religious vocation. Yet, as Basil pointed out, the school produced no priests. It was not lost on the boys that while they starved, eating only barley soup with chunks of gristle, the Fathers dined on meat and potatoes.

Basil painted a heart-breaking picture of the youngest crying and whimpering all day and night, wretchedly clinging to each other and to the knees of the indifferent priest who was in charge of them. Basil's conclusion was that the Jesuits had taken an oath upon entering the order to repudiate all feelings.

The system continued through the 1950s and into the '60s. The children were "wards of the Crown," not citizens of their own country. It was not until 1960 that First Nations people were allowed to vote without losing their status.

Though I had some understanding of Indigenous issues from reading Maria Campbell's *Half-Breed*, Basil's *Indian School Days* was the first I had heard of the horrific fate of children in government-sponsored religious schools in Canada. I didn't know that children were forcibly removed from their homes, that they were separated from friends and family, and I had no sense of the widespread abuse, the cultural genocide rooted in the Indian Act of 1876. What is just as surprising: few people knew of the "Sixties Scoop," a federal government policy that removed First Nations children from their homes in the 1960s and placed them in foster homes or put them up for adoption elsewhere. The press did not deem this worth reporting, and Canadians either didn't know or didn't care about what was done in their name.

Basil had relearned the Anishinaabe language. He taught me a few words, all of which I have now forgotten. He thought it was quite amusing that I was born in Hungary, a country with no colonizing ambitions. I remember telling him that even had there been world conquerors among us, we were unlikely to have chosen such an inhospitable land as the one inhabited—quite happily—by his own ancestors. He laughed.

I was puzzled when Basil told me about his return to Spanish for a stint of high school when he could have stayed with his family. He was not very good at menial labour, he explained, and that was all the work he could find on the Parry Island Indian Reserve. He excelled at school, went to Loyola College on a scholarship, became a teacher, an avid hockey fan, married, and raised a family.

At M&S I had fought for the publication of Basil's books *Ojibway Heritage* and *Moose Meat and Wild Rice*, the latter a series of very funny stories without the pain that pervades *Indian School Days*. At Key Porter, I didn't have to fight to publish Basil.

I think his most challenging book was *The Manitous: The Spiritual World of the Ojibway*, published in 1995.

It is the first comprehensive collection and explanation of the sacred stories that inspired and informed the life of the Ojibway before that life was subsumed by contact with the white people. In some ways, this is Basil's vindication of his heritage that the government and the priests had failed to erase.

The last of Basil's books that we published was *Crazy Dave*, a beautifully told tale of Basil's uncle Dave, born with Down syndrome yet always trying to fit in with the people on the Cape Croker reserve, struggling to be one of the guys. In our promotion of the book, reaching for a catch-all metaphor, we held him up as some sort of reflection of the Ojibways' struggle to fit into a world not eager to accept them on any—least of all their own—terms.

Basil, for me, was the kind of writer who made our entire publishing enterprise worth the effort. His unique voice, his immense knowledge, his patient perseverance have added immeasurably to our knowledge of who we all are.

The Canadian Way of Death and of Living

WHEN ROB BUCKMAN first came into the offices, he was looking at the ceiling, wondering whether it was safe to take a breath. Rob was a medical doctor, an oncologist, but most important for us, he was also a comedian, a performer, and an author, a most unusual combination for a most unusual man. He had produced and hosted, with a pleasantly unaffected British accent, a TV series called *Magic or Medicine*, which debunked many of the alternative medicine cures popular in the last few decades. He was very thin with rounded shoulders, a mop of unruly grey-brown hair, a long face, bushy eyebrows that he could move up and down to express delight or consternation. My bedraggled no-longer-white couch elicited the latter, as did the billowing dust that greeted his arrival in the boardroom.

Born in England, he had begun his acting career at thirteen. Medicine came later.

His first book at Key Porter was *I Don't Know What to Say—How to Help and Support Someone Who Is Dying*. Rob had an understanding both of the progress of disease and of the jarringly awkward ways in which medical professionals and family members try to communicate with someone who is dying. Having been diagnosed with an autoimmune disease—dermatomyositis—that was doing its best to kill him, he understood the patient's view of the medical profession, and the need for frank talk that could give a dying person a chance to say what he or she felt he/she wanted to say.

Rob had tried to demonstrate the effects of his own disease to me by pretending to choke, much to the horror of the uptight maître d' in the stylish Yonge Street restaurant where we celebrated the publication of his fourth book with Key Porter: *Magic or Medicine*, based on his TV series.

He said that he was astonished at his own longevity. The prognosis had buried him years ago.

His *What You Really Need to Know about Cancer: A Comprehensive Guide for Patients and Their Families* answers myriad questions that are obscured behind taboos and misconceptions that keep the cancer sufferer from understanding his own diagnosis. When I told him that Julian's father had been expected to keep the fact of his cancer a secret from his family, he was not surprised. Cancer was thought not to be a topic for polite conversation. Nor was dying.

Later Rob produced a series of medical information videos with his old Cambridge friend, *Monty Python*'s John Cleese, and hoped we could cooperate on a series of books based on the videos, but Key Porter was already publishing medical information books for people interested in their own diagnosis. Health guides had become one of our steady, dependable publishing fields, one that even our skeptical bankers understood. I had made a deal with the Canadian Medical Association to endorse our books on arthritis, migraines, eating disorders, epilepsy, Crohn's disease, and other common ailments. There were similar American series, but I believed that our system, medications, and medical advice were different. That was our reason for commissioning books on women's health and a large fundraiser for the Hospital for Sick Children on childhood health.

Always the comedian, in his almost-memoir, *Not Dead Yet: The Unauthorised Autobiography of Dr. Robert Buckman, Complete with Map, Many Photographs and Irritating Footnotes*, Rob predicted that "At my funeral they're going to play a recording of me saying, 'Thank you so much for coming. Unlike the rest of you, I don't have to get up in the morning.'"

The Witness

I HAD ALWAYS admired Josef Skvorecky but had not met him until we inherited his books from Lester & Orpen Dennys. Josef, who had been used to Louise Dennys's gentle ways, handled the transition with some suspicion. Not only were we a very different publishing house, but relations between Czechs and Hungarians had not been particularly amicable during the past several centuries. After a long conversation about Central European history, we decided on a new entente that would ignore both their Masaryk and our Kossuth and we got down to trying to decipher his international contracts, an exhausting effort cheered along by the arrival of some late funds from various agents and sub-agents who had imagined Josef had vanished with L&OD and were delighted to find him with us.

I already knew his formidable career as a dissident writer. His first book, *The Cowards*, published in 1958, was judged "decadent" and "reactionary" by the Czechoslovak censors. He was one of several writers the regime thought were dangerous.

He and his wife, Zdena Salivarova, came to Canada in 1969, shortly after the Soviet army put an end to Alexander Dubček's "Communism with a human face." His books banned, the jazz he loved prohibited, some of his friends jailed, Josef could not have continued to live and write in Czechoslovakia, though he was published all over the world. *The New*

Yorker named him "one of the major literary figures of our time." *The Bass Saxophone*, his first book translated into English, was a modern classic. "Superb, masterly," wrote Graham Greene. It was Greene who had first told his niece, the barely twenty-four-year-old Louise Dennys, about Skvorecky and suggested she should try to help him get published in English. Since she couldn't interest any of the established houses in publishing a Czech émigré writer with no track record in English, Louise ended up creating her own small press with antiquarian bookseller Hugh Anson-Cartwright to publish Skvorecky. After she joined Lester & Orpen, adding Dennys to the marquee, Josef followed.

His *The Miracle Game* and *The Engineer of Human Souls* are among the best, most enduring books in world literature. Both are set in Czechoslovakia under occupation, and although *Engineer*'s Smiricky leaves his native land, he carries his country with him. Both books are deeply rooted in human relationships. Josef's Lieutenant Boruvka novels were wonderfully realistic, hilarious, engaging, and, for me, full of the daily idiocies that characterized living under Communism. Very Central European. When I was a child, I had read Jaroslav Hašek's famous satire *The Good Soldier Schweik* in Hungarian and loved it. Boruvka was the good soldier Schweik's Soviet army successor.

Josef and Zdena started 68 Publishers in Canada specifically to publish writers who could not be read at home. Josef was soft-spoken but determined, gentle but with a will of iron. When he disagreed with a particular editorial comment, he would become quite taciturn. In one of his letters to me about such comments, he asserted that his way of presenting his story was exactly the way he wished to present it, and while he appreciated our editor's comments, he was not going to change anything. Naturally, I acquiesced.

In our long, meandering conversations, we used to talk about how the role of writers living in totalitarian countries differs from that of writers who live in democracies, such as Canada. There was, he believed, a moral obligation that writers in Central and Eastern Europe shared: that of being witnesses to the crimes committed by their rulers. However, in order to stay alive, they, though all their readers knew the truth, had to disguise what their characters perceived. Thus they shared perilous secrets with their audience—secrets the regime suspected but couldn't prove. That's why writers are considered dangerous in countries with no free speech.

Josef had a talent for being very still and suddenly bursting into laughter. In some ways an anachronism, a light-hearted, jazz-loving Bohemian in the rather barren Canadian university landscape—he taught creative writing—he was a great writer who had landed quietly in our midst and enjoyed not being recognized.

In Prague he would have been stopped in the streets and hugged and begged for autographs, as he was during his infrequent visits after the Iron Curtain was raised in 1989. He showed me a video of his trip to Náchod, Bohemia, his old hometown—meeting people he had known in his childhood, a dinner in his honour, speeches, compliments—but he was suspicious of some of the people who had come to celebrate him. Some of them had been Nazi sympathizers, some had been Státní bezpečnost (Czechoslovakia's singularly nasty state police) informers. He felt uneasy in Prague even while autographing books for adoring fans. Now he viewed the video with a mixture of pleasure and wry amusement.

He didn't want to go back. He said he preferred teaching at the University of Toronto, where no one cared that he was a famous Czech writer. There is a hilarious short story, "According to Poe," included in his *When Eve Was Naked.* Josef is teaching a class of would-be writers. While listening to their creative work of unvarnished pornography—they mistakenly believed that he had asked for a "lovemaking story," not a love story—Josef reflects on his own rather more restrained efforts at lovemaking when he was about the age of his students.

"Money-Grubbing Has Become Respectable"

WHEN I WAS interviewed by *Maclean's* in 1986, I mentioned how much Canadians' attitude to business had changed in the years since I had arrived. "Money-grubbing has become respectable," I said. Peter Newman's blockbuster gossipy business books would not have been of such overwhelming interest to ordinary folk in the fifties or sixties, but business leaders had somehow acquired star quality. Key Porter had started early in publishing business books.

Diane Francis, then a lead columnist for the *Financial Post*, *Maclean's*, and the *Toronto Sun*, gave us a slew of entertaining business books, including *Bre-X: The Inside Story* and *Immigration: The Economic Case*. Sandy Ross of *Canadian Business* used to stop me on my way through the Key Publishers' rabbit warren to tell me about new developments in the Southam family saga—a story he relished and had hoped to write one day—and Conrad Black became a poster guy for second-generation success with his purchase of Argus Corporation, rising to international media fame with his acquisition of the UK's *Daily Telegraph*.

The National Business Book Awards were launched in 1985. Peter Foster's *The Master Builders*, about the Reichmann family empire, was our contender in 1986, and Ken Lefolii's *Claims: Adventures in the Gold Trade*, about mining and the unusual cadre of people who prospected for, invested in, and speculated in gold, won in 1987. Conrad Black's *A Life in Progress* was a finalist in 1993.

Conrad, by then, presided over a major newspaper conglomerate, Hollinger Inc. I was, for a short time, a director of Hollinger and later of Argus Corporation. Hollinger was, by far, the most fascinating board I had been on, though I had found Maritime Life, Empire Company, Alliance Communications, and Peoples Jewellers interesting and sometimes challenging. Argus was Conrad's holding company but meetings were attended by, among others, Paul Reichmann and His Eminence Emmett Cardinal Carter.

Conrad was probably the only board chair who had no illusions about the book business when he asked me to join the Hollinger board. Most of the meetings were held in the boardroom at 10 Toronto Street, whose door had served as the cover of Peter Newman's *The Canadian Establishment*. I looked forward to the discussions of newspapers, the political situations in the United States and the UK, in Australia and Israel (Conrad had also bought the *Jerusalem Post*), and had a ringside seat at the *Daily Telegraph*'s newspaper price war with News Corporation's Rupert Murdoch, the take-no-prisoners Aussie proprietor of the London *Times* and much else besides. The *Times*, trying to beat the *Telegraph*'s circulation, had assumed that aggressively lowering the price of its papers would do it. When that didn't work, they inserted free Eurostar tickets into each copy of the Saturday paper. Conrad was, in the end, forced to lower his own paper's price.

I loved listening to Conrad's erudite, often ornate, and sometimes very funny review of his empire and its enemies.

Now and then I noted words I had never used and never heard anyone else use, a great deal more fun than the jargon of life insurance. (I had planned to commission an actuaries' joke book, but fortunately never got around to it.)

I attended days-long Advisory Board meetings that included people like David Brinkley, William F. Buckley, Lord Carrington, Henry Kissinger, billionaire financiers Lord Rothschild, Gianni Agnelli, and Jimmy Goldsmith, economist and former Chairman of the Federal Reserve Paul Volcker, global strategist and US presidential adviser Zbigniew Brzezinski, and

George F. Will. I once had a fascinating conversation with Brzezinski about the long-term effects of quick, painful economic reforms in Poland and the economic outcome of the end of the Soviet Union. Already, he had predicted Russian efforts to reestablish a sphere of influence to mirror the former Soviet empire.

Another time when I attended the advisers' meetings with a broken leg, Lady Margaret Thatcher helped me to the washroom. While I hobbled, she talked with admiration about the United States' having been founded on idealism and about civilization being in peril "as long as brutal forces of enslavement walk the earth." She was the least guarded politician I have met. The current state of the European Union, unfortunately, confirms her fears of what would happen if you tried to force together disparate nations with different objectives.

Conrad's *A Life in Progress* has a wonderful jacket: black-on-black elegant, minimalist but striking. It was designed by the preternaturally talented Scott Richardson,[*] who also designed Farley Mowat's second Key Porter book, *Born Naked*. It would be difficult to invent two people less alike than Farley and Conrad, or two books less alike than their memoirs. I think it says something interesting about Key Porter that we proudly published both. We were eclectic in our choices and, apart from our environmental dedication, not particularly ideological.

A Life in Progress, while offering interesting portraits of Henry Kissinger, Brian Mulroney, Lyndon Johnson, and Margaret Thatcher, is revealing about the private Conrad Black. Since then, he has published eleven more books, including his epic work on Roosevelt, a controversial biography of Nixon, a second autobiography, and his history of Canada. He ultimately sold his company's interests in the Southam papers to Izzy Asper, founder of CanWest Global Communications, in what Peter Newman billed as "the largest media transaction in Canadian history."

---

[*] Scott himself, as C. S. Richardson, wrote two novels, one of which, *The End of the Alphabet*, should be read by everyone who is planning a trip to Paris.

In 1998 we published a new, shortened edition of Conrad's *Duplessis* as *Render unto Caesar: The Life and Legacy of Maurice Duplessis.*

IN 2003, NEW York investment firm Tweedy, Browne initiated an investigation into Hollinger's management practices. Initially Conrad welcomed the special committee and its chairman, Richard Breeden. All corporate files and papers would be open to them, he said. He was confident, he told me, that the company's books were in order. The special committee's report, however, accused Hollinger's chief shareholders of "corporate kleptocracy" and initiated a suit against them for inappropriately acquiring Hollinger assets.

I followed the course of Conrad's trial in Chicago closely and thought American justice had failed—as it has failed in many other cases (except on television). A hallmark of the US system is a ninety-nine per cent conviction rate, ninety-seven per cent without a trial. So, just this about Conrad's case: his persecutors lacked the one essential ingredient for a fair trial: credible proof of wrongdoing. They abandoned three of seventeen counts against him even before the trial began. One more was abandoned during the trial. The jury discarded a further nine counts. Eight justices of the US Supreme Court threw out four more counts. When the Chicago appeal judges were left to reassess these four convictions, the court either had to abandon the case or try to make something stick. Two charges stuck: one for improperly receiving $285,000 from the sale of newspapers, even though corporate files showed that matter had been approved by the audit committee and the board; the second was for obstruction of justice. Conrad had removed thirteen boxes of his papers from his former Toronto office. The prosecution claimed that he had done so furtively, and in contravention of a Canadian court order. In fact, he removed them in broad daylight, under his own security cameras, having announced his intention to do so. Furthermore, there was no Canadian court order forbidding him to remove his papers.

Conrad spent three years and two weeks in jail. He was a model prisoner, witty even about his incarceration and polite to the men who shared his fate. He taught history and English and French grammar to inmates who wished to pass exams, and he learned first-hand how the US justice system discriminates against blacks and the poor—"the US system of injustice," he called it.

In *A Matter of Principle*, published in 2010 by M&S, he recounts the events leading up to his incarceration, the members of the Special Committee charged with discovering what, if any, wrongdoings there had been under his leadership of Hollinger, the trial in Chicago, the appeals, and his time in prison. Meanwhile Hollinger's value (about $2 billion) disappeared. Conrad accused his accusers: "Court-protected charlatans took $100,000 a month in directors' fees each and rifled the treasury for their own benefit."

Conrad returned to Canada and continues to write columns for the *National Post* and *National Review*, and though there are those who still insist he acted with unenlightened self-interest while running his companies, he is practically mobbed by well-wishers and admirers at social events. In 2011 he sued members of the Special Committee for libel and accepted a $5 million settlement.

The Last Decade of the Last Century

D ISASTER HIT IN 1995, when book superstores came to Canada and I first met Larry Stevenson. He was a tough-talking, Harvard-educated former paratrooper with no particular love for books: he once mentioned to me that he could have run any other business just as successfully and with a whole lot fewer complaints. With a group of venture capitalists he had taken over Smithbooks, which already owned the Classics chain, then added Coles to create a mega-chain of bookstores across Canada—all with his own brand: Chapters. His strategy, as he explained to those of us still mired in old-world publishing practices, was to modernize the industry. That included building superstores with children's play areas and coffee outlets on the American model and demanding payments for "placement," meaning if you wanted your books to be seen, you had to pay extra. What he didn't mention openly was his intention to replace all independent bookstores with slick marketing and deep discounts on bestsellers at the publishers' expense. He installed former Ontario premier David Peterson as chair of the board perhaps to distract regulators' attention from applying the government's own competition rules.

Larry's strategy took a couple of years to gel. Meanwhile, he badgered, threatened, and sweet-talked us into staying quiet. The early orders for the new superstores helped to quell our fears. But worse was to come.

In 1995 the Ontario government under Premier Mike Harris cancelled the loan guarantee program that had been Lester Publishing's main support with its bankers. Not unrelated to that fact, Key Porter's bank—bankers don't see books as assets—decided that our operating loan was too generous and our security insufficient. They demanded repayment at about the same time as we had doubled in size. Sadly, after only five years, our partnership with Malcolm ended on a grim note and Lester Publishing was wound up.

Margaret Atwood, having listened to my whining, decided to give us a little gift that could help cheer us up during the bad times. She wrote a hilarious fractured fairy tale: *Princess Prunella and the Purple Peanut*. Maryann Kovalski illustrated what was, up to then, our most successful kids' book at home and internationally. Since the book was also a celebration of the letter *P*, as in "Princess Prunella was proud, prissy and pretty," she also gave me a *P* poem to accompany the manuscript. I still have it framed on my office wall:

AttemPting
to Preserve Pretty, Personable
Porter's Precarious Publishing enterPrize,
Petite Penperson Peggy Propels
Herself Personally right over the toP
And is Pronounced Possibly Potty.

She went on to write *Rude Ramsay and the Roaring Radishes*, another hilarious alliterative masterpiece, this one about a boy called Ralph. Illustrated by Dušan Petričić, the book enjoyed several printings, with the intrepid Margaret's reading in libraries and bookstores to oceans of kids and their curious parents. She ended her alliterative kids' lit project at Key Porter with *Bashful Bob and Doleful Dorinda*, a particular favourite of my youngest grandchild, Violet.

But I still think the end of the last century was Larry's, and I still blame us publishers for our acquiescence. In 1999 he named his warehouse and distribution centre Pegasus and announced it was a wholesaler and would, therefore, be entitled to the same discounts we offered to other wholesalers: fifty per cent. Imagining that he was actually interested in my advice, I agreed to go on the Pegasus board. It never met. Unsold book returns from shipments to Chapters hit sixty per cent of sales, and Chapters stopped paying our invoices in anticipation of more returns from future shipments.* By then, whatever collegial relationship we thought we had with Chapters had vanished. That year *The Globe and Mail Report on Business* declared Larry Stevenson Canada's "Man of the Year."

That was also the year I called Larry to tell him that our new Allan Fotheringham book, *Last Page First*, had been stuck for three weeks somewhere in his commodious warehouse or in the massive tractor-trailers waiting outside, victims of his firm's growing inability to process its own orders. Since Allan was touring the country, I could assure Larry that he would mention why his books were not in Chapters stores. Larry's usual belligerent response hit operatic scales: Julian in the next room could hear him shouting at me on the phone. He threatened he would have his staff return every Key Porter book they could find in his stores, his warehouse, or in those trailers. It's what he did to Lionel Koffler's Firefly Books, when Lionel refused to give Chapters the terms Larry demanded. Lionel paid for his courage with more than one million dollars' worth of returned books. Allan MacDougall, another M&S graduate, now running Raincoast Books in Vancouver, was more successful in resisting Larry's demands, but then Allan had Harry Potter to perform his magic for him. The first two Harry Potter books had sold more than a million copies each in Canada, and the third, *Harry Potter and the Prisoner of Azkaban*, was released in 1999.

The rest of us were not so brave.

Our bank, generally skittish about granting operating loans to book publishers, moved us to its "watch" list and demanded both personal guarantees and an additional one million dollars of "key person" insurance to

---

* Unlike most merchandise, books in Canada are sold fully returnable to all retail outlets.

keep them onside. I remember the moment one of the young banking executives looked at me and said, jocularly, "At this point, Ms. Porter, you are worth more to us dead than alive."

Michael de Pencier, who had remained steadfast throughout our struggles, began to suggest that we search for a way out.

Farley: The Next Chapter

THE DECADE HAD already become a disaster when Farley Mowat's bestselling *Never Cry Wolf* and *People of the Deer* were used by journalist John Goddard to launch an attack on Farley in *Saturday Night* magazine. It was 1996 and Farley was seventy-five years old. I felt responsible because we had arranged the interview with Goddard as part of our promotion of the new book, *Aftermath*—Farley's memoir of his travels after the "charnel house of mud and rain and shells and death" that was the Second World War.

For the first part of the interview, Goddard drove to the Mowats' home in Port Hope. A second interview followed in our dingy Esplanade boardroom. Farley had been reluctant to come to Toronto, but he came because he was a McClelland-trained author and I was a McClelland-trained publisher. Both of us believed that author publicity can only help sell books.

In this case, though, we were both wrong. Goddard's second interview turned into an interrogation "during which I was accused of misrepresenting," Farley said, what he had observed and written in the 1952 and 1963 books.

In a letter to Ken Whyte, then publisher of *Saturday Night*, Farley protested that *People of the Deer* was written "to expose the unconscionable and barbarous treatment of a group of Canada's Inuit by the government, the missions, the RCMP, the traders . . ."

It was not and had never been intended as an anthropological text. He had always made it clear that he had altered some times, places, names, and dates in order to present a dramatic narrative.

Since I had met Ken Whyte on several previous occasions and knew *Saturday Night* owner Conrad Black, I phoned, wrote, and blustered to try to stop publication of the attack on Farley. I repeated what he had already written to Ken Whyte: that he had never presented himself as a traditional non-fiction writer. He had proudly declared that his talent lay "somewhere in what was then a grey void between fact and fiction." What he was writing is the non-fiction novel,* a form that has become celebrated since as creative non-fiction. In fact, the RBC Charles Taylor Prize, named after my late friend, was founded by his artist widow, Noreen Taylor, specifically to reward "the pursuit of excellence in the field of literary non-fiction."

We both failed. The hurtful article appeared and, to add insult to injury, that month's magazine cover featured Farley with a long Pinocchio nose. He retreated to his summer place in Cape Breton and wrote me a letter I have pinned on my wall at our cottage. It is vintage Farley and it used to make me feel good on bad days in publishing. This is how the letter ends: "I want to thank you (emphasis on want), you mad, bloody Hungarian, for doing all the things you did in my defence. A mother puma couldn't have done more in defence of her kitten. I'm only sorry you got shat on in the process. . . . But not to sweat: you and I can handle the stuff."

He was right. I recovered quickly from my sense of outrage for Farley. But it took a long time for him to get over it. He was still smarting from the insult to his integrity when I next visited the Mowats at their Cape Breton home to talk books with Farley. It was a long way from Halifax to River Bourgeois. After the causeway and the spewing paper mill at Port Hawkesbury on the way to Sydney, there was still that stretch of gravel road before the barn that was no longer a barn but headquarters of the

---

* Truman Capote's 1965 bestseller *In Cold Blood* was written in the same form.

Mowat Environmental Institute. Out front there was a weather-worn mailbox, arm raised to signal uncollected mail. The lettering on the mailbox announced MOWAT.

Farley and Claire lived there for the warmer half of the year in an old, white-painted wooden house with grey peaked roof, tall bramble bushes, spruce forest, and narrow paths leading to the bay below. We picked string beans and tomatoes in their vegetable plot and walked on the rough, stony beach in the late afternoon. Chester, the small black Lab, chased seagulls, pirouetting on three legs, scratching a sore spot on his side with the fourth. "His back hurts," Farley explained. The dog, like Farley, was listing slightly to the left. Though Farley had a long record of supporting the Left, this was not all political persuasion: he had hurt his back putting fresh paint on the house, getting it ready for the winter. Chester, so much younger, was aping in sympathy.

An osprey circled overhead; its thin, sharp cries stopped abruptly when it dove for its supper. Farther out a few seals popped their heads above water to peer at us. There were discarded bottles and cans amongst the stones at the edge of the sea.

"I haven't been able to change one goddamn thing," Farley declared. "I thought I could make a real difference, force people to see what I see. Devastation. Death. We're dying in our own waste. Killing everything." He stopped for a moment, watching the osprey grab a fish with its outstretched talons and struggle to lift off again. "*Sea of Slaughter* was too dark, maybe. Too grim. Once they put it down, people wouldn't pick it up again." In 1984, when it was first published, there was still a Newfoundland fishery. Cod was still king. But the age of the great whalers had already emptied the seas of most whales. The numbers were numbing. "And they are still blaming the seals," he said, his eyes scanning the horizon for those few bobbing black heads. "The slaughter goes on."

THE LAST TIME I saw Farley was in early 2014. It was sunny and cold in Port Hope, though not too cold for the Mowats' daily walk along the waterfront. He said he still missed Chester, who used to prance along on these walks, but there was no sense now in buying another dog. What, he asked, would a man his age want with a young dog?

He was wearing a green vest with his Order of Canada just above his heart. He was thin but claimed to be as healthy as anyone can expect to be at ninety-two, an age he had never anticipated he would reach. He was contemptuous of his doctors' prescriptions for operations he had invariably refused. He was grey-haired, balding, slightly stooped, but still cantankerous and still protesting the evil that people wreak. He was still mourning wolves, seals, whales, and caribou, though no longer sad for the earth. The earth would take care of itself; it was humanity, in its greed and stupidity, that was doomed. With us gone, there would be no one to tell the stories.

Earlier in April, the good ship *Farley Mowat*, captained by Farley's friend Paul Watson, had sailed to the ice floes' killing grounds with a small group of Sea Shepherd Conservation Society folk. Armed with only their cameras, they had tried to confront sealers carrying clubs and high-powered rifles.

"I couldn't go this year," Farley said apologetically. He was working on his thirty-ninth book. In one of his letters to Jack McClelland, Farley had promised not "to grow old gracefully. I'm going down the drain snarling all the way." In that too he succeeded.

The Last Berton Party

T HE SUMMER OF 1995 was the last time I had a conversation with Pierre Berton on the lawn of his Kleinburg home. The occasion was the last Berton party—billed thus on the invitation. There were fewer of us than there used to be. Some of the regulars, including Pierre's old birding friend and fellow newspaperman, Fred Bodsworth, had died.

Pierre was wearing a red apron and flipping burgers on the barbecue. He was still tall but his frame was thinner and he was bent over his cane. Even his voice had become softer, his steps less certain. But he was still eager to correct my version of the tale of Headless Valley, his first big breakthrough newspaper story. In that valley, east of the Yukon, fourteen men were said to have died in mysterious circumstances. In his series of articles, the young reporter's—Pierre was in his mid-twenties—quest for the truth turned into an adventure up the mysterious South Nahanni River, where he finally found the source of the mystery: a lonely, desolate place that is haunted only by men's imaginations. But the way he told the story established him as one of the best reporters the country had ever known.

I asked him whether his life would have been different had it not been for the Headless Valley story. "Why?" he asked.

"Because that story made you famous."

Pierre gave me one of his withering looks. "I'd have found another," he said.

Several of his seven children, most of whose first names started with a *P*, were in attendance, as was his wife, Janet, who had once told Barbara Frum that the family's lives revolved entirely around Pierre. Often it seemed to me our lives at M&S had also revolved around him.

He was still lively and enthusiastic about his lifetime birds' list, his annual trip to Point Pelee National Park in pursuit of some impossible-to-pronounce brown bird, and he was planning another book. He had already written fifty but thought he still had time to write a few more. He had won every prize that could be given to a writer, including "Man of the Century" from the Canadian Authors Association, and they were not exaggerating. Berton was, by both temperament and avocation, the man who embodied Canada's twentieth century. That he didn't share Bob Fulford's view of feminism, that he seemed unaware of Canada's Indigenous history, did not detract from his nationalism, his abiding curiosity, his passionate belief that we are a Northern people with more in common than what draws us apart. His fiftieth book, published in 2004, was *Prisoners of the North.* In the Preface he celebrates the fact that he was born in the Yukon. The North gave him all the inspiration he needed to become a writer. "It was my great good fortune, thanks to my father, the sourdough, and my mother, the journalist's daughter, that I was born in what was then the most interesting community in Canada."

Pierre Berton died on July 12, 2004. *The Globe and Mail* ran Sandra Martin's long obituary above the fold with the headline, "A Voice of Canada Is Gone." Even Farley paid him a compliment: "He was one of the real honest-to-God giants of the writing, not literary, scene." All the other dailies celebrated his life on their front pages.

Elsa Franklin produced her last Berton show in the CBC's Barbara Frum Atrium. Everybody who was anybody in the media, in publishing, in television, in political life was there, and many of them gave tearful eulogies. The only person missing was Barbara Frum herself. She had lost her battle with leukemia in 1992. I never go to that atrium without paying my respects to her.

At the end of the Berton eulogies, Elsa took the stage to say her own farewell.

Pierre's home in Dawson City has been turned into a haven for professional writers. Lawrence Hill was the winter 2017–18 writer-in-residence.

The Incomparable Dalton Camp

I HAD EAGERLY read his 1970 book, *Gentlemen, Players & Politicians*, but in those early days I was still too much a newcomer at M&S to have an editorial opinion for Dalton Camp. In any event he had shown little patience with editorial comments and even less with copy editing. He said he knew best what he wanted to say and he would be the best judge of how to say it. An intellectual, a witty and acerbic speaker, an astute political commentator on both radio and television, a columnist, a strategist, Camp was the kind of guy who could have given Pierre Trudeau a fair challenge for the leadership of the country. But given his controversial role in ending the John Diefenbaker era, he had no chance to win a seat in Parliament.

I didn't really get to know him until about his seventy-fifth year. He was a bit lonely in Toronto over Christmas, so we asked him for dinner on Christmas Eve, the traditional time for Hungarians to celebrate Christmas. He was warm, genial, considerate of my mother, but what our daughters remember most is how Dalton lay on the living room carpet with them, playing board games in front of the fire.

In the summer we were invited to spend a few days at Linda Camp's cottage at Robertson Point on Grand Lake, New Brunswick. It's the biggest body of fresh water east of the Great Lakes, brown, muddy, slippery on the rocks, but there are cottages all around, many of them belonging to the Camp family. Linda and Dalton had met while they were at Acadia University, been married very young, and had five children in quick succession. They remained friends after their divorce.

When Dalton came to visit the cottage, he sat in his "usual" chair; Linda poured him his "usual" vodka, nominally a martini, just the way he liked it; and we talked late into the evening.

The next day he drove me down to Saint John to meet with the authors of our K. C. Irving book, *K. C.: The Biography of K. C. Irving* by Ralph Costello and Douglas How. Dalton had little regard for the Irvings. He was convinced that our book would be a whitewash, leaving no blemishes on the gigantic reputation of one of the richest men in the world, who had been involved in virtually every aspect of New Brunswick business, industry, and politics. "There would not be a mention of the Irving *Whale** in that book," he said with confidence. And he was right.

THE LAST TIME I was with Dalton, he was eighty-one years old. I had gone to New Brunswick to talk about the book he thought he might be writing—his reflections about Canada and its political life.

He picked me up at Fredericton airport at around nine a.m. The people around the luggage carousel were all looking at him. "Hey, Dalt, how ya doing?" and "Whatdya make of those eejits in Ottawa?" The commissioner in charge of handing out parking tickets told him, "It's a good thing you write better than you park, eh Dalton," and gave him no ticket. We drove to the Sheraton. The doorman leaned in to shake Dalton's hand. "We missed you last week. Hope there's no truth to the rumour you've been ill." We parked near the entrance in disabled territory. "What the hell, I am likely

---

* The *Whale*, a cargo barge carrying oil and PCBs, was reputed to have been leaking for twenty-six years before it was salvaged by the Canadian Coast Guard in 2000, at a cost of $42 million (of which the Irvings, as determined by an out-of-court settlement, paid only $5 million).

disabled," Dalton said. "The air force thought I was, the buggers, that's why they wouldn't send me to active duty."

In the restaurant there was a corner with a plaque that said Dalton's Corner, and his old typewriter was on display on the shelf just above the table.

We sat and Dalton talked politics. He had been thinking about the state of the nation. There were too many "eager no-talents" seeking office, and the good people who should be serving chose to make money instead. "The world is upside down. Our system of values gone, no one wishes to give of themselves anymore unless well rewarded."

"And how is your friend Conrad?" Dalton asked. "Does he still think he can escape being one of us?" Back then, Conrad was spending most of his time in London. He had been appointed to the House of Lords and he was still the proud owner of the *Telegraph*. I think Dalton admired Conrad's independent spirit but was not sure about Conrad's Canadian loyalties.

All the way to Jemseg he talked about the past. He drove his too-large car as if the highway belonged to him. His older brother, Dalton said, had died years ago, never making peace with him. He had been Dalton's childhood hero, an alcoholic, living off old times, borrowing when he could. His younger brother was now in an institution. "Couldn't leave him in the house alone while I had my heart taken out. Might have set fire to things." Dalton had had a heart transplant.

He'd lost his best friend in the war and felt guilty about that still. I asked him why still, when most people had buried their dead long since. His friend was a pilot, shot down over the Channel, and his body was never recovered. For decades Dalton had believed that the story was not yet finished.

Why guilty? "They wouldn't take me into the air force because of this wandering eye. I had perfect vision, really. But I couldn't convince them. And later, when my regiment shipped out, I was on leave. With Linda. Somehow I just missed out on the war."

The wandering eye had failed him years ago, now the other was playing old-man tricks, barely able to focus. A few weeks earlier, searching for a car repair shop, Dalton had crashed his car when he hit a hole in the narrow highway, banged his head, broke a rib, clambered out of the car, and started walking in the heat, surrounded by blackflies, barely noticing a thunderstorm. Eventually he walked into a farmhouse and he was rescued.

Though he denied it, Dalton was somewhat deaf. Signs of aging, he said, were annoying but hardly important. What he feared was losing his memories.

We looked at pictures. Young Dalton, a blond, insecure kid. His brother strutting. Maybe that's what happened, Sandy (his name was Sanborn) took independence too far, hated their father: who wants to be a minister's son? Dalton was a mother's boy, still struggling to understand who his mother really was. The photographs don't do her justice, he said. After she died, he found these sexy, passionate, romantic poems hidden in the false bottom of her box of letters. "What do you make of these? Could she have had a lover? Did she write them herself? Or were they written to her? Why keep them for more than sixty years?" Though he remembered so much about her, loved her so much, perhaps he barely knew her?

She had been good at everything, but all along something had been missing from her life. Dalton thought it had been all about his dad, the preacher who travelled too much and maybe found some solace with other women, less demanding than his wife. He used to listen to their arguments when his father was home. Dalton had disliked his father. Though there was the time, in California, when young Dalton was hospitalized, and his father brought him books, encouraging him to read and find things out for himself. Every day, there would be more books and sometimes the preacher read to him, but never preached.

I held his mother's tiny leather-bound diary in my hand for a few minutes and let it breathe. Dalton was watching to see whether I noticed it was haunted.

At sunset we sat on his wooden porch, drinking dreadful Mouton Cadet and talking about his next book.

He showed me a photograph of his second wife. He had been quite besotted with her beauty, vivacity, and youth. It had been a wonderful late-life love affair—he was fifty-two and she only twenty-six when they met—then a short-lived marriage of six good years and, he said, a tempestuous divorce. She loved company and entertaining; she had found living in the big, isolated house too lonely. Their son, Christopher, was about twenty now. So much younger than the other Camp kids.

He searched in the fridge for something to eat. When he came up with nothing, he decided we would visit Linda at Robertson's Point. She received us graciously, eighty years old and still in love with her ex. Various children and grandchildren trooped by to see Dalton. One of them brought warm fish chowder. She knew Dalton would have forgotten to buy food. We ate in the dark as he tried to recall the words of the Browning poem "My Last Duchess."

On the way to the airport, along the road past Jemseg, Dalton saluted a lay-by. He said he did it to remind himself of who he really was. Wouldn't explain what he meant. Then we passed a church where he had slept one night after he drove off the road. He didn't salute the church. He said he was still working on whether there really is a God.

Though he tried, he never did write the book we had talked about. Too little time, still too much living to do.

After Dalton died, I signed Geoffrey Stevens, one of the best political writers in Canada, to write the biography. I think *The Player: The Life and Times of Dalton Camp* was a much more revealing book than one Dalton would have written. There were thousands of people all across Canada who wanted to know the inside story of the Diefenbaker debacle in the late 1960s, many more who were curious about Dalton, and there were those who had loved him.

I wonder what has happened to Dalton's mother's little leather-bound book.

PART THREE

Passages

Memory, Secrets, and Magic

M Y GRANDFATHER HAD been the most constant figure in my child-hood, as I have frequently acknowledged. As a land surveyor, my mother was often away, and when she was in Budapest, she worked during the day and liked to go out with her friends in the evenings. I was too young to sympathize and quite unforgiving of her second marriage to the balding Jeno, an idealistic Communist with a pugilistic son, nicknamed Jenci. Jenci's idea of a good time was to try to wrestle me into submission, and when that didn't work, he practiced his boxing skills on my head and stomach.

As she often explained, she had married my father because she was des-perate to escape the boarding school where my grandparents had parked her; she was only seventeen and he was thirty, and anyway, he was probably in love with my grandmother. She married Jeno only because he could pull strings in the Communist Party. It was the only way to extract my grand-father from prison. She did not think he would last much longer at hard labour. I was usually angry with both my mother and father when I was younger but tended to forgive my grandfather's serial infidelities.

Vili is the storyteller of my book *The Storyteller: Memory, Secrets, Magic and Lies*, the man who didn't stop telling me tales until I was in my teens and we were living in New Zealand. His form of exile was my aunt and uncle's horse farm near Hastings, mine was the Sacred Heart Convent. When I began to write about him so many years later, his fanciful stories became intertwined with my own memories of events in Hungary. His fantasies about our family's ancient past were tangled with his retelling of our country's history in a way he believed was suitable for my age. He believed he was shaping a young Hungarian to be ready to resist the depredations of the Soviet empire, Hungary being one of its outposts. I was to be a dissident poet with a large, underground following. I loved our long walks along the Danube, the hushed conversations in coffee houses, even the incomprehensible jokes his friends told and our random meetings with people he pretended not to recognize.

Later, in New Zealand, I missed those times as much as Vili did. He was always hoping that there would be another revolution, that this one would succeed against Soviet armour, and that we would return home. He thought I would return as the Hungarian poet-hero, and judging by his impassioned letters, he didn't give up on that idea even after I became a Canadian book publisher. Publishing, as it happened, was part of his own past as a magazine publisher.

During the 1980s I returned to Hungary a few times, twice with my mother, who had wanted to see a couple of her old friends, once with Julian when the TTC was planning to buy Hungarian streetcars, and again with financial wizard Andy Sarlos, who was working on his autobiography[*] while exploring ways to start new businesses with his former countrymen. Andy was a legendary Bay Street arbitrageur, tireless gossip, power broker, and another 1956 refugee.

I have always found being in Hungary stressful, in part because I have never managed to lay my childhood ghosts to rest, and in part because I find I am a different person when I speak Hungarian. The ghosts lurk behind doors where I am still expecting that late-night knock, the one

---

[*] Andy's autobiography, *Fireworks*, was published in 1993. Peter Newman contributed the foreword. It was Andy who proposed me for the board of Alliance Communications, run by another Hungarian expat, Robert Lantos.

that takes away friends and family. That different person may be the one I would have been, had we never left. She is at once scared and defiant.

I wrote much of *The Storyteller* late at night and during summer weekends on Quarry Island, over a period of several years—not an ideal way to write, but I was too busy with my family and other people's books to take a long time away. I would sit through long meetings about warehousing and distribution, about pricing and returns, and find that I couldn't focus. Being a publisher is complicated enough if you are focused, let alone when you are imagining long-forgotten events in Transylvania and Serbia.

In 1997, when my daughter Julia offered to come to Hungary with me to help with the research for *The Storyteller*, I grabbed the opportunity. Andy Sarlos lent us a friend's car and driver for the long journey to Transylvania. He was delighted that my ancestors had lived there and charmed that they had been around long enough to do battle with the Turks in the fifteenth and sixteenth centuries.

Unfortunately, Julia and I found no trace of them. Not a ruined building. Not a fallen gravestone. Nothing. But we did find Hunyadvar, the Hunyadis' castle, where one of our ancestors, my grandfather claimed, had stabbed a disloyal royal retainer. I told Julia some of the stories I had grown up with. We climbed up into the Carpathian mountains, where the great Transylvanian dragon used to thrive, and we explored the site in Arad where the Hungarian generals were executed after a failed attempt to free their lands from the Hapsburgs (another story).

It was not until a year or so later, with my mother and our cousins, that we found Vili's parents' grave in Kula, now in Serbia. There was also the wooden pew in the little church where the family had knelt on Sundays during the long sermons and where the child Vili had been fascinated by the painting of that Transylvanian dragon behind the altar.

I had wanted to keep writing *The Storyteller* long after I sent it to the publisher, but Modris Eksteins's story of escaping from the past had taught me that all stories have to end somewhere, and with the visit to Kula, Vili's story came back to its beginnings.

Key Porter's Twentieth Birthday

M Y PROMOTION OF Susan Renouf to president of Key Porter Books in 1999 was akin to Jack's appointment of Linda McKnight in 1978. I needed someone with experience, talent, and love of the business to run it so that I could focus on dealing with the nasty new challenges that had crept up on us.

We celebrated our twentieth year in the book biz with most of the staff and many former staffers, many of our authors, a few booksellers (some of them had already given up in face of the Chapters onslaught), candlelight, wine, Scotch for Farley and Foth, and, in acknowledgement of the future, a couple of agents. More than a hundred people came to our house, Bob the barman was ensconced in the alcove near the window, our daughters* served hors d'oeuvres, and Julian played some doleful music and helped fill the glasses. I toasted our two exciting decades and did not mention my fear that the next decade would not be one to celebrate.

---

* In 1997, when my daughter Julia introduced herself to June Callwood in Victoria, she said that June might not recognize her without a tray of food held high under her chin. From an early age, she and her sister usually served drinks and food at book launch parties at our home.

We took out some ads, printed a catalogue with a gold patch, and launched one hundred books, including Farley Mowat's *Walking on the Land*, Josef Skvorecky's *When Eve Was Naked*, Daphne Odjig's retrospective art book, and Fotheringham's *Last Page First* (a reference to his having been the king of the back page of *Maclean's* for more than twenty years). We trumpeted our authors' awards, including Zsuzsi Gartner's for *All the Anxious Girls* and Eric Wright's *Always Give a Penny to a Blind Man*.

With a sense of optimism for our children's future, we published Dennis Lee's new poetry for kids: *Bubblegum Delicious*, illustrated by David McPhail.

We had already reprinted his *Alligator Pie*, the collection of children's poems that had swept the country when my children were little and has successfully endured through four more decades and counting. Even our grandchildren can recite poems from it, as can most kids and their parents.

My favourite of all Dennis's children's poems is "The Cat and the Wizard," illustrated by Gillian Johnson. I can recite it all if a child is interested in hearing to the end, and I absolutely love the last two lines:

The wizard is grinning.
The wizard is me.

Yes, I do think the wizard is Dennis.

I have been an admirer of Dennis Lee since I first read his "Civil Elegies" in the 1970s, a brilliant, complex poem worth rereading to draw out its many meanings and its sadness. As with so much of his poetry, it reflects a hopelessness in the face of the devastation wrought by humanity. The ending suggests that a new beginning is still possible, but that was in my last reading of *Civil Elegies* and that ray of hope may have vanished in later versions. Dennis has—for me—a maddening habit of rewriting poems even after they are published.

Mark Dickinson, who has been writing a book about Dennis's work, told me, "Writing poetry for Dennis is like praying—a never-ending act of prayer. In this sense, his never-ending rewrites are part of a conversation between him and God." When he was very young, Dennis had wanted to be an Anglican minister.

Anansi has published his cataclysmic, difficult poetry collection *Un*. It is a lament for the earth itself. The title, says Dickinson, refers to the work of the German-language Jewish poet Paul Celan, who asked whether it is possible to reclaim the language after the Holocaust.

Dennis himself has stood the test of time. He hasn't changed much since we first met at Anansi years ago. He is still rumpled and abstracted, still wears those owlish glasses. His forehead is higher but his hair still flops on the sides and he still has that little beard and that impish (some describe it as dark) sense of humour. When I last saw him in a downtown Toronto restaurant, he offered that same look of amused attention he gave me the first time we met. But he no longer smokes his trademark pipe or the occasional cigar.

I just recently read his long love poem *Riffs*. It may be told in another man's voice, but it feels highly personal and, whatever he may tell his fans (and I am a Lee fan), Dennis is himself talking with longing and erotic joy: "We swam into/ paradise easy . . . / That was in the flesh . . ." It's Dennis at his best. Not the Dennis of *Alligator Pie* or *Bubblegum Delicious*, but Dennis wistful and in love, and mourning the loss of love.

The End of M&S

I N JUNE 2000, after fifteen years, Avie Bennett announced the sale of McClelland & Stewart. Ostensibly he was donating seventy-five per cent of the company to the University of Toronto and selling twenty-five per cent to Random House. For those of us who had been making our living in the book business, there was no mystery about who was the real buyer of the "house that Jack built": Random House was in control from the first day and the more than $5 million they paid for their twenty-five per cent stake in the company was about what its total value would have been. The university's role was window dressing designed to make the deal palatable to a government not yet ready to repeal its ownership rules for publishing companies. Knowing Bertelsmann, which had owned Random House (including Doubleday) since 1998, I know there was no chance that Random House would let the university actually control M&S. Nor did it appear that the university had any desire to do so.

What I found offensive was that between 2000 and 2011, millions in federal and provincial subsidies continued to flow to M&S as if it were still Canadian-controlled, when it was fully controlled by Random House, itself a subsidiary of the massive German conglomerate, Bertelsmann AG.

The deal had been pre-approved by the Liberal government after skilful lobbying by Avie and, probably, Rob Pritchard, then University of Toronto president. Civil servants and agency heads administering the grants and tax credit programs held their noses and continued to dole out the money. I talked with several of them. A few deplored the situation and acknowledged that the deal should never have been approved. Some regretted that their hands were tied: they had to give M&S as many government grants as it would have been entitled to under Avie's ownership, though they knew that the firm had effectively changed hands. One officer of the Canada Council said, defensively, that he was following orders "from above." A charming man in the Privy Council Office said that as far as he was concerned, the takeover had made no difference: M&S was still publishing the best Canadian writers, so who cares about ownership?

I had wanted to raise funds for a chair in Canadian literature in Jack McClelland's name, but the price tag the University of Toronto put on such a venture—a minimum of $1 million—was just too steep, so I settled for a writer-in-residency in his name at Massey College. Peter Munk contributed to the fund. Avie Bennett did not. John Fraser, master of Massey at the time, helped, and the Jack McClelland writer-in-residence program was established. It has hosted such writers as Shani Mootoo, David Bezmozgis, Camilla Gibb, Tomson Highway, Jane Urquhart, and Barbara Gowdy. The 2015–2016 Jack McClelland writer-in residence was novelist Rawi Hage. Jack would have approved.

JACK MCCLELLAND, THE prince of publishers, the man who invented Canadian author publicity tours, who "had lent his bravery and confidence to a whole generation of authors,"* and my friend, died on June 14, 2004. He was, as Gabrielle Roy wrote, "one of the few left of the breed of friendly publishers who genuinely love their writers." He would have been pleased that his life was over. The last few years had been terribly difficult, and eighty-one was an age he had never intended to reach.

The funeral was private but there was a memorial service at the stately

---

* Margaret Atwood in the University of Guadalajara's Homage Edition, 1996.

Granite Club on Bayview Avenue. It was low-key, sombre, quiet, not the kind of event Jack in his heyday would have wished as a send-off. But Leonard Cohen was there, paying tribute to his publisher and friend, who, he said, was "an open heart in Toronto." Poet and novelist Anne Michaels wrote in thestar.com that November about Jack: "the visionary, a man who had given himself over to a task, something bigger than himself—in this case, the passionate belief in, and support of, Canadian literature."

As for me, I went home and cried.

Welcome to the Twenty-first Century

IN NOVEMBER 2000, Julian and I had gone to Russia. He had been hired by *Maclean's* to examine one of the men accused of ethnic cleansing in the former Yugoslavia. I went along to see whether I was ready to face a few of my own demons. On November 7 we were in St. Petersburg—called Leningrad when I was in primary school—and watched a group of elderly Russians march under red flags displaying faded hammer-and-sickle emblems, celebrating the 1917 Revolution. I remembered the long, boring parades of my childhood, when every citizen was expected to march to Heroes Square in Budapest to honour our Soviet "liberators" and listen to endless speeches from the leading Comrades.

I also remembered them in their tanks in November 1956, when their swivelling turrets destroyed much of the city of my birth, including the small flat my mother and I had shared. As Julian and I were ambling through the Hermitage Museum looking at his beloved Rembrandts, about fifty young Red Army recruits passed by, and I had to grab Julian's arm to stop myself from screaming.

Is the past ever really past?

When the World Trade Center Towers in New York were destroyed by Islamic terrorists on September 11, 2001, I was in the third-floor Key offices watching CBS News. Someone had called me upstairs when the first plane hit. There were about a dozen of us that morning, all of us silent. Disbelieving. Downstairs in our office, I was greeted with shocked silence. I told everyone to go home and hug the people they loved and not to bother coming in the next day.

For Key Porter, the twenty-first century began not with a terrible bang but an extended whimper. Entrepreneur Heather Reisman, having wrested control of Chapters from Larry Stevenson, announced "the purge of about $40 million" of books to publishers for full credit, and the shutdown of at least twenty stores. Our bankers had not yet recovered from the 1990s, when independent bookstores kept disappearing and library budgets were being slashed. Now publishers were struggling to understand a fiercely competitive retail marketplace that included Costco and an ambitious on-line outlet called Amazon. Our distributor, General Distribution Services (GDS), was tottering under the onslaught.

In self-defence, we had been selling illustrated books directly to Chapters in Canada, to Barnes & Noble, Costco, and Price Clubs in the United States, to American promotional and remainder merchants, and to a variety of door-to-door businesses. We had even created books specifically for this market, producing heavy mock-ups with art or photographs and dummy text that I lugged to meetings often lasting only fifteen minutes. Invariably we were told to think bigger but at a lower cost. I imagined that selling non-returnable into these markets would give us operating income to support our regular publishing of Canadian books. We made Dudley Witney's *The Farm, The Children's Treasury*, several pretty wildlife books (the same animals but we billed them Canadian for Chapters, American for Barnes & Noble), a couple of books about wildflowers (who can tell the difference between our wildflowers and US ones?) and loons, an American national parks book, and other assorted stuff about mountains and rivers that we called "merch," short for merchandise.

Having just been to Romania, I proposed a book about vampires to Barnes & Noble. They liked the concept, the price, the number of pages, everything, except that they wanted it in two months. I agreed, on the assumption that I would find someone to write it very quickly. When I couldn't, I ended up writing most of the book myself with an assist from a co-author film buff who supplied words about vampires in movies. I did Vlad the Impaler and his successors. The book, I am surprised to discover, is still in print.

We also explored ways of increasing our size and, therefore, our clout in the Canadian book market, imagining that if our annual income doubled or tripled, we could demand better terms from "the chain," from Amazon, maybe even Costco.

I had had long, enjoyable meetings with my colleague Scott McIntyre to discuss how such an affiliation or even a merger could work. We had now been friends for more than thirty years, had grown to know what each of us cared about and why we were devoted book people. We had both been members of the small group—known at the time as "the junta"—elected in 1991 by the Association of Canadian Publishers to lobby the government.* Scott's company, Douglas & McIntyre, was the star of West Coast publishing. We were both known to be innovative at home and respected internationally. We both sold books all over the world.

Scott and I sometimes had dinner in Frankfurt during the Book Fair, and in Paris after Frankfurt. Scott took many pages of notes and calculated whether we could save money by merging. We thought we could, as Scott was fond of saying, "create a major." However, Scott's dream of "a major" included Jack Stoddart of General Publishing, whose sales were about the same as Key Porter's. Since Jack Stoddart's General Distribution Services supplied warehousing and shipping for all of us, it seemed to be a marvellous idea to invite Jack to our discussions. If the two of us together could be influential, imagine how influential the three of us together would be! Better still, the combined firms would prove to be an attractive investment for outsiders. Scott and I had a number of very encouraging meetings with potential investors.

I wrote a long letter to Jack Stoddart on November 7, 2001, proposing

---

* The other members of our group were Karl Siegler of Talon Books, Philip Cercone of McGill-Queen's University Press, Louise Fleming of Ragweed, and Randy Morse of Reidmore Books. Roy MacSkimming was "interim director" coordinating our efforts.

a corporate structure that was predicated on merging Key Porter, Douglas & McIntyre, and General Publishing. It was an elaborate plan, partly devised by our CFO, Allan Ibarra. I still think it could have saved all three companies. I hoped that if we merged, Scott would run the company day-to-day and I could maybe write the book that had been gnawing at me for a couple of years. It was about the Holocaust in Hungary and an unusual person who had both the courage and the imagination to come up with a plan to rescue more than seventeen hundred Jews.

We didn't know that Jack Stoddart had been teetering on the edge for a couple of years. There had been problems with his bankers, but he had found another bank, an American lender called Finova. He still had a confident strut, a cheery smile, and, I thought at the time, a great relationship with Sheila Copps, the federal Heritage minister, because Jack usually attended her functions. When he suggested that Scott and I go to Ottawa and cajole the government into a short-term investment of $5 million, we believed it was all for a good cause.

But we were wrong. After sustaining about sixty per cent returns of inventory from Chapters, and after Finova itself went bankrupt, General Publishing, including GDS, sought bankruptcy protection in April 2002.* That the announcement was a shock to me would be an understatement. GDS's gargantuan warehouse held all of Key Porter's books and we were among the many unsecured creditors. Overnight, we had no income from our Canadian sales. Our banker noted the news with alarm. Our plight was exacerbated by the decision of a judge that all our receivables belonged to GDS, which had but one secured creditor: its bank. In *The Perilous Trade*, Roy MacSkimming gives a full account of the disastrous effect on GDS's client publishers, including us.

I spent some months reeling from the blow, more months trying to get our books out of the warehouse and pick up the pieces. Most of our authors and many of Jack Stoddart's were calling in panic to see if their royalties would ever be paid (I know we paid ours). God knows, it's hard

---

* For more detail, see *The Perilous Trade*.

enough to make a living as an author even if your royalty cheques show up on time. What may have saved Key Porter was our early decision not to put all our eggs in one basket. While we had no income and, for a long time no books to sell to bookstores, we had those Barnes & Noble, door-to-door, and bulk sales to other countries. I remember a phone call from a reporter covering the story of our plight (many others, including D&M, were in the same pickle). He asked when we had last been paid by Stoddart and I told him, "Moses was still in short pants when we had our last cheque."

Eventually, we bought our books out of GDS's warehouse and moved them to H. B. Fenn, our new distributor. I had known Harold Fenn for a long time and he had always seemed stable, amiable, and reliable.

Though he was always willing to have one more discussion about Key Porter's future, Michael de Pencier was obviously preoccupied with selling Key Publishers to St. Joseph Corporation. His interests and enthusiasms had shifted from magazines to the environment. Throughout the eighties he had been involved with the Young Naturalists Foundation and with the Royal Canadian Geographical Society's *Canadian Geographic*, and he was on the board of the World Wildlife Fund. His new venture, Investeco Capital, would be Canada's first "green" investment company.

It didn't take a genius to discern that Michael had moved on. I didn't blame him. The writing was on the wall.

In 2003 I asked Harold Fenn whether he would be interested in buying Key Porter. It was a difficult decision for him because publishing required a lot of cash for author advances and manufacturing. The kind of business Harold was in—distribution—worked in reverse: you sold other companies' books, collected, took your percentage, and sent the rest to the publisher who had produced the books. Unsold copies were usually returned as well, so you didn't have to finance mountains of inventory. However, Harold's son, Jordan, had taken a course in publishing and wanted to be a book publisher. So Harold was interested.

In July 2004, Michael and I sold most of our shares in Key Porter to H. B. Fenn. There was a seemingly endless array of papers to sign in

Harold's lawyers' steel and glass tower offices. Now and then I pretended an avid interest in the skyline, walked over to the windows, and muttered something about birds. Only Julian, who had come with me that day, knew that I was crying.

As part of the deal, I had to agree to stay on in some undefined capacity to finish a few projects and to ease Jordan into the role of publisher. One of Harold's first decisions was to move our offices from The Esplanade to Adelaide Street, into one of those dull buildings that define the street east of Yonge. While I was sad to leave our lived-in premises, I was relieved that I would not be haunted by memories of happier times.

Endings

ONE OF THE last two books I worked on was George Jonas's riveting memoir, *Beethoven's Mask: Notes on My Life and Times.* Set against the grim facts of the twentieth century, it is by turns comic and tragic, bemused and opinionated. It is classic Jonas. George muses on the rise and fall of nations, on human follies and foibles, on Hitler and the pope, on political correctness, pomposity, ignorance, anti-Americanism, nationalism, on the scope and barbarity of the Holocaust, the future of the European Union, and even life and death.

In the Preface to *Beethoven's Mask,* George quotes his opera singer father: "'Europe is a carnival in Venice,' he offers, 'with assassins dressed up as lyric poets. Butchers lurk in ducal palaces wearing Beethoven's mask. The voice is Beethoven's, but the hand is Beria's.'"*

The other manuscript was Norman Jewison's *This Terrible Business Has Been Good to Me.* It's a great title for a memoir and I wish I could have used it for this book. It took me over a decade to convince Norman to tell his story. For more than forty years, Norman had been one of Hollywood's fabled filmmakers. He had directed many of the great stars of the era, from

---

* Lavrenti Beria was the chief of Joseph Stalin's secret police.

Steve McQueen ("the camera loved him") in *The Thomas Crown Affair* and *The Cincinnati Kid*, to Cher ("she is in touch with the reality of ordinary people . . . they identify with her") in *Moonstruck*. He also worked with Faye Dunaway, Goldie Hawn, Burt Reynolds, Anne Bancroft, Meg Tilly, Doris Day, Rock Hudson, and, in the very early days of television, Judy Garland and Frank Sinatra.

His landmark film, *In the Heat of the Night*, with Sidney Poitier, was shot in 1966, in a small southern corner of Illinois, to quote Norman, "as Southern as we could get without actually crossing into the Confederacy, where black men were still being lynched." It was a time when the civil rights movement in the South was held in check by brutal police forces. "Sidney said there was no goddamn way he'd go below the Mason-Dixon Line for the eight weeks we'd needed to shoot the movie." When the Poitier character, Tibbs, slapped the Rod Steiger character, Endicott, it was the first time that a black man had slapped a white man in an American movie.

The film won five Academy Awards. Norman would eventually receive the Academy's lifetime achievement award in 1999. To help nurture Canadian talent, he created the Canadian Film Centre on what used to be E. P. Taylor's estate in north Toronto, and judging by its graduates' careers, it has been a great success.

We worked on the manuscript for several weeks, most of the time in Malibu, where we started early mornings and didn't finish until after midnight. I was editing the manuscript all the way home on the plane, testing a few ideas on the flight attendants.

This Terrible Business is not a personal autobiography. Like this book, it's mostly about Norman's craft, the people he worked with, the films he directed. "I tried to be truthful and entertaining," he wrote in the Preface. And his films reflect this simple but powerful credo.

From Publisher to Writer

INEVITABLY, MY NEXT book was going to be about the Holocaust in Hungary. I had been thinking about it for some forty years, circling around it, but I couldn't find a compelling way into the story. Vili had often talked about those terrible times, the horror and the inexplicable brutality of the murder of more than four hundred thousand Hungarian Jews. Some of them had been his friends and at least one of them had also courted my seventeen-year-old mother when she was home on school holidays. The last time she saw him, he was hanging from a lamppost in a small square on the Buda side of the river.

My grandfather had hidden a few of his Jewish friends in the basement of our home during the war but thought that was too little. He should have fought a valiant battle in their cause, but under the fascist regime that had brought in the anti-Jewish laws and arranged the deportations, it was too hard to be valiant. Still, according to Martin Gilbert's book *The Righteous: The Unsung Heroes of the Holocaust*, Vili Racz is listed among the Righteous at Yad Vashem in Jerusalem.

I found the subject so overwhelming, so incomprehensible that I simply couldn't write the book while I was still in publishing. I interviewed some survivors, but remained baffled by how this horror could have happened and by the fact that those wonderful, heroic, funny, interesting people—

the Hungarians—had a major role in the murder of almost half a million of their fellow citizens. I went to Auschwitz II Birkenau, stood on the railway platform in the blazing sunshine, and tried to imagine the terror of those arriving after days of standing in tightly packed boxcars, the howls of the children, the desperation of the mothers as they were herded by dogs and whip-wielding guards into the showers—the showers that were gas chambers. Most of the victims at Birkenau were Hungarians.

The sheer magnitude of the task weighed me down.

Then, one Saturday afternoon in 2004, Peter Munk called to ask if I had time to come over for a talk. I had known Peter for some years. I had first spoken with him when M&S was planning to publish a book by Garth Hopkins about Clairtone, Peter's first business venture in Canada. Jack McClelland, disinclined to be sued for libel, had thought I was the best person to find out how Peter felt about the book, as we were both born in Hungary.

Clairtone, a company that manufactured high-end stereo equipment, had collapsed, leaving a trail of unhappy investors and politicians. Peter and his partner, David Gilmour, had left Canada and spent a few years assembling a package of hotels, real estate, and mining companies. Now, years later, he was chairman of the largest gold producer in the world: Barrick Gold.

Peter said that Garth Hopkins had the facts of the sorry tale correct. We got to know each other during the next few years of lunches and dinners and the occasional trip to his Georgian Bay island. We shared friendships with both Andy Sarlos and George Jonas.

Now he and his wife, Melanie, were moving to a new house in Forest Hill, and he had been packing up old photographs and memorabilia that got him thinking about the past. He recalled his elegant grandfather, Gabriel Munk, his almost as elegant father, his beautiful mother, and the rest of his wealthy, privileged Hungarian Jewish family.

It was the first time I had heard of Rezso Kasztner. He was the man who had saved the Munk family, part of a group of 1,684 people he had rescued from almost certain death. He had managed to do this three and a half months after the German army and Adolf Eichmann's Special Commands had marched into Hungary. Ironically, Rezso Kasztner was killed in Israel, after the war, by a fellow Jew who believed he had been a collaborator.

That was my entry into the world of *Kasztner's Train*. By the time I finished the manuscript, I had read about two hundred books, hundreds of documents in three languages, and travelled to Hungary, Poland, Israel, the United States, Germany, and Austria to interview survivors. I had endured long sleepless nights living with their stories, and I knew how my book was going to tell the story of Rezso Kasztner and of the Holocaust in Hungary.

WHILE I WAS struggling with ghosts from the past, Michael de Pencier continued to invest in green businesses, such as the Green Living Show and the Environmental Guide (co-founded with Mary Anne Brinckman), Bullfrog Power, fluorescent light bulbs, smart cars, the Green Toronto Awards (which he managed in partnership with the city), and even LongPen, the remote signing device launched in 2006 by Margaret Atwood. LongPen's plan had been to make it possible for authors to sign their books for fans without having to travel. Conrad Black, for example, could go on a virtual tour, signing his Richard Nixon book while sitting in his house.*

As chairman of World Wildlife Canada, Michael had become a poster man for the green movement. He volunteered for the International Conservation Fund and the Natural Burial Association of Canada (yes, we are considering this but it is a bit yucky). He and Honor use solar power at their farm near Rosemont, Ontario, and he has been busy planting and nurturing trees—ninety thousand at last count—on their property. I have witnessed, personally, the nurturing: Michael wrapping saplings for the winter and proudly unwrapping them in the spring.

In early 2005, to take a break from my writing, I went to Florence with Catherine for a short holiday, just the two of us. We walked, checked out the art galleries, laughed, talked, drank Prosecco, and ate. Our room looked

---

* In 2014 LongPen was proud to announce that the invention had saved 1,764 lbs of CO_2 emissions. It is now part of www.syngrafii.com.

out over the Arno, with a grand view of the Ponte Vecchio. Julian phoned from Vancouver on April 8. He was about to argue a libel case in front of the BC Court of Appeal. He was as nervous as a kid before an exam. The last time he was in a Vancouver courtroom, famous BC counsel Peter Butler had said to the judge, "Well, Mr. Porter's an Eastern lawyer. What does he know?" Julian thought being a Toronto lawyer had counted against him then, and would, perhaps, now.

When he called the next day, he was somewhere along a river, surrounded by Douglas firs. "My God," he shouted over the sound of rushing waters, "I think I won!"

While we were away, Harold Fenn fired Allan Ibarra, the best book business finance guy in Canada. Allan, who was rather more philosophical about his dismissal than I was, said he was not surprised that Harold would want his own man in place.* I quit Key Porter Books a week after Julian won his case, and I got on with writing my book.

Kasztner's Train was published in 2007 by my friends Scott McIntyre in Canada and George Gibson† of Bloomsbury in the United States. It won the 2007 Writers' Trust Non-Fiction Prize and the Jewish Book Award. I spent much of the fall on a promotion tour, including a talk at New York's famed 92nd Street Y. It was a great relief to finally share this story with the world. Vili would have been proud of me.

---

* Allan went on to be CFO at the House of Anansi.

† George was an occasional member of the Quasimodo dinner group.

Europe's Ghosts

I N OCTOBER 2006, while I was immersed in *Kasztner's Train*, the CBC
sent me to Budapest to be part of a documentary commemorating the
fiftieth anniversary of the Hungarian Revolution. We visited plot 301 in
the Rákoskeresztúr Cemetery, the burial ground of people killed by the
state after Soviet troops put down the uprising in 1956. In the country I
had come from, there was once a revolution and our prime minister had
been betrayed, imprisoned, and executed.

We walked through the House of Terror, once headquarters of both the
Hungarian fascists and their successors, the Communist state police. My
grandfather had been held in its underground cells pending his trial on
trumped-up charges. I walked, again, the old streets of what had been the
Jewish ghetto, where so many died that the dead had been stacked up like
cords of wood in the small square where now children play.

I had been curious about how my former country was dealing with its
newfound democracy, how it was weathering the shift to capitalism and
consumerism. How was it dealing with its horrific legacies of the Holocaust and of the Soviet occupation? How did it deal with the perpetrators
and what justice could it bring to the victims?

This experience is what led me to write my next book, *The Ghosts of
Europe*. I wanted to explore how Central Europe was adjusting to its pres-

ent realities twenty years after the end of the Soviet era. I wrote about Solidarity in Poland, the famous Round Table meetings that ended one-party rule and brought in free elections, about the Czechs and Slovaks deciding to put an end to Czechoslovakia, about the Library of Prohibited Books in Prague with its twenty-seven thousand books banned under Communist rule. Jiri Gruntorad, then the custodian of these books and periodicals, proudly showed me the packed shelves of Slovak, Czech, and Polish writers, including dozens of Josef Skvorecky's novels, Vaclav Havel's plays, Milan Kundera's novels, Czeslaw Milosz's poetry, Bohumil Hrabal's scripts, and Ivan Klima's novels and scripts. Now there was a free press, yet it was Ivan Klima who had remarked, "We asked for freedom and you gave us the market."

I interviewed former Polish prime minister General Jaruzelski, Hungarian prime minister Gyurcsány, legendary Czech resistance hero and first elected president Vaclav Havel, and former Slovak prime minister Vladimir Mečiar. After one of my visits to the Czech Republic, I brought Josef Skvorecky greetings from his old friend, Vaclav Havel, who told me he wished Josef would "come home" again.

"I am already home," Josef told me. Here. In Canada.

Josef and Zdena were further estranged from their former home when a group of overzealous Czechs decided that more had to be done to punish the Communist regime's informants and the collaborators. The Státní Bezpečnost, or StB as it was usually referred to, had been dispersed quickly after the fall of the old regime and little was done to retrieve its files. Havel believed that his people would be best served by moving on from the past. "Take care when judging history," he said. "Otherwise you can do more harm than good." The past is never black and white. No one was untouched by the system.

However, the group of citizens published a list, an enforced "lustration" of StB informers, and Zdena's name appeared on it. Devastated, she sued the Ministry of the Interior and won, but she felt from then on that her name had been muddied, that she would "never get rid of the dreadful suspicion." Her health, Josef said, never recovered. The zealots who had compiled "the list" had shown as little regard for the truth as they did for the consequences of their actions.

That was the story behind Josef's novel *Two Murders in My Double Life*.

Adam Michnik, one of the heroes of Poland's resistance to totalitarianism, once said that it would be well to remember that in 1989 Central Europe came "as a messenger not only of freedom and tolerance but also of hatred and intolerance. It is here that the last two world wars began."

I finished writing *Ghosts of Europe* in 2009, twenty years after Central Europe joined Western Europe. I have been back to Warsaw, Prague, and Budapest since, and I am saddened at the turn away from some of the principles of democracy that led to the creation of the European project. I fear that too many of us have become so comfortable with democracy as a backdrop to our daily existence that we no longer see it as an ideal worth fighting for.

Douglas & McIntyre published *Ghosts* and, as I discovered later, persuaded Tom Dunne at St. Martin's to buy US rights.

THROUGHOUT THE WRITING of *Ghosts* and my next book, *Buying a Better World: George Soros and Billionaire Philanthropy*, George Jonas was my sounding board.

For some years, George and I used to meet in the Coffee Mill, a Hungarian restaurant in Yorkville run by the very hospitable Martha, who had been married to a Hungarian wrestler called Laci Heczey, another Jonas friend. I had met Laci for the first time at one of Key Publishers' annual Christmas parties that stretched through the warren of offices all the way from Front Street to The Esplanade. Laci, one of the grand unpublished stories of the decade, walked through the somewhat inebriated throng with two tigers he kept as pets.

Over endless coffees, George talked about his own experiences with fascists in Budapest, and we debated his lingering appreciation of Hungary's wartime governor, Miklós Horthy. He often accused me of being influenced by left-leaning writers and politicians, and he forced me to defend and sometimes rethink what I had written. I can almost hear him talk to me when I reread some of the passages about George Soros in *Buying a Better World*. Soros is, indeed, a left-leaner, one who has had the opportunity to influence world affairs, though, as my book posits, might not for long. He had spent about $16 billion, most of it through his Open Society Foundations, by the time my book was published. "He could have become the most hated man in Central Europe for a fraction of that," George Jonas opined, "but he didn't ask for my advice."

Being a true Central European, George Jonas could recite Heine and Goethe in German, Apollinaire in French, and Pushkin in Russian. Both of us had learned Russian, unwillingly, in school in Budapest, and both of us admitted that when reading Russian literature, it was not altogether useless. When the refugee or migrant (depending on your point of view) crisis began, he had dire predictions for Europe's ability to survive. The year Hungarian Prime Minister Viktor Orban (he had succeeded Gyurcsány) built a wall and called in the military to guard Hungary's borders, George was the only columnist in Canada in Orban's corner. In one of his last columns,* he said that a country "cannot accept foreign countries imposing an immigration model on it that would dramatically change its cultural composition." Being a realist, however, he charted the downslide of Europe's aging and shrinking population and the inexorable march toward a new Eurobia, a Europe ruled by Muslims.

During the last months of his life, George wanted to hear *Eugene Onegin* again. He had, of course, heard it many times before, knew the melodies and the words in Russian, and he sang (very croakily) along with the soprano during the Letter Scene. We assembled his last book, *Selected Poems 1967–2011*, with the unusual method of my reading each poem from his collections and George indicating, sometimes impatiently, which ones he wished to leave out.†

---

* September 22, 2015.

† The book was published by Marc Côté of Cormorant, with Margaret Atwood's introduction.

When a few of us gathered to celebrate George's poetry at Harbour-front in 2015, my choice was "Landmarks," about his arrival in Canada. These are its last lines:

> with cardboard trunks, torn clothes, needing a wash,
> an evil-smelling strange boy, tall and thin,
> had asked to spend the night. And god knows why
> they took me in.

I remembered the handleless blue suitcase with all my worldly possessions, and like George, I was grateful that Canada had taken me in.

Keep the Promise

JUNE CALLWOOD'S DEATH was a shock. She seemed so vital, so ageless. Too many of us take for granted today the social initiatives she had
started. In 2007, a group of June Callwood's friends restarted June's campaign to end child poverty, Keep the Promise. On November 24, 1989, in a
unanimous all-party resolution, the House of Commons resolved to end
child poverty in Canada by the year 2000. It hadn't happened. In fact, child
poverty had increased: now one in five children in Canada live in poverty.

The last time I saw June was at a putatively celebratory lunch at Biff's
Bistro on Front Street. Her cancer had spread and she had not much longer to live. She was frail but very elegant in a soft blue outfit with a trail-
ing scarf and shapely flat shoes. She ordered some kind of fish while she
talked with considerable animation about her progress with the all-party
parliamentary agreement, and how good she felt about that. She also felt
good about her fundraising efforts on behalf of Casey House, a downtown
Toronto hospice that specializes in HIV/AIDS care. We sat near the door as
men of various shapes and sizes marched in, talking loudly on cell phones
and demanding immediate attention from the hostess. June watched them
with amusement, then she said, not too quietly, "Here come the big swinging dicks."

After our lunch she drove off in her small convertible—a gift from her children—and waved goodbye. There was her irrepressible smile and that glow June had when she felt she had accomplished something.

Unfortunately, the politicians forgot their promises and everyone went on with their lives just as before. But this time it did not just end there. With June gone, we restarted the Keep the Promise campaign with theologian and social activist Mary Jo Leddy and Rabbi Arthur Bielfeld as our leaders. They had both been friends of June. We lobbied governments at all levels, mobilized thousands of children and teachers across the country. In November 2015 children from every province and territory came to the Keep the Promise National Summit in Ottawa. During the 2015 federal election, all major parties promised to take action.

I do not know whether they will honour that commitment, but June would have been glad that we tried to hold them to it.

June 2 is June Callwood Children's Day in Ontario, a special day for a very special woman, a day, as my daughter Catherine wrote in the *Toronto Star*, "to imagine a better world and make a plan to achieve that. It's a day to be unexpectedly kind to strangers."*

---

* Catherine was appointed the *New York Times*'s Canadian Bureau chief in 2017.

A Footnote to Canadian Publishing History

I N 2012, HAVING enjoyed eleven years of government financial assistance through its control of M&S, Random House Canada announced
that it had now acquired the University of Toronto's seventy-five per cent
shares in M&S—for one dollar. Elaine Dewar's 2017 book *The Takeover* is
an interesting account of the loss of "The Canadian Publishers." To some
extent, the book answers my questions about how and names a few of the
individuals who had so cleverly engineered the original deal.

My one remaining question is what took them so long.

In a long letter to Mordecai Richler, dated September 13, 1974, Jack
McClelland wrote about his views on the American publishing presence
in Canada.

There is no doubt in my mind that US publishers (and for that you
could read British publishers and any other publishers because it
has nothing to do with the USA per se) are a real problem in Canada. . . . A publisher operating a subsidiary in another country does
not identify with the culture of that country. His purpose in having a subsidiary can only be twofold. First, he is interested in moving his publishing product, and second, he is interested in making
money. Those are his sole objectives. . . . Nobody can object to those

objectives. The problem in Canada, however, is the almost total takeover of the industry by foreign interests; this means that many vital forces in the cultural growth of the country can be lost because of inability to compete with massive foreign presence.

I am glad Jack was not alive to see "the house that Jack built" become part of a German subsidiary.

The Inimitable Jack Rabinovitch

I T IS UNUSUAL to become close friends late in life with someone you have just met. But Jack Rabinovitch had a unique talent for friendship. We met in November 1994 and remained friends for the next twenty-two years. Our friendship started with exchanging jokes, a few of them in Yiddish, and stories the evening of the first Giller Prize party. I loved his ability to size up people and situations, his silly jokes, his delight in new discoveries, new places where we could get lost, and new faces, such as the young priest's who showed us around the pope's private galleries in Rome. And I loved his stories.

Jack's father had been a ballroom dancing instructor in Bucharest: a dapper man with dark hair, charm, fast feet, and a determination to do better. Except for the colour of his hair, Jack inherited most of his characteristics. Jack's mother and aunt had escaped across the Ukrainian border to Romania when another wave of Cossack pogroms threatened to end their youthful ambition to stay alive. The two sisters were barefoot but had the family's wealth in jewels sewn into the linings of their threadbare coats. When the border guard's wife told them how much they would have to pay, they pleaded abject poverty, and since they were both barefoot in the snow, she believed their lie.

Had Jack's parents not married and had three children so soon after they arrived in Canada, Jack's father might have had a bright future as a businessman. As it was, he became a newspaper vendor on a Montreal street corner.

Jack hawked newspapers at his father's stand. Later, when his father opened a fast-food restaurant, he and his brother, Sam, helped out behind the counter. During those years, they ate well. Otherwise, it was his mother's cooking, and she had an unerring talent for serving burnt, soggy, greasy, colourless food.

Jack and his brother went to school with the kids of other immigrants. All except two families in Jack's neighbourhood were Jewish. A few blocks over, the Catholic kids ran with their own crowd and provided lively exercise for Jack and his friends, who had to run the gauntlet of battle-scarred fists and metal-heeled boots on the way to school. It was a quick, if not painless, method of learning French, and Jack spoke a fine *joual*. His nickname was '*ti carotte*, little carrot, because he was a redhead.

His best friend back then was a kid called Archie, a small boy with big dreams about joining a band. He danced along the streets and up and down stairs, as if he could hear music. Archie's father was a bookie, his older brother, a tank of a man, was the enforcer. One day, after Archie was bashed in the face by Tarzan, one of the school's "repeaters," Archie's brother showed up at school and decked the guy. After that, Tarzan never touched Archie. It was a timely lesson for Jack on how to survive as a scrawny kid: ally yourself with a large protector. From then on, he traded his reading and maths skills for protection. It was a great incentive to stay ahead of the class.

Without that incentive, Jack was not sure he would have made it to Baron Byng High, the school where most of the immigrant kids went and where Irving Layton had preceded him. And without high school, he would not have gone to university, studied literature, or fallen in love with books and with Doris Giller.

It was at Baron Byng that Jack first met Mordecai Richler. They were not especially friendly to start with because Mordecai's sole interest in Jack was Jack's friendship with Lefty, or Hyman Berger as the class teacher insisted on calling him, the best athlete, the best ball player, runner, pitcher, pool player at school. There was no better way to acquire prestige than to be connected with Lefty.

When Jack went to McGill to study literature, he lost touch with both Lefty and Mordecai. He rarely talked about his McGill years but did like to tell tales about working for the Steinbergs and what he learned as executive VP of Trizec. Later he became an independent developer and builder. Along the way he acquired some wealth. As a volunteer, he helped build the new Princess Margaret Hospital in Toronto, "on time and under budget," he told us.

It was only after Mordecai became a friend of Jack's wife, Doris Giller, that the two men reconnected.

I HAD FIRST met Doris near the end of the seventies in the Roof Lounge of the Park Plaza Hotel. She was at that time entertainment editor at the *Montreal Star*, a fast-talking, opinionated, hard-drinking, hard-swearing buddy of Jack McClelland's. She could match him for every "fuck" he tossed at her. She was also curvaceous, strikingly beautiful, flamboyant, a chain-smoking wonder of a woman who told funny stories and insisted that Canada needed less mealy-mouthed book reviewers. Jack McClelland, of course, agreed with her. Doris Giller and Jack Rabinovitch moved to Toronto in the mid-eighties and I met her again when she was assistant books editor at the *Toronto Star*. She was impatient with much of what she considered "the Toronto elite." She had an unfailing nose for bullshit.

Doris was the love of Jack's life. They were inseparable. They had big parties and long sun-drenched holidays, went dancing, frequented the clubs, read books together. Doris died in 1993 and Jack never stopped mourning. The Giller Prize was to honour her memory. Jack first tried the idea on Mordecai at Woody's on Bishop Street in Montreal. Woody's used to be one of Montreal's famous pubs, a dark room with wooden seats in narrow booths, a hangout for writers and other creative types. Though he was not enamoured of literary prizes, Mordecai liked this idea because he had been very fond of Doris and shared her discerning nose for the "fraudulent." That's why he agreed to be one of the judges. For the first year of the awards, Mordecai was joined by Alice Munro and literary critic and university professor David Staines.

The Giller Prize is awarded to the best Canadian fiction work published in English the previous year. The prize, then, was $25,000.* The first Giller evening, Doris's friend Joey Slinger was the MC. Jack, in his tuxedo, looked splendid, as did everyone else—writers, editors, booksellers, many of whom had never worn a tux or a long dress until that night. Yet despite the formal wear, the party was, somehow, less formal and more relaxed than other literary get-togethers because Jack, smiling, welcoming, easygoing in a great celebratory mood, put all of us at ease.

From the very start, the Giller represented literary quality. The first three winners were M. G. Vassanji, Rohinton Mistry, and Margaret Atwood. Mordecai did not win until 1997, when he was no longer a judge. Alice Munro followed a year later. Rohinton Mistry, the 1995 winner, also won the Commonwealth Writers' Prize. He commented after the evening that the crowd of guests had swelled to five hundred, that the tables had been moving closer and closer together to make room for more, and now also for the television cameras bobbing about filming the evening. No one minds, he said, because they are also here to celebrate literature.

I read Rohinton's winning book, *A Fine Balance*, while travelling in India and called to tell Jack that the book had ruined what I had planned as a relaxing, sightseeing journey. All I could think about each day as we visited temples and bazaars and tea plantations was the fate of the benighted characters who were the anti-heroes of the novel. I had so desperately wanted a different ending that one evening I asked Rohinton whether he had ever considered a less terrible fate for those two. He said, no. He hadn't.

Both Margaret Atwood (a winner for *Alias Grace*) and Alice Munro (winner for *Runaway* and *The Love of a Good Woman*) won other prizes—Margaret, the Man Booker Prize, and Alice, the Nobel Prize in Literature. One evening, years before the Booker and the Nobel, I told Alice that she

---

* In 2005 the Giller was renamed Scotiabank Giller, and the award has been increased to $100,000.

was only one of two Canadian writers I had read before I arrived here. She was amused and wondered why, after reading her stories, I had persisted in staying.

The 2001 winner was Richard B. Wright's *Clara Callan*, published by Phyllis Bruce at HarperCollins, the same Phyllis who had urged me to start publishing fiction when she was at Key Porter. The 2011 winner was Esi Edugyan's *Half-Blood Blues*, a book that had been scheduled to be published by Key Porter Books before H. B. Fenn declared bankruptcy. The 2016 Scotiabank Giller Prize winner was Madeleine Thien's *Do Not Say We Have Nothing*, and in 2017 the winner was Michael Redhill's *Bellevue Square*.

People talk of the Giller effect. It's evidenced by all the books on the short lists. Zsuzsi Gartner (her *All the Anxious Girls* had been published by Key Porter) told me that the prize changed her life. She is now invited to festivals around the world. The awards ceremony is viewed by 1.3 million people. There is even an anti-Giller faction and a big, casual-dress Giller-Lite fundraising party for all those who have not been invited to Jack's glamorous gala.

Every year, at the Giller party, Jack repeated the same simple suggestion: "For the price of a meal in this town, you can buy all the short-listed books. So eat at home and buy the books."

Is it any wonder that I loved him?

For the Love of Books

IN A SHORT piece for Carol Shields and Marjorie Anderson's *Dropped Threads*, June Callwood observed about old age: "I don't know what death is, but it can't be worse than the curse of an optimistic nature that learns nothing from discouragement." Though June had meant this to apply to herself, it would also be a very astute observation about book publishers.

Writing this memoir has forced me to think about both my love of books and the business of books. I think that publishing is more of an avocation than a business. It lacks predictability. It sells books fully returnable or, as it often seemed to me, lends them to booksellers with an option to buy, should they choose to do so. Publishing, then, requires some government funding, though not on the scale that Bombardier or the film industry does. If English Canada's population were triple its present size, and if our country didn't share a language with the United States, Canadian publishers could probably manage without subsidies. Had the French forces prevailed instead of the British on the Plains of Abraham in 1759, I think we would have a relatively healthy book industry.

At both McClelland & Stewart and Key Porter we were publishing more than a hundred books a year, and every one of them had the potential to be plagued by gremlins: typesetters who lost pages, indices that were five or six pages out, jackets that didn't fit, chapters gone missing from the printed book, entire shipments gone off the rails or into the ocean. My favourite book disaster is the one where an army of hungry weevils ate two skids of an expensive art book and the binder chose bankruptcy over paying for the damage. Today's computer-based production systems have reduced the frequency of errors on the page, but they have created a new set of problems. Yet publishers persist, always hoping for that perfect book.

Our industry relies on the brilliance of writers who may or may not produce a manuscript in any given year. Without them, there would be no book business. And it relies on a dedicated group of people (many more than those I have acknowledged in this book) who believe in the value of books.

I grew up believing that those who have the power of words can shape our memory and our history. My wise grandfather used to tell me that smart dictators first jail the writers. It's always been thus in Russia, whether under the czars or Stalin or Vladimir Putin. In 1989, the Iranian Ayatollah Ruhollah Khomeini issued a fatwa ordering Muslims to kill novelist Salman Rushdie. I was proud of Canada for being the first country to welcome Rushdie and of Ontario Premier Bob Rae for being the first government leader to appear on stage with him during the 1992 PEN Canada benefit. In his short speech, thanking all those responsible, Rushdie reflected not so much on his own fate but on the fate of all writers who were killed or imprisoned.

Publishing is still a very personal endeavour, relying on the talents and commitments of a few inspired, grievously underpaid stalwart individuals. We call them editors and publishers. At a gathering of lawyers—I have attended several of these over the years—a very successful corporate lawyer asked me why I would want to be in the book business. I told him it was because I loved it. Much has changed during the years since I first entered 25 Hollinger Road, there have been some winners and some losers, but the essentials have remained the same. There has also been much to celebrate: for example, the House of Anansi fiftieth anniversary in 2017 with the publication of Dennis Lee's *Heart Residence*; the happy handover of ECW Press to its co-publisher, David Caron; the continuing efforts by Chapters/

Indigo's CEO Heather Reisman to support books in Canada even as US bookstore chains decline. Digital books have not destroyed the audience for books; in fact they may have expanded it. The television series based on Margaret Atwood's *The Handmaid's Tale* became the most successful drama series on TV in 2017, and the second season started in 2018. The Amazon Canada First Novel Award celebrated its 42nd year in 2018 with Michael Kaan's *The Water Beetles* taking the first prize. Past winners include Michael Ondaatje, Nino Ricci, and Madeleine Thien.

Over my forty-year career, I can honestly say that I looked forward to every day at M&S and Key Porter Books, and more than a few days at Doubleday and Seal. Like many of my colleagues, I have enjoyed being a publisher and miss the companionship of my peers, the moment of recognition when a new manuscript reveals itself to be a work of art or insight, or sheer brilliance. I miss the delight of holding one of our new books in my hands; I love even the smell of fresh book pages. I can rarely resist wanting to share books with friends and family. Though I still worry about some of my stupid decisions, in hindsight, I do not think I would have chosen a different life.

In reflecting on my own writing, I have come to realize that I invariably return to my childhood. I have written about Hungary and Hungarians— both real and imagined—about the troubles faced by Central Europe, about the defunct Hapsburg empire and its descendants, and about my own strange family. Even *The Appraisal*, my 2017 novel, relies on what I have learned about the realities of today's confused Central Europe. Most of my writing is a way to understand the world.

Margaret Atwood said that writing involves "negotiating with the dead." I have been aware of this throughout the years it took me to complete this memoir, much as Atwood herself had negotiated with Susanna Moodie, and Pierre Berton had negotiated with the men who built the railway, and Basil Johnston had negotiated with his school friends and his ancestors. I negotiated with Jack and Al, Margaret and Irving, Leonard and Farley, George and Doris, and what I ended up with is never the whole truth, but it is as truthful as I could make it.

I give the last word to Margaret Laurence. From *The Diviners*: "Look ahead into the past, and back into the future, until the silence."

Acknowledgements

I N THE COURSE of researching the past, confirming or correcting my own recollections, I have contacted a lot of people in the publishing world—writers, poets, editors, publishers, journalists. I thank them all for their own memories: Phyllis Bruce, Susan Renouf, Jennifer Glossop, Michael de Pencier, Dennis Lee, Annie McClelland, Sylvia Fraser, Scott McIntyre, Graeme Gibson, John Macfarlane, David Berry, John Neale, Sandra Martin, Gloria Goodman, Jack David, Lily Miller, Beverley Slopen, Jim Marsh, Paul Dutton, Angel Guerra, Sheila Douglas, Linda Pruessen, David Shaw, Barbara Berson, Dean Cooke, Linda McKnight, Roy MacSkimming, John Pearce, Tom Best, Jim Polk, Ken Rodmell, Suzanne Drinkwater, Stephen Anderson, Charis Wahl, Jonathan Webb, and Margaret Atwood.

I am grateful to all the extraordinary people I have had the privilege to work with at McClelland & Stewart and Key Porter, at Seal and Doubleday, Douglas & McIntyre, ECW, and the Association of Canadian Publishers. I am thankful for all the great independent booksellers who have continued to promote new books by Canadian authors—in particular, Book City, Munro's Books, Ben McNally Books, A Different Drummer, The Bookshelf, The Odd Book, Café Books, McNally Robinson, Woozles, Paragraphe Bookstore, Mabel's Fables, and all those who have soldiered on through the decades of my life in the book business. I will always miss the Book Room, once Canada's oldest bookstore, and I am sad to see that Bryan Prince Bookseller has closed its doors. They were some of the best.

The McMaster Library and Archives have helped enormously by allowing me access to documents. McMaster has Key Porter's, McClelland & Stewart's, Pierre Berton's, and Farley Mowat's archives. I would be remiss if I did not mention here that the Key Porter fonds at McMaster would not exist had Sheila Douglas not packaged them, labeling each box with great care, and dispatched them to Hamilton. I want to thank the McClelland family for giving me access to the M&S fonds and Sheila Turcon for spending many weeks digging up information, memos, dates, and letters in the files.

Dr. Norman Allan's manuscript about his father, Ted, was a great source of inspiration, as was Frank Newfeld's *Drawing on Type*, Roy MacSkimming's *The Perilous Trade: Publishing Canada's Writers*, and Bruce Meyer's *Portraits of Canadian Writers*, published by Porcupine's Quill.

Thank you also to Marc Côté of Cormorant Books for publishing George Jonas's *Selected Poems: 1967–2011* in time for George to be able to hold the book in his hands and, later, for allowing me to reprint the poems in this memoir.

Julian Porter has been kind enough to read the whole manuscript twice to remind me of what I had missed, and to make some suggestions to save us from libel suits.

A heartfelt thank you to Phyllis Bruce for her patience as my editor bringing this book to life and to Kevin Hanson and his talented Simon & Schuster team.

Catherine, Julia, Jessica, Suse, Graeme, and Cam have all contributed in various ways to filling in the blanks. Sometimes just being there is great encouragement. My mother, as always, remained generous with her own memories of the events and the people who make up this book.

Index

Abella, Irving, and Harold Troper, *None Is Too Many,* 342, 349–50

Abella, Rosalie, 274, 349–50

Achebe, Chinua, 148

Acorn, Milton, 50, 54–55, 122

Adams, Ian, *S: Portrait of a Spy,* 212, 288

Agnelli, Gianni, 364

Aldana, Patsy, 139, 142, 144

Alexander, Clare, 327

Alexander, Lincoln, 328

Alfons (Anna's mother's third husband), 8–9, 17, 19, 102, 156–57

al-Ilah, Crown Prince Abd, 288

Allan, Norman, 33

Allan, Ted, 31–34, 275
  Lies My Father Told Me, 33
  The Scalpel, the Sword (with Sydney Gordon), 31
  This Time a Better Earth, 33n
  Willie the Squowse, 33

Allen, Charlotte Vale, 320

Alliance Communications, 247n, 343, 390n

Al Purdy Was Here (documentary), 54

Amazon, 402, 403

Amazon Canada First Novel Award, 431

American Booksellers' Association, 182, 255, 318, 338

Amiel, Barbara, 219, 289

Amis, Kingsley, 167

Amis, Martin, 342

Anderson, Doris, 193, 194, 197–201, 252
  Rebel Daughter, 197n, 201
  Rough Layout, 199
  The Unfinished Revolution, 200–201, 320

Anderson, Marjorie, 192, 429

Andrews, Keith, 45

Anishinaabe people, 134, 353, 355

Anne of Green Gables (TV), 217

Apollinaire, Guillaume, 416

Aquin, Hubert, 83, 137

Arany, János, 6, 57

Argus Corporation, 177, 363, 364

Arthur, Eric:
  The Barn: A Vanishing Landmark of North America, 42, 79, 80n, 269, 270
  Toronto, No Mean City, 79

Ashevak, Kenojuak, "Enchanted Owl," 135

Ashoona, Pitseolak, 135

As It Happens (CBC radio), 159–60, 162

Asper, Izzy, 365

Association of Canadian Publishers, 84, 139, 403

Atkins, Norman, 294

Atwood, Margaret, 58, 61–67, 81, 82, 108n, 122, 124, 151n, 166, 211, 295, 305, 335, 398n, 416n

  Alias Grace, 67

  Angel Catbird (with Johnnie Christmas and Tamra Bonvillain), 67

  awards and honors to, 61, 64, 426

  Bashful Bob and Doleful Dorinda, 370

  Bodily Harm, 64

  Cat's Eye, 63, 64

  The Circle Game, 61

  Edible Woman, 61–64, 67

  and Gibson, 65–66

  Hagseed, 67

  The Handmaid's Tale, 64, 431

  inventions of, 66, 411

  The Journals of Susanna Moodie, 63

  Lady Oracle, 64, 180

  Life Before Man, 64

  and M&S, 61–65, 137, 138, 180, 279, 305

  and McClelland, 61–62, 65, 309

  "Owl and Pussycat, Some Years Later," 64

  Princess Prunella and the Purple Peanut, 370

  Rude Ramsay and the Roaring Radishes, 370

  Surfacing, 64

  Survival: A Thematic Guide to Canadian Literature, 107–8

  "True North," 67

  and women's issues, 193, 194, 232

  "Writing the Male Characters," 192

  The Year of the Flood, 66–67

  "You Fit into Me," 64

Auden, W. H., 54, 59

Auschwitz Birkenau, 349, 410

Austen, Jane, 8, 117

Axworthy, Lloyd, 200, 223

Azzopardi, Trezza, 348

Bacque, Jim, 83

Balzac, Honoré, 6

Bantam Books, 179–80, 182, 186, 214, 217, 241–42, 253, 292

Bantam Doubleday Dell International, 318, 331

Barfoot, Joan, 348

Barlow, Maude, 261

Barnes & Noble, 402, 405

Baron, Carole, 292

Barreto-Rivera, Rafael, 43

Bassett, Isabel, 176n, 193, 287

Bassett, John, 176, 287, 289

Bata, Tom, 128

Batten, Jack, 210–11, 258–59, 267

  Judges, 262

Bedford, Brian, 224

Bellow, Saul, 167

Belushi, John, 143

Benchley, Peter, 180, 218

Bennett, Avie, 279, 305–7, 309, 313, 315, 321, 397

Bennett, Bill, 284

Bennett, James Leslie, 212, 288

Bentley, Peter, 129

Beny, Roloff, 49, 78, 169–74

  Iran, Elements of Destiny, 139, 150, 171–74, 309

  People: Legends in Life and Art, 174

  Persia, Bridge of Turquoise, 139, 150, 170–72, 173, 270, 309

  To Every Thing There Is a Season, 169

  and *A Visual Odyssey, 1958–1968: Roloff Beny*, 169

Bergen, David, 138

Berger, Hyman "Lefty," 424–25

Bernstein, Harriet, 120

Berry, David, 41

Berson, Barbara, 137

Bertelsen, Ruth, 252

Bertelsmann, 317–19, 321–23, 326, 329–31, 347, 397

Berton, Janet, 93, 212, 378

Berton, Pierre, 77, 78, 81, 91–97, 130, 151n, 245n, 258, 309, 431
  The Comfortable Pew, 91
  death of, 378–79
  Drifting Home, 93n
  and Franklin, 93–95, 96, 378–79
  The Great Railway Illustrated, 105, 108
  The Last Spike: The Great Railway, 1881–1885, 97, 99, 101, 105, 108
  and M&S, 94–95, 107, 182, 279
  The National Dream: The Great Railway, 1871–1881, 92–93, 97, 105, 108
  The Pierre Berton Show (TV), 94
  Prisoners of the North, 378
  The Smug Minority, 91–92
  socializing with, 95–96, 99, 212, 377–78
  as storyteller, 92–93, 97, 166
Besant, Derek Michael, 243
Best, Tom, 259, 274
Bethune, Norman, 31, 32
Bevington, Stan, 253
Bezmozgis, David, 398
Bielfeld, Rabbi Arthur, 420
Bird, Heather:
  Conspiracy to Murder: The Trial of Helmuth Buxbaum, 284n
  Not Above the Law, 284
Birdsell, Sandra, 342
Birney, Earle, 50, 51, 81, 111–14, 118, 123, 182, 245n
  "David," 111, 113
  and Low, 41, 111, 112, 113
  "The Moon of Pooh Chi," 111–12
  poem to Catherine, 109
  and Puci, 111–12
  Turvey, 113
Black, Conrad, 130, 175–78, 363–66, 374, 383, 411
  Duplessis, 175–77, 366
  A Life in Progress, 364, 365
  A Matter of Principle, 367
Blackwood, David, 72
Blais, Marie-Claire, 81, 83

Blaise, Clark, *A North American Education*, 82
Blatty, William Peter, 180, 218
Bodsworth, Fred, 377
  Last of the Curlews, 95n
Boggs, Jean Sutherland, 189
Bonner, Margerie, 114
Bonvillain, Tamra, 67
Bookmen's/Bookperson's Lunch Club, 66
Book of the Month Club, 97, 142, 254
Borovoy, Alan, *Uncivil Disobedience*, 349
Bourgault, Pierre, 83
Bowering, George, 53, 122
Braithwaite, Max, 81
  The Night We Stole the Mountie's Car, 139
Brand, Dionne, *Ossuaries*, 123–24
Braunschweiger, Jürgen, 266–67
Breakwater Books, 254
Breeden, Richard, 366
Brinckman, Mary Anne, 247, 333, 411
Brinkley, David, 364
Bronfman, Peter, 343
Bruce, Harry, 267
  Down Home: Notes of a Maritime Son, 246n
Bruce, Phyllis, 137, 280, 281, 299, 313, 344, 427
Bruemmer, Fred, 336
  The Arctic World, 271, 337–38
  Encounters with Arctic Animals, 78
  Seasons of the Eskimo, 78, 135
  Survival: A Refugee Life, 135n, 277
Brzezinski, Zbigniew, 364–65
Buckler, Ernest, 21, 220n
Buckley, William F., 364
Buckman, Bob:
  I Don't Know What to Say—How to Help and Support Someone Who Is Dying, 357–58
  Magic or Medicine, 357
  What You Really Need to Know About Cancer, 358
Bukowski, Denise, 254

Bull, William Perkins, 25
Burnard, Bonnie, 254
Burnford, Sheila, *The Incredible Journey,* 41
Burroughs, William S., *Naked Lunch,* 22
Burton, Richard, 342
Bush, Jack, 39
Butler, Peter, 412
Butterfield, George and Martha, 239–40
Buxbaum, Helmuth, 284

Calgary Conference on the Canadian Novel
    (1978), 150–51
Callaghan, Morley, 21, 166
    Winter, 29n
Callwood, June, 95, 131, 159, 161, 193, 194,
    227, 295, 350, 393n, 419–20, 429
Calvino, Italo, 320, 342
Cameron, Dorothy, 100
Cameron, Stevie, *Ottawa Inside Out,*
    261–62, 283
Camp, Dalton, 76, 285, 294, 381–85
    Gentlemen, Players & Politicians, 381
Camp, Linda, 381–82, 383, 385
Campbell, Maria, *Halfbreed,* 45–46, 354–55
Canada:
    Anna's arrival in, 3–4, 9
    Arctic region of, 78, 133–36, 271, 277–78,
        334, 337–38, 378
    "Baie Comeau" policy, 317
    bookstores in, 77–78, 101, 280, 369–72,
        402
    censorship in, 113, 149–50, 213
    Centennial (1967), 18, 246
    Constitution of, 298
    First Nations, *see* Indigenous peoples
    foreign influence on economy of, 84, 86,
        92, 127–28, 175, 218n, 421–22
    landscape painters of, 44
    literary agents in, 254
    literary journals in, 123
    nationalism in, 75–77, 84–86, 92, 108,
        127–28, 133, 217, 223, 330, 407, 417
    national parks of, 338

non-fiction novels, 374
October Crisis (1970), 13
poets of, 50–52, 64, 122–24, 253
political books, 283–86
publishing industry in, 75–79, 83–85,
    138–39, 150–51, 179–80, 240, 253–54,
    280, 283, 313–15, 317–32, 369–72, 397,
    402–5, 421–22, 429–32
Quebec, *see* Quebec
"Sixties Scoop," 355
Soviet spies in, 288
theatre in, 254–55
universities in, 84–85
vastness of, 81, 82
victory in Canada-Russia hockey (1972),
    108–9, 253
writers in, 42–43, 81–84, 107–8, 150, 179,
    253, 430
Canada: A Celebration, 29n, 267–68, 344
Canada: Year of the Land, 246
Canada Council for the Arts, 134, 139, 223,
    398
Canadian, The, 53, 244, 246
Canadian Abortion Rights League, 192
Canadian Advisory Council on the Status of
    Women, 200
Canadian Art Club, 44n
Canadian Authors Association, 81, 378
Canadian Book Publishers Council, 84
Canadian Booksellers Association, 149, 301
Canadian Business, 241, 245, 246
Canadian Children's Treasury, 344
Canadian Conference of the Arts, 153
Canadian Encyclopedia, 85
Canadian Film Centre, 408
Canadian Geographic, 241, 405
Canadian Living, 248, 249
Canadian Medical Association, 358
Canadian National Exhibition (CNE; "the
    Ex"), 153–54, 185
Canadian Pacific Railway, 92–93, 97, 105
Canterbury University, Christchurch, 8, 17,
    19, 63

Canyon Club, 341–42
Capote, Truman, *In Cold Blood,* 374n
Cariou, Len, 224
Carney, Pat, 199–200n
    Trade Secrets, 200n
Caron, David, 430
Carrier, Roch, 82
Carrington, Lord, 364
Cary, Joyce, 148
Cassell & Co., 4, 9, 191
CBC, 58, 378
CBC radio, 12, 81, 159, 213–14, 249
CBC TV, Anna's job quest at, 13–15
Celan, Paul, 117, 395
Cercone, Philip, 403n
Chamberlain, Neville, 125
Chapters bookstores, 369, 371, 393, 402, 404, 430–31
Chatelaine magazine, 197, 198–99, 211
Chaucer, Geoffrey, 8, 111
Cheetham, Anthony, 320
Chickadee, 241, 247
Chrétien, Jean, 260
    Straight from the Heart, 297–301
Christmas, Johnnie, 67
Citytv, 14–15, 213
Civil Liberties Association, 159
Clairtone, 410
Clan Macmillan, 154
Clark, Joe, 237, 253, 289n
    A Nation Too Good to Lose, 277
Clarke, Austin, 81
Clarke Irwin, 280n, 319
Clarkson, Adrienne, 214, 248
Classic Book Shops, 77–78, 369
Cleese, John, 274, 358
Cockwell, Jack, 343
Cohen, Leonard, 22, 50, 81, 118, 315, 399
    Beautiful Losers, 121–22
    Death of a Ladies' Man, 137, 187–88
    Elizabeth and After, 144
    The Energy of Slaves, 122

    as ghost writer, 143
    Selected Poems 1956–1968, 122
    The Spice Box of Earth, 121
Cohen, Matt, 87–89, 182, 218, 219, 232, 344
    Columbus and the Fat Lady, 89
    The Disinherited, 141–42
    Johnny Crackle Sings, 87–89
    Korsoniloff, 87, 88, 89
    The Leaves of Louise, 142
    The Spanish Doctor, 143–44
    The Sweet Second Summer of Kitty Malone, 142
    Typing, a Life in 26 Keys, 143
Cohen, Nathan, 99–100
Cohon, George, 129
Colbert, Nancy, 254
Colbert, Stan, 254
Cole, Carl, 78
Cole, Jack, 78
Coleridge, Samuel Taylor, 8
Coles Bookstore Canada, 77, 78, 369
Collier Macmillan, 4, 9, 10–11, 14, 19, 191
Collins, William, 79
Colombo, John Robert, 26
Colville, Alex, 82
Committee for an Independent Canada, 84, 127
Communists, 31, 33–34
    Fourth International, 113
    Hollywood blacklist, 32
    in Hungary, 5, 91, 156, 191, 351, 401
Conklin, Jimmy, 100, 153–54
Connor, Ralph, 21
Cooke, Dean, 254, 321–22
Cools, Anne, 296n
Copetti, Livio, 277
Copper Thunderbird (Morrisseau), 134
Copps, Sheila, 404
Costello, Ralph, 382
Coward, Noel, 174
Craig, Janet, 92
Crean, Patrick, 41

Creeley, Robert, 54
Creighton, Donald, 289
Crites, Michael, 174
Crittenden, Yvonne, 176, 211, 287
Cronyn, Hume, 224
	A Terrible Liar, 276
Cross, James, 13, 159
Crozier, Lorna, 253
Cry of the Wild (film), 280–81
cummings, e. e., 9
Czechoslovakia:
	German invasion of, 125
	Library of Prohibited Books in, 414
	list of informants in, 414–15
	Soviet control of, 359–60

Daily Telegraph, 363, 364, 383
Dalai Lama, 288
Daniels, Alan, 344
David (journalist), 11–13, 15, 213
David, Jack, 83n
Davies, Alun, 215, 217, 222, 235, 242, 318,
	322, 332
Davies, Robertson, 82, 145–46, 167, 253,
	270, 304
Davis, Bill, 127, 287, 294–95
Davis, Fred, 95
Davis, Glen, 334–35
Davis, Nelson, 128, 334
Davison, Peter, 70–71
Delaney, Marshall (pseud.), 39–40, 252
de la Roche, Mazo, 21
DeLillo, Don, 342
Dennys, Louise, 320, 341, 343–45, 359, 360
Derry, Ramsay, 270
Desmarais, Paul, 128, 129
Deutsch, Andre, 79, 182
Deverell, Bill, Needles, 215
Dewar, Elaine:
	"The Mysterious Reichmanns: The
	Untold Story," 321
	The Takeover, 421
Di Cicco, Pier Giorgio, 123, 253

Dickinson, Mark, 394–95
Diefenbaker, George, 154
Diefenbaker, John, 294, 296, 381, 385
Dietrich, Karsten, 329
Doubleday (publisher), 271, 317–22, 397
Doubleday, Nelje, 270
Doubleday Book Clubs, 319, 329, 347
Doubleday Canada, 319–20, 330–31, 431
Douglas, Jim, 23, 45, 138
Douglas & McIntyre, 45, 138–39, 253, 339,
	403–5, 415
Dryden, Ken, 109
Dubček, Alexander, 359
Dudek, Louis, 117
"duke and fork" question, 150
Dundurn Press, 84
Dunne, Tom, 327, 415
Duplessis, Maurice, 175–77, 366
Durham, Lorraine, 265–66, 274
Dutton, Paul, 43
Dystel, Oscar, 179–80

Eaton, John, 252
Eaton, Signy, 169
ECW Essays on Canadian Writing, 83
Edmonds, Alan, 213, 269
Edugyan, Esi, 427
Eichmann, Adolf, 410
Ekstein, Modris, 350–51, 391
	Rites of Spring, 349, 350
	Walking Since Daybreak, 350, 351
Eliot, T. S., 8, 54, 59
	The Waste Land, 124
endangered species, 70, 72, 107, 233, 334,
	337–39
Engel, Howard, 165–66
Engel, Marian, 81, 137, 165–67, 182,
	183–84, 193, 232, 270
	Bear, 166–67
environmental issues, 133, 333–39, 373–75,
	376, 405, 411
Environment Canada, 337
European Union, 365, 407

Faludy, George, 59
  My Happy Days in Hell, 59n
Farewell to the 70s: A Canadian Salute to a Confusing Decade, 211, 252–53
Felker, Clay, 241
Fenn, Harold B., 405–6, 412, 427
Fenn, Jordan, 405–6
Fennario, David, 254
Fetherling, Doug (later George), 49–50
Feyer, George, 93
Fielding, Joy, 320
Findley, Timothy, 183
Firefly Books, 338n, 371
First Nations people, 354–56
  see also Indigenous peoples
First World War, 4–5, 351
Fischman, Sheila, 82
Flaubert, Gustave, 6
Fleet Books, 280
Fleming, Allan, 246
Fleming, Louise, 403n
FLQ (Front de libération du Québec), 13, 167
Foster, Peter, *The Master Builders,* 363
Fotheringham, Allan, 95, 210, 245n, 257–61, 283, 295, 297, 300, 393
  Last Page First, 371, 394
  Malice in Blunderland: or How the Grits Stole Christmas, 257, 259, 261
Francis, Diane:
  Bre-X: The Inside Story, 363
  Immigration: The Economic Case, 363
Frankfurt Book Fair, 4n, 78, 254, 265–68, 292, 297, 320, 323, 326–27, 338, 403
Franklin, Elsa, 93–95, 96, 182, 378–79
Fraser, Fil, 252
Fraser, John, 398
Fraser, Russell, 106, 227
Fraser, Ruth, 45–47, 210
Fraser, Sylvia, 22, 47, 81, 96, 109, 116, 186, 192, 194, 210, 227–30, 344, 350
  The Ancestral Suitcase, 348
  Berlin Solstice, 228
  The Candy Factory, 228

The Emperor's Virgin, 227–28
"Hurricane June," 350n
My Father's House: A Memoir of Incest and Healing, 229, 320
Pandora, 105–7
The Rope in the Water: A Pilgrimage to India, 229
Frayne, Trent (Bill), 95, 159, 161
Free Trade Agreement, 200n
Friedan, Betty, *The Feminine Mystique,* 192
Fritz (Alfons's brother), 102
Front Page Challenge (TV), 94, 96n, 260
Frost, Leslie, 100, 154, 293
Frum, Barbara, 96, 118, 159–63, 192–93, 214, 248, 262–63, 378–79
  As It Happened, 161
Frum, David, 161
Frum, Linda, 161
  Linda Frum's Guide to Canadian Universities, 263
Frum, Murray, 96, 159, 162, 244, 263, 305
Fry, Pamela, 21–22, 62
Frye, Northrop, 63
  The Bush Garden: Essays on the Canadian Imagination, 108n
Fulford, Robert, 37, 38, 49, 66, 95, 161, 162, 183, 193, 210, 232, 250, 267, 295, 378
  as Delaney, 39–40, 252
  Marshall Delaney at the Movies, 40

Gage Publishing, 212
Gal, Laszlo, 347
Gallagher, Smiling Jack, 129
Garner, Marion, 278
Garr, Allen, *Tough Guy,* 284
Gartner, Szuszi, *All the Anxious Girls,* 394, 427
Gatenby, Greg, 41, 150, 253
General Distribution Services (GDS), 402, 404–5
General Publishing, 403–4
Georgian Bay, 155–56, 163, 185, 210–12, 270, 333

Gerstgrasser, Walter, 329

Gibb, Camilla, 398

Gibson, George, 412

Gibson, Graeme, 65–66, 77, 85, 151n, 211, 231–33
  Five Legs, 66, 231
  Gentleman Death, 232–33
  Perpetual Motion, 231, 232

Gibson, Shirley, 66

Gilbert, Martin, *The Righteous: The Unsung Heroes of the Holocaust,* 409

Gill, Brendan, 269–70
  Summer Places, 269

Giller, Doris, 424, 425

Giller Prize, 117n, 425–27

Gilmour, David, 410

Ginsberg, Allen, 37

Glassco, Bill, 254

Glazer, Milton, 241

Globe and Mail, The, 27, 161, 259n, 304, 305, 333, 371, 378

Glossop, Jennifer, 42, 62, 137, 166, 218n

Godard, Mira, 252

Godbout, Jacques, 83

Goddard, John, 373–74

Godfrey, Dave, 83, 154

Godfrey, Gina, 154

Goethe, Johann Wolfgang von, 416

Goldsmith, Jimmy, 364

Goodman, Eddie, 84, 85, 289
  Life of the Party, 261, 296

Goodman, Gloria, 274, 319

Gordon, Alison, 125

Gordon, Sydney, 31

Gordon, Walter, 84, 85

Gorky, Maxim, 117

Gottlieb, Allan, 161

Gould, Allan, 225

Gouzenko, Igor, 288

Governor General's Award, 107, 122, 144, 166, 233

Gowdy, Barbara, 398

Graham, Bill and Cathy, 239

Graham, Billy, 186, 211

Graham, Ron, 299
  One-Eyed Kings, 298

Grant, George, 27, 89, 142
  Lament for a Nation, 85–86

Graves, Robert, 4, 9

Gray, John MacLachlan, 254

Greenberg, Clement, 39

Greene, Elaine, 345

Greene, Graham, 148, 185, 342, 343, 344, 360

Greenpeace, 336

Greer, Germaine, *The Female Eunuch,* 192

Greey, Phil, 241, 273

Greey de Pencier Books, 241, 247

Grescoe, Paul, 221

Gretzky, Wayne, 249

Greystone Books, 339

Griffin, Krystine, 124n

Griffin, Scott, *My Heart Is Africa: A Flying Adventure,* 124

Griffin Prize, 123–24

Griffin Trust, 124

Griffith, Linda, 254

Groundwood, 139, 142

Group of Seven, 44–45, 189

Grove, Frederick Philip, 21

Gruntorad, Jiri, 414

Guggenheim, Peggy, 169, 174

Guinness, Alec, 225

Gustafson, Ralph, 122

Guthrie, Tyrone, 225

Gwyn, Richard:
  The Northern Magus, 81
  Smallwood: The Unlikely Revolutionary, 81

Gwyn, Sandra, 252

Gzowski, Peter, 137, 193, 213–14, 240–41, 248–50, 267, 280
  The Game of Our Lives, 249
  The Sacrament, 248

Gzowski, Sir Casimir, 249

Hage, Rawi, 398

Haliburton, Thomas, 21

Halpenny, Francess, 198n

Hapsburg Empire, 57, 232, 431

Hardy, Thomas, 54

HarperCollins, 79n, 274, 281, 313, 427

Harris, Marjorie, 192, 210–11, 242, 252–53, 258–59, 292

Harris, Mike, 370

Harron, Don, 252

Hašek, Jaroslav, *The Good Soldier Schweik,* 360

Havel, Vaclav, 414

Hay, Elizabeth, 138

Heaps, Leo, *The Quebec Plot,* 219

Hebb, Marian, 217

Hébert, Anne, 82

Heine, Heinrich, 58, 117, 416

Henderson, Paul, 108–9, 253

Henry, Martha, 224

Herriot, James, 180

Herrndorf, Eva, 161

Herrndorf, Peter, 161, 214

Highway, Tomson, 398

Hill, Lawrence, 379

Hirsch, John, 224

Hirtle, Sheila, 244

Hitler, Adolf, 117, 350, 407

Hodgeman, Marge, 21, 70, 146–47, 307

Hollinger Inc., 364, 366–67

Hollywood blacklist, 32

Holocaust, 143, 349–50, 395, 404, 407, 409–11, 413

Honderich, Beland, 130

Hope, Bob, 154, 221

Hopkins, Garth, 410

Horthy, Miklós, 415

House of Anansi, 58, 65–66, 83, 88–89, 107–8, 124, 231, 254, 395, 430

Houston, James, 81, 135–36, 309

  Aurora Borealis, 136

  Spirit Wrestler, 136

  Whiteout, 136

How, Douglas, 382

Howard, Gillian, 249

Howard, Kirk, 84

Hoy, Claire, 261

  Friends in High Places: Politics and Patronage in the Mulroney Government, 283–84, 294

Hrabal, Bohumil, 414

Hudson's Bay Company, 64

Hummel, Monte, 233, 333–34

  Arctic Wildlife, 334

  Endangered Spaces: The Future of Canada's Wilderness, 334

  Wintergreen, 339

Hungary:

  Anna's early years in, 5–8, 31, 34, 156, 325, 326, 390–91, 401, 431

  Anna's return trips to, 390–91, 413

  Arrow Cross in, 350

  art of, 44

  Communist government in, 5, 91, 156, 191, 351, 401

  Hapsburgs in, 57, 431

  Holocaust in, 143, 349–50, 404, 409–11, 413

  poets in, 57

  Revolution (1956), 7–8, 31, 34, 57, 58, 59, 72, 126, 325, 326, 347, 390, 401, 413

  siege of Budapest (1945), 156, 350–51

  Szigethy family's origins in, 6, 351, 391

Hunt, Don, 289

Hurst, Christopher, 78

Hurtig, Mel, 84, 85

Hurtig Publishers, 83, 85

Hussein, king of Jordan, 288

Hutchinson, Helen, 245n

Hutt, William, 224

Ibarra, Allan, 404, 412

Illustrated History of Canada, The, 342, 349

Independent Publishers Association, 84

Indian Act (1876), 355

Indigenous peoples, 45–46, 93, 133–36, 146, 277, 278, 333, 354–56, 374, 378

Ines (Alfons's daughter), 8, 9, 334
International Festival of Authors, 41, 55, 118, 253
International Organization of Books for Young People, 139
In the Wake of the Flood (documentary), 66–67
Irving, John, 73n, 304n, 345n
Irving, K. C., 382
Irwin, John, 292
Ishiguro, Kazuo, 342, 344

Jackson, A. Y., 45, 82
Jacobs, Jane, 39
Jaffe, Marc, 179–80, 182, 186, 255, 292
Jam, Teddy (pseud.), 142
James, Henry, 8
James, P. D., 320, 342, 345
Janson-Smith, Patrick, 327
Jarislowsky, Stephen, 128
Jewison, Norman, 321
    This Terrible Business Has Been Good to Me, 407–8
Jews:
    anti-Semitism, 79, 117–18, 350
    and the Holocaust, 143, 349–50, 395, 404, 407, 410–11, 413
Johnson, Lyndon B., 365
Johnston, Basil, 93, 353–56, 431
    Crazy Dave, 355–56
    Indian School Days, 354
    The Manitous: The Spiritual World of the Ojibway, 355–56
    Moose Meat and Wild Rice, 355
    Ojibway Heritage, 355
Johnston, Moira, 270
Jonas, George, 58–59, 415–17
    The Absolute Smile, 58
    Beethoven's Mask: Notes on My Life and Times, 407
    By Persons Unknown: The Strange Death of Christine Demeter (with Barbara Amiel), 219, 289

Final Decree, 219
The Happy Hungry Man, 58
"Landmarks," 417
"Memories," 58–59
Politically Incorrect, 349
Selected Poems, 59, 124, 416
Jones, Doug, 122
Jones, Judith, 146
Joyce, James, 8

Kaan, Michael, 431
Kahlo, Frida, 113
Karsh, Malak, *Canada: The Land That Shapes Us*, 271
Karsh, Yousuf, 94, 271
Kassem, Abdel Karim, 288
Kasztner, Rezso, 410–11
Keats, John, 117
Keep the Promise, 419–20
Kemper, Fried, 237
Kennedy, Betty, 96
Kenton, Stan, 130, 131
Kertész, André, 243
Kevin Sullivan Productions, 217
Key Porter Books, 242, 243–50, 257–63, 301, 429
    Anna as president of, 194, 393, 431
    Anna's resignation from, 412
    authors published by, 36n, 54n, 72, 135, 136, 200n, 261, 269–71, 275, 276–78
    and Bertelsmann, 317–19, 321–23
    books about the environment, 233, 338
    business books, 363–66
    and Doubleday, 271, 317–22, 330–31
    expansion of, 341–45
    financial issues of, 278, 348, 370, 402–6
    and Fleet Books, 280
    health guides, 358
    international market, 265–68, 348
    and L&OD, 341, 342–44, 348, 359
    launch of, 33, 257–60, 274
    and M&S, 250, 257, 303–5, 313
    magazines of, 297

and Mowat, 72, 278, 335–36, 365, 393, 394
offices of, 273–74, 280, 406
photographic books, 269–71
sale to Fenn, 405–6
and Seal, *see* Seal Books
staff of, 246–48, 265, 273–75, 277, 278, 280, 281, 327, 330, 393, 427
twentieth anniversary of, 393–95
and *Where*, 251
Key Publishers Company Ltd., 321, 415
Khomeini, Ayatollah Ruhollah, 174, 430
Khrushchev, Nikita, 33, 34
Kiakshuk (artist), 135
Kidd, Bruce, 241n
King, Thomas, 347, 348n
Kinsella, W. P., 244
  Shoeless Joe, 182
Kissinger, Henry, 364, 365
Klein, A. M., 21, 117
Klima, Ivan, 414
Knelman, Martin, 223
Knopf Canada, 344–45
Kobrak, Fred, 4, 10
Koffler, Lionel, 371
Kogawa, Joy, 342
Kolber, Leo, 128
Kovalski, Maryann, 370
Krantz, Judith, 180
Kundera, Milan, 414

LaMarsh, Judy, 252
  Memoirs of a Bird in a Gilded Cage, 43n
L'Amour, Louis, 180, 218
Lane, Patrick, 123
Lansdowne, Fenwick, 270
Laporte, Pierre, 13, 159
Laurence, Margaret, 19, 77, 81, 137, 145–51, 165, 166, 173, 183, 192, 193, 228, 253
  A Bird in the House, 42, 145, 146
  The Diviners, 146–47, 149–50, 310, 431
  The Olden Days Coat, 42, 182n
  The Stone Angel, 145, 148, 150, 311
  This Side Jordan, 309

Lautens, Gary:
  How Pierre and I Saved the Civilized World, 276n
  Peace, Mrs. Packard and the Meaning of Life, 276
  Take My Family . . . Please!, 276n
Lawrence, D. H., 54
Lawrence, R. D., 336–37
  In Praise of Wolves, 336
  The Natural History of Canada, 336
  The Shark, 336
  Trail of the Wolf, 336
Layton, Aviva, 103, 117, 118, 120, 186, 187n
Layton, David, 117, 120, 187
Layton, Irving, 53, 81, 115–20, 121, 122, 166, 182, 186–87, 228, 424
  "The Bull Calf," 115–16
  The Collected Poems of Irving Layton, 118–19, 120
  "The Death of Moishe Lazarovitch," 116
  Engagements: The Prose of Irving Layton, 120
  "For Anna," 103
  Love Where the Nights Are Long, 50
  Nail Polish, 120
  Selected Poems, 124
  "Song for Naomi," 120
  The Swinging Flesh, 121
  "There Were No Signs," 119
  The Uncollected Irving Layton, 119–20
  "A Wild Peculiar Joy," 116
Leacock, Stephen, 21
League of Canadian Poets, 123
Leah, Aunt "Lilo," 62–63, 191, 203, 209–10
Leddy, Mary Jo, 420
Lee, Alma, 77
Lee, Bruce, 94
Lee, Dennis, 52, 55, 88, 107n, 123, 137, 144, 231, 303, 394–95
  Bubblegum Delicious, 394, 395
  "The Cat and the Wizard," 394
  "Civil Elegies," 394
  Heart Residence, 430

Lee, Dennis (*cont.*)
  Riffs, 395
  Un, 395
Lefolii, Ken, 267–68, 292
  Claims: Adventures in the Gold Trade, 284, 363–64
Lemelin, Roger, 83, 150
Lenin, V. I., 7, 34
Lennox, John, 310n
Lespérance, Pierre, 299, 300
Lessing, Doris, 275
Lester, Malcolm, 341, 343–44, 348, 370
Lester & Orpen Dennys (L&OD), 320, 341, 342–45, 348, 359, 360
Lester Publishing, 348–50, 370
Lévesque, René, 253, 259, 298
Levine, Michael, 307
Levine, Norman, 344
Lewis, David, 117, 305
Lies My Father Told Me (film), 33
Lighthouse, The (text by Edmonds and Porter), 269
List Verlag, 326–27
Literary Guild book club, 21, 319
Livesay, Dorothy, 113
Livingston, John, 333
  One Cosmic Instant: A Natural History of Human Arrogance, 233
  Rogue Primate: An Exploration of Human Domestication, 233
Loewen, Charles, 342
LongPen, 66, 411
Lorenzini, Amleto, *Assyrian Sculpture in the British Museum*, 119
Lorimer, Jim, 84
Lougheed, Jeanne, 295, 296
Lougheed, Peter, 253, 284–86, 294, 295, 296, 298
Low, Wailan, 41, 111, 112, 113
Lowry, Malcolm, 53, 114
Ludwig, Jack:
  A Woman of Her Age, 109n
  and Canada-Russia hockey, 109

Lumumba, Patrice, 288
Lunn, Janet, and Christopher Moore, *The Story of Canada*, 344
Lynch, Charlie, 261, 285

MacDonald, Flora, 85
MacDougall, Allan, 45, 371
MacEwen, Gwendolyn, 123
Macfarlane, John, 241, 244
MacInnis, Joe, 277
  Saving the Oceans, 338
Mackenzie, John (Jack), 338n
MacLaren, Roy, 245
Maclean Hunter, 241, 289
Maclean's, 108, 125, 127, 193, 199, 220n, 248, 258, 363, 394, 401
  mass walkout (1964), 267
MacLennan, Hugh, 183, 253
MacLeod, Alistair, 220n
  As Birds Bring Forth the Sun, 22
  The Lost Salt Gift of Blood, 22, 253
MacSkimming, Roy, 83, 166, 403n
  The Perilous Trade: Publishing Canada's Writers, 139, 254n, 331n, 404
Magic or Medicine (TV), 357, 358
Maillet, Antonine, 83
Mandelstam, Nadezhda, 117
Manguel, Alberto, 327–28, 342, 345n
Manguel, Polly, 327–28
Mann, Ron, 66
Márai, Sándor, *Embers*, 59
Marchand, Philip, 22–23, 41
Markle, Robert, 100
Marsh, Jim, 85
Martel, Yann, 254, 345n
Martin, Lawrence, *Breaking with History*, 320
Martin, Paul, 301
Martin, Sandra, 378
Marty, Sid, 123
Mason, Bill:
  Path of the Paddle, 280
  Song of the Paddle, 280
Masse, Marcel, 317, 318

Matas, Carol, 137
Matthews, Robin, and James Steele, *The Struggle for Canadian Universities*, 85
Maupassant, Guy de, 6
May, Elizabeth, 334–35
  At the Cutting Edge: The Crisis in Canada's Forests, 335
  How to Save the World in Your Spare Time, 335
May, Karl, 6
Mayer, Peter, 307
Mayo, Charles, 193
McCaffrey, Steve, 43
McClelland, Elizabeth, 307, 313, 314
McClelland, Jack, 18–21, 44, 102, 106, 117, 118, 166
  and Anna's children, 109, 180
  and Atwood, 61–62, 65, 309
  authors critiqued by, 28, 37, 38, 112–13, 122
  authors given support by, 31, 50–52, 81, 83–85, 94, 95, 121, 130, 135, 146
  and backlist, 343–44
  and Beny, 170–74
  and Berton, 94–97
  and Bookmen's Lunch Club, 66
  and Canadian publishing, 75–79, 84–85, 179–80, 187–88, 240, 280, 321
  death of, 398–99
  Drawing on Type (memoir), 18n
  and Laurence, 146–47, 149–51, 310–11
  letters of, 114, 315
  listening to authors, 32, 39, 40
  as literary agent, 306–7
  and M&S, *see* McClelland & Stewart
  and Mowat, 20, 69–71, 73, 95, 135, 173, 279, 309, 311, 376
  My Rose Garden (unfinished), 303, 307, 313–15
  nationalism of, 77, 83–85, 127, 133, 151, 175, 421–22
  publishing authors, not books, 82, 83, 120, 240, 315
  retirement of, 306–7, 313, 335
  and Seal Books, 188, 215, 304, 306, 321, 331
  and staff, 35–36, 41, 95
  and Second World War, 78–79
McClelland, Sarah, 307
McClelland & Stewart (M&S), 17–23, 429
  Anna's early days in, 21–23
  Anna's interview for, 18–20
  Anna's responsibilities in, 181–84, 431
  Anna's titles in, 23, 35, 94, 96, 154, 182
  archives of, 113, 228n, 315
  and Atwood, 61–65, 137, 138, 180, 279, 305
  and Bantam, 179–80, 189, 193, 214
  building of, 21, 36, 43, 274, 306
  Canadian authors published by, 81–82
  Carleton Library series, 85
  editorial meetings in, 43–44
  end of, 397–99
  financial issues of, 20, 35, 38, 43, 75–77, 94, 96n, 113, 173–74, 178, 179–80, 257, 279–80, 303–5, 306–7, 398
  Four Horsemen (poetry group), 43
  and Key Porter, 250, 257, 303–5, 313
  and lawsuits, 129
  and Mowat, 137, 173, 180, 182, 220, 279
  New Canadian Library, 20–21, 43, 121, 122n, 150
  in 1972 (a year to remember), 105–8
  sales conferences of, 45, 228
  sale to Bennett, 306, 307, 313, 315
  sense of mission in, 42–43
  slush pile of, 22–23, 41–44, 150, 231, 253
  staff of, 82, 137–39, 181
  and Taylor, 36, 43, 44, 95, 99, 138, 188, 215, 228
  warehouse of, 43, 75, 242, 303
McClelland-Bantam Limited, 180, 189
McCutcheon, Fred, 342
McCutcheon, Susan, 102, 177n, 296
McCutcheon, Wallace, 101, 177, 293
McDermid, Anne, 254

McDougald, Bud, 128, 177
McDougall, Barbara, 199n
McEwan, Ian, 320, 342
McFadden, David, 123
McGraw-Hill Book Company, 76
McIntyre, Scott, 23, 45, 138, 403–4, 412
McKeon, Clare, 281
McKnight, Linda, 22, 137–38, 257, 281,
    303–4, 393
McMichael, Robert and Signe, 45
McMurtry, Roy, 165
McPhail, David, 394
Mellen, Peter:
    Group of Seven, 44–45
    Landmarks of Canadian Art, 189
Melzack, Louis, 78
Métis, oppression of, 45–46
Michaels, Anne, 399
Michnik, Adam, 415
Miller, Lily Poritz, 22, 137, 313
Milne, David, 252n
Milosz, Czeslaw, 414
Milton, John, 117
Mint, Morty, 10, 17
Mistry, Rohinton, 426
Mitchell, Merna, 221
Mitchell, W. O., 82, 148, 219–21
    How I Spent My Summer Holidays, 220
    Jake and the Kid, 220
    The Kite, 220
    The Vanishing Point, 220
    Who Has Seen the Wind, 46n, 220
Mobutu, Sese Seko, 288
Mohn, Reinhard, 322
Molnár, Ferenc, *The Boys of Paul Street,* 6
Monette, Richard, 223, 224
Monk, Lorraine, 169, 281
    Between Friends: Entre Amis, 65
Montgomery, Lucy Maud, 20, 217
Montreal International Book Fair, 83,
    187–88
Monty Python, 239, 358
Moodie, Susanna, 431

Moore, Brian:
    Catholics, 42, 107
    The Doctor's Wife, 180
    The Revolution Script, 42, 107
Moore, Christopher, 344
Moore, Jean, 107
Moore, Mavor, 223
Mootoo, Shani, 398
Morgenthaler, Henry, 198
Móricz, Zsigmond, 6
Morningside (CBC), 249–50
Morrisseau, Norval, 134
Morse, Randy, 403n
Motovun Group, 266–67
Mouland, Michael, 338n
Mowat, Claire, 70, 72, 375
Mowat, Farley, 19, 69–73, 77, 81, 253, 304n,
    373–76, 378
    Aftermath, 373
    And No Birds Sang, 69
    The Boat Who Wouldn't Float, 70–71
    Born Naked, 335, 365
    The Desperate People, 220
    The Dog Who Wouldn't Be, 69
    and the environment, 107, 133, 333,
        336–37, 375, 376
    Goddard's attack on, 373–74
    High Latitudes, 335
    and *In Search of Farley Mowat* (film), 220
    and Key Porter, 72, 278, 335–36, 365, 393,
        394
    and M&S, 137, 173, 180, 182, 220, 279
    and McClelland, 20, 69–71, 73, 95, 135,
        173, 279, 309, 311, 376
    My Father's Son, 335
    Never Cry Wolf, 69, 72, 373
    People of the Deer, 70, 335, 373
    Sea of Slaughter, 336, 375
    Sibir: My Discovery of Siberia, 71–72
    Wake of the Great Sealers, 72
    Walking on the Land, 394
    A Whale for the Killing, 107
Mulroney, Brian, 130, 262, 283–84, 294, 365

Munk, Peter, 398, 410

Munro, Alice, 9, 19, 82, 166, 220n, 232, 426–27

Murdoch, Rupert, 364

Musgrave, Susan, 122
  The Impstone, 123
  A Man to Marry, A Man to Bury, 123

Naked Came the Stranger (literary hoax), 166

Nash, Knowlton, 96

National Business Book Awards, 363–64

National Film Board, 280
  Still Photography Division, 65, 169, 267, 281

Neale, Gladys, 198

Neale, John, 138–39, 181, 242n

Nehru, Jawaharlal, 288

Neurath, Eva, 171

Newfeld, Frank, 18, 19, 23, 37, 38, 71, 133, 139
  The Group of Seven (designer), 45

Newhouse, Si, 255

Newlove, John, 50, 112, 122
  Lies, 95

Newman, Alvie, 130

Newman, Camilla Turner, 130

Newman, Christina, 126, 128, 130

Newman, Peter C., 71, 77, 81, 84, 87, 88, 99, 125–31, 176, 182, 244, 252, 258, 279, 283–84, 390
  The Canadian Establishment, Volumes One and Two, 128–30, 180, 214, 364
  Distemper of Our Times, 87
  The Establishment Man, 177–78
  Here Be Dragons, 126, 128n, 131
  Home Country: People, Places, and Power Politics, 127, 128
  "Hudson's Bay" books, 307
  and *Maclean's,* 53, 108, 125, 127, 258, 363
  Renegade in Power: The Diefenbaker Years, 87

New Press, 83, 85, 241n, 254

New Yorker, The, 32, 67, 269, 359–60

New York Times, The, 64, 322

New Zealand, 12–13
  Szigethy family as refugees in, 7–9, 17, 205, 389

Nichol, bp, 43

Nichols, Marjorie, 258

Nietzsche, Friedrich Wilhelm, 117

90 Minutes Live (TV), 248

Nixon, Richard M., 127, 365, 411

Nowell, Iris, 38, 39
  Harold Town, 39n
  Hot Breakfast for Sparrows: My Life with Harold Town, 39n

Obe, Don, 244

Odjig, Daphne, 134, 394

Official Secrets Act, 213

Olson, Peter, 322

Ondaatje, Christopher, 341–43

Ondaatje, Michael, 22, 81, 124, 138, 253, 341, 342, 431
  "Letters and Other Worlds," 123
  Running in the Family, 123
  There's a Trick with a Knife I'm Learning to Do: Poems 1963–1978, 123

Onley, Tony, 82

Ontario (sesquicentennial book), 294

Orban, Viktor, 416

Ouellet, Fernand, 83

OWL, 241, 247

Pachter, Charlie, 62, 64

Paddle to the Sea (film), 280

Pagurian, 342, 343

Painters Eleven, 37

Parliamentary Press Gallery "boys," 258

Parry Island Indian Reserve, 355

Patterson, Freeman, 277, 280–82
  The Garden, 282
  The Last Wilderness: Images of the Canadian Wild, 271, 281
  Namaqualand: Garden of the Gods, 281
  Photography and the Art of Seeing, 281
  Portraits of Earth, 281

Patterson, Tom, 224–25
  *First Stage: The Making of the Stratford
    Festival,* 225
Pattison, Jimmy, 129, 221–22, 259n
  Jimmy: An Autobiography, 221
Pearce, John, 138, 292, 319–20
Pearsall, Patricia, 348
Pearson, Lester, 12, 87, 294, 398
Pegasus, wholesaler, 370–71
Pelletier, Gérard, 127
PEN Canada, 138, 430
Pencier, Honor, 240, 411
Pencier, Michael de, 76, 240–42, 243, 245,
    247–48, 251, 252, 280, 304–5, 320–21,
    338n, 372, 405, 411
Penguin Books Canada, 10, 274
Pennell, Nicholas, 224
Peterson, David, 369
Peterson, Eric, 254
Peterson, Roy, 295
Petőfi, Sándor, 57
Petričić, Dušan, 370
Philby, Kim, 288
Phillips, Eric, 177
Pinsent, Gordon, *A Gift to Last,* 222
Pockell, Les, 327
Polar Bears (Key Porter), 334
Polk, Jim, 108
Poole, Jack, 129
Porcupine's Quill, 254
Porter, Anna Szigethy:
  The Appraisal, 431
  and Bertelsmann, 317–19, 326, 329–32
  The Bookfair Murders, 265n, 326–27
  *Buying a Better World: George Soros and
    Billionaire Philanthropy,* 415–17
  Canadian nationalism of, 127–28, 253,
    255, 325, 417
  on corporate boards, 193–94, 364–65
  early years of, *see* Szigethy, Anna
  environmentalism of, 333–35
  The Ghosts of Europe, 137, 413–15
  Hidden Agenda, 291–92, 319n, 326, 345

Kasztner's Train, 137, 349, 409–12,
    413
  and Key Porter, *see* Key Porter Books
  Mortal Sins, 250, 292, 319n, 326
  and pink lady (ghost), 210
  resignation from M&S Board, 257
  and Seal, *see* Seal Books
  search for her father, 203–5
  *The Storyteller: Memory, Secrets, Magic
    and Lies,* 5n, 291, 351, 389–90, 391
  vampire book by, 402–3
  wedding of Julian and, 102–3; *see also*
    Porter, Julian
Porter, Catherine (daughter), 73n, 109, 150,
    153, 154, 156, 182–83, 184, 185, 210,
    214, 227n, 237, 239, 247, 261, 262, 266,
    295, 304n, 328, 411, 420
Porter, Jessica (stepdaughter), 101, 103,
    177n, 209, 237, 295
Porter, Julia (daughter), 46, 148n, 180–81,
    182–83, 184, 185, 210, 214, 239, 249,
    266, 295, 325–26, 348, 391, 393n
Porter, Julian (husband), 99–101, 106,
    130–31, 173n, 239–40, 266, 305, 328,
    341, 358, 401
  and Georgian Bay cottage, 156–57, 163,
    185, 210–12, 270
  and law, 100, 103, 113, 129, 153, 160,
    184, 212–13, 217n, 223, 224, 239, 262,
    283–84, 321, 412
  and politics, 108, 159, 284, 285, 287,
    293–96
  and Stratford Festival, 223–25
  and "the Ex," 153–54, 185
  and Toronto Transit Commission, 223,
    296
  wedding of Anna and, 102–3
Porter, Suse (stepdaughter), 101, 103, 177n,
    209
Potter, Harry (fict.), 45, 371
Pound, Ezra, 54
Powis, Alf, 128
Pratt, Christopher, 82, 252

Pratt, E. J., 50, 54
Preminger, Otto, 193
Price, Tim, 343
Princess Royal Island, 337
Pritchard, Rob, 397
Pruessen, Linda, 137, 348
Purdy, Al, 27, 50–55, 71, 81, 112, 115, 118, 123, 148, 182, 253, 310
   Al Purdy Was Here (documentary), 54
   "At the Quinte Hotel," 53–54
   The Cariboo Horses, 51
   "The Country North of Belleville," 55
   "For Margaret," 311–12
   Love in a Burning Building, 50, 52
   Morning and It's Summer, 53
   Naked with Summer in Your Mouth, 124
   Reaching for the Beaufort Sea, 52
   "Say the Names," 52
   Storm Warnings, 122–23
   and Town, 50–52
Purdy, Eurithe, 50, 51
Pushkin, Aleksandr, 58, 416

Quarrington, Paul, 320
Quasimodo dinner group, 327, 412n
Quebec:
   civil liberties suspended in, 159–60
   Referendum (1980), 298
   separatism in, 12–13, 82–83, 85, 118, 167, 175–76, 298
Quintus Press, 252

Rabinovitch, Jack, 116–17, 423–27
Racz, Therese (grandmother), 7, 102
Racz, Vili (grandfather):
   and Anna's childhood, 5–6, 325, 389
   death of, 206
   in Hungary, 7, 79, 156, 204, 291, 349, 391, 409, 413
   Jolan (Vili's mother), 102
   letters to Puci, 111
   marriage of, 102

   in New Zealand, 7, 205, 389
   as storyteller, 5, 7, 33, 34, 126, 156, 291, 325, 349, 389–90, 412, 430
   in First World War, 351
Rae, Bob, 430
Raincoast Books, 45, 371
Rákosi, Mátyás, 7, 34
Ranch, The: Portrait of a Surviving Dream (Derry, Ed), 270
Random House, 79, 255, 397
   and Bertelsmann, 322, 397
Random House Canada, 139, 331, 345, 421
Rathgeb, Charles, 128
Ray, Justina C., 334n
RCMP (Royal Canadian Mounted Police), 92, 212–13, 260
Rea, Michael, 246, 305
Redhill, Michael, 427
Red Tories, 25, 27, 261
Reeves, John, 102
Reichmann family, 321, 363
Reid, Fiona, 224
Reisman, Heather, 402, 431
Rendell, Ruth, 320
Renouf, Harold, 278
Renouf, Susan, 137, 278, 319, 329, 335, 347–48, 393
Ricci, Nino, 431
Richardson, Scott, 365
Richler, Florence, 32, 107
Richler, Mordecai, 81, 86, 117, 137, 142, 151, 166–67, 250, 421, 424–26
   A Choice of Enemies, 32
   Cocksure, 21
   St. Urbain's Horseman, 107
Rilke, Rainer Maria, 54, 58, 310
Ripley, Donald, *Bagman,* 261n
Ripley Entertainment, 221, 222
Ritchie, Larry, 76
Ritter, Erika, 137, 348
   The Hidden Life of Humans, 254
Rivera, Diego, 113

Robarts, John, 294

Roberts, Charles G. D., 21

Rodmell, Ken, 246, 252

Rohmer, Richard, 76, 182
  Balls, 218n
  Exodus/UK, 218
  Exxonoration, 218
  Separation, 218
  Ultimatum, 218–19

Roosevelt, Franklin D., 365

Rosenblatt, Joe, 122

Ross, Gary, 244n

Ross, Krystyna, 275

Ross, Malcolm, 20, 121–22, 150

Ross, Sandy, 245–46, 363
  Canadians on the Nile, 245n
  publishing ventures of, 245
  The Risk Takers, 245

Ross, Sinclair, 21, 81, 148

Roth, Joseph, 143
  The Radetzky March, 232

Roth, Philip, 79, 167

Rothschild, Lord, 364

Rotstein, Abe, 84

Roy, Gabrielle, 82, 150, 165, 309, 398
  The Tin Flute—Bonheur d'Occasion, 21,
    150
  Windflower, 42

Royal Canadian Geographic Society, 241

Royal Canadian Yacht Club, 126–27, 130

Royal Commission on Book Publishing,
  75–77

Royal Commission on the Status of Women
  in Canada, 198

Royal Geographic Society, 19, 405

Royal Ontario Museum, 353

Runyon, Damon, 244

Rushdie, Salman, 430

Russell, Charlie, 336
  *Spirit Bear: Encounters with the White
    Bear of the Western Rainforest*, 337

Ryan, Claude, 84

Ryerson Press, 76

Sacred Heart Convent School, New
  Zealand, 7, 8, 91, 111, 126, 148n, 203,
  210, 390

St. Joseph Corporation, 405

St. Martin's Press, 415

St. Peter Claver school, Ontario, 354–55

Salinger, J. D., 180

Salivarova, Zdena, 359–60, 414

Sandberg, Sheryl, *Lean In: Women, Work
  and the Will to Lead*, 198

Sari, Aunt, 7, 203

Sarlos, Andy, 390–91

Saturday Night, 37, 38, 183, 193, 220, 298,
  373–74

Saul, John Ralston, 214

Savage, Candace, 339

Schlesinger, Joe, 245n

Schroeder, Andreas, *Founding the Writers'
  Union of Canada*, 31n

Schwarz, Herbert:
  *Norval Morrisseau: Travels to the House of
    Invention*, 134
  Tales from the Smokehouse, 134
  Windigo and Other Tales of the Ojibways,
    134

Scientologists, 284

Scotiabank Giller Prize, 426n, 427

Scott, Ian, 296

Seal Books, 180, 189, 242
  Anna as president and publisher of, 213,
    215, 217–22, 231, 243, 292, 321, 330,
    431
  First Novel Award, 180, 182, 188, 214, 347
  and McClelland, 188, 215, 304, 306, 321,
    331
  sale of, 331

Sears, Dennis T. Patrick:
  Aunty High Over the Barley Mow, 42
  The Lark in the Clear Air, 41–42

Sears, Val, *Hello Sweetheart, Get Me Rewrite*,
  261

Sea Shepherd Conservation Society, 336,
  376

Second World War, 69, 72, 78–79, 125, 135, 156, 322, 336, 349, 373
Seligman, Ellen, 62, 65, 138
September 11 attacks, 401–2
Service, Robert, 96–97
Sessions, Bob, 327
Sewell, John, 252
Shah and Shahbanu of Iran, 150, 170–74
Shakespeare, William, 8, 117, 224, 310
Shaw, David, 45, 139
Shebib, Donald, 252
Shelley, Percy Bysshe, 8
Sherman, Geraldine, 95, 161, 162, 192, 210
Sherrin, Muriel, 224
Shields, Carol, and Marjorie Anderson, *Dropped Threads: What We Aren't Told,* 192, 429
Shipton, Rosemary, 137
Shorter, Ned, 252
Shulman, Morton, 284
Siegler, Karl, 403n
Silcox, David, 252
Sinclair, Gordon, 260
68 Publishers, 360
Skalbania, Nelson, 129
Skvorecky, Josef, 342, 344, 359–61, 414
   The Bass Saxophone, 360
   The Cowards, 359
   Two Murders in My Double Life, 415
   When Eve Was Naked, 361, 394
Slaight, Allan, 126n
Slaight, Annabel, 247, 333
Slater, Ian, *Firespill,* 219
Slavin, Bill, 347
Slinger, Joey, 426
Slopen, Beverley, 254
Smith, A. J. M., 123
   poem to Julia, 180–81
Smith, Peter, 22
Smith, W. H., 77, 78
Smithbooks, 369
Snow, Michael, *Canada Geese,* 262
Sogides, 299

Solecki, Sam, *Imagining Canadian Literature: The Letters of Jack McClelland,* 114, 315
Sordsmen's Club, 96
Soros, George, 415–16
Souster, Raymond, 50, 122
Southam Press, 244, 365
Southey, Tabatha, 348
Soviet Union:
   Anna's vehement dislike of, 7, 31, 34, 39
   end of, 365, 414
   Hungary invaded by (1956), 7, 8, 31, 34, 72, 401, 413
   spies in Canada, 288
   Twentieth Congress of Communist Party (1956), 33
   writers persecuted by, 31n
Soyinka, Wole, 79, 148
Spanish, Ontario, 353–54, 355
Spanish Civil War, 32, 33n, 336
Spark, Muriel, 167
Spencer, Steven, *see* Szigethy, István
Spinoza, Baruch, 117
Staines, David, 122n, 426
Stalin, Joseph, 7, 33, 34, 430
Stanfield, Robert, 108, 253, 285, 293–94, 296
Starowicz, Mark, 214
Steele, James, 85
Stendahl, 6
Stephen Leacock Memorial Medal for Humour, 32, 71, 139n
Stevens, Geoffrey, *The Player: The Life and Times of Dalton Camp,* 385
Stevens, Sinclair, 283
Stevenson, Larry, 369, 371, 402
Stoddard, Jack, 403–5
Stratford Festival, 223–25
Stravinsky, Igor, 350
Struzik, Ed, and Mike Beedell, *The Northwest Passage,* 271
Styron, William, 180
Supreme Court of Canada, 198
Susann, Jacqueline, 180

Sutton, Joan, 252

Swinton, George, 133–34, 137
  Eskimo Sculpture, 78
  Sculpture of the Eskimo, 133

Symons, Scott, 25–29, 116, 129, 231–32
  Civic Square, 25–28
  Helmet of Flesh, 29
  *Heritage: A Romantic Look at Early
    Canadian Furniture,* 28–29
  Place d'Armes, 26

Szigethy, Anna:
  Canada as home of, 81–83, 102, 109
  childhood of, 5–8, 156, 325, 326, 389,
    390, 401, 431
  family background of, 4–5, 6, 102, 351,
    391
  and Hungarian Revolution, 7–8, 34, 39,
    57, 58, 72, 126, 325, 326, 401, 413
  jobs taken by, 8, 9, 10–11, 62, 191
  languages of, 7, 18, 57, 416
  last name of, 18, 71, 103
  at M&S, *see* McClelland & Stewart
  marriage of, *see* Porter, Anna Szigethy
  in New Zealand, 7–9, 17, 205, 389
  in Sacred Heart Convent School, 7, 8, 91,
    111, 126, 148n, 203, 210, 390
  travels of, 14, 82

Szigethy, István (father; a.k.a. Steven
    Spencer), 5, 6, 18, 71, 156, 203–5

Szigethy, Maria "Puci" (mother), 59, 126,
    266
  Alfons (third husband), 8–9, 17, 19, 102,
    156–57
  and Anna's childhood, 6, 389
  and Anna's wedding, 102
  and Birney, 111–12
  and Charlotte, 109
  in Hungary, 156, 191, 326
  Istvan (first husband), 5, 6, 18, 71, 156,
    203–5
  Jeno (second husband), 7n, 389
  memorabilia of, 111–12
  move to Canada, 157, 239

Tandy, Jessica, 276

Taro, Gerda, 275

Tarragon Theatre, 254–55

Taylor, Charles, *Radical Tories: The
    Conservative Tradition in Canada,* 27

Taylor, E. P., 27, 128, 177, 408

Taylor, Firp, 129

Taylor, Ken, 172

Taylor, Noreen, 374

Taylor, Peter, 242n
  at M&S, 36, 43, 44, 95, 99, 138, 188, 215,
    228
  *Watcha Gonna Do Boy . . . Watcha Gonna
    Be?,* 36

Templeton, Charles, 81, 94, 96, 153, 182,
    211–12, 293
  Act of God, 180, 185–86
  and Georgian Bay, 155–56
  inventions of, 155
  The Kidnapping of the President, 155, 180

Templeton, Madeleine, 156, 211

Thackeray, William Makepeace, 8

Thames & Hudson, 170, 171

Thatcher, Colin, 284

Thatcher, Lady Margaret, 365

Thien, Madeleine, 427, 431

This Country in the Morning (CBC radio),
    192, 213

Thistledown Press, 253

Thom, Ron, 145

Thomas, Audrey, 81

Thomas, Dylan, 54, 311

Thomson, Judith, 254

Thomson, Lorraine, 96

Thomson, Roy, 128

Thomson, Tom, 45

Thomson organization, 280

Thorsell, William, 161

Thury, Fredrick, 347

Tomašević, Bato, 266–67
  Life and Death in the Balkans, 266n

Torgov, Morley, 254

Toronto International Film Festival, 54

Toronto Life, 99, 240–41, 243, 321
Toronto Scottish Regiment, 135
Toronto Star, 23, 37, 127, 130, 166, 227n,
    233, 244, 262, 276, 306, 420, 425
Toronto Sun, 176, 252, 289, 290
Toronto Telegram, The, 288, 289
Toronto Transit Commission, 223, 296
Totten, Sam, 22
Town, Harold, 96, 106–7, 116, 133, 252n
    Bald Is Beautiful, 36n
    Birney drawing by, 111
    Christmas trees of, 39
    Drawings, 36–38, 39, 40, 49
    fame of, 37
    and Nowell, 38, 39
    and Purdy, 50–52
Transylvania, Szigethy family's origins in, 6,
    351, 391
Treaty of Trianon (1920), 4–5, 351
Tremblay, Michel, 137, 254
Trinity College School, Port Hope, 26–27
Trivial Pursuit, 15
Troper, Harold, 342, 349
Trotsky, Leon, 113
Trudeau, Justin, 237, 238
Trudeau, Margaret, 235–38, 253
    Beyond Reason, 235
    Changing My Mind, 237–38
    Consequences, 235–38, 300
Trudeau, Pierre Elliott, 53, 108, 118, 127,
    170, 260, 296, 297, 298, 381
    and Canadian publishing, 85–86
    and Margaret, 235–37, 253, 300
    Memoirs, 300
    opponents of, 43n, 259, 289, 293
    and Quebec, 159–60
    and "Trudeaumania," 11–12, 252, 253
Trudeau, Sacha, 237
Truth and Reconciliation Commission,
    353
Tupper, Sir Charles, 92–93
Turnbull, Janet, 304
Turner, Camilla, 130

Turner, John, 245n, 299, 300
Tweedy, Browne, 366–67

Ubyssey, The, 245, 258
UNESCO Copyright Convention, 102
University of Toronto, 397–98, 421–22
Updike, John, 79
Urquhart, Jane, 138, 398
US Supreme Court, 366–67

Vaile, Sig, 40
Vallières, Pierre, *Nègres blancs d'Amérique,*
    82–83
Vancouver International Writers' Festival,
    77
Vanderhaeghe, Guy, 138
van Herk, Aritha, *Judith,* 188, 214
van Kampen, Vlasta, 347
Van Nostrand Reinhold, 280
Vardey, Lucinda, 254
Vassanji, M. G., 254, 426
Verne, Jules, 6
Versailles Treaty (1919), 5
Villiers, Marq de, *Into Africa: A Journey*
    through the Ancient Empires, 244
Villon, François, 59
Visser, John de, 29, 267–68
Vitale, Alberto, 318–19, 321, 322, 330,
    331–32
Vizinczey, Stephen, *In Praise of Older*
    Women, 59
Volcker, Paul, 364
Vörösmarty, Mihály, 6, 57

Wahl, Charis, 21, 42, 137
Waldock, Peter, 274
Wales, Johnny, 348
Walker, Norris, 262
Wall, Robert, *The Canadians* (series), 219
Walter, Jan, 244n
Walters, Barbara, 193
Ward family, 9
War Measures Act (1970), 118

Watson, Paul, 376
  *Ocean Warrior, My Battle to End the
    Illegal Slaughter on the High Seas,* 336
Waugh, Evelyn, 167, 211
Webb, Jonathan, 246n, 274–75, 338n
Webb, Ken, 172
Webster, Ben, 14n
Webster, Jack, 260–61, 284
Weekend magazine, 53, 135
Wente, Peggy (Margaret), 245–46
West, Rebecca, 211
West Coast Review, 232
Weston, Galen, 128
Westwood, Bruce, 254
Where magazine, 251
Whitcombe and Tombs, 8, 19
Whitman, Walt, 54
Whyte, Ken, 373–74
Wiebe, Rudy, 81, 137
  Big Bear, 42
Wieland, Joyce, *Reason Over Passion,* 236
Wilhelm, Marcus, 322–23, 329, 331
Wilkie, Robert, 23, 274
Will, George F., 365
Williams, William Carlos, 54
Wilson, Catherine, 95
Wilson, Ethel, 82
Wiseman, Adele, 166, 219, 310
Witney, Dudley, 79, 80, 157, 269–71, 277,
    402
  American Journey by Rail, An, 271
  The Moorlands of England, 271
  Railway Country: Across Canada by Train,
    271
Wolf, Naomi, *The Beauty Myth: How Images
    of Beauty are Used Against Women,* 194
women:
  and #MeToo, 195
  and abortion, 192, 198
  on corporate boards, 193–94

equality for, 200
feminism, 183, 191–95, 197–201, 232
glass ceiling vs., 191, 199
Métis, 45–46
roles for, 198
unequal pay for, 181, 191–92
Wood, David, *The Lougheed Legacy,* 285–86
Woodward's, Vancouver, 271
Woolf, Virginia, 8
Workman, Carolan, 327
World Wildlife Canada, 411
World Wildlife Fund (WWF), 233, 334, 337,
    405
Worthington, Peter, 176, 211, 212, 213, 239,
    245n, 287–90, 297
  Looking for Trouble, 290
Worthington, Yvonne, 193, 239
Wright, Eric, *Always Give a Penny to a Blind
    Man,* 276, 394
Wright, L. R. "Bunny," *The Suspect,* 219
Wright, Richard B., 427
Writers' Trust, 73, 151, 231
Writers' Union of Canada, 31n, 66, 77, 123,
    139, 149, 166, 183, 231
Wynne-Jones, Tim, 347
Wynveen, Tim, 137, 348

Yaffe, Phyllis, 247
Yeats, William Butler, 54
Yevtushenko, Yevgeny, *Don't Die Before
    You're Dead,* 54
Young, David, 151n
Young Naturalist, 247
Young Naturalist Foundation, 333, 405

Zed, Dr., 247
Znaimer, Moses, 13–14, 186, 213
Zolf, Larry, *Survival of the Fattest: An
    Irreverent View of the Senate,* 296
ZoomerMedia, 14

About the Author

ANNA PORTER was born in Budapest, Hungary, and escaped with her mother during the 1956 Revolution to New Zealand. In 1968 she arrived in Canada and was soon swept up in the cultural explosion of the 1970s. In 1982 she founded Key Porter Books and published such national figures as Farley Mowat, Jean Chrétien, Conrad Black, and Allan Fotheringham. She went on to write both fiction and non-fiction works, including *Kasztner's Train,* which won the Writers' Trust Non-Fiction Prize and the Jewish Book Award, and *The Ghosts of Europe,* which won the Shaughnessy Cohen Prize for Political Writing. She has published four mystery novels.

Porter is an Officer of the Order of Canada and a recipient of the Order of Ontario. She lives in Toronto with her husband, Julian Porter.

Permissions and Credits

The excerpt from the poem "Landmarks" in *Selected Poems: 1967–2011* by George Jonas, © 2015 Cormorant Books, is reprinted with permission of the publisher.

The excerpt from the letter from Jack McClelland to Mordecai Richler (September 13, 1975) is reprinted by permission of Suzanne Drinkwater, literary executor for the estate of Jack McClelland.

The excerpt from June Callwood's essay "Old Age" in *Dropped Threads* has been reprinted by permission of Jill Frayne, literary executor for the estate of June Callwood.

Photo Credits

First Insert

Page 1

Vili Racz portrait. Image courtesy of Anna Porter.

Anna on the catwalk. Image courtesy of Anna Porter.

Therese and Anna. Image courtesy of Anna Porter.

Page 2

Margaret Atwood in 1969. Image reprinted by permission of Graeme Gibson.

Graeme Gibson in a canoe. Image reprinted by permission of Margaret Atwood.

Peter C. Newman, Anna Porter, and Pierre Berton. Image courtesy of Anna Porter.

Page 3

Harold Town outside the Art Gallery of Ontario. John McNeill / The Canadian Press.

Scott Symons in 1979. Jack Dobson / The Canadian Press.

Al Purdy in his A-frame. Reprinted from *Portraits of Canadian Writers* by Bruce Meyer by permission of the Porcupine's Quill. Copyright © Bruce Meyer, 2016.

Page 4

Matt Cohen. Image courtesy of Patricia Aldana.

Julian and Anna Porter wedding. Image courtesy of Anna Porter.

Sylvia Fraser and Catherine. Image courtesy of Anna Porter.

Page 5

Puci in 1986. Image courtesy of Anna Porter.

Irving Layton and Isabel Bassett. Image courtesy of Anna Porter. Copyright © Doug Griffin.

Catherine, Anna, and Julia Porter. Image courtesy of Anna Porter.

Page 6

Earle Birney. Reprinted from *Portraits of Canadian Writers* by Bruce Meyer by permission of the Porcupine's Quill. Copyright © Bruce Meyer, 2016.

Jack McClelland in his office. Reg Innell / *Toronto Star* / Getty / 502498229.

Anna Porter and Mordecai Richler. Image courtesy of Anna Porter.

Page 7

Farley Mowat. Bill Becker / The Canadian Press.

Margaret Trudeau. Tibor Kolley / The Canadian Press.

Aritha van Herk and Jack McClelland with Seal Books First Novel Award. Image courtesy of McMaster University Archives and McClelland & Stewart.

Page 8

Anna Porter and Alun Davies. Image courtesy of Anna Porter.

John Irwin, Janet Turnbull, and Anna Porter. Image courtesy of Anna Porter.

Leonard Cohen. Reprinted from *Portraits of Canadian Writers* by Bruce Meyer by permission of the Porcupine's Quill. Copyright © Bruce Meyer, 2016.

Second Insert

Page 1

Margaret Laurence at the Authors at Harbourfront series. Image courtesy of Anna Porter.

Barbara Frum. Image courtesy of The Canadian Press.

Conrad Black and Joe Clark. Image courtesy of Conrad Black.

Page 2

Doris Anderson. Image courtesy of Stephen Anderson.

Peter Worthington election button. Image courtesy of Anna Porter.

Peter Gzowski Invitational golf tournament. Image courtesy of Anna Porter.

Page 3

Linda McKnight, Bella Pomer, Anna Porter, and Lucinda Vardey. Image courtesy of Anna Porter.

Lorraine Durham, Anna Porter, and Annabel Slaight. Image courtesy of Anna Porter.

Dudley Witney. Image courtesy of Anna Porter.

Page 4

Peter Lougheed and David Wood. Image courtesy of Anna Porter.

Gloria Goodman. Image courtesy of Anna Porter.

Brian Mulroney. Image courtesy of Anna Porter.

Page 5

Jean Chrétien. Image courtesy of Anna Porter.

Allan Fotheringham. Image courtesy of Phyllis Bruce.

Jack McClelland and Avie Bennett. Keith Beaty / *Toronto Star* / Getty / 502495471.

Page 6

Fred Bruemmer. Tony Bock / *Toronto Star* / Getty / 502545143.

Norman Jewison and Margaret Atwood. Image courtesy of Anna Porter.

Basil Johnston. McMaster University Archives.

Page 7

George Jonas. Bob Olsen / *Toronto Star* / Getty / 502544875.

June Callwood. Hans Deryk / The Canadian Press.

Scott McIntyre. Photo Tom Sandler.

Page 8

Peter Munk and Anna Porter. Image courtesy of Anna Porter.

Anna Porter and Jack Rabinovitch. Image courtesy of Anna Porter.

Anna Porter in Budapest. Image courtesy of Anna Porter.